# Accounting, Finance, Sustainability, Governance & Fraud: Theory and Application

**Series Editor**

Kıymet Tunca Çalıyurt, Iktisadi ve Idari Bilimler Fakultes, Trakya University Balkan Yerleskesi, Edirne, Turkey

This Scopus indexed series acts as a forum for book publications on current research arising from debates about key topics that have emerged from global economic crises during the past several years. The importance of governance and the will to deal with corruption, fraud, and bad practice, are themes featured in volumes published in the series. These topics are not only of concern to businesses and their investors, but also to governments and supranational organizations, such as the United Nations and the European Union. Accounting, Finance, Sustainability, Governance & Fraud: Theory and Application takes on a distinctive perspective to explore crucial issues that currently have little or no coverage. Thus the series integrates both theoretical developments and practical experiences to feature themes that are topical, or are deemed to become topical within a short time. The series welcomes interdisciplinary research covering the topics of accounting, auditing, governance, and fraud.

More information about this series at https://link.springer.com/bookseries/13615

Bernur Açıkgöz · İbrahim Attila Acar
Editors

# Pandemnomics: The Pandemic's Lasting Economic Effects

Springer

*Editors*
Bernur Açıkgöz
Faculty of Business Sciences
and Economics
Izmir Katip Celebi University
Izmir, Turkey

İbrahim Attila Acar
Department of Economics
Izmir Katip Celebi University
Izmir, Turkey

ISSN 2509-7873 ISSN 2509-7881 (electronic)
Accounting, Finance, Sustainability, Governance & Fraud: Theory and Application
ISBN 978-981-16-8023-6 ISBN 978-981-16-8024-3 (eBook)
https://doi.org/10.1007/978-981-16-8024-3



This Springer imprint is published by the registered company Springer Nature Singapore Pte Ltd.
The registered company address is: 152 Beach Road, #21-01/04 Gateway East, Singapore 189721, Singapore

# Foreword by Marc Willinger

"Pandemnomics" addresses the major challenge of the COVID-19 pandemic for the global economy and for the Turkish economy in particular. Deeper than the economic shock of the 2018 financial crisis, the COVID-19 health crisis is likely to have lasting and far-reaching effects, not only on the economy, but on society, on health and on our way of living and seeing the world. The global challenge launched by the pandemic is widely discussed in this book, which builds on an original conceptual framework, in terms of global public goods (bads). The book offers us diagnoses and relevant perspectives on the future of our societies, with a global and a local vision. A special focus is given on some key economic issues, e.g. public spending, taxation, monetary policies, cryptocurrencies and digitalization of the economy, and some key social issues, e.g. migrations and viral information. I am proud to recommend this book to curious and demanding readers, as it was co-authored by a talented woman, Bernur, who is also my good friend.

Marc Willinger
Professor of Economics at the
University of Montpellier (UM) and
Member of the Center for
Environmental Economics of
Montpellier (CEE-M)

# Foreword by Ronald M. Harstad

A sensible economic analysis of the pandemic due to the virus commonly called COVID-19, and policies responding to its outbreak, is timely and much needed. Naturally, epidemiologists and virologists have taken centre stage in efforts to push political responses in sensible directions. Yet the long-run and possibly the near-term economic impacts may exceed the medical impacts.

This book is thus a fine and key contribution. Surely by early 2023, there will be many books about economic effects of the pandemic. The lasting contribution of Açıkgöz and Acar in *Pandemnomics* will lie in large part from the Turkish perspective being prominent, affecting not just Chapter Two, but also the tenor in much of their writing here. Turkey presently sits outside the US-EU-Japan-Canada-Australia accord, including South Korea, Taiwan and other allied nations with fairly similar per-capita incomes and political systems. Turkey also sits outside those nations noted for being politically inimical to that accord; here, Russia, China, Iran and North Korea are prominent. Of the "double-outsider" nations in neither of these groups, Turkey has perhaps the highest incomes, greatest educational accomplishments and about the most advanced medical industry and medical research community. Its policy-reaching and policy-implementation structure is somewhat typical of double-outsider nations, as is the ongoing nature and breadth of political opposition. For these reasons, *Pandemnomics* will remain particularly relevant both to understanding of likely future pandemics and to policy consideration in many nations totalling at least a couple billion population. Wealthier nations who seek to help them may also gain by taking notice; for this, I particularly call attention to Part III.

I have known, and deeply respected, Prof. Dr. Bernur Açıkgöz for a decade. Well-schooled, she continues to add to her research tools and is a thoughtful, upbeat and persistent scholar. I have not yet had the opportunity to interact with her co-author, Prof. Dr. İbrahim Attila Acar.

Ronald M. Harstad

# Acknowledgements

The world faces a new and more dire threat after the Spanish Flu, which killed 50 million people in 18 months 100 years ago. The fact that science and technique are so advanced is not enough to eliminate this threat. The risk is higher as people live in more crowded places today. The epidemic has more severe impact, the risk is deadly, and life has come to a standstill. It should not be forgotten that the contamination not only is intent on human life, but also affects all areas of life.

It has been seen that the COVID-19, affecting the whole world along with Turkey in March 2020, is not only a health issue. We live in a time that continues only with the suggestions and directions of the political power and the Ministry of Health. The motto of this period, formulated with the trilogy of social distance, masks and hygiene, will continue to be remembered for many years. However, their effect will not only be to get rid of the pandemic; the period will also be referred to with its different aspects.

Although the coronavirus itself, which emerges with the pandemic, is seen as a problem, the main issue is the insufficient service and impotence of the health sector due to the epidemic. After all, mass deaths in places such as bed and intensive care will trigger social anger and panic. Consequently, this concern is the catalyst of the process; it will accelerate the process. Panic and fear will increase the effects of the epidemic on the life as a whole. Public administration will also be insufficient to tidy up the order. Therefore, countries will not be able to have healthy reactions in times of panic.

At the beginning of the period, the USA announced a package of 1 trillion dollars to get its economy out of this crisis. The FED made a commitment to purchase $700 billion in bonds. After IMF President Kristalina Georgieva said "We are ready to give the necessary support to every country", the first application came from Iran. Unconditional surrender: as long as support is given… In the period of March 2020, the number of countries that met with the IMF, including Iran, reached 100.

The most important deficiency about this period, which reshapes our whole lives today, is that the issue is treated as a pure health issue. However, the lifestyle is forced to change as a whole. Therefore, it is necessary to examine the areas that the pandemic has forced to change, apart from health.

The subject has many historical, legal, social, psychological, technical and economic dimensions. It is not just about a simple flu case. We are at the beginning of a process that can have an impact for many years. In this process, this book aims to discuss the pandemic issue in depth, by bringing the field experts together.

The book is composed of three Parts:

Part I addresses the global public nature of the COVID-19 pandemic, the fiscal policies implemented in epidemics from past to present and increasing public expenditures.

Part II is composed of the studies addressing the issue in terms of Turkish economy. Four studies are included in this part. The evaluation of COVID-19 in terms of Turkish Tax Law and an empirical research on tax perception in this period includes evaluations on the income side of this part. Evaluations on the cost side are addressed in two different studies. The first one analyses the transfer expenditures dimension, whereas the other study analyses the support provided by various countries during the pandemic and the evaluations on the budget management in Turkey.

Part III includes projections regarding the COVID-19 pandemic. There are four studies in this part. Of course, attention has been drawn to the future of possible financial trends after the epidemic. In addition to the technological side of the subject and robotization, digital currencies are examined in this part. The issue of refugees, who are the victims of the deepest problems of the world and one of the most vulnerable segments, has also taken its place in this book as the victims of this age. The study, in which the content of the increasing social media shares of people staying at home and living with social distancing concerns are subjected to big data analysis, constitutes the final study of the book.

The book is a product of great effort and self-devotion. We thank all researchers and experts who contributed to the process and we hope that the study will be beneficial to students, researchers and everyone who are interested in the subject.

İzmir, Turkey
March 2021

Prof. Dr. Bernur Açıkgöz
Prof. Dr. İbrahim Attila Acar

# Contents

# Editors and Contributors

## About the Editors

**Prof. Dr. Bernur Açıkgöz** was born in 1979 in Ankara. After attending Ankara Finance High School, she continued her undergraduate studies at Dokuz Eylül University, Department of Finance. She received her master's degree in Financial Law from Dokuz Eylül University. In 2006, she was awarded her Ph.D. degree from Dokuz Eylul University Department of Public Finance. Her Ph.D. thesis covered the topics of poverty and development.

In 2006, she won the Harvard University Project scholarship and worked as a visiting professor at Harvard University. In 2009, she received a scholarship from the Swiss Government for a post-doctorate degree in economics at the University of Neuchatel/Switzerland, and taught courses at Bern Universities. She then began to work in the fields of experimental economics and game theory, and for three consecutive years as a guest lecturer in the economics laboratory of the Montpellier University in Montpellier, France. Afterwards, she went to Missouri University, Indiana University and Arizona University with a scholarship from Missouri University. She then worked as a visiting professor at the University of East Anglia and took some courses from Exeter Universities in the UK with a Tubitak scholarship.

She has books, articles and papers on foreign direct investments, economic growth, panel econometrics, experimental economics and game theory. She is currently working at the Department of Public Finance and Financial Management at Izmir Katip Çelebi University/Turkey. In addition, Açıkgöz teaches at the Department of International Trade and Finance at Izmir University of Economics/Turkey and the Department of Economics at University of Life Sciences in Poznań (Uniwersytet Przyrodniczy w Poznaniu)/Poland.

**Prof. Dr. İbrahim Attila Acar** graduated from Department of Management, Faculty of Economics and Administrative Sciences at Dokuz Eylül University in 1990. He received his master's degree in Public Finance from Dokuz Eylül University. He was awarded his Ph.D. degree from Dokuz Eylul University Department of Public Finance.

He has books, articles and papers on public strategic management, public financial management and control law (Law No: 5018), health and education economy, refugees crisis, auditing, financial management and budgeting. He is a member of the Specialization Commission in the 9th, 10th, 11th Development Plans and involved in quality, effectiveness, university rankings, European University Association higher education assessment and rating studies in higher education.

He worked as a panelist and independent evaluator of TÜBİTAK and Development Agencies. He participated in programs in written and visual media. He prepared and presented the Economic Agenda program at TRT for many years. The analyzes are located in its own website, acarhoca.com. He worked at Süleyman Demirel University for 10 years. And he is currently working at the Department of Economics, Faculty of Economics and Administrative Sciences at Izmir Katip Çelebi University. He was the Vice Rector and the founding dean at the same university.

## Contributors

**İbrahim Attila Acar** Department of Economic Policy, Department of Public Finance and Financial Management, İzmir Katip Çelebi University, İzmir, Turkey

**Bernur Açıkgöz** Department of Public Finance and Financial Management, İzmir Kâtip Çelebi University, İzmir, Turkey

**Doğancan Akata** Department of Public Finance and Financial Management/Post-Graduate Study, İzmir Kâtip Çelebi University, İzmir, Turkey

**Volkan Altıntaş** Akhisar Vocational High School Computer Technologies Programme, Manisa Celal Bayar University, Manisa, Turkey

**Sibel Aybarç** Finance, Banking and Insurance Program, Manisa Celal Bayar University, Ahmetli, Manisa, Turkey

**Turgay Çağlayan** Ministry of National Defense, Ankara, Turkey

**Zeynep Demirci Çakıroğlu** Department of Fiscal Theory, İzmir Katip Çelebi University, İzmir, Turkey

**Tülin Canbay** Department of Finance Theory, Manisa Celal Bayar University, Manisa, Turkey

**Ümit Çevik** Ziraat Participation Bank, İstanbul, Turkey

**Hilal Balcı Cura** Department of Protection of Ownership and Security Social Security Programme, Manisa Celal Bayar University, Manisa, Turkey

**Alper Doğan** Department of Fiscal Theory, İzmir Katip Çelebi University, İzmir, Turkey

**Yaprak Karadağ Duymazlar** Department of Financial Management, İzmir Kâtip Çelebi University, İzmir, Turkey

**Abdulcelil Gazioğlu** Department of Budget and Financial Planning, İzmir Kâtip Çelebi University, İzmir, Turkey

**Elif Ayşe Şahin İpek** Department of Public Finance and Financial Management, İzmir Kâtip Çelebi University, İzmir, Turkey

**Melih Kabayel** Department of Public Finance and Financial Management/Post-Graduate Study, İzmir Kâtip Çelebi University, İzmir, Turkey

**Halis Kıral** Social Sciences University of Ankara, Ankara, Turkey

**Burhanettin Onur Kireçtepe** Faculty of Law Department of Financial Law, Tokat Gaziosmanpaşa University, Tokat, Turkey

**Belgin Yakışan Mutlu** Ziraat Participation Bank, İstanbul, Turkey

# List of Figures

# List of Tables

# Part I
# Pandemic and Public Economy

# Chapter 1
# Evaluation for COVID-19 Outbreak Public Policies in the World Within the Scope of Global Public Goods (GPGs)

**Bernur Açıkgöz**

**Abstract** Due to the global impact of the COVID-19 pandemic, states and international organizations must implement a variety of economic and financial practices to combat the pandemic and its adverse effects on the economies. These public policies require the most efficient use of resources under a serious resource scarcity. Nations must re-imagine the ways how they cooperate as they fight to COVID-19. Global public bads are public goods with costs that extend across countries, across rich and poor population groups, and even across generations. We can consider the COVID-19 pandemic as a global public bad. This chapter looks at definitions and concepts of GPGs and global public bads, and then, the public policies implemented within the scope of COVID-19 will be evaluated within this framework.

**Keywords** COVID-19 · Pandemic · Public policies · Global public goods · GPGs · Global public bads · Fiscal policy · Health · International organizations · Government response

## 1.1 Introduction

Being put on the agenda upon the COVID-19 outbreak, GPGs are actually an issue that has never become out-of-date due to globalization in many fields such as environment, health, information, peace and governance. Although still acting with incomplete information, the relationship between globalization and GPGs is clear, yet the solutions are quite complex. The countries around the world are becoming increasingly interdependent and they remain more vulnerable to problems beyond their borders in the fields of health, environment, etc. For example, in many industrialized countries, where people born in foreign countries make up almost half of the population, tuberculosis has become a major problem. Likewise, the refugee problem causes the re-emergence of old diseases that are no longer seen in host countries.

B. Açıkgöz (✉)
Department of Public Finance and Financial Management, İzmir Kâtip Çelebi University, İzmir, Turkey
e-mail: bernur.acikgoz@ikc.edu.tr

 
B. Açıkgöz and İ. A. Acar (eds.), *Pandemnomics: The Pandemic's Lasting Economic Effects*, Accounting, Finance, Sustainability, Governance & Fraud: Theory and Application, https://doi.org/10.1007/978-981-16-8024-3_1

However, despite their increasing vulnerability, countries can also take advantage of new opportunities offered by globalization to promote GPGs. Today, countries can expand their knowledge limits by creating international research networks for health and supporting international research. Public–private partnerships can be established to create new generation product groups, making medicines, vaccines and diagnosis much easier. Countries can share the burden of dangerous and communicable diseases in the world through R&D studies, innovation, joint projects, screening programs, surveillance activities and other means to be carried out in cooperation, and at the same time, they can minimize their health, environmental and financial risks that may stem from cross-border movement of people, animals and foodstuffs and thereby increasing connections.

The interdependence of socio-ecological systems and increased access to human activities resulted in significant political and scientific difficulties in managing the environmental resources. Human activities and the physical environment interact with each other. Therefore, the main challenge for governance in environmental and health issues is to link physically-linked actions each other also institutionally. It is necessary to question whether the core institutions of the economies are set up to address this challenge thoroughly (Vatn 2012). In modern economies, generalized dependency and complex coordination problems prevail. While the basic structure of markets and firms is strong in facilitating economic expansion, it is weak in addressing the dependencies created (Brousseau et al. 2012). Of course, states and international organizations have made various arrangements to try to overcome these difficulties. However, these arrangements are not at a sufficient level, as we have seen in the COVID-19 outbreak.

Governance problems of environmental GPGs and GPGs for health are evident. First of all, it is necessary to develop institutions and governance mechanisms working on the right spatial and temporal scale. Then, it is necessary to match the governance structure with the nature of public goods at risk. For example, considering the open oceans and global disease risks, promoting collaboration in their governance is now an imperative. When it comes to disease risks, although global cooperation is easier due to the high potential cost of global outbreaks, collaboration efforts in the field of environment appear to be a more complex problem (Perrings 2012).

Collective action problems vary in scale, from the very small problems that concern only a few people, such as the farmer-managed irrigation system, to the enormous problems involving global resources such as the atmosphere and oceans. If we are to effectively solve collective action problems, we should consider restructuring existing market and government institutions. We must recognize the importance of entrepreneurship in both public and private spheres. We also need to understand that the presence of a large number of government units at multiple scales is not automatically a negative indicator of performance. However, when governance systems are organized in a multicenter system, collective action problems can be handled more effectively on multiple scales (Ostrom 2012). In other words, the plurality of decision makers will bring along more efficient solutions.

It seems that being dependent on the management tools, in which change is assumed in the effort to manage complex and dynamic socio-ecological systems, is already costly and a highly unwanted obligation in the future. In a world where change is often nonlinear, sudden and irreversible, we need to formulate a set of principles that will help (re)establish environmental and health policies that can produce sustainable results (Young 2012).

Promoting sustainable use of world resources and a harmonious relationship between people and ecosystems requires setting up market-based and self-financing mechanisms that do not require donations for implementation and reduce the wealth gap between rich and poor countries and more generally between high and low income people, women, men and children. In the event of crises, government intervention is possible and legitimate, where mobilizing the means rapidly and massively enables citizens and stakeholders to accept major policy measures and reforms. Nevertheless, the emergency plans rarely result in the optimal measures. Thus, the main objective of common policies should be crisis avoidance. At this point, it is necessary to rely more on decentralized and reflexive governance, as all stakeholders must feel accountable. Furthermore, this will enable better management and producing the required knowledge.

## 1.2 Global Public Goods

Global public goods are goods whose benefits and costs extend across countries and generations; that is, global public goods are goods in which political and geographical boundaries disappear (Savaşan 2012). At the same time, these goods bring along passing down of external cost or benefit from one generation to the other. When evaluated from this point of view, "intergenerational externality" and "cross-country externality" are the most important features of global public goods (Sandler 2011).

When talking about a public good or GPG, we are actually talking about an economic term and this economic term has two main characteristics. The first one is ***non-excludability*** from consumption which means that the good can also be used by those who do not pay or it is impossible to prevent its consumption. The second one is ***non-rivalry*** in consumption; that is, for any production level, the marginal cost of delivery of the goods to an additional consumer is zero. In both cases, the price mechanism does not work properly in finding the balance between supply and demand. Among the most widely-known examples are law and order, defense and lighthouses. Public goods released on the free market face the problem of inadequate presentation, largely because of non-excludability and non-rivalry. Therefore, governments must take additional measures to finance, subsidize and present them, or they must make the presentations themselves. This is a public responsibility area that is accepted by even the most liberal thinkers.

On the other hand, when discussing GPGs' issue, broad-based and multi-sectoral discussions were typically held. For example, environmental, information, international security, peace and trade agreements are the subject of these broad-perspective discussions, while discussions on healthcare GPGs mostly focus on medical technologies (Kaul et al. 2003).

We need to distinguish global and non-global public goods. Our global understanding here is not only geographical, i.e., rather than being local, national or regional, it also covers both countries and generations. In other words, it is actually multi-dimensional as it has a sociological and temporal dimension along with its geographical dimension. If a public good would only benefit one country or region, it would be a national or regional public good, not a global one. Similarly, NATO's security services and alliances for the Western bloc countries during the Cold War are club goods, not GPGs. Again, when a multilateral investment guarantee agreement only benefits private international investors per se, it would be a worldwide club good and probably a private good. Contrarily, a poverty reduction program for sub-Saharan Africa, preventing conflict and contributing to international peace by addressing the needs of local people potentially, has international consequences, and reducing environmental damage and improving global health conditions is a GPG. Again conversely, donations to disaster victims are redistribution of private goods voluntarily from one owner to another, and they are mainly motivated by empathy not with global concerns. Private transfers and public goods procurement are not morally or ethically different. They only have different technical features. In other words, the non-excludability and non-rivalry in their consumption distinguish GPGs from private goods. These are the properties that should be considered in the classification of public goods as global or non-global or as GPGs and private goods (Kaul et al. 1999a, b) (Fig. 1.1).

The publicness level of the public goods that differ geographically and politically in the publicness cube appears to also differ among themselves. In other words, regardless of the spreading level of costs and benefits geographically and politically, each good and service (global, national, local, etc.) may show different characteristics according to a competition and exclusion factor (Açıkgöz 2011).

If we start with private goods, they are usually traded in the markets, and buyers and sellers trade through the price mechanism. If they jointly decide on a price, they transfer ownership or use of the good (or service). Therefore, private goods are excludable and rivalrous in consumption as their ownership is clearly defined. For example, bread, car and ice cream are private goods. Public goods have the

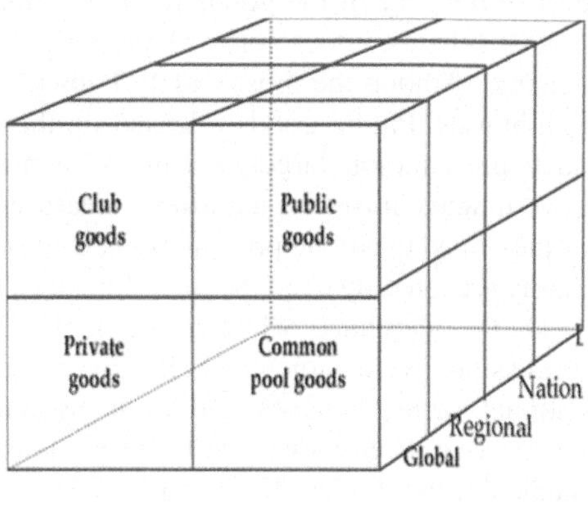


**Fig. 1.1** Publicity cube and global public goods. *Source* (Smith 2004; Açıkgöz 2011, p. 229)

opposite features. It is not possible to exclude people from consumption and there is no competition in their consumption. Street signs, traffic lights or fresh air are examples of public goods. Even if a large number of people look at it, the street sign will not wear out and it will be nearly impossible, costly and inefficient to limit its use to just one or a few people and to prohibit other people from looking at it.

The question of who provides public goods is also important. They are ready for everyone to use, right after their delivery. Therefore, overuse problems arise. In the absence of some kind of collective action mechanism, they risk inadequate provision. Oppositely, without collective action, public bads, namely pollution, noise, street crime, risky bank lending, etc., would be over-provided (Kaul 2000).

Global public goods are public goods whose benefits and costs extend across borders, generations and population groups. For example, if international social peace is achieved, everyone can benefit from this. This also applies to well-functioning international markets. Likewise, when global climate change is prevented, widespread intergenerational and geographical benefits will be provided, although people around the world can benefit in different manners. Likewise, civil aviation, postal services and telecommunications have similar features.

Most of the time, governments take action to facilitate the collective action required to prevent over-production of public bads or under-provision of public goods. There is no such an institution at international level. However, if GPGs correspond to national needs and self-interest, countries are able to conclude agreement on coordinated action. The main difficulty is to encourage countries not to let public bads extend across their borders and transform from national public bads into global public bads. This requires cooperation and cohesion between cross-border policies (Kaul 2000).

Therefore, when talking about a commodity, it is important to recognize that not all people give the same value to it. Poor people, who cannot bear the expense of traveling, may not place maximum value on international passport regime. Yet, traders may prefer global health endangerment to free trade as they wish their products find new markets (Drager and Beaglehole 2001). Others may put the control of international terrorism or stability of international financial markets at the highest rank. Thus, when an agenda is established for GPGs, equitably taking into account the priorities of different population groups is important (Kaul 2000).

Civil society and business actors make contribution to delivery of public goods, including GPGs, from human rights to technical norms. In fact, these actors have highlighted the importance of balancing the globalization of private activities with that of public goods. State actors appear to make limited contribution, maybe because nation states are defined differently at regional level. In order to maximize their contribution, GPGs should be closely linked to national interests (Kaul 2000). It is also necessary to take into account the need for stronger international platforms where state actors as well as non-state, transnational actors can discuss how to balance private goods with public goods. Such balance will contribute to people's well-being. Public goods, including GPGs, are essential even for the wealthiest person. International markets cannot operate in the absence of provision of such goods.

Property rights, legal institutions, educated people, absence of epidemics, peace and security are necessary for efficient functioning (Thorsteinsdóttir et al. 2003).

## 1.3 Global Public Bads

Public bads, which we can define as the opposite of GPG, are negative externalities that cause negative effects on people and societies. If these negative externalities spread across countries and/or generations, they are called global public bads. The spread of infectious diseases such as COVID-19, human trafficking, financial crises, global warming, eradication of biodiversity, malware, income and wealth inequalities is example of global public bads.

Many international organizations (IMF, regional development banks, non-governmental organizations, the UN, the World Bank, the World Trade Organization, etc.) and governments around the world assume duties with the aim of adequate delivery of global public goods, which includes external aid and foreign military interventions to correct "global public bads." If we take a brief look at the studies on global public bads, for instance, Cook and Sachs (1999) and Jayaraman and Kanbur (1999) investigated the impact of foreign aid on the prevention of global public bads. Similarly, Ferroni (2000) examined the issue of reforms in the provision of foreign aid for the prevention of global public bads. Again, Ferguson (2004) examined the United States and its role in ensuring global stability. In his study, Mendez (1999) discussed the importance of the UN for peacekeeping. Collier (2008), in his study, investigated the effect of properly timed foreign military interventions on the prevention of military coups. Mitchener and Weidenmier (2005) and Ferguson and Schularick (2006) analyzed the historical foreign intervention cases of the United States and tried to reveal the necessary conditions for intervention and willingness to use the declared military force by emphasizing the GPGs produced by the UK and the army.

While the COVID-19 outbreak is considered a global public bad, the improvement of health care is considered a GPG. The presentation of health GPG requires both individual and public actions, and especially, the health of the poor population requires collective actions both within and between countries. Infectious diseases such as COVID-19, AIDS, tuberculosis and malaria which can be defined as negative externality caused by GPG or as global public bads, provision of GPG will begin if some initiatives such as global fund for combating AIDS, tuberculosis and malaria are established. Now these initiatives, already established around the world, reflect the growing awareness of this fact. Nonetheless, globally initiating, organizing and financing collective actions for health pose serious problems for existing international organizations (Drager and Beaglehole 2001).

As mentioned before, factors resulting in considerable environmental damage with negative consequences on health are public "bads" and reducing them is in the public interest. Important examples are the reduction of biodiversity, environmental and air pollution, global warming and depletion of the ozone layer. Air pollution in the big cities of countries typically occurs in a country and in a limited area such as Istanbul, New York and London. For this reason, governments intervene in the market through regulation, taxation or other means and provide the presentation of this public good in order to provide the public benefit (consuming fresh air) that citizens cannot buy for them individually. Where air pollution reaches country borders, such as the former East Germany, the Czech Republic and Poland, affected countries can act together to reduce a public bad to which they are collectively exposed (and collectively contributed) (Feachem and Medlin 2002).

Health is the major concern on the global agenda today. It is discussed at meetings of the G-8, and organizations and relevant actors establish worldwide health coalitions to overcome the global disease burden. Some of the mentioned organizations include the Global Alliance for Vaccines and Immunization (GAVI); Medicines for Malaria Venture (MMV); Global Tuberculosis Drug Facility (GDF); Stop Smoking Campaign; and the Global Health Fund to fight acquired immunodeficiency syndrome (AIDS) and other infectious diseases in Africa. Before the outbreak of COVID-19, the initiatives are mostly concerned with human immunodeficiency virus (HIV)/AIDS, tuberculosis (TB) and malaria, and their overall goal is to encourage to address the health problems mostly the poor suffer by means of medical research and development (R&D). Helping poorer countries purchase medicines and strengthen their national health care services is among their other goals (Kaul and Faust 2001).

The problem of equity in accessing health care is also very important. Although public goods are defined as neither divisible nor excludable, they carry risks such as unequal access to public health services, biased priorities or negligence. The poor have different health priorities than the rich, and the rich can access preventive and protective healthcare services more than the poor. In addition, the spread of the global private market accelerates the privatization of healthcare services and the commercialization of health information. Private markets are naturally unequal because the poor, without purchasing power, are excluded from commercial services and healthcare technologies. Another problem in this regard is whether new opportunities will be used to meet human health needs equally. For example, the average life expectancy in developed countries (about 80 years) is twice that of the most backward countries (about 40 years) in terms of health. There are equally large healthcare differences across countries. Even in the United States, the life expectancy of the healthiest men in the best county is twice that of the most unhealthy men in the worst county (Lopez and Murray 1998).

Control of many global diseases that concern the poor more can be considered a GPG. For example, successful elimination of smallpox, nearly eliminating polio and activities related to primary health care are global efforts for the public good. Global efforts are absolutely egalitarian. Different health problems offer to the rich population different priorities created by ready access to effective vaccines and antibiotics that are not accessible to many poor populations financially or logistically. Adopting only a global commodity perspective does not resolve the dilemma of which disease should be a global priority or how to prioritize limited global resources (Lincoln et al. 1999).

Currently, emergency interventions are carried out against increasing disease burden, as it is not sustainable in many developing countries. The main issue is what health policies are necessary to sustain such efforts and prevent similar future crises? Analyzing current health challenges from the perspective of a GPG, following a number of policy options is necessary for putting the current dispersed initiatives into a wider framework. These policies should offer a comprehensive rationale for international cooperation on health issues and propose new arrangements for financing. Policies for more efficient delivery of health information and a new "matrix" approach to management of global health issues and initiatives are discussed nowadays. Globalization has currently created interdependencies dimming the difference between domestic and external relations. When the understanding of "the best way to ensure one's own well-being is to be concerned about that of others" is acceptance all over the world, the parties will place more emphasis on cooperation for solution (Kaul and Faust 2001).

However, some public bads—such as global warming and ozone depletion—affect large regions or even the entire world. For this reason, it is difficult to establish fast collaborations. For the public goods corresponding to such public bads, the properties of non-excludability and non-rivalry apply, this time, to countries instead of individual consumers. Ideally, the global or regional reach of these properties will inspire countries to act collectively to encourage (or discourage) global public goods (or bads) delivery. If global warming could be slowed down by means of collective action, a country having made no contribution cannot be prevented from benefiting, and the cost of that benefit to the dissenting country would be zero. A GPG should be deemed a good that a "world government" would finance, subsidize or otherwise encourage, if such kind of organization were present (Feachem ve Medlin 2002).

The concept of GPG suggests a possible framework to consider these issues (Kaul 2000). In this statement, "goods" encompass a range of physical products (such as bread, books and shoes), but also include services (such as security, information and travel) that distinguish between private and public goods. Most of the goods are "private" as their consumption can be stored until a payment is made in return and cannot be reconsumed once consumed. On the contrary, when "public" goods are provided, no one can consume (non- excludable) and the consumption by one person does not prevent anyone else (non-rivalry in consumption) from consuming it (Kaul et al. 1999a, b). For example, all individuals in one country benefit from reducing the risk of epidemics, and one who benefits from this reduction in risk does not prevent anyone else from taking advantage of it.

The fact that international travel is now easy, changes in technology and the rapid liberalization of trade also bring different features to healthcare GPG. Today, infectious diseases (often drug-resistant) are spreading faster (Smith and Coast 2002), with our environmental damage, access to fresh air and clean water is reduced worldwide, and new information about traditional and modern medical technologies is increasingly patented. These new changes coming with globalization disrupt the non-excludability characteristic of the GPG goods, making them artificially excludable (Thorsteinsdóttir et al. 2003). It also allows GPG to worsen existing inequities. Some healthcare services are open to the public, yet some may not be accessible to the poor. Practices such as the free trade regime in an unequal world can cause the rich to have all the resources. If these exclusion concerns are not taken into account, people's and states' willingness to cooperate will suffer and so will the presentation of GPGs. Equity is an important component of an effective GPG presentation strategy (Kaul 2000).

Equity is very important in effective presentation of GPGs, but equity is itself a GPG. GPGs are non-rival, such that treating a person equitably does not reduce the chance of another person to be treated the same, and if equity in access to health care is accepted as a norm-like other global norms and principles such as human rights, no one can be excluded from accessing the health care. Hence, equity in accessing the health care should be ensured globally, as a universal principle, in the best and most predictable way (Kaul 2000).

The COVID-19 outbreak brought to mind a new question about GPG. Why a new class of global public goods emerge? Based on other studies on global trends (Hirst and Thompson 1999; Rodrik 1997; Kaul et al. 2003), it is clear that a variety of factors contributed to the emergence of new GPGs. Countries have become more vulnerable to risks by reducing cross-border controls, as well as increasing political pluralism and democracy. Considered along with technological developments, this has promoted more international economic activity, more foreign trade, more foreign investment and more international travel and communication. Lincoln et al. (1999) stated in their study that even non-communicable diseases are a global health problem with the integration of markets and internationalization of marketing. The authors, among other things, refer to the fact that ads around the world do not contain healthy information and the spread of unhealthy consumption patterns such as smoking.

When defending their own interests, countries should never build conservative obstacles, or they should work to maximize the welfare of the country by combining national interests with international imperatives, not to defend the country against external influences. In other words, it is necessary to address the interrelated, internal and external issues posed by the new global public goods class (Kaul et al. 1999a, b).

International cooperation is an active area. As Young (2012) stated, "we live in the world of international regimes." In some regions, international cooperation, information exchange and consultation activities on common concerns work very well. However, actors must cooperate fully to transform intentions into policy actions. There are many obstacles to the implementation and follow-up of international agreements. The first one is the uncertainty about the feasibility of possible policy practices. Therefore, international organizations are very important for providing information and reducing the uncertainties of the governments in the negotiation process (Haas 1992). The second one is, despite the emergence of new GPGs and the activities of non-state actors related to these new goods, countries do not want to present GPGs at an adequate international level. This causes problems to deepen in areas that are not operated and are idle (Kaul et al. 1999a, b).

## 1.4 Global Fiscal Policies Implemented Within the Scope of Fight Against COVID-19, a Global Public Bad

Governments' responses to COVID-19 are considerably different from each other. One of the first measures taken is to shut schools. Some countries have closed all the schools; whereas some countries closed universities on a different calender than primary schools; in other countries, though, only the children of essential workers can go to schools. It is observed that wide variety of practices have been implemented in countries, even only in the case of schools (Hale et al. 2020).

The COVID-19 outbreak has the capacity to create more damage in underdeveloped countries than developed countries, due to their underdeveloped health systems and infrastructures, insufficient budget resources, shallow financial systems, and poor government authority and capability. This impact also reflects incomplete reporting and/or fewer tests for COVID-19 in underdeveloped and developing countries. Policy makers in these countries should first focus on the implementation of health-related measures and then focus on economic measures to reduce negative economic effects and support employees.

Countries are counting on social distance, quarantine and isolation to cope with COVID-19, as the coronavirus is spreading very rapidly with human contact and currently has no vaccine or definitive treatment. Goal of these measures is to "flatten the health curve"; therefore, limited healthcare facilities and resources can accommodate patients without over-care, preventing unnecessary deaths due to poor care. In the absence of widespread testing and monitoring, these are the best methods known to reduce the spread, but these actions have great economic costs, especially on tourism, trade and foreign investment (Hale et al. 2020).

Unprecedented slowing down of economic activities has resulted in significant economic costs, including widespread unemployment. The duration of the crisis and the following recovery rate are unknown; thus, it is hard to assess all of these costs. The longer the crisis lasts, the more costly the losses will be.

Under normal circumstances, countries in crisis can ask for help from external resources, namely the World Bank and the International Monetary Fund, but due to the global nature and magnitude of this crisis mentioned external resources will not be sufficient and it is necessary to support external resources by domestic funding. Comprehensive policy packages must be prepared for individual countries and global bodies. The negative effects caused by sudden decrease of economic activities must be alleviated by means of fiscal policy. As a short-term solution, direct payments to taxpayers, for instance, could help individuals, especially the unemployed. Businesses can make use of canceled or delayed tax payments when coping with their losses. Fiscal and monetary policies serve to mobilize government resources by providing an adequate flow of liquidity to businesses and households, yet it must be ensured that they are supported with private sector financing instruments. Central banks of many developed countries cut the interest rates, and some accelerated their asset purchases process. Many middle-income countries can alleviate pressures on the balance of payments arising from the recent drop in oil prices, if their exchange rate regimes are fixed and if they can provide financing that will not allow the exchange rate to depreciate in the face of the decline in exports and the rise in the dollar (Hinh 2020).

The governments should set up assistance programs for manufacturing firms to survive the downturn, bounce back faster and stronger, and produce higher-value products. To this end, the governments must reallocate their budget and utilize the limited resources more efficiently. These expenditures could also be made by means of foreign borrowing.

Financial assistance with the aim of helping firms not shrink and retain workforce must be provided in the short term, but if it is not supported with technical training and assistance, the long-term benefits will be minimal. Policies to be implemented in the short term are as follows (Hinh 2020):

Firmaların küçülmeye gidip, mevcut çalışanlarını işten çıkarmaması için mali yardımların kısa vadede dağıtılması gereklidir ancak teknik eğitim ve yardımla desteklenmediği sürece uzun vadeli faydalar asgari düzeyde olacaktır. Kısa vadede uygulanabilecek politikalar

- Financial assistance must be provided as grants or low-interest loans to manufacturing firms retaining at least some of their employees during the idle time.
- The governments must provide especially the SMEs with assistance for providing raw materials and other intermediate inputs as well as technical assistance regarding appropriate technologies used to make the medical products and equipment.

These actions may be taken during the lockdown, and during the transition period before all economic activities fully resume.

## 1.5 Conclusion

In the IMF (2020) study, it is mentioned that this period, which is called The Great Lockdown, will cause the biggest economic collapse since 1929 great depression. The IMF predicted that the world economy will shrink by 3% in 2020. It is stated that even if there is a recovery in 2021, the level reached will fall behind the pre-virus period. IMF underlined that the policymakers will need to take measures in the fiscal, monetary and financial markets to support affected households and businesses domestically, and the IMF also emphasized that strong and multilateral cooperation is necessary to channel aid to countries with financially inadequate and weak health systems facing health and financial shocks, to overcome the effects of the epidemic at the international level.

Economic indicators for 2020 were revised in the interim report published by the OECD evaluating the economic effects of the rapid spread of the COVID-19 outbreak worldwide. It was emphasized that COVID-19 virus threatens human life and global economy more than SARS virus and spread rapidly in the world even if increase in the number of cases in China ceased abruptly. It was emphasized that there were significant decreases especially in the tourism and supply chain, which made the global economy extremely fragile. In this context, it invited governments to take urgent measures without underestimating this outbreak in any way. It proposed policies such as limited working hours, increased health resources, cash aid to individuals, tax deferral or reduction to the most affected sectors, making public payments to companies which have been delayed and increasing the liquidity of banks (OECD 2020).

In the joint study of the World Economic Forum and Harvard Health Institute, the effects of epidemic diseases before the COVID-19 outbreak on human health and the economy were discussed in detail. It has been stated that combating the flu pandemic is almost as costly as combating climate change and will cause more costs than climate change in the coming years. The socio-economic costs caused by the COVID-19 pandemic, which are on the agenda of the world today, support that report published in the previous months (World Economic Forum 2019).

The European Commission has listed the measures to be taken to alleviate the effects of the crisis caused by the COVID-19 outbreak. The list includes measures such as making investments and necessary expenditures for the control and treatment of the pandemic, protection of employees against income losses and providing necessary liquidity support to enterprises, especially SMEs, increasing state aids, shortening the working time of workers, offering tax expenditures and export subsidies, securing the supply chain of medical materials and equipment among EU countries, inter-agency cooperation to monitor and revive the tourism sector (European Commission 2020).

Even though the measures proposed by international institutions are necessary and sufficient to combat COVID-19 in the short term, both states and international organizations should prepare for the dangers in the future that we do not know yet and cannot foresee which are called "black swan" and, as long-term solutions, strong cooperation networks and common funds should be established.

## References

Açıkgöz B (2011) Globalization and global public goods. In: Pachura P (ed) New knowledge in a new era of globalization. Intech Publications, pp 225–242

Brousseau E, Dedeurwaerdere T, Jouvet PA, ve Willinger M (2012) Introduction: global environmental commons: analytical and political challenges in building governance mechanisms. Brousseau E, Dedeurwaerdere T, Jouvet PA, Ve Willinger M (eds), vol 1. Oxford University Press, UK. https://doi.org/10.1093/acprof:oso/9780199656202.003.0001

Collier P (2008) The bottom billion: why the poorest countries are failing and what can be done about it. Oxford University Press, Oxford

Cook LD, ve Sachs J (1999) Regional public goods in international assistance. In: Kaul I, Grunberg I, Stern MA (eds) Global public goods: international cooperation in the 21st century. Oxford University Press, New York, pp 436–449

Drager N, ve Beaglehole R (2001) Globalization: changing the public health landscape. Bulletin World Health Org 79:803

European Commission (2020) Coordinated economic response to the COVID-19 Outbreak. https://eur-lex.europa.eu/legal-content/EN/TXT/?uri=CELEX%3A52020DC0112. Accessed on 30 Apr 2020

Feachem R, ve Medlın C (2002) Global public goods: health is wealth. Nature 417:695. https://doi.org/10.1038/417695a

Ferguson N, ve Schularıck M (2006) The empire effect: the determinants of country risk in the first age of globalization, 1880–1913. J Econ Hist 66(2):283–312

Ferguson N (2004) Colossus: the price of America's empire. The Penguin Press, New York

Ferroni M (2000) Reforming foreign aid: the role of international public goods. OED working paper series, No 4. The World Bank

Haas PM (1992) Introduction: epistemic communities and international policy coordination, Int Org 46(1)(Winter):1–35

Hale T, Angrist N, Kıra B, Petherıck A, Phıllıps T, Ve Webster S (2020) Variation in government responses to COVID-19, BSG working paper series, University of Oxford

Hırst PV, Thompson G (1999) Globalization in question, 2nd edn. Polity Press, Cambridge

Hınh TD (2020) COVID-19 and government policies, https://www.policycenter.ma/opinion/covid-19-and-government-policies#.XueQZG5uLIU. Accessed on 17 June 2020

IMF World Economic Outlook (2020) The great lockdown. https://www.imf.org/en/Publications/WEO/Issues/2020/04/14/weo-april-2020. Accessed on 30 Apr 2020

Jayaraman R, Ve Kanbur R (1999) International public goods and the case for foreign aid. In: Kaul I, Grunberg I, Stern MA (eds) Global public goods: international cooperation in the 21st century. Oxford University Press, New York, pp 418–435

Kaul I, Conceição P, Le Goulven K, ve Mendoza RU (2003) Providing global public goods: managing globalization. Oxford University Press, New York

Kaul I, Faust M (2001) Global public goods and health: taking the agenda forward. Bulletin World Health Org 79:869–874

Kaul I, Grunberg I, ve Stern MA (1999a) Global public goods: international cooperation in the 21st century. Oxford University Press, New York

Kaul I, Grunberg I, ve Stern MA (1999b) Defining global public goods, UNDP, Oxford University Press, New York

Kaul I (2000) Global public goods https://www.globalpolicy.org/component/content/article/215-global-public-goods/46038.html. Accessed on 30 Apr 2020

Lincoln C, Evans TG, ve Cash RA (1999) Health as a global public good, UNDP. Oxford University Press, New York

Lopez AD, ve Murray CC (1998) The global burden of disease, 1990–2020. Nat Med 4:1241–1243

Mendez RP (1999) Peace as a global public good. In: Kaul I, Grunberg I, Stern MA (eds) Global public goods: international cooperation in the 21st century. Oxford University Press, New York, pp 382–416

Mıtchener KJ, ve Weidenmier M (2005) Empire, public goods, and the roosevelt corollary. J Econ Hist 65(3):658–692

OECD (2020) OECD interim economic outlook corona virus: the world economy at risk. https://www.oecd-ilibrary.org/docserver/7969896b-en.pdf?expires=1588321881&id=id&accname=guest&checksum=D85CE785DB3E618ED3BADA6410A44297. Accessed on 30 Apr 2020

Ostrom E (2012) Polycentric systems: multilevel governance involving a diversity of organizations. In: Brousseau E, Dedeurwaerdere T, Jouvet PA, Ve Willinger M (eds) Global environmental commons: analytical and political challenges in building governance mechanisms. Oxford University Press, UK.https://doi.org/10.1093/acprof:oso/9780199656202.003.0005

Perrıngs C (2012) The governance of international environmental public goods. In: Brousseau E, Dedeurwaerdere T, Jouvet PA, Ve Willinger M (eds) Global environmental commons: analytical and political challenges in building governance mechanisms. Oxford University Press, UK. https://doi.org/10.1093/acprof:oso/9780199656202.003.0003

Rodrik D (1997) Has globalization gone too far? Institute for International Economics, Washington DC

Sandler T (2011) Understanding global public goods. OECD Observer. http://www.oecdobserver.org/news/fullstory.php/aid/540/Understanding_global_public_goods.html. Accessed on 15 May 2020

Savaşan F (2012) İki Başarısızlık Arasında Kamu Ekonomisi. Trabzon: Celepler Matbaacılık

Smith RD, ve Coast J (2002) Antimicrobial resistance: a global response. Bulletin World Health Org 80:126–133

Smith RD (2004) Public goods & health, health economics lecture notes (lecture 20), Autumn 04/05

Thorsteınsdóttır H, Daar A, Smith RD, ve Singer P (2003) Genomics is a global public good? Lancet 361:891

Vatn A (2012) Environmental governance: the aspect of coordination. In: Brousseau E, Dedeurwaerdere T, Jouvet PA, Ve Willinger M (eds) Global environmental commons: analytical and political challenges in building governance mechanisms. Oxford University Press, UK. https://doi.org/10.1093/Acprof:Oso/9780199656202.003.0002

World Economic Forum (2019) Outbreak readiness and business impact: protecting lives and livelihoods across the global economy. http://www3.weforum.org/docs/WEF%20HGHI_Outbreak_Readiness_Business_Impact.pdf. Accessed on 30 Apr 2020

Young OR (2012) Navigating the sustainability transition: governing complex and dynamic socio-ecological systems. In: Brousseau E, Dedeurwaerdere T, Jouvet PA, Ve Willinger M (eds) Global environmental commons: analytical and political challenges in building governance mechanisms. Oxford University Press, UK. https://doi.org/10.1093/acprof:oso/9780199656202.003.0004

**Bernur Açıkgöz** was born in 1979 in Ankara. After attending Ankara Finance High School, she continued her undergraduate studies at Dokuz Eylül University, Department of Finance. She received her master's degree in Financial Law from Dokuz Eylül University. In 2006, she was awarded her Ph.D. degree from Dokuz Eylul University Department of Public Finance. Her Ph.D. thesis covered the topics of poverty and development. In 2006, she won the Harvard University Project scholarship and worked as a visiting professor at Harvard University. In 2009, she received a scholarship from the Swiss Government for a post-doctorate degree in economics at the University of Neuchatel/Switzerland, and taught courses at Bern Universities. She then began to work in the fields of experimental economics and game theory, and for three consecutive years as a guest lecturer in the economics laboratory of the Montpellier University in Montpellier, France. Afterwards, she went to Missouri University, Indiana University and Arizona University with a scholarship from Missouri University. She then worked as a visiting professor at the University of East Anglia and took some courses from Exeter Universities in the UK with a Tubitak scholarship. Professor Dr. Bernur Açıkgöz has books, articles and papers on foreign direct investments, economic growth, panel econometrics, experimental economics and game theory. She is currently working at the Department of Public Finance and Financial Management at Izmir Katip Çelebi University/Turkey. In addition, Açıkgöz teaches at the Department of International Trade and Finance at Izmir University of Economics/Turkey and the Department of Economics at University of Life Sciences in Poznań (Uniwersytet Przyrodniczy w Poznaniu)/Poland.

# Chapter 2
# Global Outbreaks from a Historical Perspective and Fiscal Policy: An Analysis for COVID-19 Outbreak

**Sibel Aybarç**

*Do not be afraid of the epidemic, avoid the disease,*
*Do not leave your patients,*
*Stay at home and be cheerful,*
*The disease escapes from joy.*
Master of Doctors İbn-i Sina (Avicenna (İbn-i Sina is better known in the West by the name Avicenna.)),
(930–1037)

**Abstract** Outbreaks that have changed the era throughout history affected the course of wars and have largely steered the destruction of economic order and understanding are the ancient desperation that the human beings have paid social, psychological, economic, and financial costs. In this section addresses, especially starting from 431 BC (Athens), the global outbreaks that have shaped the fate of people, empires, and nation states, the fiscal policy measures implemented in the fight against the epidemics, and particularly the policy measures that have been implemented in the context of combating COVID-19. The times of epidemics have made some state interventions inevitable; such as, on one hand, announcing support packages for the elimination of economic stagnation, on the other hand, health expenditures, personnel training, vaccine and treatment efforts, social security expenditures for the sustainability of public health, as a requirement of being a social state. In the last century, anticipation of an increase in epidemic diseases arising from the environmental destruction (especially due to the prevalence of plastic production, which is shown innocent due to its lightness, population growth, unbalanced urbanization, and excessive consumption habits) necessitates intervention through all policy instruments. The tax regulations that are taken rapidly during the epidemics are pragmatic-based and temporary. However, environmental sustainability can be ensured and preparation can be made for extraordinary periods such as epidemics and natural disasters, through the Pigovian taxes and environmentally friendly standards that will be applied in the ordinary periods. In addition, an Epidemic Tax, which will be

S. Aybarç (✉)
Finance, Banking and Insurance Program, Manisa Celal Bayar University, Ahmetli, Manisa, Turkey



B. Açıkgöz and İ. A. Acar (eds.), *Pandemnomics: The Pandemic's Lasting Economic Effects*, Accounting, Finance, Sustainability, Governance & Fraud: Theory and Application, https://doi.org/10.1007/978-981-16-8024-3_2

set up to be applied in the usual periods, will strengthen the countries' hand in terms of eliminating the possible risks in the first place, and on the other hand, it will create the social environment and financial awareness in the carbon-epidemic-externality spiral.

**Keywords** Pandemic history · Global outbreaks · Black Plague · COVID-19 · Financial highlights · Fiscal policy · Pandemic tax

## 2.1 Introduction

While it is assumed that the human beings have gained momentum of development throughout the history, they have gained the power to dominate nature and have endured the negative consequences of living in a community and as settled. The most important of these are fatal epidemic diseases. Transition from hunter-gatherer life to agricultural society, killing animals' habitats; the spread of intercontinental trade with geographical discoveries; the destruction of nature and the employment of people in crowded work environments upon transition from the agricultural society to the industrial society; the emergence of globalization's unlimited transportation opportunities upon transition from industrial society to information society, and disruption of the ecological balance along with convenience of technology upon transition from the information society to the super smart society has also brought the appropriate ground to reproduce and contamination ability for the invisible virulent microbes.

In human development momentum, the cornerstone for preparing the suitable ground for microbes can be considered as approximately 10,000 years ago. Most of the microbes that cause infectious diseases, especially in crowded societies, with the transition to the settled life required by the agricultural society, were derived with the mutation of microbes in animals (smallpox, 1600 BC, mumps, 400 BC, leprosy 200 BC) with which food producers had close relation (Diamond 2010). Outbreaks, which generally occur due to war, migration, climate change, famine, malnutrition during periods of drought, poor hygiene, have shaped not only the city and castle architecture (Özlü and Tiryaki 2019), but also world history. While the mankind was trying to overcome the process, at first, by seeking help from the gods[1] in the face of global pandemics, which he caught unpredictably and helplessly, they, in time, tried to manage the process with tax and other obligations, various public services, and legal regulations (Labour Law, easy citizenship) in a way that differs from country to country. Today, both nation states and international organizations have entered the process of combating the epidemic with economic, financial, social, and political policy measures.

---

[1] In the face of the epidemic, remedies were sought in the Christian world from religious offerings, talismans, spells, religious rituals, and priests, while quarantine, which was a public measure, was applied in time in line with the approach of the Prophet Muhammed, "*not entering any place with the plague and not going out from that environment*" (Bayat 2016).

The times of epidemics have made some state interventions inevitable; such as, on one hand, announcing support packages for the elimination of economic stagnation, on the other hand, health expenditures, personnel training, vaccine, and treatment efforts, social security expenditures for the sustainability of public health, as a requirement of being a social state. This section addresses, especially starting from 431 BC (Athens), the global outbreaks that have shaped the fate of people, empires, and nation states, the fiscal policy measures implemented in the fight against the epidemics, and particularly the policy measures that have been implemented in the context of combating COVID-19.

## 2.2 Global Outbreaks from an Historical Perspective

The historical origin of the contagious diseases, which constitute global public problems, goes back to human beings start settling and cultivating the soil.

The life of hunter-gatherer groups varied according to regional and climatic factors, but it was more comfortable and healthier than the life of the settled societies. Destruction of forests over time in order to reach cultivable agricultural areas narrowed the living space of various animals (such as mice, ticks, mosquitoes, bats) and forced them to live with people. Various infectious diseases such as tuberculosis, malaria, plague, typhus, measles, and smallpox have found an environment suitable for the spread of an epidemic, especially after domestication of animals (Table 2.1). In the historical development process, upon the geographical discoveries, overseas trade, industrial revolution and the working environment, population growth, and the change in settlement style, most people had to live in stuck collective dwellings that are far from hygienic conditions that paved the way for the spread of infectious diseases (Harari 2015). In line with these developments, working, living, and transportation conditions were the main determinants for creating an environment suitable for the infectious disease to become an epidemic.

We have arranged the heaviest fatal epidemic diseases experienced throughout human history, benefiting from the historical development table outlined by LePan

**Table 2.1** Domesticated animals and human diseases that they'll be able to cause

| Human diseases | Animal that carries a close relative of the microbe |
|---|---|
| Measles | Cattle (Rinderpest) |
| Tuberculosis | Cattle |
| Smallpox | Cattle (Smallpox in cows) |
| Flu | Pig and duck |
| Whooping cough | Pig and dog |
| Falciparum Malaria | Birds (Chickens, ducks) |

*Source* Diamond (2010)

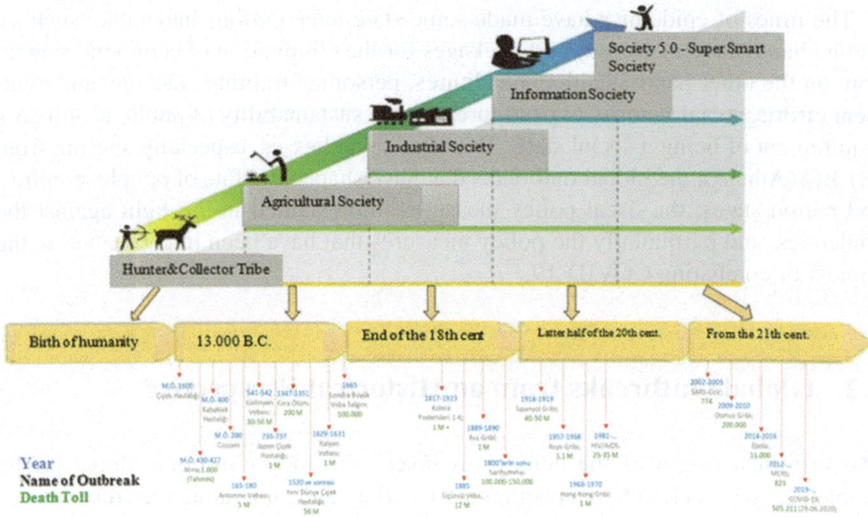


**Fig. 2.1** Pandemic history from hunter society to super intelligent society. *Source* (Generated by the author by compiling the data in Fukuyama 2018; Yıldız 2018; LePan 2020)

(2020) and the social development map visualized by Fukuyama (2018), Yıldız (2018) (Fig. 2.1).

Table 2.2 shows the global outbreaks experienced throughout human history, the pathology of the disease, and the number of deaths caused.

## 2.3 Epidemic Diseases in Primeval Era

While the most frightening epidemic diseases which demands the most time for its elimination throughout the history of humanity spontaneously emerged, at first, due to the change in social life and consumption conditions, they were then developed as biological threats in line with strategic goals.

The Peloponnesian War, which lasted 27 years between Athens and Sparta (and the allies of these two city states) in the Ancient Greek geography between 431 and 404 BC, paved the way for the Athens Outbreak, which was the first outbreak in history and resulted in the death of a third of the population (History.com Editors 2020).

Although it is called the plague outbreak in the beginning, it is thought, as inferred from the related works of Thukydides, the second great historian of Ancient Greece, that it might have been bubonic plague, smallpox, measles, typhoid, typhus, and even Ebola. However, in the last quarter of the twentieth century, it was understood that the epidemic was caused by typhoid, a water-based pathogen, upon examining the mass graves determined to belong to the Peloponnesian War period. As Thukydides

**Table 2.2** Global pandemic examples: period, host, death toll

| Name of outbreak | Time period | Type/pre-human host | Death toll |
|---|---|---|---|
| Athens outbreak | B.C. 430–427 | Waterborne Pathogen Typhoid | 1000 (Tahmini) |
| Antonine plague | 165–180 | Estimated to be either smallpox or measles | 5 M |
| Plague of justinian | 541–542 | Yersinia pestis bacteria/Rats, fleas | 30–50 M |
| Japanese smallpox outbreak | 735–737 | Variola major virus | 1 M |
| Black death | 1347–1351 | Yersinia pestis bacteria/Rats, fleas | 200 M |
| New world smallpox outbreak | 1520 and then | Variola major virus | 56 M |
| İtalian Plague | 1629–1631 | Yersinia pestis bacteria/Rats, fleas | 1 M |
| Great Plague of London | 1665 | Yersinia pestis bacteria/Rats, fleas | 100.000 |
| Cholera pandemics 1–6 | 1817–1923 | Vibrio cholreae bacteria | 1 M+ |
| Third Plague | 1885 | Yersinia pestis bacteria/Rats, fleas | 12 M (China and India) |
| Russian Flu | 1889–1890 | Estimated to be $H_2N_2$ (possibly avian origin) | 1 M |
| Yellow fever | End of 1800s | Virus/Mosquitoes | 100,000–150,000 (U.S.A.) |
| Spanish Flu | 1918–1919 | $H_1N_1$ virus/Pigs | 40–50 M |
| Asian Flu | 1957–1958 | $H_2N_2$ virus | 1.1 M |
| Hong Kong Flu | 1968–1970 | $H_3N_2$ virus | 1 M |
| HIV/AIDS | 1981–present | Virus/Chimpanzees | 25–35 M |
| SARS-CoV | 2002–2003 | Coronavirus/Bats, Civet cats | 774 |
| Swine Flu | 2009–2010 | $H_1N_1$/Pigs | 200,000 |
| Ebola | 2014–2016 | Ebolavirus/Wild animals | 11,000 |
| MERS | 2012–present | Coronavirus/Camels, Bats | 823 |
| COVID-19 | 2019–present | Coronavirus/Unknown (possibly pangolins, bats) | 507,518 (30.6.2020) |

*Source* LePan (2020)

stated in his writings, it was found that those who were sick threw themselves into the surrounding wells due to high fever and the epidemic spread rapidly from these wells (Turan 2018).

In the Roman Empire, The Antonine Outbreak (Galen Outbreak), which was effective between 165 and 180 AC, was the biggest epidemic ever seen. The origin/contamination point of the outbreak caused by smallpox was thought to be the

Parthia Expedition of Roman Legions, especially in 165. On the one hand, the Roman soldiers who returned to their posts after the expedition and on the other hand, the active use of the Silk Road caused the spread of the epidemic in a large geography from Asia to Europe and the death of more than 5 million people (Diamond 2010). Most of the Roman army was lost due to the epidemic, and commercial activities were interrupted. This process was perceived as the beginning of the end for the Roman Empire.

### 2.3.1 Three Plague Outbreaks and Financial Practices

The epidemic that human history has had to struggle with the most has been the plague. Although having a complicated chronology and painful results from the Middle Ages up to the twentieth century, plague outbreaks are gathered under three main episodes. These are (Achtman et al. 1999; Abbott and Rocke 2012, Snowden 2019): Justinian plague outbreak (fifth century-seventh century); Black Death (thirteenth-fifteenth century); and modern plague outbreak (after 1870).

### 2.3.2 Justinian Plague Outbreak and Financial Practices

The Justinian Plague outbreak, which was the first plague outbreak in the Middle Ages and occurred in 541–542, started in Ethiopia and turned to Anatolia through the Mediterranean and Middle East, and from there to the east and west, and affected the continents. The bubonic plague[2] epidemic spread by black rats and fleas on them carried by cereal ships and cars sent as tribute to Istanbul, which was the center of Byzantium, resulted in the death of 50 million people in 3 years. The death of 16,000 people in Constantinople (Istanbul) in just one day has led to the perception of the epidemic as “the wrath of God.” The vast majority of the population going down with the disease brought agricultural and economic activities to a standstill, and as a result, a spiral of scarcity and inflation was introduced (Arık 1991; Horgan 2014). The impact of the epidemic continued with eighteen aftershocks in a wide geography from the Balkans to North Africa from the Middle East to Europe, in the years 558, 560–561, 571, 573–574, 591–592, 597, 598, 599, 599–600, 600–601, 618–619, 698, 747–748 (Stathakopoulos 2007).

As a result of the interruption of production and consumption during these periods, the fact that the tax-generating event could not happen resulted in a decrease in tax revenues. Despite such a collapse of the economic system, Emperor Justinian

[2] Plague ocuurs in three types: (i) bubonic plague (the lightest form of the disease that grows in the spleen, liver, and lymph nodes, the duration of death is 3–6 days), (ii) lung plague (the type of plague caused by the spread of bacteria that have passed into the blood as a result of bubonic plague, the duration of death is 2–4 days), (iii) plague sepsis (plague that poison the blood, duration of death is very short) (Arık 1991).

(Justinyen) continued to collect the same level of tax from the declining population. In addition, despite the economic, financial, and demographic conditions of the day, the Emperor started wars on other principalities and even engaged in public investment projects despite the lack of resources (such as the capital Hagia Sophia and church construction) (Horgan 2014; Huremovic 2019). The church construction work continued as it was believed that it was possible to get rid of the existing diseases by praying.

### 2.3.3 *Black Death Epidemic Period and Financial Practices*

The bubonic plague epidemic, which played an important role in the collapse of the Roman Empire, was the deadliest epidemic in history under the name of Black Death[3] because it caused the death of 200 million people between 1347 and 1351 (Acemoğlu and Robinson 2013). The plague carried by the fleas living on the rats was spread from China to the Mediterranean through the merchants using the Silk Road; by the Mongolian armies to Kefe; and to Istanbul, Sicily, and Europe through the Genoese who fled Kefa. Living conditions of medieval Europe (living in the same house with animals in the narrow living spaces in the city surrounded by high stone wall for protection from invasion, low immune system due to food shortage), religious traditions (especially some churches see "pollution" as a form of holiness), and increasing population accelerated the spread of the plague. As a public service in the face of this two-headed illness mutating in Europe and turned into a lung plague, Parisians were tried to be warned with black flags hanging on the bell towers (Özden and Özmat 2014).

In the early fourteenth century, when the plague began, unequal power relations in medieval Europe deepened economic depression and poverty, causing the epidemic to particularly increase its financial impact. This is summarized by the paleoecologist Per Lageras as follows (Snowden 2019):

> Even under normal circumstances, ordinary people are poor in medieval Europe. They are faced with high tax burdens, rentals, 10% of landowner taxes on the product in England (tithes) and heavy working burdens. In the European economy based on agriculture, while the upper class of the period did not want to compromise on the level of well-being and luxury spending, the population is growing in Europe and revenues are insufficient and the period of economic recession began. Especially with the effect of climate conditions, revenues declined rapidly, which disturbed the upper class, and thus, taxes and rents were increased. As a result of the stagnant economy and unsustainable agriculture, people have reached the limit of hunger.

The scarcity of labor supply as a result of the plague epidemic encouraged the surviving peasants and made them demanding about the wage increases and decrease in their liabilities and chores. Despite various legal arrangements (such as the control of the increase in wages by the Labour Law, imprisonment for those who leave

[3] Referred to as "home-destroying plague" by Ibn Khaldun (İbn-i Haldun 2018).

work without the consent of the employer) aiming at eliminating the developments unsettling the feudal structure, the desired success was not achieved (Acemoğlu and Robinson 2013). In fact, the Peasants' Revolt was initiated in 1381 under the leadership of Watt Tyler as a result of; the removal of various privileges after the epidemic in England which were introduced during the plague epidemic (such as the allocation of land to be paid in time by working), the obligation to work in the church for at least two days a week as a tax in kind, and the poll tax, which was enacted in 1380 to finance the French war (5 pound fixed tax collected in cash). The poll tax was abolished in 1382 to prevent a new rebellion attempt as a result of the revolt that was suppressed in a short time (Aktan et al. 2002; Gök 2007). In Vienna, in order to revive the economy after the epidemic, taxes were removed, the people were granted the right of ownership, and those who wanted were immediately granted citizenship (Wish 2017). In Medieval Europe, where medicine is seen as a sub-branch of natural philosophy, and physicians as the wise persons that wealthy families can reach, public health and disease control have spread to the social base and the public started to be provided with public health services (Özden and Özmat 2014).

The age-changing victory, the conquest of Istanbul (1453), brought about the continuous expansion of the Ottoman Empire. The Ottoman Empire lived three phases of plague (Varlık 2018):

- "First phase" between 1453 and 1517 through caravan routes in the Balkans and European ports in the Mediterranean,
- "Second phase" between 1517 and 1570 as a result of the conquest of Syria, Egypt, Mecca, and Medina and the increasing population and centralized policies implemented,
- "Third phase" between 1570 and 1600 as a result of Istanbul becoming the nodes of the disease that affected Europe, North Africa, and Near East.

During his visit to Egypt, Evliya Çelebi emphasized the financial impact of the epidemic by stating that a village was abandoned nine times within three months due to the ta'un[4] epidemic; the tax farmers gave up their tax collection rights because they could not collect income (Ertaş and Eğnim 2011).

The Ottoman Empire, which spread to three continents during its strongest era, was affected by outbreaks due to its geographical location. In this process, especially Suleiman the Magnificent built thousands of health institutions across the continents with the idea of, "*There is no respected object in the public as state / there is no such thing in the world as health*". However, despite the public measures taken, hundreds of thousands of people lost their lives (Başağaoğlu et al. 2015).

The epidemic, which continued until the mid-eighteenth century, reappeared in 1640 in Scotland, 1665–1666 in the UK, 1710 in the Netherlands, 1720–1722 in France, and 1743 in Italy. Therefore, the impact of the 2nd plague epidemic, called Black Death, continued in Europe from 1347 to 1743, albeit intermittently with different waves (Snowden 2019).

[4] Name given to the plague in the Ottoman Empire.

In eighteenth-century France, a privileged class corresponding to 5% of the 25 million population consisted of nobles and clergies, while 95% consisted of the non-privileged class of bourgeoisie, craftsman and (22 million) peasants. The peasants were obliged to pay "tax" to the state, "feudal tribute" to the noble class, and "tithe" to the clergy class (Huberman 2009). In the last quarter of the eighteenth century, the poor people in France were almost crushed under the taxes that the king and the nobility who paid no tax but had the privilege to impose feudal tax applied to reduce the budget deficit. French peasants were subject to heavy tax and financial obligations, such as tithes to the church, 20% income tax (vingtieme), poll tax (capitation), salt tax (gabelle), cash feudal rent (cens), rent in kind (champart), land purchase and sale tax (lods et ventes), corporal tax (corvee) as a participation in the compulsory road construction work (Rude 2015). Despite the fact that feudalism was in the process of dissolving in the eighteenth century, the villagers were exposed to heavy feudal obligations for a long time. The heaviest of these was the taxes on salt and wine (Yakut 2010). As a matter of fact, salt had been used to protect foods for a long time and to prevent the spread of outbreaks throughout history. In times when the salt, also called white gold, was insufficient, famine and outbreaks were seen. The fact that French villagers had to spend about 15% of their income on salt tax, persecution in tax collections, salt smuggling, and heavy penalties led to reduced salt consumption, causing food to deteriorate and weaken the people against epidemics. It was even an important factor on the road to the French Revolution of 1789 (Sharman 2019).

### *2.3.4 Modern Plague Outbreak and Financial Practices*

With the industrial revolution that started in the UK, especially the production of steam machines increased international trade and economic development, while causing the rapid transport of epidemic diseases. In this context, the third major epidemic, referred to as the Central Asia-origin Modern Plague Outbreak, was inevitable. The plague epidemic that emerged in China in 1855 had its effect in Canton and Hong Kong in 1894. Thanks to international trade with steamships, not only goods but also rats with fleas moved to the cities of Buenos Aires, Honolulu, Sydney, Cape Town, Naples, Oporto, and San Francisco (Abbott and Rocke 2012; Snowden 2019).

Apart from the plague, the nineteenth-century world also witnessed outbreaks such as cholera and typhoid (Karalöse 2017). After the plague epidemic in Aleppo at the beginning of the nineteenth century, the fact that Christians, who carried out the majority of commercial activities, quarantined themselves at home, disrupted the economic life. The governor of Aleppo introduced new taxes to this segment, who resisted staying at home and discontinuing commercial activity (Marcus 2013 cited in Çalışkan Eyicil, 2019). Having a dynamic and active structure with activities such as military expeditions, trade relations, pilgrimage visits, the Ottoman Empire faced a strong epidemic again in 1894 (Turna 2011).

Diseases such as plague (cattle plague) and cholera were combatted during the nineteenth century by some measures such as increasing the taxes on sheep and goats for Aleppo's cleaning expenses, collecting taxes for cord costs in Damascus, building new hospitals, assigning doctors, pharmacists, and veterinarians from the center (Çalışkan and Eyicil 2019). Since the epidemic caused the death of many people and animals, it affected the economic and social life negatively.

Although different diseases were observed during the modern plague epidemic period, the result did not change. It is stated that the modern plague epidemic ended in the 1960s by the World Health Organization. However, occasional plague cases are accepted as the aftershocks of the modern plague epidemic (Varlık 2018).

## 2.4 Epidemics and Financial Practices from the Twentieth Century to Today

The twentieth century, when human beings stepped on the moon, transitioned into the information age with technological developments, and marked an era in science by developing robots, was also the scene of various and deadly outbreaks. As a matter of fact, the two major world wars, the globalization trend and the mobility and migration movements, brought along outbreaks. The difference from previous epidemic adventures is that it shows a faster spread especially with the improvement in transportation opportunities. In addition, climate change (extreme heat and drought) caused by the increase in carbon emissions due to the increasing population and excessive consumption habits paved the way for the occurrence of various epidemics. It was perceived in another scenario as the most vital tool of war strategy. Although new measures were taken within the framework of developing economic and financial policies, collective deaths were inevitable.

### *2.4.1 Spanish Flu (1918–1919) and Financial Practices*

Considered to be the deadliest disease of the modern age, Spanish flu is estimated to have infected a 30–50% of the world's population and killed 50 million people. The deadly virus $H_1N_1$, which emerged during World War I, was detected in the troops of both sides and the flow of information was restricted due to war reasons. Two possibilities were considered regarding the origin of the virus. In this context, the virus either started in China and came through the Chinese who migrated to North America or spread to the whole world in March 1918 from a military camp and prison in America where the first cases were seen. The epidemic was called the Spanish flu, as the world public learned about this through Spanish newspapers that did not participate in the war and were exempt from embargo (Lina 2008).

The second wave, which started in Europe and North America in August 1918 and when 90% of deaths were recorded, increased the number of cases that could not make it possible to fight in October 1918. This created a strong belief that the outbreak was responsible for the end of the war. The third wave that took place in January 1919 showed a striking effect (Lina 2008). The number of people who lost their lives due to the epidemic is estimated to be 5 to 10 times more than those who died in World War I (Cotter 2020). In fact, according to some estimates, the deaths toll is thought to exceed 100 million. The Spanish flu, which spread from America to Asia, from Africa to the Pacific Islands, resulted in the grave picture in one year which the Black Death caused throughout a century. In addition, the epidemic was the first in terms of observability of long-term effects. Increased physical disability, low-income level, low socio-economic status, and higher transfer payments were identified in the post-epidemic (especially births and born generation) studies (Almond 2006; Huremovic 2019).

Information on the economic impact of Spanish flu is limited, both due to the fact that most governments have limited the flow of information because of the war, and that national income accounting was in its infancy at the time. The study of the Canadian Ministry of Finance suggested that the decreases in the industrial and commercial activity index resulted in only 0.4% loss in annual production (IMF 2006). The 1960s study investigating the effect of the outbreak in India suggested that agricultural production decreased by more than 3% (Schultz 1964 cited in IMF 2006). In addition, it was estimated that 8% of the agricultural workforce was infected and the heavy cost of the epidemic (through taxes and similar liabilities) was laid on the surviving section (IMF 2006).

### 2.4.2 *HIV/AIDS Virus (1981– …) and Response Through Financial Policy Instruments*

The HIV/AIDS epidemic, which started in the early 1980s in America and spread slowly throughout different continents and generations, has caused the death of more than 35 million people (Huremovic 2019). Evolving from wild African apes to humans, the virus produces new antigens while in the victim's body and causes a person's immune system to collapse (Diamond 2010).

As of the end of 2018, 37.9 million (36.2 million adult individuals, 1.7 million children under the age of 15) people live with HIV worldwide, while 1.7 million new people was infected with the epidemic. The epidemic has been infected by 74.9 million people since its inception in 1981 and killed more than 32 million people. The death toll, which peaked in 2004 with 1.7 million people, decreased to 770 thousand in 2018, especially with the policies pursued in underdeveloped countries where the virus was common. Since 2010, there has been a 33% reduction in the fatality rate arising from AIDS (UNAIDS 2019).

AIDS was declared by the World Bank as an economic development crisis in 2000. In some countries in sub-Saharan Africa, growth per capita was estimated to have decreased by 0.5% to 1.2% each year as a direct result of AIDS (Zakaria 2015). The vast majority of people with HIV worldwide live in East and South Africa (UNAIDS 2019). In the post-2010 period, Esvatini (Swaziland), Botswana, and Lesotho in South Africa were the countries with the highest adult HIV/AIDS prevalence in the world, with rates of respectively 25.9%, 24.8% 23.6%. While the epidemic, which is an important threat to development, decelerate the growth rate and increases medical care and health expenditures in the short term due to the sudden reaction in many countries' economies, whereas in the long term, losses especially in human capital affect the transfer of information between generations and cause a risk (Anyanwu et al. 2013).

Untimely deaths due to AIDS reduce the qualified workforce and cause a long and costly replacement process. This was supported by findings in a study conducted in Tanzania that an estimated 40 billion dollars should be spent to train new teachers instead of teachers who died from AIDS by 2010 (Çilingiroğlu 1998). Direct and indirect visible and invisible costs must be determined in order to determine the economic and financial dimension of the outbreak and to intervene in this direction (Çilingiroğlu 1998). These costs are:

- "direct visible costs" such as diagnostic tests, health and personnel training, consultancy services, R&D activities,
- "direct invisible costs," such as care services provided by patients' relatives and charities, for free,
- "Indirect visible costs," such as production losses due to illness and untimely death,
- "indirect invisible costs," such as physical and psychological decline due to factors such pain, ache, anxiety, fear, blame, isolated life, depression as well as deterioration in quality of life.

Measures to combat AIDS are implemented according to the development level of the countries on a national scale, the priorities of health policies, and the effectiveness of donors and activists on an international scale. Within the scope of combating the AIDS epidemic, 90-90-90 global HIV targets set by UNAIDS are listed as follows (UNAIDS 2014):

- By 2020, 90% of individuals infected with HIV will know their HIV status.
- By 2020, 90% of all individuals diagnosed with HIV infection will receive continuous Antiretroviral Therapy (ART).
- By 2020, 90% of individuals in the ART process will have viral suppression (Fig. 2.2).

In the fight against AIDS, which is a global public good, diagnosis is very important for the detection and course of the disease. As seen in Fig. 2.3, rapid diagnostic tests are offered as public service. The most humane approach in the fight against AIDS is the production of vaccines and drugs that are still in the experimental stage in the public sphere (Saçaklıoğlu 2006).

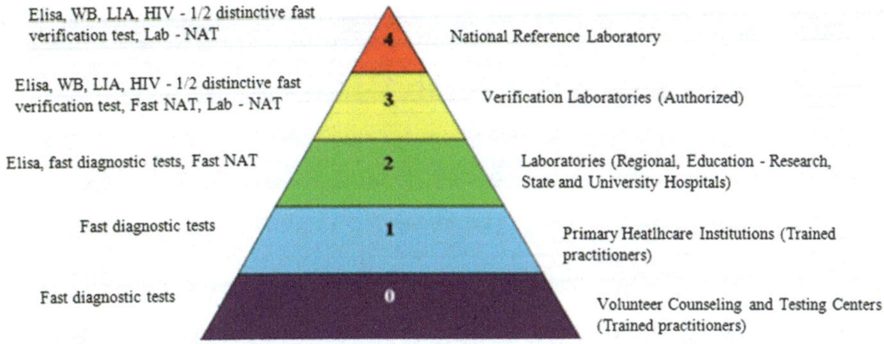


**Fig. 2.2** Level based test centers and the responsibilities of laboratory. *Source* (By using WHO 2015, T.R. Ministry of Health, 2019)

In Turkey, among the main duties of the Turkish Ministry of Health is "to perform preventive, curative medicine and rehabilitation services by fighting infectious, epidemic and social diseases".[5] In addition to the health services provided to the patients by the Ministry of Health, in-service trainings (such as Epidemic Intelligence Service, Basic Training Courses, Extended Immunization Program Trainings) are provided under investment current expenditures for the purpose of infectious disease surveillance and control (Durusoy et al. 2011).

Upon the publication of "HIV/AIDS Control Program (2019–2024)" and "HIV/AIDS Diagnosis and Treatment Guideline 2019" by the Turkish Ministry of Health, the effort to strengthen the fight against disease is revealed. In addition, patients diagnosed with HIV/AIDS in Turkey (regardless of whether they already have insurance) can benefit from examination and innovative treatment services free of charge within the scope of Global Health Insurance (T.C. Sağlık Bakanlığı 2019).

Public spending on health can be increased by increasing the financial capacity of governments, collecting more taxes, or prioritizing health spending from the government budget. The health ministries of the countries should work in an intervening and active manner in the framework of the budget, public financial management systems, and fiscal space/opportunities, together with the ministries of finance. Investments on HIV/AIDS should support the fair distribution of public resources devoted to combating HIV (WHO 2016).

[5] Official Gazette of 13.12.1983 No. 181: 14.12.1983 O.G. No 18251. Decree Law on the Organization and Duties of the Ministry of Health.

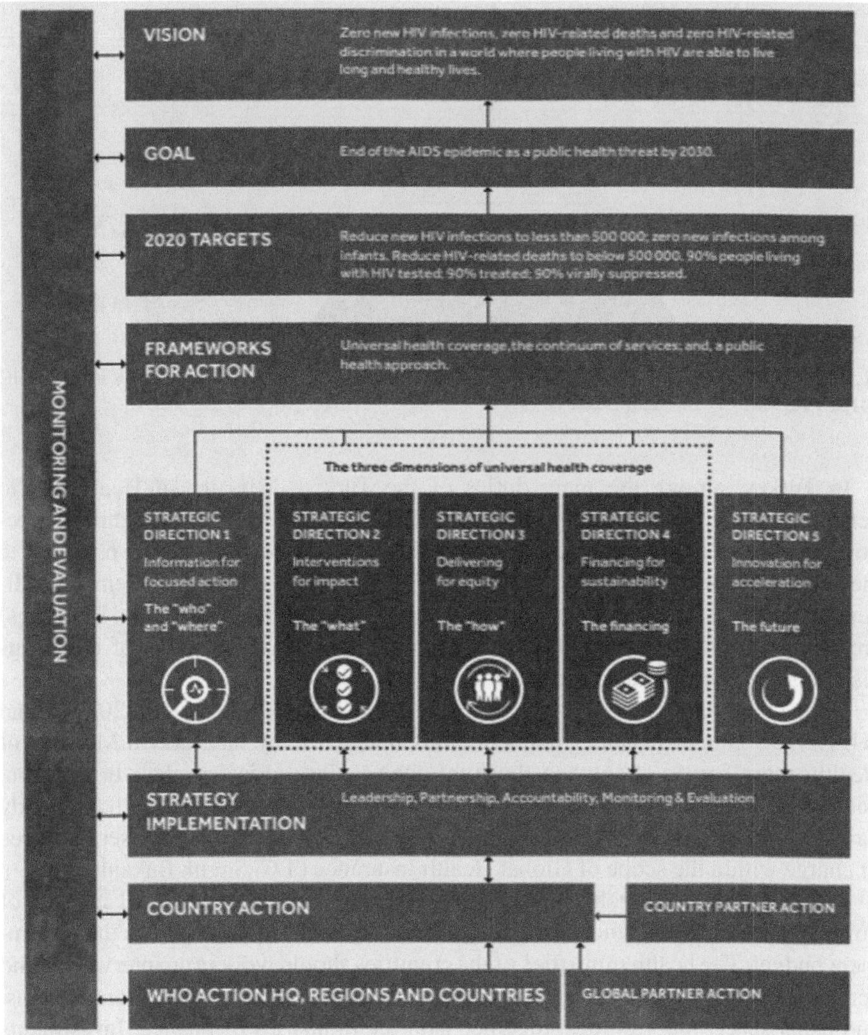


**Fig. 2.3** Global health sector strategy (2016–2021). *Source* WHO (2016)

## 2.5 Corona Virus-Based Millennium Outbreaks and Intervention Through Fiscal Policy Instruments

The use of fossil fuels in production and the popularization of plastic production introduced by the industrial revolution has been the beginning of the inevitable end for human beings on the sustainable environment; such that global economic growth has not been possible without plastic since World War II. In this case, plastics are both driving force and problem of globalization (HBF, BFFP 2019).

In addition to the change in production methods and tools, crowding cost, consumption increase, technological development, increase the emission of chlorofluorocarbon gases, creating greenhouse gas effect. These gases, which hold the heat reflected on the earth, act as a covering around the atmosphere, creating an average surface temperature of 15 °C. Increased drought due to climate anomalies brings along the decrease in agricultural yield in most regions, water shortage, the risk of epidemic disease such as malaria and related economic problems (Kadılar 2010). As a matter of fact, especially in underdeveloped countries, poor nutrition (consumption of wild meat through live animal markets), heavy working conditions, strict adherence to traditions, common diseases also prevent the efficiency of manpower (Tütengil 1971) and the economic bottleneck may deepen.

Geographies (Amazon, Central Africa, Asia), where medium and severe food insecurity are experienced in the world, also have the forests with the largest biological diversity. However, the destruction of forests for timber trade, mining, and palm oil production from palm trees for generating income has affected all balances of the environment. As a result of deforestation, wild animals, who had to live closer to humans, found an environment to transfer viruses that can turn into epidemics.

The coronavirus family causing respiratory infection which was discovered by K. McIntosh, PhD, and his team in 1968 was observed in the form of SARS-CoV-1 (2003), MERS-CoV (2012) since the beginning of the twenty-first century and made its striking effect with SARS-CoV2-COVID-19 (TÜBA 2020).

## 2.6 Epidemics Before COVID-19 and Intervention Through Fiscal Policy Instruments

The coronavirus family circulating among the people consists of HCoV-229E, HCoV-OC43, HCoV-NL63, HKU1-CoV, and SARS-CoV-1, MERS-CoV, and COVID-19, which have an epidemic effect. SARS-CoV, which first appeared in China in 2002, was effective in 29 countries between 2002 and 2003. SARS-CoV, which is thought to have been transmitted from bats to palm cats and from there to people, infected 8,098 people worldwide and caused 774 deaths (Akyol 2005; Şengöz 2013; Maden 2014; TTD 2020).

MERS-CoV, a member of the coronavirus family, also appeared in Saudi Arabia in 2012, infecting 2206 people in 27 countries, causing 823 deaths. Bat-origin virus is thought to have been transmitted to humans through camels (Maden 2014; TTD 2020; TÜBA 2020). While the fatality rate as a result of SARS-CoV was 9.5%, this ratio was recorded as 37.3% with a fourfold increase in MERS-CoV.

Publishing a report in mid-2003, the Asian Development Bank conducted a review of possible losses in GDP if the SARS outbreak ends in one financial quarter and two financial quarters. According to the findings, in the first case, the annual GDP growth rate of 2003 fiscal year was 0.4% compared to the starting point where there was no epidemic in East Asian countries, while in Southeast Asian countries, the

**Table 2.3** Economic impact prediction of SARS: selected asian countries (2003)

| Countries | Possibility of ending in 1 quarter—loss of GDP growth | Possibility of ending in 2 quarter—loss of GDP growth |
|---|---|---|
| East Asia | 0.4 | 1.0 |
| China | 0.2 | 0.5 |
| Hong Kong | 1.8 | 4.0 |
| South Korea | 0.2 | 0.5 |
| Taiwan | 0.9 | 1.9 |
| Southeast Asia | 0.5 | 1.4 |
| Indonesia | 0.5 | 1.4 |
| Malaysia | 0.6 | 1.5 |
| Philippines | 0.3 | 0.8 |
| Singapore | 1.1 | 2.3 |
| Thailand | 0.7 | 1.6 |

*Source* Fan (2003)

ratio in question was estimated to have decreased by 0.5%. In the second case, it was estimated the annual GDP growth rate of 2003 fiscal year was 1.0% compared to the starting point where there is no epidemic in East Asian countries; while in the Southeast Asian countries, the ratio in question was estimated to have decreased by 1.4% (Table 2.3) (Fan 2003).

In the face of the vulnerability brought by the outbreaks that occurred one after another, countries have entered the process of struggling with all their policy instruments. As can be understood from the above economic picture, Asian countries, when faced with SARS under the impact of the previous crisis, fiscal balances were out of control. In Hong Kong in particular which was severely affected, the government revenues declined by more than 35% nominally between the fiscal year 1997/1998 and the fiscal year 2002/2003, as a result of the decline in the private sector and the asset market and increases in health and social security spending. This loss of income caused increased budget deficits from fiscal year 1998/1999 (excluding fiscal year 1999/2000) to fiscal year 2003/2004. Reforms were made to balance the financial position. Considering the process as a whole, 40% of financial reserves (approximately HK $182 million) were spent on financing health expenditures in Hong Kong (HKMA 2012).

Especially in Far Eastern countries where tourism has a large share in national income, epidemic exacerbated the economic crisis by disrupting travel and tourism. For example, according to a study investigating the impact of the MERS epidemic on the South Korean tourism industry, the industry suffered a loss of approximately $ 2.6 million (Delivorias and Scholz 2020).

## 2.7 COVID-19 Pandemic and Intervention Through Fiscal Policy Instruments

The SARS-CoV2 (COVID-19) outbreak has marked the twenty-first century, defined as the "super smart society" (Baykal 2018), which aims at the high level integration of the cyberspace and the physical life space, where the concepts of Industry 4.0 and Society 5.0 are discussed.

COVID-19, which was seen in the local seafood market in Wuhan, China in December 2019, is thought to have derived from the bats (even a rhinolophus) but, as it was not sold in the market in question, it is thought to have passed from pangolin (scaly anteater) as an intermediate host to humans (TÜBA 2020; Ak 2020). The epidemic that influenced the whole world infected 10.402.637 people and caused the death of 507.518 people as of 30 June 2020 (Worldometer 2020). The fatality rate of approximately 5% in a period as short as 6 months from the first death of January is a signal that it will have a more severe effect than other outbreaks if individual, national, and international measures are disrupted.

During the epidemic periods before the Keynesian economic theory that emerged in the 1930s, the role of the state in the economy was limited. However, with the Keynesian theory, with the state interventionism becoming effective in the economy, the process of struggling through public fiscal policies and instruments was initiated in the next epidemic periods. In the face of the COVID-19 outbreak, which left its mark on 2020, countries quickly implemented government support packages as large as those not seen apart from the long war periods. This suggests that the epidemic will cause a long-term economic crisis, when viewed from a broad perspective, and will lead to increased role and scope of state interventionism even in developed liberal economies (Pamuk 2020).

Stating that there are no institutions to meet this expectation in the USA and European countries, which are expected to assume such an enormous role, Acemoğlu (2020) points out the need for the formation of strong non-governmental organizations and new democratic institutions, which are powerful and can balance the power of the state, from the examples of Singapore, Taiwan, Japan, and South Korea (Acemoğlu 2020).

The pandemic has stimulated the cooperation platforms both nationally and globally, shaping economic, financial, and social policies with legal institutional arrangements in cooperation. Tax policy should be coordinated with other policy levers (health, trade, labor market policy and social, financial, and monetary policies). For example, in some countries, social spending may be more efficient in providing financial support to households; tax policies can support the cash flow to the private sector with the specified measures; the capacity of companies to manage corporate debt burdens can be increased by facilitating their credit access. Providing liquidity support to businesses, especially through tax delays, has been a priority policy instrument in most countries. Tax delays provide cash flow support to businesses, especially when applied to taxes to be paid during the fiscal year (such as Value Added Tax, taxes on wage income, and social security contributions) (Table 2.4). Similarly, fiscal

**Table 2.4** Tax regulations in combating COVID-19: country examples

| Countries | Income tax and social security withholdings | Corporata tax | Value added tax |
|---|---|---|---|
| China | – Healthcare personnel bonuses are excluded from tax<br>– Social security premium payments have been postponed regionally | – Donations to anti-epidemic institutions have been reduced in determining the tax base | – Discounts and exceptions have been introduced for specified products and services |
| Germany | – The period for submitting annual income tax returns to directly affected sectors has been postponed | – The period for submitting annual corporate tax returns to directly affected sectors has been postponed | – The deadline for submitting value added tax (VAT) declaration to the directly affected sectors has been postponed |
| France | – Income payments of self-employed persons have been delayed for a while<br>– Social security premium payments have been postponed for a while | – The period for submitting annual corporate tax returns to directly affected sectors has been postponed | – VAT refund processes have been accelerated |
| Turkey | – The annual income tax declaration submission period has been postponed in all sectors<br>– In the directly affected sectors, the period of withholding tax return on wages has been postponed | | – VAT declaration has been postponed for a short time, valid for all sectors<br>– VAT declaration has been delayed for a long time in directly affected sectors |
| USA | In order to be valid for tax bases that do not exceed a certain limit, the period of submitting an income tax declaration has been postponed<br>– The period of submitting a withholding return regarding wage income has been postponed, to be valid for tax bases not exceeding a certain limit | – The period of submitting a corporate tax declaration has been postponed to be valid for tax bases not exceeding a certain limit | – Practices that will vary according to the state in the sales tax have been made |

*Source* PWC (2020a, b)

policy should be coordinated with monetary policy. On the other hand, if there is a risk that the epidemic crisis may negatively affect public debt sustainability, the alternative of monetarization of debt (emission) may be considered (OECD 2020).

The cost of the support packages announced by the countries will increase public spending (establishment of pandemic hospitals, personnel training, etc.) with the aim of alleviating health and economic losses, and the loss of tax revenues due to the epidemic crisis will cause worsening of public debt levels and budget balances, resulting in significant increases in public borrowing. Such that, the ratio of the average public debt level to GDP in OECD countries was 73% in 2007 due to the 2008 global financial crisis. This ratio increased to 101% in 2011. The economic impact of the COVID-19 outbreak is expected to be more severe than the global financial crisis in the framework of the 2020 financial balances forecast (OECD 2020).

Especially considering the financial position of low-income countries, it is highly likely that they will face difficulties in terms of credibility and debt costs in international debt markets (OECD 2020). However, these countries urgently need grants and zero-interest loans to finance their health expenditures. Past epidemic experiences such as SARS, Ebola, and MERS show how important the providing privileged funding rate is in controlling the spread of the epidemic (Gaspar and Mauro 2020).

## 2.8 Conclusion

Outbreaks have many direct and indirect effects, both visible and invisible. Outbreaks that have changed the era throughout history affected the course of wars and have largely steered the destruction of economic order and understanding are the ancient desperation that the human beings have paid social, psychological, economic, and financial costs.

It is argued that, in spite of the enormous multi-sided costs that occur after the epidemic, it is less costly to establish the concept of "preparedness" in the epidemic. Such that, as a result of costing the public health capacity gaps determined by using the Joint External Evaluations (JEEs) process executed by WHO, it is claimed that most countries should spend an average of $1.69 per person per year in order to reach the appropriate level of epidemic preparedness. In addition to cost efficiency, investments to be made on epidemic preparations are thought to contribute to the reduction of poverty by providing an economic business area (WB 2019).

Plastics, which constitute a significant barrier to environmental sustainability, will cause approximately 56 billion tons of carbon emission by 2050 if not intervened. In this case, plastic production will cost 10–13% of the carbon budget created by the effort to keep global warming below 1.5 °C (HBS, BFFP 2019).

In the last century, anticipation of an increase in epidemic diseases arising from the environmental destruction (especially due to the prevalence of plastic production, which is shown innocent due to its lightness, population growth, unbalanced urbanization, and excessive consumption habits) necessitates intervention through all policy instruments. The tax regulations that are taken rapidly during the epidemics are pragmatic-based and temporary. However, environmental sustainability can be ensured and preparation can be made for extraordinary periods such as epidemics and natural disasters, through the Pigovian taxes and environmentally friendly standards that will be applied in the ordinary periods.

While Environmental Cleaning Tax, Motor Vehicle Tax are applied in order to reduce environmental damage and internalize the cost of crowding worldwide, more specific Emission Taxes (Carbon Tax, Energy Tax, Mineral Oil Tax, Transport Data, Solid Waste Tax) such as Drought Tax, Accommodation Tax, and Plastic Bag Tax are tried to be applied, albeit partially. Financing will be provided in the case of possible risks such as the outbreak and ensuring environmental sustainability by expanding the efficiency and application areas of the said taxes. In addition, an Epidemic Tax, which will be set up to be applied in the usual periods, will strengthen the countries' hand in terms of eliminating the possible risks in the first place, and on the other hand, it will create the social environment and financial awareness in the carbon-epidemic-externality spiral.

## References


Abbott RC, Rocke TE (2012) Plague, National Wildlife Heatlh Center Circular *1372, U.S.G.S.: Virginia*

Acemoğlu D (2020) Daron Acemoğlu Salgının Ekonomiye Etkilerini Değerlendirdi, www.finansgundem.com/haber/daron-acemoglu-salginin-ekonomiye-etkilerini-degerlendirdi/1481836. Accessed date: 1 May 2020

Achtman M, Zurth K, Morelli G, Torrea G, Guiyoule A, Carniel E (1999) YersiniaPestis, the cause of Plague, is a recently emerged clone of Yersinia Pseudotuberculosis. Proc Natl Acad Sci 96:14043–14048

Acemoğlu D, Robinson JA (2013) Ulusların Düşüşü - Güç, Zenginlik ve Yoksulluğun Kökenleri (trans: Velioğlu FR). Mega Press, İstanbul

Ak Ö (2020) Soğukalgınlığından Ölümcül Salgına! Küresel Kabus, TÜBİTAK Bilim ve Teknik Dergisi, Y. 53, I. 628:12–27

Aktan CC, Dileyici D, Saraç Ö (2002) Avrupa ve Amerikan Tarihinde Vergi İsyanları, https://docplayer.biz.tr/6981589-Avrupa-ve-amerikan-tarihinde-vergi-isyanlari.html. Accessed date 15 Apr 2020

Akyol AD (2005) Şiddetli Akut Solunum Yetmezliği Sendromu (SARS) ve Korunma Önlemleri, Ege Üniversitesi Hemşirelik Yüksek Okulu Dergisi 21(2):107–123

Almond D (2006) Is the 1918 Influenza pandemic over? Long-Term Effects of in UteroInfluenza exposure in the post-1940 U.S. population. J Pol Econ 114(4):672–712

Anyanwu JC, Siliadin YG, Okonkwo E (2013) Role of fiscal policy in tackling the HIV/AIDS epidemic in Southern Africa. Afr Dev Rev 25(3):256–275

Arık FŞ (1991) Selçuklular Zamanında Anadolu'da Veba Salgınları. Tarih Araştırmaları Dergisi 15(26):27–59

Başağaoğlu İ, Uçar A, Doğan O (2015) Osmanlı'da Salgın Hastalıklarla Mücadele, Çamlıca: İstanbul

Bayat AH (2016) Tıp Tarihi. Pınarbaş Press, İstanbul

Baykal N (2018) Endüstri 4.0'dan Toplum 5.0'a Japonya'da Değişimin Mimarı TateoArimoto ile Söyleşi, TÜBİTAK Bilim ve Teknik Dergisi 52(612):48–53

Cotter C (2020) From the "Spanish Flu" to COVID-19: lessons from the 1918 Pandemic and First World War. https://blogs.icrc.org/law-and-policy/2020/04/23/spanish-flu-covid-19-1918-pandemic-first-world-war/. Accessed date: 1 May 2020

Çalışkan A, Eyicil A (2019) XVIII. Ve XIX. Yüzyılda Halep ve Civarında Salgın Hastalıklar, Bingöl Üniversitesi Sosyal Bilimler Enstitüsü Dergisi 9(18), Autumn 2019, 1289–1319

Çilingiroğlu N (1998) HIV/AIDS Epidemisi ve ekonomiye olan yükü. HIV/AIDS Tıp Dergisi 1(3):111–116. www.hatam.hacettepe.edu.tr/ekonomi.shtml. Accessed date: 05 May 2020

Diamond J (2010) Tüfek, Mikrop ve Çelik- İnsan Topluluklarının Yazgıları. TÜBİTAK Popüler Bilim Kitapları: Ankara

Durusoy R, Emek M, İnci R (2011) İl Sağlık Müdürlüklerinde Bulaşıcı Hastalıklar İnsan Gücünün Değerlendirilmesi. Türk Halk Sağlığı Dergisi 9(2):70–85

Delivorias A, Scholz N (2020) Economic impact of epidemics and pandemics. EPRS—Euro Parliamentary Res Service Briefing PE 646:195

Ertaş MY, Eğnim K (2011) Evliya Çelebi Seyahatnamesi'nde Hastalıklar, Pamukkale Üniversitesi SBE Dergisi. 10:83–108

Fan EX (2003) SARS: economic impacts and implications, Asian Development Bank. Economics and Research Department Policy Brief Series No. 15

Fukuyama M (2018) Society 5.0: Aimingfor a new human-centered society. Japan Spotlight 2018:47–50

Gaspar V, Mauro P (2020) Fiscal policies to protect people during the coronavirus outbreak, IMF Blog. https://blogs.imf.org/2020/03/05/fiscal-policies-to-protect-people-during-the-corona virus-outbreak/. Accessed date: 2 May 2020

Gök K (2007) Vergi Direncinin Gelişimi, Marmara Üniversitesi İİBF Dergisi. XXII, I. 1:143–163

Harari YN (2015) Hayvanlardan Tanrılara Sapiens İnsan Türünün Kısa Bir Tarihi, 7. Press. (trans: Genç E) Kolektif Kitap - 63. Kolektif Kitap Bilişim ve Tasarım: İstanbul.

HBF, BFFP (2019) The child of global trade (in plastic atlas facts and figures about the world of synthetic polymers), Heinrich Böll Stiftung and Break Free From Plastic. Druckhaus Kaufmann - Lahr: Germany

History.com Editors (2020) Pandemics That Changed History. www.history.com/topics/middle-ages/pandemics-timeline. Accessed date: 25 Apr 2020

Hong Kong Monetary Authority (2012) The importance of fiscal prudence under the linked exchange rate system in Hong Kong SAR. BIS Paper No. 67k, pp. 173–177

Horgan J (2014) Justinian's Plague (541–541 CE). www.ancient.eu/article/782/justinians-plague-541-542-ce/. Accessed date: 20 Apr 2020

Huberman L (2009) Feodal Toplumdan Yirminci Yüzyıla. İletişim Publications, İstanbul

Huremovic D (2019) Brief history of pandemics (pandemics throughout history). In: Humerovic D (ed) Psychiatry of pandemics. Springer Nature, Switzerland

IMF (2006) The global economic and financial impact of an Avian Flu pandemic and the role of IMF. The Avian Flu WorkingGroup: IMF

Haldun İ-i (2018) Mukaddime. Dergah Publications, İstanbul

İstek E (2017) Avrupa'da Veba Salgını ve Salgında Din Faktörü (Viyana Örneği). Tarih Araştırmaları Dergisi 36(62):173–204

Kadılar R (2010) Karbon Fırsat mı, Tehdit mi? Destek Publisher, İstanbul

Karalöse H (2017) Halep'te Sosyal, Ekonomik ve Kültürel Durum (1876–1918 Yılları Arası), Uluslararası Sosyal Araştırmalar Dergisi 10(51):289–301

Lepan N (2020) Visualizing the history of pandemics. www.visualcapitalist.com/history-of-pandem ics-deadliest/.(Accessed date: 23 Apr 2020

Lina B (2008) History of influenza pandemics. In: Raoult D, Drancourt M (eds) Paleomicrobiology: past human infections. Springer, Berlin, pp 199–211

Maden E (2014) SARS, MERS-CoV, Hanta Virüs Pulmoner Sendromu. Güncel Göğüs Hastalıkları Serisi 2(1):18–26

Marcus A (2013) Modernliğin Eşiğinde Bir Osmanlı Şehri Halep (trans: Baş ME) Küre Publications, İstanbul

OECD (2020) Tax and fiscal policy in response to the coronavirus crisis: strengthening confidence and resilience. OECD Tackling Coronavirus (Covid-19) Contributing to a Global Effort
Özden K, Özmat M (2014) Salgın ve Kent: 1347 Veba Salgınının Avrupa'da Sosyal, Politik ve Ekonomik Sonuçları. İdeal Kent 12:60–87
Özlü Z, Tiryaki K (2019) Osmanlı'da Seferberlik Dönemlerinde Salgın Hastalıklara Karşı Halk Sağlığı Muhfazasına Dair Bulgular, Zeugma II. Uluslararası Multidisipliner Çalışmalar Kongresi, 18–20 January 2019, Gaziantep
Pamuk Ş (2020) Tarihte Küresel Salgınlar ve İktisadi Sonuçları. https://sarkac.org/2020/04/tarihte-kuresel-salginlar-ve-iktisadi-sonuclari/. Accessed date: 15 Apr 2020
PWC (2020a) Navigate tax, legal and economic measures in response to COVID-19. www.pwc.com/gx/en/services/tax/navigate-the-tax-measures-in-response-to-Covid-19.html?c=Turkey%3BGermany%3BFrance%3BChina%3BUSA&finance-andliquidity=general%3Bindividuals%3Bsmes%3Bcorporates%3Binsolvency-law%3Bfurther-information%3Bother&operations=contract-law%3Bcyber-privacy-law%3Bcorporate-law&tax-trade-regulatory=vat-gst. Accessed date: 29 June 2020
PWC (2020b) Covid-19 Salgını Kapsamında Dünyada ve Türkiye'de Vergi Önlemleri. www.pwc.com/gx/en/services/tax/navigate-the-tax-measures-in-response-to-Covid-19.html Accessed date: 29 June 2020
Rude G (2015) Fransız Devrimi. İletişim Press, İstanbul
Schultz T (1964) Transforming traditional agriculture. Yale University Press, New Haven
Snowden FM (2019) Epidemics and society- from the black death to the present. Yale University Press, London
Stathakopoulos D (2007) Crime and punishment. In: Little LK (ed) Plague and the end of antiquity: the pandemic of 541–750. Cambridge University Press, Cambridge, pp 99–118
Saçaklıoğlu F (2006) AİDS'in Ekonomi Politiği. https://docplayer.biz.tr/955361-Aids-in-ekonomi-politigi-feride-sacaklioglu.html. Accessed date: 20 Apr 2020
Şarman K (2019) Devrimin Tuzu: Arc-et Senans. Atlas Dergisi, December. www.atlasdergisi.com/kesfet/kultur/devrimin-tuzu-arc-et-senans.html. Accessed date: 20 Apr 2020
Şengöz G (2013) MERS CoV. www.klimik.org.tr/wp-content/uploads/2013/10/MERSCoV.pdf. Accessed date: 4 May 2020
T.C. SAĞLIK BAKANLIĞI (2019) HIV/AIDS ile Mücadelede 2019–2024 Yol Haritası Oluşturuldu. www.saglik.gov.tr/TR,55913/hivaids-ile-mucadelede-2019-2024-yol-haritasi-olusturuldu.html. Accessed date: 18 May 2020
T.C. SAĞLIK BAKANLIĞI (2019) HIV/AIDS Tanı Tedavi Rehberi, T.C. Sağlık Bakanlığı Yayın No. 1133. Artı6 Medya Press, Ankara
TTD (2020) Her Yönüyle COVID-19. Türk Toraks Derneği COVID-19 E-Book Series: Ankara
Turan O (2018) Thukydides'in Aktarımına Göre Atina Salgınının Gerçek Etkileri. Tarih ve Gelecek Dergisi 4(2):89–108
Turna N (2011) İstanbul'un Veba ile İmtihanı: 1811–1812 Veba Salgını Bağlamında Toplum ve Ekonomi. Stud Ottoman Domain 1(1):1–36
TÜBA (2020) Covid-19 Pandemi Değerlendirme Raporu, TÜBA Raporları No. 34. Türk Bilimler Akademisi Press, Ankara
Tütengil CO (1971) Az Gelişmenin Sosyolojisi. Toplum Publisher, Ankara
UNAIDS (2014) 90-90-90 An ambitious treatment target to help end the AIDS epidemic. www.unaids.org/sites/default/files/media_asset/90-90-90_en.pdf. Accessed date: 23 May 2020
UNAIDS (2019) UNAIDS Data 2019, Reference. www.unaids.org/sites/default/files/media_asset/2019-UNAIDS-data_en.pdf. Accessed date: 23 May 2020
UNAIDS (2019) FactSheet- World AIDS Day 2019. www.unaids.org/sites/default/files/media_asset/UNAIDS_FactSheet_en.pdf. Accessed date: 23 May 2020
WB (2019) Pandemic preparedness financing status update. WB Group Health, Nutrition, Population, September
WHO (2016) Global health sector strategy on HIV 2016–2021 Towards Ending AIDS. WHO Document Production Services, Switzerland

Worldometer (2020) Covid-19 coronavirus pandemic. www.worldometers.info/coronavirus/. Accessed date: 29 June 2020

Varlık N (2018) Osmanlılarda Veba Salgınları. Toplumsal Tarih 296:30–36

Yakut K (2010) Fransız İhtilali, Açıköğretim Fakültesi: Eskişehir. www.tarih.gen.tr/Arsiv/Fransizihtilali.pdf. Accessed date: 2 May 2020

Yıldız MS (2018) Toplum 5.0: Japonya'nın İnsan Odaklı Yaklaşımı. https://tr.linkedin.com/pulse/toplum-50-japonyan%C4%B1n-insan-odakl%C4%B1-yakla%C5%9F%C4%B1m%C4%B1-mustafa-said-yildiz-phd?trk=articles_directory. Accessed date: 2 May 2020

Zakaria Y (2015) Macroeconomic policy impacts on the fight against HIV/AIDS in Ghana, AFRODAD. www.africaportal.org/publications/macroeconomic-policy-impacts-on-the-fight-against-hivaids-in-ghana/. Accessed date: 05 May 2020

**Sibel Aybarç** was born in 1981 in Izmir. After graduating from Izmir Anatolian Vocational High School, she continued her undergraduate education at Manisa Celal Bayar University, Department of Finance. She received her master's degree in the field of Finance Theory from Manisa Celal Bayar University. She was awarded her Ph.D. degree from Manisa Celal Bayar University Department of Public Finance in 2012. Her Ph.D. thesis is on the efficiency analysis of higher education public expenditures. In 2014, she lectured in Poland within the scope of Erasmus exchange mobility. She took part as an executive and researcher in various institutions and organizations, especially the EU project. Sibel Aybarç has books, articles and papers on public fiscal policies in the fight against drought and water scarcity, epidemic economy, efficiency in public expenditures, efficiency in tax audits, environmental sustainability, carbon tax and accounting, vocational national qualification training, Tobit regression. She has participated in many seminars and conferences on public finance, fiscal policy and social sciences around the world. She is still working in the Banking, Finance and Insurance Program at Manisa Celal Bayar University Ahmetli Vocational School. She is also the Deputy Director of Manisa Celal Bayar University Population and Migration Application and Research Center.

# Chapter 3
# Increasing Public Expenditures Due to COVID-19 Pandemic Crisis: An Assessment According to Peacock-Wiseman Hypothesis

**Melih Kabayel and Alper Doğan**

**Abstract** Although the COVID-19 pandemic crisis is basically a health crisis, it does not only concern health policies due to its economic and social effects. In the fight against the pandemic, it is important to implement economic, social and financial policies as well as health policies. In this context, effectively using the public spending tools of fiscal policy in the fight against the COVID-19 pandemic has become a priority rather than a political choice for governments. In times of pandemics, sufficient increase in public expenditures is an effective political tool for governments in order to prevent the decline of the economic growth process, loss of welfare, large-scale unemployment and supply problems. Considering the Peacock-Wiseman Hypothesis in the public finance literature, if public expenditures are used as an effective policy tool in the COVID-19 pandemic crisis, a leap in public expenditures is likely. This study evaluates the relationship between the COVID-19 pandemic crisis and public expenditures and reveals the public expenditure policies of selected countries in the fight against COVID-19. It can be said that there is a positive relationship between the level of development of countries and the increase in public expenditures in the COVID-19 pandemic crisis. It is seen that developing economies mostly resort to credit instruments, while developing countries mainly use public expenditure instruments, they also use credits and supports sufficiently. However, due to the continuation of the COVID-19 pandemic crisis, obtaining definitive results will emerge in post-pandemic studies. For this reason, the final results of this study will become clear with the studies carried out after the pandemic crisis.

**Keywords** COVID-19 · Pandemic · Public expenditures · Peacock-Wiseman hypothesis · Public policies · Economic crisis

---

M. Kabayel
Department of Public Finance and Financial Management/Post-Graduate Study, İzmir Katip Çelebi University, İzmir, Turkey

A. Doğan (✉)
Department of Finance Theory, İzmir Katip Çelebi University, İzmir, Turkey
e-mail: alper.dogan@ikc.edu.tr

 
B. Açıkgöz and İ. A. Acar (eds.), *Pandemnomics: The Pandemic's Lasting Economic Effects*, Accounting, Finance, Sustainability, Governance & Fraud: Theory and Application, https://doi.org/10.1007/978-981-16-8024-3_3

## 3.1 Introduction

Public expenditures, as an instrument of fiscal policy, are important expenditure instruments in the production of goods and services of the state. Every state that generates public revenue, as required by the power of the purse, reveals a social benefit by making public expenditures in various fields, providing employment, investing and providing services with the authority vested by the nation. However, during extraordinary periods (war, disaster, epidemic, etc.), public expenditures are rapidly increased regardless of financial constraints in the short term, and it is aimed to ensure the security of citizens and properties. This is accepted as a possible trend by the fiscal theory, as public spending increases in similar ways during past extraordinary periods. With the Peacock-Wiseman Displacement Hypothesis, this is accepted by the detection of the increasing public spending tendency during the war periods. A similar situation was experienced with the 2008 Global Financial Crisis and a successful policy was followed by shortening the impact and duration of the crisis with public expenditure instruments in many countries.

With the COVID-19 Outbreak in 2020, many countries have started to use various spending packages to continue the fight with emergency additional budget plans and to maintain the continuity of the economy. It is also predicted that the COVID-19 Outbreak Crisis reveals negative externality and that public expenditure instruments are the most efficient means to compensate and reduce the resulting costs. On the other hand, it does not seem correct to assume that this situation is temporary. After the epidemic, many countries (including developed countries) that want to strengthen their health service delivery infrastructure need to invest through public spending on a budget basis.

The COVID-19 pandemic crisis has greatly affected the twenty-first-century society and economy. The aim of the study is to compensate for missing information and contribute to the literature in the short term, accompanied by economic and financial evaluations. On the other hand, the study emphasizes that public expenditure instruments are saviors contrary to the neo-classical view and are very important in terms of transformation-sustainability. Finally, the study aims to evaluate the displacement effect in public expenditures, which is the most important tool in the hands of the public sector during natural disasters, wars and finally epidemics.

## 3.2 The Concept of Public Expenditure

Public expenditures are mainly current, investment and transfer expenditures made by the public sector through the budget. The scope of public expenditures is divided into two: narrow and wide. While public expenditures made through the central government budget are called "*narrow public expenditures*," the public expenditure calculated by including the expenditures made by local administrations, social security institutions and state economic enterprises (SEE) are defined as the concept of "*large public expenditure*" (Mutluer et al. 2016).

Public expenditures are the most important positive tool of public economy in a broad sense and of fiscal policy in a narrow sense. Because public expenditures contribute positively to the economic growth and development process, as they create purchasing power within the national economy. Therefore, the share of public expenditures in GDP is very important. Public expenditures are used as an effective tool in times of economic recession, crisis and take off. Although public expenditures, which are used in the Keynesian economic model to increase the aggregate demand function and eliminate underemployment, appear to be a bit behind in today's liberal economic model, it appears as an important dynamic in the economy. However, public expenditure management is an expenditure policy developed within the budget management since it is the expenditure function of the budget. That is, an expenditure policy independent of revenue policy cannot be considered in the medium and long term (Allen and Tommasi 2001).

### *3.2.1 Public Expenditures in a Historical Perspective*

Public expenditures are tools for financing the goods and services produced by the public sector. While public goods and services are financed by public expenditures, public expenditures are mainly met by tax revenues. Therefore, there is a financial proportion in the provision of public goods and services. In the long run, public spending and tax revenues are likely to increase in a coordinated manner (Gurdal et al. 2020).

When public expenditures are examined historically, it has been in a rapid increase trend since 1870 and the increase rate has slowed down after 1980. Considering the global economic growth after 1980, although public expenditures have increased nominally, their increase has slowed proportionally (compared to GDP). This is the result of the post-1980 global economic order and the implementation of liberal policies in many countries (Tanzi and Schuknecht 2000). When this policy change is evaluated periodically, as the inflationary environment emerging due to the inefficiency in collecting public revenues and public expenditures resulted in excessive budget deficits, public debt stocks increased linearly and fiscal sustainability became an urgent requirement in many countries. This led to the discussion of liberal policies as a solution tool in the mid-1970s (Buchanan 1975).

Public expenditures and tax revenues are the basic expenditures and revenues of the public sector. The state makes basic public expenditure in order to produce/provide public goods and services, and earns compulsory and sin non-quid pro quo tax revenues. However, public spending is much more important as the provision of goods and services is more important in the short term. Tax revenues, on the other hand, are increased in the medium and long term and the balance that preserves fiscal discipline is maintained. Throughout the history of the economy,

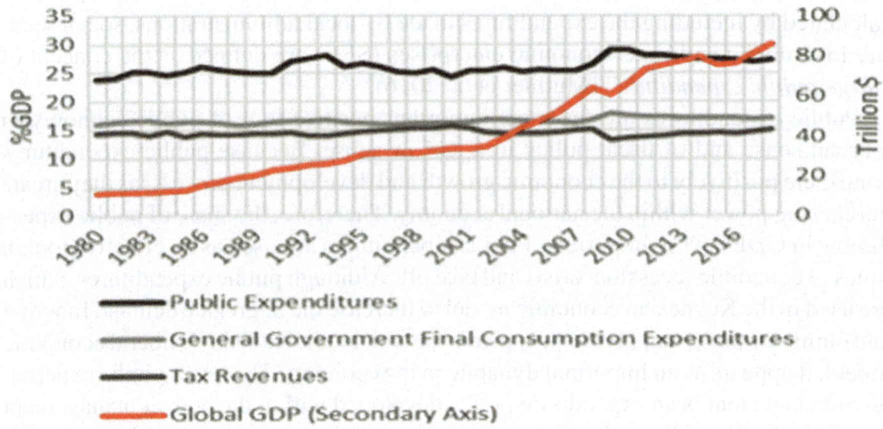


**Fig. 3.1** Global GDP growth, public expenditures and public revenues by year-1980–2018 (World Average-% GDP). *Source* World Bank (2020a)

public expenditures have had an increasing trend in times of recession, disaster, war and epidemic. After the 2008 Global Economic Crisis, many countries tried to compensate the economic loss in the market with public spending packages. As for the global public expenditure average, the public expenditure average, which was around 25% in 2007, increased and reached 29% in 2009. It was observed that there was a 20% increase in public expenditure during crisis periods. On the other hand, there was a decrease in tax revenues. The rate of tax revenues, which was around 20% in 2007, decreased to 13% in 2009. This shows that there is a 13% decline in tax revenues. The public sector, which expanded with 20% spending and lost 13% tax revenue, endured a 33% financial burden in total. This is a period in which global gross domestic product suffers a loss of 5%. The fact that the public sector is under a financial burden of 30% shows the benefit of the existence of the public sector and that liberal policies are not successful in market failures and crises, and that the public sector is in the role of "*a global automatic stabilizer*" with the fiscal policy tool (Horton and El-Ganainy 2020).

Figure 3.1 reveals that the public expenditure break occurred in 1990s and 2008. The 1990s can be described as the cradle of global crises. Many countries encountered new generation crises that had a global spillover effect in the 1990s and tried to compensate for the economic loss caused by the crisis by means of public expenditure packages with Keynesian reactions.[1] However, as a result of non-cyclical Keynesian policies, economic costs increased in the following periods. For this reason, Keynesian policies were used inefficiently by many countries for political purposes in the 1990s. However, in the 2008 Global Financial Crisis, Keynesian policies being using in a conjunctural manner gained importance again (Eatwell and Milgate 2011).

[1] At this point, it should be said that the Keynesian policies implemented in the 1990s led to new crises in the later periods.

Figure 3.2 gives the public expenditure rates (% GDP) in selected countries as of 2018. The high share of public expenditures in GDP indicates the percentage of GDP that belongs to the public sector. The higher the rate of public expenditure in GDP, the higher the competence of the public sector in the economy. For example, in the figure above, the public expenditure rate of France is 47%, while the rate of the United States is 22%. This shows the effect of the public economy in total economic activities. While the French economy is much more sensitive to the size and scope of public spending, this effect is lower in the United States (Timbeau 2017).

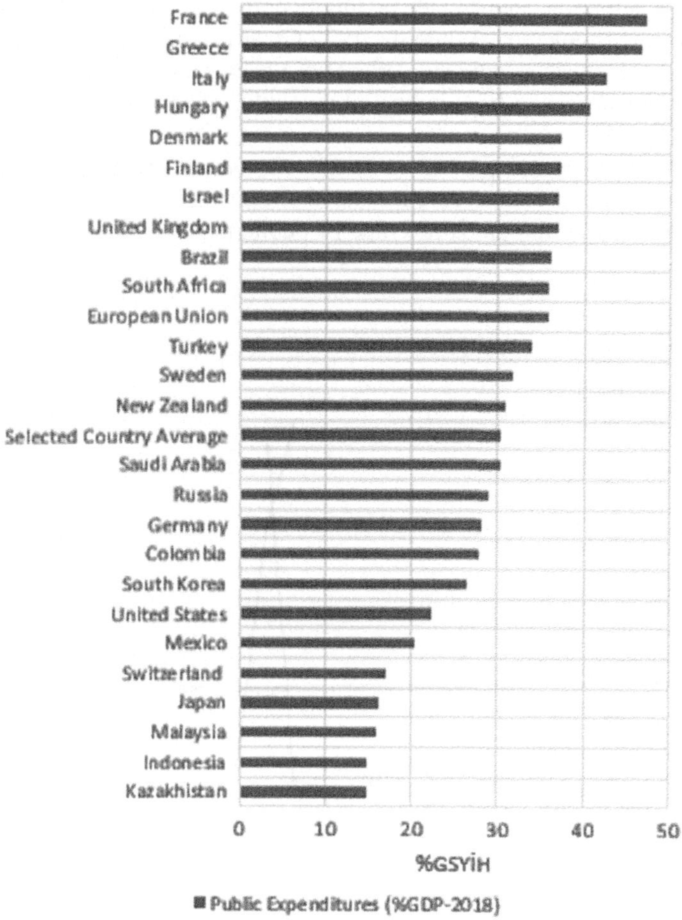


**Fig. 3.2** Public expenditure levels of selected countries—2018 (% of GDP). *Source* World Bank (2020b)

### 3.2.2 *Economic Crisis and Public Expenditures*

Even though economic crises vary in themselves, they simply express periods of economic and financial breakdown. The inconsistencies in the economy dynamics cause an economic crisis. For example, excessively increasing the debt burden may lead to an economic breakdown by eliminating economic and financial sustainability (Koh et al. 2020). In this case, financial markets collapse and the crisis is reflected in the real sector. In some cases, crises arise on the basis of the real sector. Such crises negatively affect the production chain and create longer-term negative effects. On the other hand, a definition can be made as supply or demand crises based on the point at which the crisis emerged. While the 1929 Great Depression can be cited as the first demand-side crisis, supply-side crises have been experienced due to increased production growth arising from industrial revolutions and are much rarer (Cencini and Rossi 2015).

Figure 3.3 shows the "*displacement*" effect of economic fragility in crisis periods on public expenditures and tax revenues. With the emergence of the crisis, a sudden leap was observed in the global average of public expenditures from 25 to 29%.

**Fig. 3.3** The impact of 2008 global economic crisis on public expenditures and tax revenues. *Source* World Bank (2020c, d)

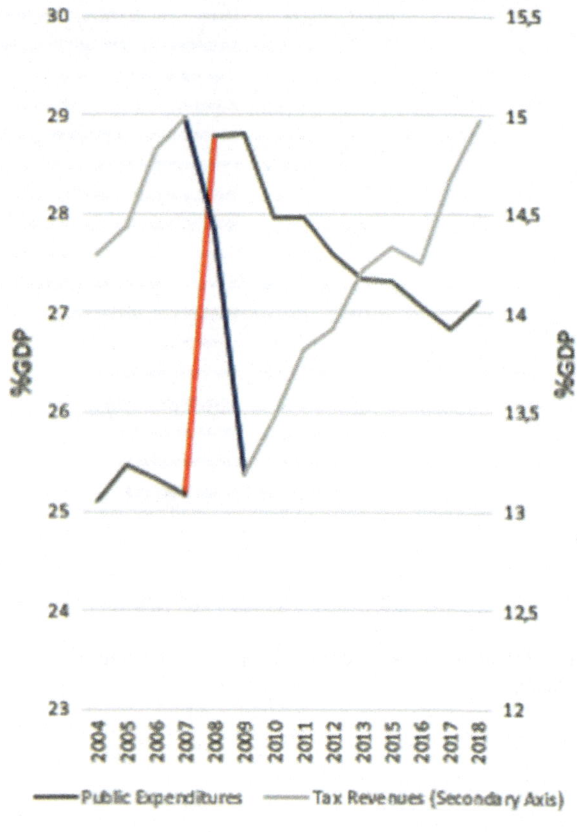

Considering that the average increased by 20% in the short term, it is clear that countries use public expenditure tools to compensate for the negative externalities of the crisis. However, it is observed that there was a decrease in tax revenues during this period. The global average of tax revenues (% GDP), which dropped from 15 to 13.5%, barely recovered in the 10 years after the crisis. At this point, it can be said that the crisis periods damage the balance of the public economy in macroeconomic terms.

Crises and emergencies cause a sudden increase in public spending, which is considered as a compensatory fiscal policy. On the other hand, in some studies, the total of public expenditures is given together with social security expenditures (Ostojić and Žmegač 2014). However, since the social security system is established in order to compensate for economic, social and physical risks, including it in the total amount may be misleading in understanding the depth of budget-based public expenditures. As a result, the actual depth of public spending, especially in countries with high elderly population density, can be misleading. However, during the 2008 Global Financial Crisis, public spending increased rapidly in all countries within the EU-15 and a conjunctural Keynesian policy was implemented (Ostojić and Žmegač 2014).

Although the 2008 Economic Crisis increased public expenditures in total, there were differences in the types of public expenditures. For example, in most countries, capital-investment expenditures declined despite increasing current expenditures. This is the policy choices put into practice by policymakers in order to find quick solutions. This situation is observed when examining the statistics of the public finance of Italy, which was deeply affected by the crisis. However, a negative opinion was presented that the relationship of this policy with growth was positive (Grisorio and Prota 2016). This relationship is mostly not observed in South American countries. Because public expenditures in these countries increased by an average of 4% during the crisis period. This shows that conjunctural Keynesian policies are not fully implemented in every region after the crisis. Essentially, this is also related to the impact area of the global financial crisis and the economic size of the countries (Garry and Rivas 2017). In a study conducted in the former Soviet countries, it was observed that post-crisis countries had shifted to a tendency of increasing the expenditures from a tendency of limiting them on the basis of basic public services (education-health as semi-public goods) (Chubrik et al. 2011). In another study, an analysis covering the crisis period shows that public expenditures in central and Eastern European countries contribute positively to economic growth. However, during the crisis period, no significant increase/leap in public expenditures was observed in terms of GDP in many of these countries (Zugravu and Sava 2014).

Increasing public spending increases the borrowing tendency and as a result, the public debt stock increases (Tanzi and Davoodi 2002). Increasing the public debt stock is important in terms of debt sustainability and fiscal discipline. On the other hand, the increase in debts increases the share of debt interest payments in the budget. After the last global crisis the world faced, the share of interest payments in total expenditures also increased. However, there are discussions about whether this has positive or negative effects. In some opinions, it is argued that public expenditures through borrowing lead to economic inefficiency (d'Agostino et al. 2016).

Figure 3.4 shows that the borrowing tendency of countries increased by income groups after the 2008 Global Economic Crisis. Since the 2008 Global Economic Crisis was a finance-based crisis and developed countries were at the center of this crisis, the first increase in the borrowing tendency was seen in the group of high-income countries. Especially the public expenditure packages implemented by the European Union and the United States in this period and the loss of tax income as a result of the reflection of the crisis on the real sector created the need for financing in high-income countries. However, it is observed that these countries reduced their borrowing tendency after the crisis (proportional decrease in interest payments). This shows that "cyclical borrowing policy" was implemented. With the increasing borrowing tendency of low-income and middle-income countries after 2011, these countries, which had financing problems due to capital shortage, implemented borrowing policies for economic growth and development after the crisis and this was reflected in interest payments as "*solid public expenditure*" (World Bank 2020e) (Fig. 3.5).

The increase in the share of interest payments in public expenditures is an indicator of the borrowing tendency that emerges in the medium term. Because the reflection of interest payments on the budget occurs 1–3 years later. However, the impact of the 2008 Crisis on the borrowing tendency showed itself with an increase of approximately 20% (according to 2009–2010 data) in the borrowing tendency in 2009 right after the crisis. The increase in public spending increased the borrowing tendency (World Bank 2020g). This was reflected in interest payments. Increasing borrowing tendency is an indicator of this situation. A study found evidence in this direction.

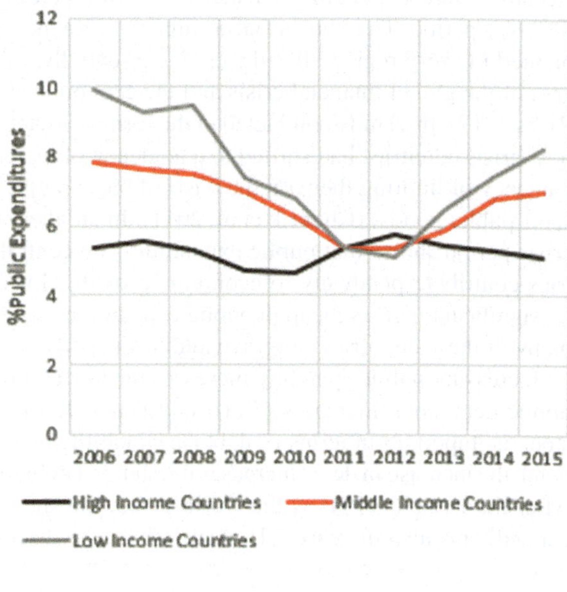


**Fig. 3.4** The course of interest payments by country groups before and after the crisis (2006–2015). *Source* World Bank (2020e)

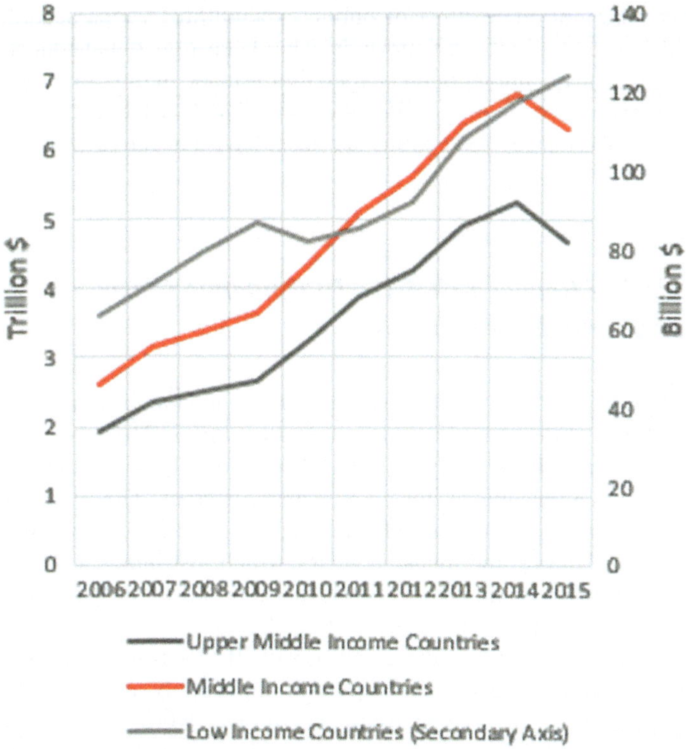


**Fig. 3.5** Post-crisis external debt tendency by country groups (2006–2015). *Source* World Bank (2020f)

However, it is clear that borrowing poses the danger of "deterioration." Excessive borrowing creates inefficient public spending. For this reason, it is essential to establish advanced control mechanisms. Otherwise, the share of solid public expenditures will increase with the tendency to borrow, and the situation will become unsustainable in the medium and long term (Del Monte and Pennacchio 2020). However, this situation is a result of the "conjunctural" fiscal policy as a Keynesian approach. However, this was misunderstood by Keynesians and by using continuous fiscal policy tools, high inflation, unproductivity-inefficiency, except for full employment, was created.

Especially developing countries fell into debt trap and ignored fiscal discipline. A study carried out contains new opinions in this direction. When the public expenditure data of OECD countries between 1981 and 2014 are examined, it is shown that the "asymmetric public expenditure" tendency is much higher in developing countries (Çulha 2016). In a study conducted among developed countries such as the European Region, it was emphasized that the asymmetric public spending tendency was low (it is also said that the multiplier effect was exaggerated), and countries made restrictions on spending and especially borrowing after the crisis (Boitani and Perdichizzi 2018). However, at this point, it is useful to distinguish between public expenditures. The multiplier effect of public expenditures varies according to the function of the expenditure. In another study, it has been argued that education-health expenditures, which are among public expenditures made in the same region, have a multiplier effect on the economy, while other expenditures (defense, social development, economic assistance, basic public services) have a negative effect (Lupu et al. 2018).

### 3.2.3 *Relation Between COVID-19 Epidemic Crisis and Public Expenditures*

The Global Economic Crisis of 2008 created a global economic crisis by shaking the economic stability of developed and developing countries. The crisis that emerged was overcome, especially with cyclical fiscal policies. However, the 2008 Global Economic Crisis is a financial sector-based economic crisis. The economic damage suffered by the finance sector caused a damage to the financial resource flow of the real sector. Therefore, the financial sector which lost blood was compensated economically through financial recovery packages. However, the COVID-19 Global Outbreak is very different from the 2008 Global Economic Crisis. It is an economic crisis that emerges as a result of the effect of COVID-19 as global public good (as global public bads) on the economic system in both supply and demand sides in a functioning economic exchange environment. In other words, the crisis caused an "*economic breakdown*" by putting all sectors in a real downsizing tendency on a global basis (Antipova 2020). This is described as "black swan"[2] in the economic literature (Morales and Callaghan 2020.

The COVID-19 Outbreak Crisis has revealed the tendency to contribute to economic policy with public expenditure tools in many countries. Because the supply and demand-side economic crises that started with the epidemic threatened economic stability. As a result of the pause in the supply and supply chain in the market due to the epidemic and the decrease in production and consumption demand due to the epidemic, the global economy entered a "forced recession-shrinkage" period. As a result of the period lived, the ordinary work flows of the sectors are decreasing. Additional financing needs arise with the change of work flows. Otherwise, economic stability will deteriorate in many countries and basic economic problems will deepen. For this reason, a cyclical public spending increase policy will ensure that the supply in the market is sustained and demand is maintained through the real sector channel. In this context (Fig. 3.6.) shows the revenue that the public sector has given up on (tax expenditure) in order to protect the market supply and demand and the ratio of

---

[2] Black Swan, the Turkish translation of which is "*siyah kuğu*" refers to events that are unlikely to occur, that are ignored and that when they occur cause shocking, destructive effects (Taleb 2007). In this context, economic crises are the types of economic shocks most commonly referred to as the black swan. Especially as the generations of crises develop, they present more destructive and difficult-to-recover situations (Açıkgöz and Çiloğlu 2020).

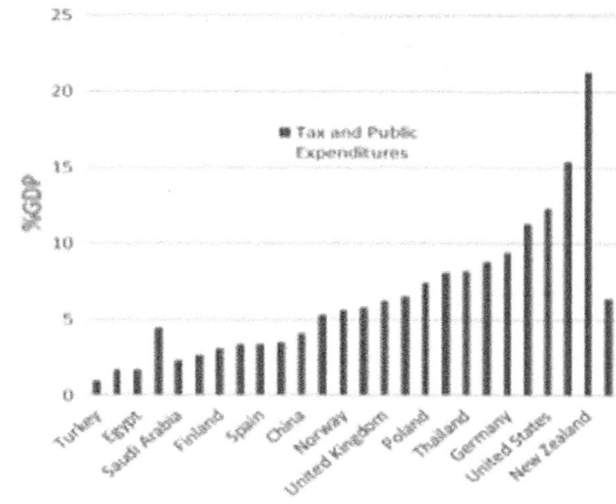


**Fig. 3.6** Public expenditures after the COVID-19 outbreak in selected countries. *Source* IMF (2020a)

public expenditures to GDP on country basis. The selected countries in the relevant chart have been selected from the prominent countries during the epidemic period and developed and developing country groups. The rate of increase in public expenditures in terms of GDP of selected countries is 6.38. Considering that the global public expenditures increase in 2008 was around 20%, it can be said according to preliminary estimates that public expenditure instruments were preferred at a lower rate during the COVID-19 outbreak. However, trends in this direction may increase in the future. Because the European Union approved a large expenditure budget of 1.8 Trillion Euros to support member countries to combat the epidemic crisis (AB 2020) (Fig. 3.7).

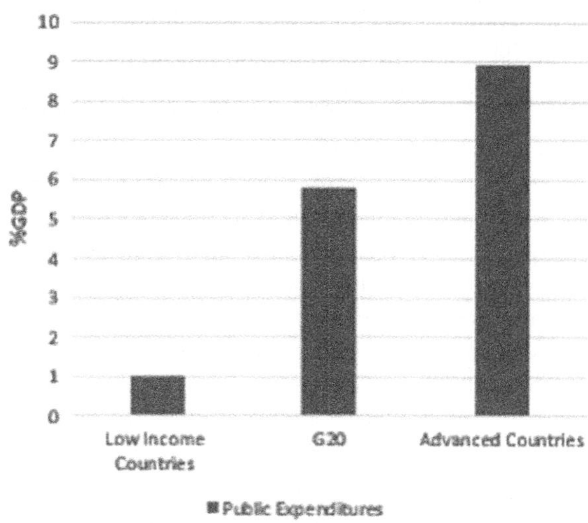


**Fig. 3.7** Public expenditure growth by country groups after the global outbreak (% of GDP). *Source* IMF (2020a)

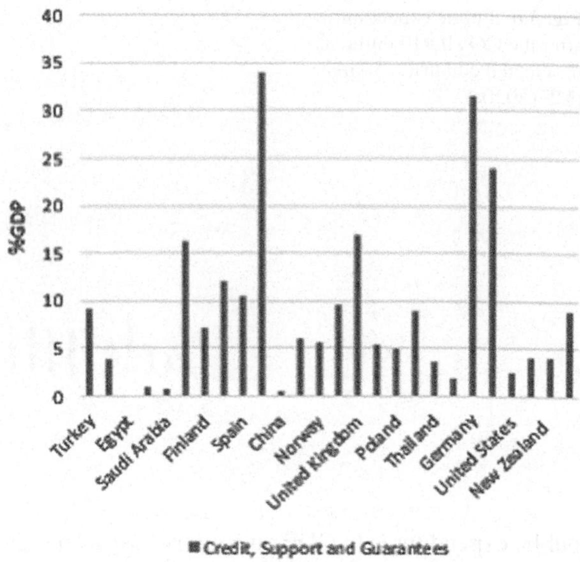


**Fig. 3.8** Credit, support and guarantees (% GDP) in combating the COVID-19 outbreak. *Source* IMF (2020a)

Considering the average of the public expenditures of the countries according to the country groups during the COVID-19 Outbreak, it is seen that the most spending was made by the developed countries. This shows that high-income capitalist countries do not hesitate to use public expenditure instruments. It is observed that as the income level of the countries decreases, the tendency to use public expenditure instruments decreases. Some countries, on the other hand, used much lower rates of public expenditure instruments, contrary to income groups. Turkey,[3] Mexico, France, Russia, Saudi Arabia, Spain, Italy and Indonesia have lagged behind the average public expenditure on using the tool. This is the result of the decisions taken by governments and the country's economic and financial structure.

In addition to the use of public expenditures during the fight against the COVID-19 Outbreak, it is seen that many countries have used credit-supported financing tools.

Figure 3.8 reveals the economic magnitude of loans, supports and guarantees in selected countries. When the two charts (Chart-7 and Chart-8) are compared, an inverse preference method is observed between public expenditure and loan-guarantees. It is observed that the countries that have used public expenditure instruments extensively, used credit support and guarantees less as a policy tool. On the other hand, it is seen that countries that use public expenditure instruments insufficiently prefer policies with credit support and guarantees (Fig. 3.9).

Credit support and guarantees are liquidities that are offered to the market as an alternative to public spending instruments. Loans, supports and guarantees offered

[3] In the first stage of COVID-19 Outbreak, Turkey opted for credit and support package. In addition, it preferred tax expenditures in various fields through tax cuts. However, as of December (2020), it turned to a grant policy especially for tradesmen. When the public spending made in this field is disclosed, indicators for Turkey will relatively increase.

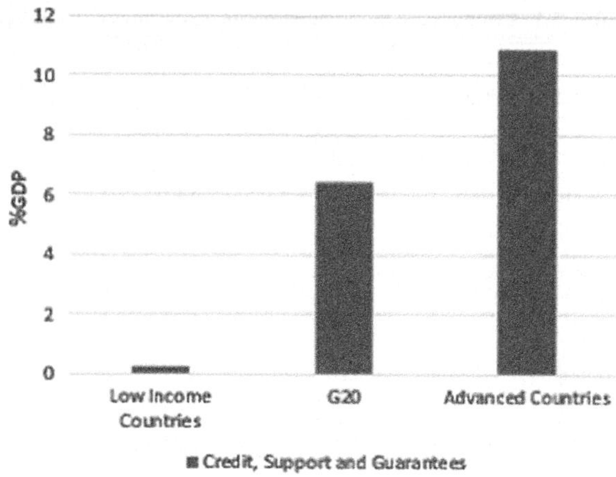


**Fig. 3.9** Credit support and guarantee utilization increase by country groups after the global outbreak (% of GDP). *Source* IMF (2020a)

to the market in order to avoid an economic crisis with the disruption of the flow of money in the market as a result of the disruption or slowdown of the business flow are mutual borrowing instruments. In this context, loans, supports and guarantees, which were used as a policy tool to compensate for the external costs and economic risks caused by the COVID-19 Outbreak, were used as an alternative tool of fiscal policy. Considering the use of public expenditures and loans, supports and guarantees in GDP, it is seen that loans, supports and guarantees are used more, depending on the level of development. It is seen that only low-income countries use loans, supports and guarantees less than public expenditures. The reason for this situation is the insufficient financial power of low-income countries and the relatively less borrowing power of the market. On the other hand, with the COVID-19 Outbreak, it is seen that the borrowing tendency of low-income developing economies to make investment increased by 9% of their GDP (IMF 2020b: 12).

The evaluation of public spending and loans supports and guarantees in terms of GDP shows how much the countries use fiscal policy tools in combating the COVID-19 Outbreak. However, it will be useful to evaluate in terms of quantity as well as evaluation in terms of GDP. In this respect, looking at the health expenditure dimensions of countries and countries with public expenditures over 48 billion dollars ($) by proportioning them to the population will reveal which government spends more per capita.

With the COVID-19 Outbreak, many countries have increased their spending instruments by ignoring their fiscal constraint in order to combat the epidemic. However, the study reveals that as the income level of the country decreases, the effect of the fiscal constraint factor increases and public expenditure instruments are used less. On the other hand, 12 countries that spend the most in terms of amount based on IMF data are evaluated in Table 3.1. In the research, it is seen that although countries increase their public expenditures, health expenditures remain at a relatively low level within the epidemic expenditures. In Table 3.1., it is seen that the country that uses public expenditure instruments the most in the fight against the

**Table 3.1** Countries with the most public spending with COVID-19 Outbreak (Billion $)

| Countries | Public expenditures (Billion $) | Health expenditures (Billion $) | Public expenditures/population | Health expenditures/population |
|---|---|---|---|---|
| Germany | 332 | 25 | 3.9 | 0.29 |
| Australia | 110 | 3 | 4.0 | 0.12 |
| Brazil | 86 | 12 | 0.4 | 0.05 |
| United States | 2.443 | 304 | 7.4 | 0.92 |
| United Kingdom | 155 | 8 | 2.27 | 0.11 |
| China | 625 | 22 | 0.43 | 0.01 |
| France | 63 | 9 | 0.94 | 0.13 |
| Japan | 551 | 38 | 4.37 | 0.30 |
| Canada | 86 | 3 | 2.26 | 0.07 |
| South Korea | 48 | 4 | 0.94 | 0.07 |
| Singapore | 52 | 1 | 9.45 | 0.18 |
| Italy | 60 | 7 | 1.0 | 0.11 |
| Average | 384 | 36 | 3.1 | 0.19 |

Zeros are not taken into account in the Expenditure/Population accounts. Color saturation is in 4 varieties across 12 countries. The 4 countries with the highest values in the respective category have dark boxes. As the darkness decreases, the rating goes down
*Source* IMF (2020a)

COVID-19 Outbreak is the United States. Japan and Germany, on the other hand, show the best performance in all categories (excluding public expenditure/population for Germany) following the United States. On the other hand, among the selected countries, Singapore is seen to among the average country with the highest per capita epidemic expenditure. When traveling to the Far East, it is seen that Japan and China use public spending tools. However, it is clear that more spending should be made, as the per capita public expenditure of China is very low. Brazil is similar to China in this regard. Brazil's public spending was relatively inadequate compared to the population.

Loans, supports and guarantees have been a preferred financial tool by many countries in combating the COVID-19 Pandemic. The use of public spending as a fiscal policy tool in combating the COVID-19 Pandemic has been more limited compared to loan support and guarantees. On the other hand, some countries (generally developed economies) followed a balanced policy and used both public spending and financial supports together. Some countries (Turkey, India) intensely used loans, support and guarantees as policy tools. Loans, supports and guarantees enable economic activities to continue by borrowing through increasing the liquidity required by the market.

Some of these borrowings are guaranteed. Guarantees are guaranteed by official and semi-official funds. Looking at the table above (Table 3.2.), Japan and Germany

**Table 3.2** Countries with the most credit support and guarantee with the COVID-19 outbreak (Billion $)

| Countries | Credit, support and guarantees (Billion $) | Credit and supports | Guarantee and semi-official financial operations | Credit, support and guarantees/population |
|---|---|---|---|---|
| Germany | 1.155 | 219 | 896 | 13.9 |
| European Union | 443 | 372 | 71 | 0.99 |
| Belgium | 57 | 0.2 | 56.8 | 3.8 |
| Brazil | 71 | 14.5 | 56.5 | 0.33 |
| United States | 510 | 56 | 454 | 1.5 |
| United Kingdom | 423 | 1 | 422 | 6.22 |
| China | 80 | 20.8 | 59.4 | 0.05 |
| France | 380 | 23 | 357 | 5.67 |
| India | 145 | 7.3 | 124.3 | 0.10 |
| Japan | 1.169 | 0 | 1.169 | 9.1 |
| Canada | 50 | 3 | 47 | 1.31 |
| South Korea | 149 | 0 | 149 | 2.9 |
| Spain | 126 | 0 | 126 | 2.68 |
| Italy | 583 | 4 | 579 | 9.71 |
| Turkey | 63 | 3 | 60 | 0.75 |
| Average | 360 | 48 | 308 | 3.9 |

*Source* IMF (2020a)

are the countries that use the most financial resources on a global scale. However, only Germany is the top country in all categories. Although loan supports and guarantees are important for the functioning of the market and the financing requirement, they carry financial risks. Some countries and sectors are likely to experience a financial crisis in the medium term as the loans, supports and guarantees given increase borrowing tendency and increase their debt stock ratios. For this reason, revitalizing the market with cyclical Keynesian policies is important in terms of ensuring economic recovery without derailing.

In this context, the International Monetary Fund (IMF) pointed out that, if governments cut public spending to compensate for economic costs of the pandemic and for a smooth economic recovery, that would be "a *policy that will derail the economic recovery*" (Gaspar and Gopinath 2020) (Fig. 3.10).

While public expenditures constitute the spending pillar of the fiscal policy, taxes and public debts constitute the revenue and borrowing policy and general fiscal policy. It is not correct to consider only expenditure policy in order to increase and measure the efficiency of fiscal policy. In this context, addressing borrowing and taxing trends

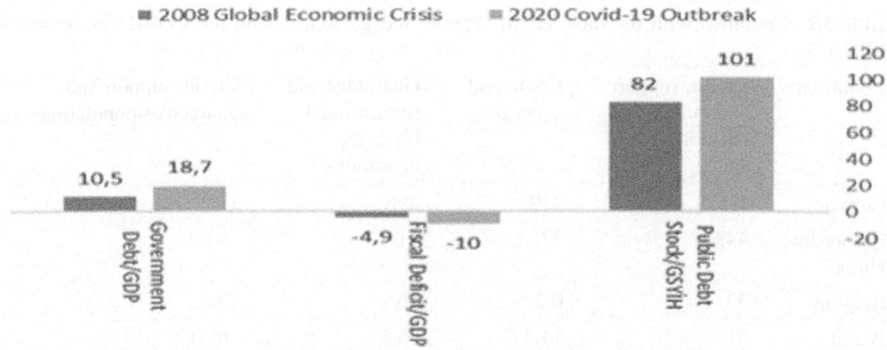


**Fig. 3.10** Comparison of COVID-19 outbreak and borrowing-COVID-19 outbreak with 2008 global economic crisis according to debt statistics. *Source* IMF (2020c)

during the COVID-19 Outbreak will reveal the fiscal policy trend of many countries at the global level. Considering the global financial trends, it is seen that the borrowing tendency increased and the fiscal balance deteriorated more during the epidemic period. The increase in the spending trend has created a borrowing requirement in many countries,[4] and according to IMF estimates, the global borrowing rate exceeded 100% (this rate was 82% in 2009) with the COVID-19 Outbreak, compared to the 2008 Global Economic Crisis (IMF 2020c: 20).

The public sector, whose financial power has increased with the increase in borrowing tendency, should follow a progressive policy in taxation policy in the long run in terms of sustainability of financial power (Gopinath 2020). However, the COVID-19 Outbreak does not make it possible to implement this policy in the short term. Governments whose tax efforts and tax capacity rates have declined due to the pandemic will bear the loss of tax revenues in order not to decrease the monetary capability of the market and to deepen the economic recession. During this period, the taxation policy should be flexible and reliable. A tax policy that increases the tax burden of individuals and institutions that strain the sectors during the crisis will increase the recession and increase the duration and depth of the crisis (OECD 2020: 36). For this reason, flexibility and determination should be based on the new tax rules. It is necessary to provide financial support to households and institutions and control the increase in unemployment. Contribution to economic recovery should be made by applying tax expenditure instruments. However, the efficiency of tax policy is directly proportional to the adaptation of tax systems to economic and social structure. Increasing digital activities with the COVID-19 Outbreak caused commercial activities to shift onto digital channels. Moreover, there are many other processes that are expected to change. Therefore, tax administrations and governments need to modernize their tax systems (OECD 2020).

[4] On the other hand, borrowing has become more attractive (compared to before COVID-19) due to declining rates in many countries (IMF 2020d: 6).

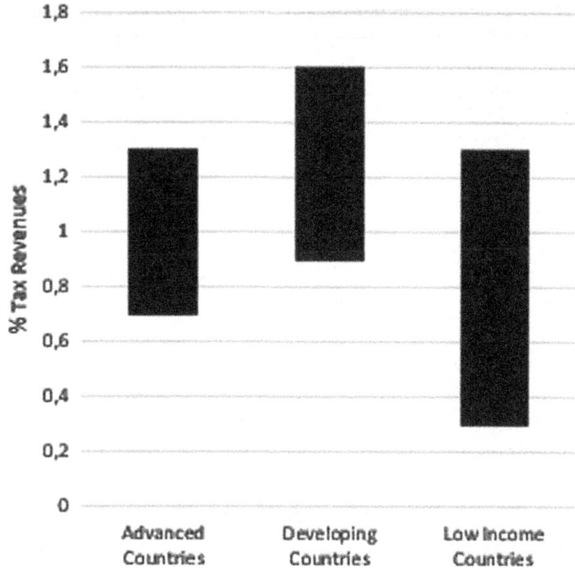


**Fig. 3.11** Effect of GDP on Tax Income by Country Groups (The relevant chart shows the effect of a 1% GDP change that will occur in country groups on tax revenues. The shaded area gives all possibilities with the top and lowest points). *Source* OECD (2020: 38)

On the other hand, the COVID-19 Outbreak also complicates the prediction of tax revenues. The continuity of tax revenues is important in terms of fiscal discipline and continuity of public services. The uncertainty that arose with the COVID-19 outbreak threatens the continuity and sustainability of economic activities. As a result, an uncertainty may arise regarding the generation of public revenues (IMF 2020e). Therefore, the effect of GDP change on tax revenues is important. In this context, the relevant chart (Fig. 3.11) shows the effect of a 1% GDP change in country groups on tax revenues. The shaded area gives all possibilities with the top and lowest points. According to Fig. 3.11, the effect of GDP change on tax revenues is the highest in developing economies. It can be said that the countries with the highest risk of tax revenues during the COVID-19 Outbreak are those with a developing economic structure.

On the other hand, private sector expenditures are decreasing contrary to the increasing public expenditures trend. As for the direct foreign capital-investment tendency, which shows the spending tendency of the private sector best among the global economic indicators, the expenditure tendency of the private sector for investment purposes decreased by 40%, and the total investment was much lower than the 2008 Global Economic Crisis (UNCTAD 2020a) (Fig. 3.12).

The COVID-19 Outbreak Crisis has had direct impacts on foreign direct investment and will have potentially lasting consequences. The sudden and simultaneous interaction of supply and demand-side shocks, combined with policy responses to the global crisis, triggers a series of effects on foreign direct investment (UNCTAD 2020a). Upon the COVID-19 Outbreak, the expenditure and investment trends of the private sector have decreased as a result of the epidemic affecting the amount of supply and demand and the disruption of the supply chains. For this reason, in this

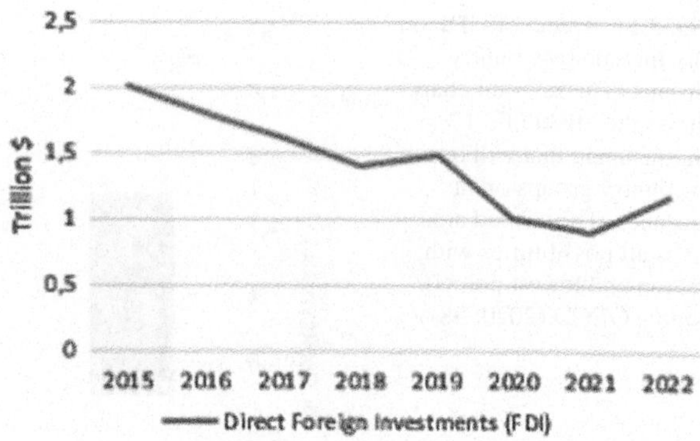


**Fig. 3.12** Direct foreign investment as COVID-19 outbreak and private sector expenditure (2015–2022). *Source* UNCTAD (2020a)

period, governments should protect and support critical sectors and companies from the adverse economic conditions after the epidemic. At this point, a great burden falls on the public economy. Conjunctively, it is normal that the share of the public economy in the total economy increased in this period. In this context, many countries resort to expropriation by purchasing the shares of important companies in the sectors affected by the crisis. Such methods are preferred to protect national capital and continue post-epidemic economic activities (UNCTAD 2020b).

Otherwise, because the crisis is unlike any previous modern crisis, it is likely that socio-economic effects will emerge and the crisis will deepen. In this context, evaluations are made on the possibility of the crisis turning into a social crisis as a result of the unemployment explosion with the COVID-19 Outbreak Crisis (OECD 2020). In fact, comparing the impact of the epidemic crisis on unemployment with the 2008 Global Economic Crisis, experts point out that the COVID-19 Outbreak caused a much deeper unemployment (IMF 2020e).

## 3.3 An Assessment of Pandemic Expenditures in the Context of Peacock-Wiseman Displacement Hypothesis

The Peacock-Wiseman Displacement Hypothesis is a fiscal theory asserting that the amount of public expenditure increases and private sector expenditures decrease during extraordinary periods (Ay 2014). According to the Displacement Hypothesis, public expenditures decrease and private sector expenditures increase as the extraordinary periods end. However, it is emphasized that the level of public spending will never decrease before the extraordinary period (Yılmaz 2018) (Fig. 3.13).

When the Peacock-Wiseman Displacement Hypothesis is evaluated regarding the COVID-19 Outbreak, it is seen that the epidemic period will cause an extraordinary leap in the amount of public expenditures. As a result of the researches, the country group with the highest leap in public expenditure is the developed economies.

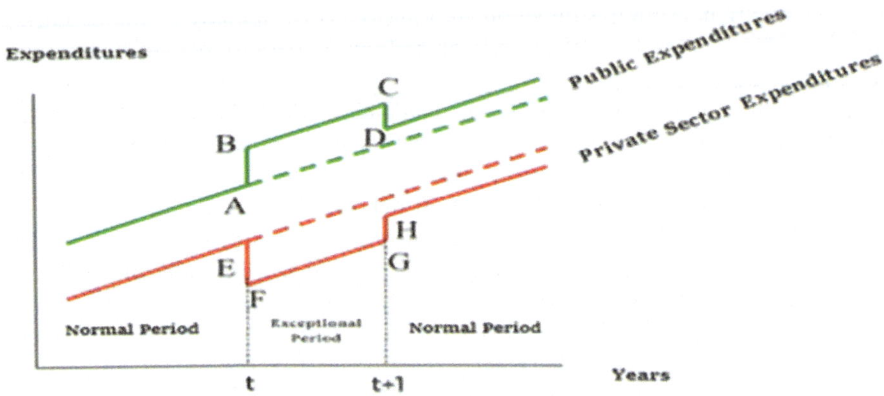


**Fig. 3.13** Peacock-Wiseman hypothesis. *Source* Created by author

Developing economies and low-income economies tend to use public expenditure instruments relatively less. This is due to structural problems and financial concerns these countries have. However, the COVID-19 Outbreak has been described as an "*unprecedented crisis*" due to its supply and demand-side economic effects, and it is emphasized for all country groups that public expenditure instruments are not cut in order for the economic recovery to develop smoothly in the future. In this context, developing countries and low-income countries other than developed economies are likely to experience a deeper economic recession during the epidemic period.

It is likely that the investment tendencies of developing countries, whose investment tendencies are relatively lower even in normal periods, will decrease due to the COVID-19 Outbreak. Moreover, due to the sharp decline in foreign direct investment worldwide, it would be difficult for these countries to make a leap forward in the medium term. Therefore, actively using fiscal policy is a national policy method as required by the conjuncture. On the other hand, policies developed by governments in this direction are likely to have a positive impact on global trade and global finance. Therefore, in this extraordinary period, governments should activate their "*shocking (counter) fiscal policies*" without acting on ordinary period conditions and indicators (Yılmaz 2018). Otherwise, the negative externalities brought about by the epidemic will deepen the economic crisis environment and threaten the future of governments (politically) and entrepreneurs by increasing the economic costs. On the other hand, increasing unemployment, deterioration in income distribution and disruption of the education-health system will make it easier for the crisis to become an unprecedented crisis with a socio-economic nature (UN 2020).

The COVID-19 Outbreak has revealed a period of great uncertainty on a global scale. Pre-epidemic predictions and predictions changed upon the epidemic, resulting in economic, political and social uncertainties. With the increasing risk factor in an environment of uncertainty, it becomes possible to experience market failure (missing information/asymmetric information). At this point, the public sector is expected to act with its regulatory and compensatory function. With the COVID-19 Outbreak, it is seen that policies in this direction are followed even in many liberal countries. However, at this point, flexible and reliable political capability becomes important. For example, the "*delays problem*" of fiscal policy makes it difficult to compensate for the risk in many countries during the epidemic period. The problem of delays decreases the compensatory ability of fiscal policy instruments (Öğretir 2017).

In other words, the efficiency of public expenditure tools in combating the epidemic may decrease with the problem of delays. The problem of delays stems from the fact that fiscal policy is made voluntarily without being based on fiscal rules. In fact, the problem of delays, which is often referred to with monetary policy, is more common in voluntary fiscal policies. This is because indicators are not read with rules and bureaucracy and politics are delayed in decision making. As a result of such delays or misdiagnosis, the market balance deteriorates and economic stability disappears as a result of following opposite policies (OECD 2010). In order to avoid such situations, it is necessary to benefit from the stabilization of the budget. Governments should use their budgetary policy effectively to ensure economic stability (Sakal and Karadeniz 2019). However, the public spending policy, which will complicate the budget policy, should be supported by the revenue policy. In ordinary periods, increasing public expenditures followed by increasing the tax burden resulting in the increase in tax revenues may create tax pressure on taxpayers. This can have negative political consequences. However, as public spending increases in extraordinary periods will force the public sector financially, taxpayers may voluntarily participate in the increase in the tax burden. This is the tax compliance effect included in the Peacock-Wiseman Displacement Hypothesis. This situation is also referred to as the "*Inspection Effect*" in the finance literature.

Due to the state of emergency, society's resistance to tax is decreasing. It is a situation that allows governments to make the arrangements they want in their revenue policy. Because governments that want to get rid of the fiscal constraint act in a more disciplined way financially when they get the necessary tax revenues. In this context, in order to compensate for the costs of the economic and social crisis that started with the COVID-19 Outbreak, many countries have also put tax packages[5] on the agenda after spending packages. However, it is very difficult to implement these policies due to structural problems, especially in low-income country groups where there is a war (Akitoby et al. 2020). On the other hand, another factor that should be noted at this point is the inspection effect. The inspection effect arises as a result of the state's need for public spending. Public expenditures are made to compensate for economic and social costs. If a government takes steps to increase the tax burden during the extraordinary period without increasing (or slightly increasing) the amount of public expenditure, this will further deepen the crisis environment and even reduce the tax effort rate.

On the other hand, tax expenditures per se will not be the solution. The market economy is based on financial mobility, and business downtime will pause this financial flow. As a result of the deterioration of financial indicators, tax revenues will

[5] In this context, the Argentine government has implemented the wealth tax plan to meet the financial burden of the COVID-19 outbreak (BBC 2020). At this point, some countries have similar plans.

shrink and companies will begin to go bankrupt. At this point, tax expenditure will only be political, not real.

## 3.4 Conclusion

The COVID-19 Outbreak has created an economic and social impasse on a global scale. This impasse has been described as an unprecedented socio-economic crisis. On the other hand, much more destructive effects are predicted compared to the 2008 Global Economic Crisis. In addition, the unpredictability of the end of the epidemic and the uncertainty that the subsequent epidemic waves will create a much deeper effect, causing uncertainty in the policies of economic and political actors. This makes it easier for the economic recession to lead to economic collapse. Because the factor that affects the economic order the most is uncertainty. Even in the economies of countries that can be described as developed and robust, uncertainty may negatively affect all economic activities and cause a deep break in economic indicators. However, it should not be forgotten that developed economies are relatively stronger in compensating external costs. While this crisis creates more of a social crisis rather than an economic one in developed countries, it may have deeper economic and social effects in developing and low-income countries. Thus, the political process in developing and low-income countries can be much more uncertain.

COVID-19 Outbreak unexpectedly affected economic and social life negatively. However, it should not be forgotten that there are solution tools to eliminate the negativities. The first of these is the discovery of a vaccine that will solve the problem radically. However, this solution, which is not possible in the short term, brings up fiscal policies that will support economic and social life. In particular, it is necessary to establish an environment in which the market and households are supported by public expenditure instruments. Considering the decline in foreign capital investments, a leap in public expenditures rather than private sector expenditures is important for the economic and social order. In this context, it is seen that many countries have developed policies in this direction.

On the other hand, the increase in the spending tendency increases the income need and taxation and borrowing tendencies are also increasing. Although it is seen that borrowing tendencies increase in the short term, it can be observed that tax resistance decreases and tax revenues increase in the medium term to compensate costs. In this study where we discuss the efficiency of fiscal policy and country trends in the context of the Peacock-Wiseman Displacement Hypothesis, it is seen that the displacement hypothesis is valid in many countries. However, it does not seem possible to predict the public revenue-expenditure course after the COVID-19 Outbreak Crisis, which is considered a state of emergency. On the other hand, the studies that will emerge in the future (transition to the ordinary period) will be complementary to our related work.

## References


AB (2020) Report on the comprehensive economic policy response to the COVID-19 pandemic. In: Press release, vol 223. Retrieved from https://www.consilium.europa.eu/en/press/press-releases/2020/04/09/report-on-the-comprehensive-economic-policy-response-to-the-covid-19-pandemic/

Açıkgöz B, Çiloğlu T (2020) Kriz Modelleri ve Finansal Krizlere Genel Bakış. In: Açıkgöz B (ed) Siyah Kuğu: Ekonomik Krizler, 1st ed. Dora Yayıncılık, Bursa, pp 3–16

Akitoby B, Honda J, Primus K (2020) Tax revenues in Fragile and conflict-affected states—why are they low and how can we raise them ? (No. 143). New York

Allen R, Tommasi D (2001) Managing public expenditure : a reference book for transition countries. In: OECD

Antipova T (2020) Coronavirus pandemic as black swan event. In: Antipova T (ed) Lecture notes in networks and systems, vol 136, pp 356–366. https://doi.org/10.1007/978-3-030-49264-9_32

Ay H (2014) Kamu Maliyesi, 2nd edn. Nobel Yayıncılık, Ankara

BBC (2020, December 7) Covid: Argentina passes tax on wealthy to pay for virus measures - BBC News. Retrieved from https://www.bbc.com/news/world-latin-america-55199058

Boitani A, Perdichizzi S (2018) Public expenditure multipliers in recessions: Evidence from the Eurozone. Retrieved from Università Cattolica del Sacro Cuore, Dipartimento di Economia e Finanza (DISCE) website: http://hdl.handle.net/10419/202842

Buchanan JM (1975) The limits of liberty: between Anarchy and Leviathan. Retrieved from https://books.google.com.tr/books?id=J2941eaDjRwC&printsec=frontcover&hl=tr&source=gbs_ge_summary_r&cad=0#v=onepage&q&f=false

Cencini A, Rossi S (2015) Economic crises and their relationship to global supply and global demand. In: Cencini A, Rossi S (eds) Economic and financial crises, 1st edn, pp 129–148. https://doi.org/10.1057/9781137461902_7

Chubrik A, Dabrowski M, Mogilevsky R, Snitsina I (2011) The impact of the global financial crisis on public expenditures on education and health in the economies of the Former Soviet Union, vol 100. CASE-Center for Social and Economic Research on behalf of CASE Network, Warsaw

Çulha AA (2016) Asymmetric government expenditure: a comparison of advanced and developing countries. In: Research and monetary policy department series. https://doi.org/10.1080/17487870.2017.1374863

d'Agostino G, Dunne JP, Pieroni L (2016) Government spending, corruption and economic growth. World Dev 84:190–205. https://doi.org/10.1016/j.worlddev.2016.03.011

Del Monte A, Pennacchio L (2020) Corruption, government expenditure and public debt in OECD countries. In: Comparative economic studies, vol 62. https://doi.org/10.1057/s41294-020-00118-z

Eatwell J, Milgate M (2011) The fall and rise of Keynesian economics. Retrieved from https://books.google.com.tr/books?hl=tr&lr=&id=-fFoAgAAQBAJ&oi=fnd&pg=PP1&dq=new+generation+economic+crisis+and+keynesianism&ots=sPOUS5FHbs&sig=FyGRFU584lf8gZIK8quxqHZUcZM&redir_esc=y#v=onepage&q&f=false

Garry S, Rivas JC (2017) An analysis of the contribution of public expenditure to economic growth and fiscal multipliers in Mexico, Central America and the Dominican Republic, 1990–2015. In: Economic Commission for Latin America and the Caribbean (ECLAC) (No. 173). Mexico City

Gaspar V, Gopinath G (2020) Fiscal policies for a transformed world. Retrieved August 10, 2020, from IMF Blog website: https://blogs.imf.org/2020/07/10/fiscal-policies-for-a-transformed-world/?utm_medium=email&utm_source=govdelivery

Gopinath G (2020) Reopening from the Great Lockdown: uneven and uncertain recovery. Retrieved August 20, 2020, from IMFBlog website: https://blogs.imf.org/2020/06/24/reopening-from-the-great-lockdown-uneven-and-uncertain-recovery/

Grisorio MJ, Prota F (2016) Public Expenditure in time of crisis: are Italian policymakers choosing the right mix? Economia Politica 35(2):337–365. https://doi.org/10.1007/s40888-018-0124-4

Gurdal T, Aydin M, Inal V (2020) The relationship between tax revenue, government expenditure, and economic growth in G7 countries: new evidence from time and frequency domain approaches. In: Economic change and restructuring. https://doi.org/10.1007/s10644-020-09280-x
Horton M, El-Ganainy A (2020) Fiscal policy: taking and giving away. Retrieved September 25, 2020, from IMF (Finance and Development) website: http://www.imf.org/external/pubs/ft/fandd/basics/fiscpol.htm
IMF (2020a) Policies to support people during the Covid-19 pandemic/fiscal measures in selected economies in response to the COVID-19 pandemic. New York
IMF (2020b) Expenditure policies in support of firms and households. New York
IMF (2020c) A crisis like no other, an uncertain recovery. World Economic Outlook Update, (June 2020), 1–20
IMF (2020d) Policies to support people during the COVID-19 pandemic. Fiscal Monitor, 1(April), 1–26. Retrieved from https://www.imf.org/en/Publications/FM/Issues/2020/04/17/Fiscal-Monitor-April-2020-Chapter-1-Policies-to-Support-People-During-the-COVID-19-Pandemic-49278
IMF (2020e) Challenges in forecasting tax revenue. In: Fiscal affairs. Retrieved from https://www.imf.org/~/media/Files/Publications/covid19-special-notes/en-special-series-on-covid-19-challenges-in-forecasting-tax-revenue.ashx
Koh WC, Kose MA, Nagle PSO, Ohnsorge F, Sugawara N (2020) Debt and financial crises. In: SSRN electronic journal (No. 9116). https://doi.org/10.2139/ssrn.3535970
Lupu D, Petrisor MB, Bercu A, Tofan M (2018) The Impact of public expenditures on economic growth: a case study of central and Eastern European Countries. Emerg Mark Financ Trade 54(3):552–570. https://doi.org/10.1080/1540496X.2017.1419127
Morales L, Callaghan BA (2020) Covid19: Global stock markets “Black Swan” critical letters in economics & finance Covid-19—global stock markets “Black Swan.” Crit Lett Econ Fin 1(1):1–14
Mutluer MK, Öner E, Kesik A (2016) Teori ve Uygulamada Kamu Maliyesi. İstanbul Bilgi Üniversitesi Yayınları, İstanbul
OECD (2010) Fiscal consolidation : requirements , timing , instruments and institutional arrangements. OECD Economic Outlook, 2, 219–265. Retrieved from https://www.oecd.org/finance/monetary/46435606.pdf
OECD (2020) Tax and fiscal policy in response to the Coronavirus crisis: Strengthening confidence and resilience. In: Tackling Corona virüs: contributing to a global effort. Paris
Öğretir AH (2017) Maliye (5th edn, Y. Bilgili, Ed.). 4T Yayınevi, İstanbul
Ostojić A, Žmegač D (2014) Public expenditure and global economic crisis-EU 15. In: 3rd International M-Sphere conference for multi-disciplinarity in business and science, pp 137–145.
Sakal M, Karadeniz M (2019) Devlet Bütçesi ve Yerel Yönetimler Maliyesi, 1st edn. Savaş Yayınevi, Ankara
Taleb NN (2007) The black swan : the impact of the highly improbable. Retrieved from https://search.library.wisc.edu/catalog/9910038828402121
Tanzi V, Davoodi HR (2002) Corruption, growth, and public finances. In: Abed GT, Gupta S (eds) Governance, corruption, and economic performance, 1st edn. International Monetary Fund, Publication Services, Washington, D.C., pp 197–224
Tanzi V, Schuknecht L (2000) Public spending in the 20th century: a global perspective. Retrieved from https://books.google.com.tr/books?hl=tr&lr=&id=kHl6xCgd3aAC&oi=fnd&pg=PR11&dq=increasing+public+spending&ots=WigACiBaVL&sig=HYT4vd7LG5VVaSChlyUarvM7f5M&redir_esc=y#v=onepage&q&f=false
Timbeau BX (2017) Is government expenditure in France too
UN (2020) Economic and social survey of Asia and the Pacific 2020. In: Towards sustainable economies. Bangkok, Thailand
UNCTAD (2020a) World investment report 2020. New York
UNCTAD (2020b) Investment policy responses to the COVID-19 pandemic. In: Investment policy monitor. Geneva, Switzerland

World Bank (2020a) General government final consumption expenditure (% of GDP)—World | Data. Retrieved July 6, 2020, from World Bank Data website: https://data.worldbank.org/indicator/NE.CON.GOVT.ZS?locations=1W

World Bank (2020b) Expense (% of GDP) - Denmark, France, Greece, Turkey, Sweden, Brazil, Germany, Israel, Saudi Arabia, United States, United Kingdom, New Zealand, Korea, Rep., Russian Federation, European Union, South Africa, Finland, Malaysia, Indonesia, Colombia, Japan,. Retrieved July 6, 2020, from World Bank Data website: https://data.worldbank.org/indicator/GC.XPN.TOTL.GD.ZS?locations=DK-FR-GR-TR-SE-BR-DE-IL-SA-US-GB-NZ-KR-RU-EU-ZA-FI-MY-ID-CO-JP-MX-CH-KZ

World Bank (2020c) Expense (% of GDP) - World | Data. Retrieved July 6, 2020, from World Bank Data website: https://data.worldbank.org/indicator/GC.XPN.TOTL.GD.ZS?locations=1W

World Bank (2020d) Tax revenue (% of GDP)-World. Retrieved July 6, 2020, from World Bank Data website: https://data.worldbank.org/indicator/GC.TAX.TOTL.GD.ZS

World Bank (2020e) Interest payments (% of expense) - High income, Middle income, Lower middle income | Data. Retrieved July 6, 2020, from World Bank Data website: https://data.worldbank.org/indicator/GC.XPN.INTP.ZS?locations=XD-XP-XN

World Bank (2020f) External debt stocks, total (DOD, current US$) - Middle income, Lower middle income, Upper middle income | Data. Retrieved July 6, 2020, from World Bank Data website: https://data.worldbank.org/indicator/DT.DOD.DECT.CD?locations=XP-XN-XT

World Bank (2020g) World bank international debt statistics. https://doi.org/10.1596/978-1-4648-1461-7

Yılmaz EB (2018) Maliye. İstanbul Yayınevi, İstanbul

Zugravu B-G, Sava A-Ş (2014) Patterns in the composition of public expenditures in CEE countries. Proc Econ Fin 15(14):1047–1054. https://doi.org/10.1016/s2212-5671(14)00668-6

**Melih Kabayel** is a Ph.D. Candidate of Public Finance and Fiscal Management at İzmir Kâtip Celebi University, Institute of Social Sciences. Melih Kabayel received his BA from the Department of Public Finance, Celal Bayar University, Manisa, Turkey in 2013. He received M.D. in Public Finance with his thesis entitled as "Applicability of Obesity Taxes As Tool of Public Policy In Turkey and Selected Countries" from Izmir Katip Celebi University, Izmir, Turkey in 2017. His research focuses on fiscal theory, public goods theory, obesity taxes, international taxation, public debts, public expenditures, economic and fiscal crises, and Industry 4.0 with aspect of taxation. Ph.D. Candidate Melih Kabayel has authored and contributed to book chapters and articles on these research areas.

**Alper Doğan** received his BA from the Department of Public Finance, Celal Bayar University, Manisa, Turkey in 2003. He received Ph.D. in Public Finance with his thesis entitled as "Gender Budgets: An Evaluation for Turkey" from Celal Bayar University, Manisa, Turkey in 2012. He presently serves as an associate professor at Izmir Kâtip Çelebi University, Faculty of Economics and Administrative Sciences, Izmir, Turkey. He was also a visiting fellow at the University of Utah, Salt Lake City, USA between 2009 and 2010. Dr. Doğan's research interest includes Fiscal Theory, Gender Studies, Industry 4.0, International Taxation.

# Chapter 4
# Internal Audit in Times of Crisis: The Case of COVID-19

**Turgay Çağlayan and Halis Kıral**

**Abstract** COVID-19, which was declared a global epidemic by the World Health Organization (WHO) as of March 11, 2020, affected all the countries in the world in a short time. This epidemic, which is called the global crisis, poses a serious threat at every scale, from a large-scale structure such as the state to small organisations. In such a crisis, the institutions' ability to protect their assets and ensure their continuity depends on the timing and effective implementation of the measures to be taken against the crisis. Crisis management, which is the mechanism that ensures the pre-planning of the measures to be taken against the crisis and their implementation when necessary, is also included in the scope of internal control as a measure to be taken by institutions in case of extraordinary situations. Internal audit is a mechanism that adds value to the activities of the institution by measuring the effectiveness of the risk management, internal control and corporate governance processes of the institution. An evaluation of the design and implementation effectiveness of the controls planned within the scope of crisis management will also be needed during the crisis, which can be provided by the internal audit activity. This study aims to determine the role of internal audit activity in the crisis process before, during and after the crisis. Within the scope of the tasks determined in the study and evaluated to be carried out in the stages of the crisis, it will be of vital importance to direct the internal audit in a way that adds value to the activities of the institution. As a result, institutions that can use their internal auditors effectively in different phases of the crisis will be able to make more successful managerial decisions than other institutions, overcome threats to their sustainability more easily and with the least damage, and even turn the crisis into an opportunity.

**Keywords** COVID-19 · Risk · Crisis · Risk management · Crisis management · Internal audit

T. Çağlayan (✉)
Ministry of National Defense, Ankara, Turkey

H. Kıral
Social Sciences University of Ankara, Ankara, Turkey

 
B. Açıkgöz and İ. A. Acar (eds.), *Pandemnomics: The Pandemic's Lasting Economic Effects*, Accounting, Finance, Sustainability, Governance & Fraud: Theory and Application, https://doi.org/10.1007/978-981-16-8024-3_4

## 4.1 Introduction

A virus first appearing in Wuhan province of China in December 2019 and which is too small for the human eye to see has turned into a phenomenon that has affected all the humanity within six months. This virus, which was declared pandemic and named COVID-19 by the World Health Organization (WHO) as of 11 March 2020 due to its rate of spread and the threat it poses, has been reported to have affected all the countries in the world. The outbreak has been considered as a global crisis, as it affects people's living standards and quality and has multidimensional macro-effects such as economy, communication, tourism, transportation, sports, supply and even international relations.

This global threat posed by COVID-19 outbreak around the world is considered to be the biggest crisis in modern history in terms of its impact after World War II—when compared to SARS, HIV, MERS, Ebola, Malaria outbreaks, etc. (ILO 2020: 2). In addition, some points out that the impact of the mentioned global crisis, which is still ongoing, will be heavier and irreversible when compared to the two major events World War I and II that affected the world negatively in the last hundred years. There are approaches that its effects will be more negative and irreversible compared to World Wars. These inferences provide insight into the size and comprehensiveness of threats posed by the COVID-19 outbreak not only for human health, but also for organisations.

Mentioned threat is mostly about the physical distribution of employees in the workplace and incompatibility of employee and customer relations with the "social distancing criteria". In this process, the ability of the organisations to survive and ensure their continuity depends on the timing and effective implementation of the measures to be taken against the crisis, in which the management assume great responsibilities. The role of internal audit, which is a strategic control factor in fulfilling these responsibilities, which are evaluated within the scope of crisis management, has not been clearly defined in the literature.

This study aims to determine the role of internal audit activity before, during and after the crisis. The study consists of two parts. In the first part, in order to evaluate the crisis environment caused by COVID-19, conceptual information about the concept of crisis and the crisis process is provided and an assessment is made on the crisis management that organisations will implement during the crisis. In the second part, the duties of the internal auditors in the crisis process phases are examined based on the COVID-19 outbreak example in order to help the organisations efficiently cope with the crisis during such a large-scale global crisis.

## 4.2 Conceptual Framework of Crisis and Crisis Management

The crisis is defined as "*time of difficulty, depression in a country or between countries, observed in the life of a society or an organization*" (TDK 2019). Derived from the Greek word "krisis, krit", it is borrowed by Turkish language from the French word "*crise*" (depression). Its Greek origin is used in the meaning of "judgment, ruling, turning point of the disease", and it can be defined as "the difficult period, depression that needs to be decided immediately".

Phillips (2004: 302) defined the crisis as unexpected events that endanger the existence and continuity of the organisation and occur differently from daily activities. Tağraf and Arslan (2003: 150), on the other hand, have defined the crisis as a tension that is not expected and cannot be perceived, which needs immediate response when faced, and threatens its existence and continuity by disabling the reaction and decision mechanisms of the organisations. The crisis is "*threatening situation caused by unpredictable changes in environmental conditions and the management of the organization is insufficient in intervention*" (Tekin 2015: 122).

From a corporate point of view, the crisis in its broadest sense can be considered as a destructive and distressing situation with a negative impact on management, planning and decision mechanisms of the organisation, which threats the achievement of the goals and continuity of an organisation and may fail the measures determined within the scope of enterprise risk management and which requires the exposed organisation to take unplanned and sudden measures. However, when the crises are managed well, though destructive, they can sometimes create an environment that will enable the organisation to come across with new opportunities and gain experience.

Examining the conceptual and institutional definitions, it is seen that the crisis has some basic features. These basic features can be listed as follows (Marie and Petra 2019):

- The crisis is sometimes unpredictable or the organisation's crisis prediction mechanisms are inadequate;
- The crisis threatens the organisation's goals, assets and sustainability;
- The crisis is mostly caused by environmental factors that are out of management's control;
- Lack of sufficient time, resources and plans to solve the events and threats that emerged as a result of the crisis;
- The crisis requires urgent intervention and if not intervened in a timely manner, it has destructive effects,
- The crisis causes stress on decision-makers and employees;
- The crisis poses threats, yet sometimes creates occasional opportunities.

The crisis is not an event or situation that occurs at a time but has a beginning and an end. Therefore, it should be considered as a process. If we divide the crisis process into phases, the phases can simply be the pre-crisis period, the moment of crisis and the post-crisis period. Some crises give clear, understandable signals before

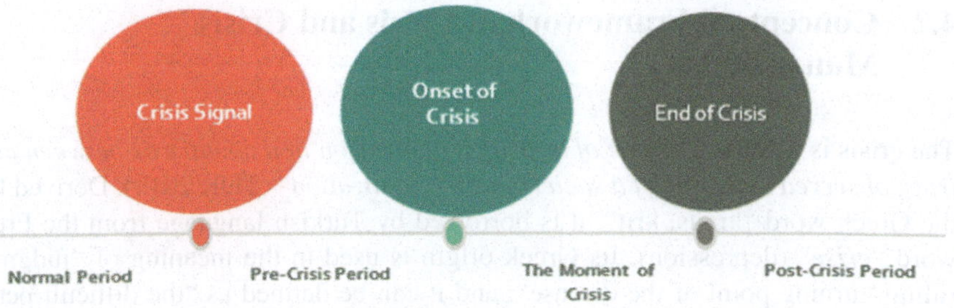


**Fig. 4.1** Phases of crisis. *Source* Prepared by the authors

they occur. As can be understood from Fig. 4.1, if a specific, understandable signal cannot be detected before the crisis, the "Normal Period" and the "Pre-Crisis" period should be evaluated together.

## 4.3 Crisis Management

If the organisations cannot take any measures against the events (crises) that occur in the internal or external environment and lead to unpredictable changes, it will be difficult for them to keep up with the changing environment or survive. For this reason, they should take some measures by evaluating the probability and effects of these events that threaten their existence in advance. The process of determining the measures as a result of this evaluation and implementing these measures during the crisis is called "Crisis Management". In other words, crisis management is a management model that includes detecting and evaluating the signal of the crisis and designing the necessary measures in order to recover from the crisis process with the least damage to the organisation and to operate at the moment of crisis. Thus, the problems causing the crisis will be solved by operating the crisis management, and it will be ensured that the organisation will be able to survive this process with the least loss (Pearson and Clair 1998: 3–4).

The main goal of the crisis management is to prepare organisations for the crisis. This process consists of five phases, as can be seen in Fig. 4.2. In cases where the proactive approach is taken by the organisations, the effects of the crisis will either last very short or there will not be any effect at all, which will increase the possibility of coming across with opportunities. Further in the study, crisis management styles that are compatible with proactive and reactive approaches will be examined separately.

Crisis management is neither a strategic formula for solving the crisis nor a plan consisting of standard processes and documents prepared to be shown upon request. Crisis management procedures prepared superficially and a perfunctory crisis management team will not be enough for the organisation to survive the crisis. Crisis management is a complex process that requires careful and detailed planning

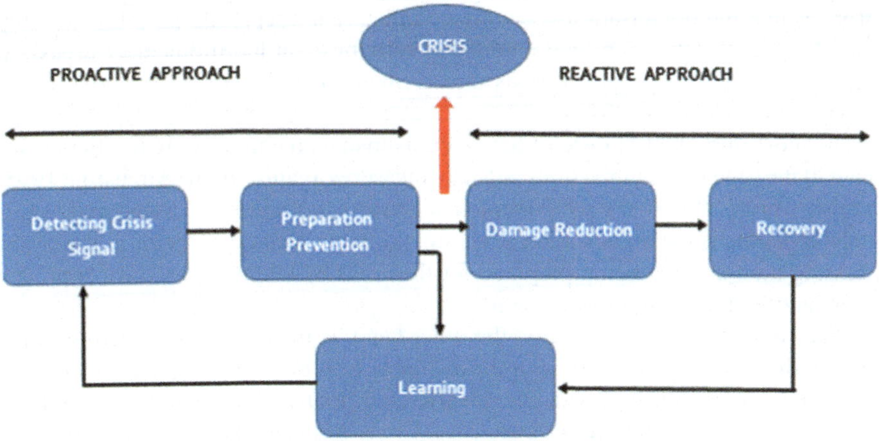


**Fig. 4.2** Phases of crisis management. *Source* Tağraf and Arslan (2003:152)

and a functional distribution of tasks. As such, it will ensure the efficient management of the crisis by steering the decisions and actions of the organisations during the crisis (Pearson 1997: 52).

Based on the above definitions, the characteristics of crisis management can be listed as follows (Bhasin 2020):

- It gives stakeholders and the organisation the ability to recognise and manage crises;
- Creates an experienced crisis management team that can react to unexpected situations;
- It needs to be designed and updated as specific to each crisis;
- Needs a "Risk Management" approach that can predict and evaluate the probability and impact of crises;
- It contains different plans (Continuity Plan, Remote Access and Work Plan, etc.);
- Beneficial when applied as designed.

Examining these features, the relationship between crisis management and risk management is remarkable. However, it is known that crisis and risk management are two processes that are often confused and sometimes considered the same. We mostly encounter some situations which are called risk management but are crisis management in deed or vice versa (Satılmış 2019).

Analysing the relationship between the concepts of crisis and risk management, it is seen that crisis management is divided into two according to the need for risk management. The first one is the onset of crisis management when any of the critical risks determined by the risk management process and whose controls are planned occur, which is called "Active Crisis Management". The second is that the incident in question is not within the scope of risk management. In large scale and devastating surprises that the organisation is caught completely unprepared, the effort to eliminate this event with urgent and unplanned activities—at the moment of crisis—is addressed within the scope of crisis management. This is called "Reactive Crisis Management" (Satılmış 2019).

The most important feature of active crisis management is to predict the events that will threaten the organisations and take measures against them (Augustine 1995) In other words, "*The best way to manage a crisis is to prevent it*". What makes this model dynamic is the organisation's risk management techniques prior to the crisis, assessing the risks and being prepared for the crisis by taking a proactive approach before getting the crisis signal.

Reactive crisis management, on the other hand, is the process of reacting to the crisis in the most optimal way with the available resources, waiting for the crisis to start. It is even possible to divide the reactive crisis management into two as "Offensive Crisis Management" and "Defensive Crisis Management". While Offensive Crisis Management means taking effort to overcome the crisis by taking measures to control the crisis at the moment of the crisis, Defensive Crisis Management can be expressed as the termination of the organisational activities, if necessary, by acknowledging the risks of crisis (Anges 2016) (Fig. 4.3).

Within the scope of the evaluations above, main activities that organisations need to do to effectively manage the crisis are; to take into account and evaluate the risks that are low in probability and high in impact, in their risk management studies; to create a "Crisis Management Plan" as specific to crisis types and support this process with complementary plans. Then, it will be possible to run these plans during the crisis, to eliminate the negative situation or to adapt, and even to turn the crisis into an opportunity.

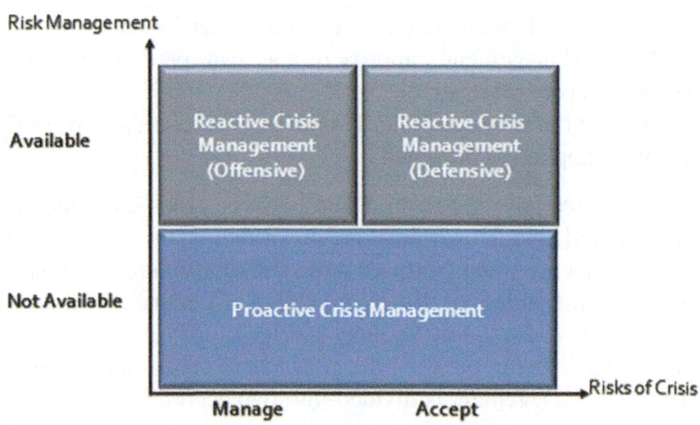


**Fig. 4.3** Ways of crisis management. *Source* Prepared by the authors

## 4.4 Role of Internal Audit in Crisis

According to the definition of The Institute of Internal Auditors-IIA, "*Internal audit is an independent and objective assurance and consultancy activity aimed at improving an organization's activities and adding value to them. Internal audit helps the organization achieve its goals by bringing a systematic and disciplined approach to evaluate and improve the effectiveness of the risk management, control and governance (corporate governance) processes of the organization*". As can be understood from this definition, internal audit will add value to the organisation's activities by measuring the effectiveness of the risk management, internal control and corporate management processes of the organisation. Crisis management is also included in the scope of internal control as a measure that organisations will take in case of extraordinary situations, and it is natural for internal auditors to add value to this process. In addition, the organisation will need an assessment of the design and implementation effectiveness of the planned controls while achieving its crisis management objectives, which can be presented by the internal audit activity.

Examining the cyclical flow chart of the crisis in Fig. 4.4, the controls named as preventive measures or solutions to be taken during the crisis process can be operated, as designed, at every phase of the process and if the desired effect is provided, the results of the crisis can be converted to benefit. The internal audit activity plays a role as a strategic mind partner for the organisation, developing and ensuring taking precautionary measures in advance, with a process- and mistake-oriented approach that suggests doing things right as well as doing the right things. When this phenomenon is considered together with the questioning of the possibility of turning the crisis into an opportunity, the internal audit activity will also contribute to the management board and senior management in the management of the crisis process.

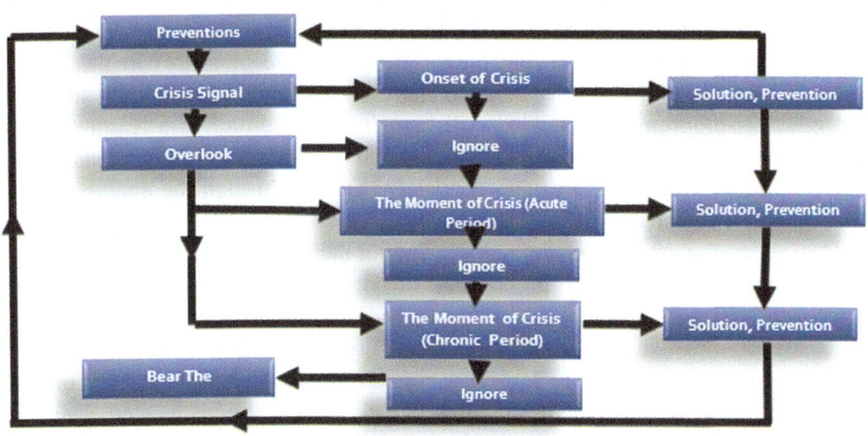


**Fig. 4.4** Cyclic flow chart of the crisis. *Source* Kash and Darling (1998:181)

In order to reveal the contribution of the internal audit activity, it is necessary to explain what the organisation needs to do in the phases of crisis defined in Fig. 4.1 and the duties of the internal auditors in accordance with the scope.

## 4.5 Duties of Internal Auditors in Pre-crisis Period

What is important for organisations in times of crisis is not trying to stave off or fudge the crisis. An organisation that can detect the crisis signal and sense that the crisis is coming before it starts and take advantage of this in the way to success will get the most out of the crisis (Ofluoğlu and Mısırlı 2001: 3).

In order for the organisations to enter the crisis preparedly, they should make some preparations in the normal period before the crisis signal in Fig. 4.1 and, if the proper detection can be made, after the detection of the crisis signal, i.e. before the crisis.

If we define the pre-crisis period, this period begins with the feeling of all kinds of actions, events, measures and indicators that will create the crisis and ends with the emergence of the crisis. During this period, crisis symptoms increase. The first activity to be carried out in this process is to identify the crisis risks and confirm that the crisis has begun to occur. Even if the crisis signal is not enough to prevent the crisis, it is of great importance in terms of managing the crisis in an efficient and least harmful way and even turning it into an opportunity. In fact, making preparations in the pre-crisis period is directly proportional to prevent the crisis before it deepens by sensing the signals before the crisis or to prevent the crisis from becoming chronic during the crisis (Campbell 2004).

In the "Normal Period" before the crisis signal is detected, two important processes that organisations will operate in order to detect the crisis signal are "Early Warning System" and "Environmental Analysis".

The early warning system is a process that is used mostly in the process of detecting financial crisis signals, guides the organisations to take measures in the face of extraordinary situations, and it allows to analyse some early indicators of the crisis and make assumptions about what will happen in the future as a result of these analyses. By means of this process, it is possible to take a position in advance after determining the time, intensity and depth of the crisis through the analyses in the relevant sector (Yeniçeri 1993: 224).

Environmental analysis is defined as a step in the early warning system, but it is also considered as a different process used to determine the crisis signal alone. In this context, the indicators of the crisis can be determined by constantly following and analysing positive and negative events occurring in the near outer environment such as countries, regions which closely concern the organisation, and the internal environment, i.e. the local environment where the organisation is located. The positive and negative cases occurring in the internal environment, such as the, can be monitored and analysed continuously to determine (Ofluoğlu and Mısırlı 2001: 13).

Apart from these activities carried out to sense the crisis signal, some management processes that need to be designed and operated in order to support crisis management are also beneficial for the organisation. The leading management process is "Enterprise Risk Management", which is the most important process that supports corporate managers to make the right decision, achieve the targets set by the organisations and develop strategies to that end.

Enterprise Risk Management, carried out under the responsibility of the organisation's senior management, is defined by The Committee of Sponsoring Organizations of the Treadway Commission (COSO) as, "*a process, effected by an entity's board of directors, management and other personnel, applied in strategy setting and across the enterprise, designed to identify potential events that may affect the entity, and manage risk to be within its risk appetite, to provide reasonable assurance regarding the achievement of entity objectives*". The important point in this process is the ability to detect "the black swans" without any ignorance, such as the COVID-19 outbreak, which are unpredictable during the risk assessment process to be carried out with the participation of stakeholders, develops circumstantially and have a very high impact when it occurs (İnce and Özbozkurt 2020: 128). Instead of stereotyped methods such as developing measures based on previously identified risks, more detailed analysis should be made in the risk assessment process by identifying all kinds of risks including new, current, those with an enormous impact, surprise events that are not seen probable to occur and evaluating the results of early warning systems and environmental analysis. It should be noted that the main cause of the crises are the risks that are known but ignored and thus against which no measure is taken since they are not likely to occur due to their low probability.

One of the efficient risk measures is "Business Continuity Management". Business continuity management system is, "*a process that is carried out in order to plan, establish, implement, monitor, review, maintain and continuously improve a written management system with a view to, in the event of a breach causing an interruption, protecting against the breach, reducing the likelihood of the breach occurring again, being prepared for the breach and take the necessary recovery action in the event of the breach*" (TSE 2014). This process is a set of written procedures protecting especially the interests of stakeholders and the brand, reputation and value-creating activities of the organisation and increasing the resilience of the organisation by ensuring continuity of its crucial activities, in the event that the risks identified by the organisation occur and pose a threat. The most comprehensive of these written procedures is the "Business Continuity Plan" and is supported by auxiliary procedures. These auxiliary procedures are mainly;

- Business Impact Analysis
- Remote Access Plan
- Remote Working Plan
- Stakeholder Communication Plan.

In addition to these processes, determining the procedures for ensuring "Organisational Resilience" will also help the organisation to carry out its activities with the least loss in the threat environment it will be exposed to. In today's world, organisational resilience with increasing popularity in the VUCA (volatile, uncertain, complex and ambiguous) environment in which organisations operate emphasises the importance of not only increasing profits but also protecting organisations against unexpected developments. Basic approaches to be applied in this process are, flexibility, backup, rapid mobility, decentralisation, transparency, learning from mistakes and turning into opportunity (Marva and Milner 2013). Some of the road maps that should be prepared in order to ensure organisational resilience:

- Emergency and Contingency Plan
- Back-up Plan
- Disaster Recovery Plan
- Evacuation Plan.

For the preparation of these plans, there is a need for "Business Impact Analysis", which enables the analysis of activities that may have an impact on business interruption and that enables to analyse the impact. In general, these plans are procedures that can be evaluated within the scope of business continuity management.

When the important processes and plans mentioned above are designed by the organisations in the "Normal Period", the crisis management process is supported in pre-crisis period. These plans should not only be designed, but also updated regularly, and their integration into the crisis management process should be carried out by rehearsals and drills to determine the accuracy, suitability and whether they provide the expected benefits.

Considering that it is difficult for the senior management to design and execute the aforementioned plans and processes in addition to its routine duties, efficiency and quality of these works will be questionable. In this context, it is vital for the board of directors and senior management that the above-mentioned plans and processes, which are planned, prepared and implemented together with crisis management and part of the internal control system, are evaluated by the internal auditors in a way to add value to the organisation.

In the normal period before the crisis, internal auditors will continue their auditing and consultancy activities in their annual plans. In this plan, it will be appropriate to periodically evaluate crisis management, business continuity management, organisational resilience and early warning systems and environmental analysis, which are already designed and that some of them are likely to be operated during the crisis period.

Considering the crisis example caused by the COVID-19 outbreak, in the "Normal Period" before COVID-19, internal auditors can carry out the activities listed below:

- During the enterprise risk management process, which is carried out periodically by the employees of the organisation, they can guide the management, within the scope of consultancy, about management of risks.
- Risk management process can be reviewed periodically. They can also provide assurance that risks related to different crisis situations have been identified and measures have been developed against them.

- Internal auditors can contribute to enterprise risk management by reporting this situation to senior management when they determine that there are high-level changes in a risk previously defined during the audit and consultancy duties, by means of the micro-risk assessment results performed at least once a year in macro-risk, audit and consultancy processes.
- They can offer improvement suggestions by testing the applicability of the plans prepared for the crisis process to different crisis scenarios and the rehearsals and drills made by the organisation for the plans (Chambers 2020a; IAAA 2020; McCafferty 2020).
- They can perform audits involving the analysis and evaluation of data obtained as a result of early warning systems and environmental analysis.
- In the "Pre-Crisis Period", which is the phase between the detection of the crisis signal and the onset of the crisis, the organisations should, along with their routine activities, review the crisis management procedures and the plans that have been prepared in accordance with the specific conditions of the crisis they will face. It would be appropriate for them to update their plans by predicting the cause, magnitude, severity and duration of the crisis they will be exposed to and rehearse these plans if the time allows. In the example of the crisis caused by the COVID-19 outbreak, the internal auditors of the organisations detecting the crisis signal of COVID-19 can carry out the activities listed below in the "Pre-Crisis Period".
- They can prepare a short-term, flexible and changeable "Agile Audit" plan that enables issues such as; remote auditing, as specific to only times of crisis, if necessary, which will enable performance of critical audits; cooperation between internal auditors and stakeholders; unlimited communication; efficient use and allocation of resources, use of technology and rapid reporting, by discussing with the management on whether to make the necessary changes in the annual audit plan in accordance with the magnitude, severity and duration of the crisis (Chambers 2020b; PEMPAL-IACOP 2020).
- They can prepare for information systems infrastructure and security within the scope of "Remote Access and Work Plan" to ensure that critical audits are performed remotely.
- With the evaluation of internal auditors' performance, competencies and their capacity to carry out their duties under pressure, a plan can be made on what kind of issues they can help the organisation during the crisis (McCafferty 2020).
- They can lead the redefinition and evaluation of financial, operational and security risks that they will be exposed to in the changing environment during the crisis, by meeting with the board of directors and senior management. They can update the plans designed in this context and prepare short-term action plans (McCafferty 2020).
- If the management decides that there will be a change in the risk appetite of the organisation regarding the crisis process, they may recommend that the enterprise risk management process be re-evaluated and updated.

## 4.6 Duties of Internal Auditors in Times of Crisis

The time of crisis is the phase in which the symptoms of the crisis are ended and the consequences begin to be felt intensely, the damages of the crisis are felt the most and the crisis must be urgently intervened. Using all the resources of the organisation to prevent the crisis during this intervention may lead to imbalance and confusion in the organisation (Kash and Darling 1998: 182). As there may also be disruptions in the decision-making processes of the corporate management in this period, this may cause panic and conflict among the employees (Yeniçeri 1993: 223).

The time of crisis is also a phase in which information pollution and false news are common. In this phase, all stakeholders exposed to the crisis want clear, precise and accurate information about the crisis. However, due to the high level of uncertainty in this phase, it may not be possible to have sufficient and accurate information about the crisis.

Time of crisis is composed of two phases:

i. Escalation phase (acute period)
ii. Standstill and de-escalation phase (chronic period).

The escalation phase is the period when the first shock, turmoil and panic are experienced. The escalation phase ends with the first response to the symptoms and the escalation slows down. As the crisis management process for the solution of the crisis is operated, the escalation stops and the crisis enters de-escalation phase (Campbell 2004).

If the signals and symptoms in the pre-crisis period are detected and measures are taken, the severity of the threat to be exposed in time of crisis will be softer. In this period, the corporate management focused on priority tasks such as maintaining the organisational existence within the scope of crisis management and put routine operational tasks into the background. In this phase, it is likely that some problems will occur in the processes of operating the controls designed with the routine activities of the organisation.

In an unpredictable crisis environment such as an epidemic disease that is very unlikely and has a devastating effect when it occurs, internal audit services should first be offered to mitigate the effects of the crisis and then return to routine activities. Considering the example of the crisis caused by the COVID-19 outbreak, internal auditors should quickly adapt to the outbreak environment in the "Time of Crisis", which is considered to have started with the acceptance of COVID-19 as an epidemic, as the above symptoms are seen all over the world, and then evaluate carrying out the following activities;

- Since the management carries out more crisis-oriented activities during the crisis, there may be difficulties especially in complying with the legal regulations. This may create a legal sanction and reputational risk for organisations in the post-crisis period. Therefore, internal auditors can provide legal compliance-oriented assurance service in managing critical activities by working in coordination with legal units, if necessary.

- As a result of the management's focus on managing the time of crisis, ensuring routine controls to be operated efficiently is of secondary importance. In this case, internal auditors can provide an assurance service for monitoring controls designed specifically against critical and high-level risks (IAAA 2020).
- Increasing the awareness of the management regarding the possible abuse risks that are likely to happen in this process and can work on internal control weaknesses that will lead to abuse in all areas (Chambers 2020a).
- They can offer consultancy services for new situations (such as disinfection, employee health, social distance, transportation problems, remote working, lack of staff and twin assignment), especially in an unpredictable crisis environment such as the COVID-19 outbreak (Coderre 2020).
- Since it is a control of critical nature, internal auditors can oversee the fulfilment of some duties such as; staying at home for a certain period of time the employees showing fever, cough, headache and other defined symptoms and working from home until the situation is clear, following the isolation rules, applying to health institutions and the follow-up of their health conditions to be carried out by human resources units
- They can assess whether the employees who continue to provide services in the workplace comply with the occupational health and safety rules set out in the COVID-19 outbreak. Thus, they take an active role in preventing the spread of the epidemic among employees.
- They can evaluate the performance of alternative procurement and product distribution processes or alternative service delivery methods designed and operated within the scope of business continuity, which are considered as the most important activities for the organisation to survive.
- They can evaluate the performance and safety of the technological infrastructure, which provides uninterrupted internal and external communication of the organisation, within the scope of the "Communication Plan" and "Remote Access and Working Plan", taking into account the information security procedures.
- They can follow the state of the organisation with regard to benefiting from local and/or international supports.
- By encouraging more frequent risk assessments with employees and helping identify particularly potential risks that may arise during a crisis, they can play a facilitating role in reducing the potential hazards the organisation will face (Chambers 2020b).
- They can actively take part in any position, when necessary, especially in crisis management teams—as staff with sufficient knowledge of all the processes of the organisation, to maintain its existence and continuity[1] (Coderre 2020).

---

[1] Although this process is a movement that would be against the International Internal Auditing Standards and would disturb independence and impartiality in the normal period, the important thing in times of crisis should be to ensure the survival of the organisation, because if there is no organisation, then is no internal auditor. In the event that these activities are audited after the crisis, performing a task by a different auditor who has not taken responsibility in that position or getting service from an independent audit firm can be evaluated.

## 4.7 Duties of the Internal Auditors in Post-crisis Period

The post-crisis period is the phase that begins with the end of the crisis and the effects continue despite its declining severity. In this period, the crisis has been brought under control in general and after the crisis, normalisation and restructuring efforts has started. These studies are also useful for learning the measures to be taken against the crises that may be exposed to in the future (Erten 2010: 16).

This period can be briefly called "*Solution or Collapse Stage*". The organisation can bring a new momentum to its activities by eliminating the crisis with the solutions it applies at the moment of crisis. In organisations that cannot develop solutions during the crisis to successfully overcome the crisis, the possibility of a solution decreases depending on the severity of the crisis and the collapse begins (Komorowski 2017). The organisation's relations with its environment are disrupted, and increased labour turnover, employee complaints, stress and panic can lead to the resolution of the organisation.

In the example of the crisis caused by the COVID-19 outbreak, internal auditors can perform the activities listed below during the crisis time in some countries, and during the post-crisis period, in others, when it is assumed that the crisis time is over, and they shift to the stage of returning to normal;

- They can update the audit universe and risks to the universe by taking into account the experiences gained during the crisis in the macro-risk analysis of the annual plan to be prepared for the following period.
- By informing the management and audit committee about the disrupted parts of the annual plan prepared before the crisis and the activities carried out at the time of the crisis, they can lead the regulation regarding the disrupted parts in the plan to be prepared for the following period.
- If there are some deficiencies regarding the performance of internal auditors when they encounter some cases in the crisis period different than the normal period, they can plan training to increase their competencies within the scope of continuous professional development.
- They can work to develop an internal audit software that has remote access to the internal audit activity, provides an infrastructure for the review of digital data, not document-oriented, integrated with other IT software of the organisation, can communicate with all stakeholders, record all of the work in the database and is accessible to the relevant people.
- They can act as consultants to update the risk management activity of the organisation within the framework of the experience gained during the crisis.
- In consultation with management, they can provide consultancy services to make an objective assessment of the crisis and to transfer the experiences gained to the business processes (IAAA 2020). Thus, managers have the opportunity to see the deficiencies of the system they have established more easily. Moreover, both planning will be completed for completing these deficiencies in the following period and new scenarios will be produced for possible crises (Erten 2010:16).

The tasks of internal auditors mentioned above, which are for the crisis environment caused by the COVID-19 outbreak, can be improved and diversified according to different crisis scenarios by considering the internal audit legislation and regulations.

## 4.8 Conclusion

The speed and accessibility offered to the business world by the modern era have brought the external environmental risks fed by the factors of uncertainty and complexity in its wake. Crises are among the most severe of these external environmental risks. Regardless of their size, organisations are exposed to different types of crises throughout their lifetimes and in which cases they have to face the problems of continuity of their existence and sustainability. The crises they face often occur at an unexpected time and can have devastating effects. However, before the crisis occurs, it often reveals itself by giving certain signals. If the organisation managers can detect these signals and operate the crisis management process they planned before, they can ensure the continuity of the organisation by turning the crisis into an opportunity.

This study addresses the duties that the internal auditors should fulfil during the crisis process in three main phases, namely before, during and after the crisis. It will be vital to direct the internal audit in a way that will add value to the activities of the organisation within the scope of the duties that are considered to be carried out in the mentioned phases.

In the "Pre-Crisis Period", which is the phase between the detection of the crisis signal and the onset of the crisis, the internal auditors, on the one hand, carry out their audit and consultancy duties within the scope of the current audit plan, on the other hand, they should be in contact with the senior management about whether to make the necessary changes to the annual audit plan in accordance with the probable magnitude, severity and duration of the crisis that started to be felt. Thanks to this communication, internal auditors can contribute to the organisation by recommending the senior management review of the financial, operational and security risks that the organisation is likely to be exposed to during the crisis and by providing guidance in this regard. Thus, internal auditors can lead the update of enterprise risk management processes by taking into consideration the risk appetite that is likely to be revised in crisis conditions. On the other hand, internal auditors can also make preparations, in this phase, for the information systems infrastructure and security related to remote execution of critical audits planned to be conducted during the crisis.

Given that the uncertainty is high and the turmoil and panic is likely to happen during the crisis which starts when COVID-19 is considered an epidemic, the internal auditors may provide legal compliance-oriented assurance services in the management of critical activities. Thus, it is possible to manage the legal sanction and reputation risk for the organisation in the post-crisis period. In addition, while internal auditors monitor the efficiency of controls against critical and high-level risks, they may also make internal control weaknesses that may lead to abuse be the subject of audit. In addition to assurance services, they can also offer consultancy services on new working conditions (such as disinfection, employee health, social distance, remote working, lack of staff and twin assignment), especially after the COVID-19 outbreak.

In the post-crisis period in which the effects continue despite its declining severity, lessons should be learned from the experiences gained during the crisis and the competencies of the internal auditors should be increased in the required areas, the internal audit plans and programmes should be updated, and the deficiencies in the remote execution of auditing and consultancy activities should be eliminated. Thus, the value that internal audit will add to the organisation will also increase.

As a result, organisations that can use their internal auditors efficiently in different phases of the crisis will be able to make successful management decisions and will overcome the threats to their sustainability more easily and with the least harm, and they can even turn the crisis into opportunities.

## References

Anges M (2016) When is it ok to implement an offensive crisis management strategy? https://melissaagnes.com/when-is-it-ok-to-implement-an-offensive-crisis-management-strategy/. Access 22 June 2020

Augustine NR (1995) Managing the crisis you tried to prevent. Harward Bus Rev

Bhasin H (2020) Crisis management—meaning, need, steps and examples. https://www.marketing91.com/crisis-management/. Access 19 June 2020

Campbell R (2004) Crisis control: preventing and managing corporate crises. Prentice Hall of Australia Ply Ltd.

Chambers R (2020a) In the face of the coronavirus, internal auditors must do more than don masks. https://iaonline.theiia.org/blogs/chambers/2020/pages/in-the-face-of-the-coronavirus-internal-auditors-must-do-more-than-don-masks.aspx. Access 05 Apr 2020

Chambers R (2020b) Covid-19 quick poll: internal auditors cope with threats while embracing opportunities. https://iaonline.theiia.org/blogs/chambers/2020/pages/covid-19-quick-poll-internal-auditors-cope-with-threats-while-embracing-opportunities.aspx. Access 24 Apr 2020

Coderre D (2020) Covid and internal audit, https://www.linkedin.com/pulse/covid-internal-audit-david-coderre?articleid=6654881892241854464. Access 22 Apr 2020

Erten Ş (2010) Türk Kamu Yönetiminde Kriz Yönetimi Anlayışı, Yüksek Lisans Tezi, Uşak Üniversitesi, Uşak

IAAA (The Institute of Internal Auditors of Australia) (2020) Factsheet: internal audit and pandemics. https://dl.theiia.org/documents/fact-sheet-internal-audit-and-pandemics-iia-australia.pdf. Access 18 Apr 2020

Ilo (2020) Covid-19 Ve Çalışma Yaşamı, Ilo Gözlem Raporu 2nd ed.

İnce M, Özbozkurt OB (2020) Siyah Kuğuyu Yönetmek. Uluslararası Toplum Araştırmaları Dergisi 15(23):125–144

Kash JT, Darling JR (1998) Crisis management: prevention, diagnosis and intervention. Leadership Org Dev J 19/4:179–186

Komorowski P (2017) The life cycle of a crisis—a model of the course of an economic collapse. Wydawnictwo Uniwersytetu Ekonomicznego W Katowicach

Marie M, Petra H (2019) Prepared for a crisis? Basicelements of crisis management in an organisation. Econ Res-Ekonomska Istraživanja 32(1):1844–1868

Marva Sm, Milner Cd (2013) Underwriting corporate resilience via creativity: the pliability model. Total Quality Manage Bus Excellence 24:835–846

McCafferty J (2020) Five internal audit imperatives for handling the coronavirus pandemic. https://misti.com/internal-audit-insights/five-internal-audit-imperatives-for-handling-the-coronavirus-pandemic. Access 10 May 2020

Ofluoğlu G, Misirli K (2001) İşletme Ve Kriz Yönetimi. Kamu-İş 2(6):1–29

Pearson VD (1997) Managing the unthinkable. Org Dynamics 26(2):52

Pearson CM, Clair JA (1998) Reframing crisis management. Acad Manag Rev 23(1):59–76

Pempal (Public Expenditure Management Peer Assisted Learning)—Iacop (The Internal Audit Community of Practice) (2020) The impact of covid-19 on the role and activities of internal audit. https://www.pempal.org/knowledge-product/impact-covid-19-role-and-activities-internal-audit. Access 04 May 2020

Phillips D (2004) Handbook of corporate communication and public relations, chapter 19. Routledge, New York

Satılmış M (2019) Risk Yönetimi Ve Kriz Yönetimi, https://www.dunya.com/kose-yazisi/risk-yonetimi-ve-kriz-yonetimi/452613. Access 18 Apr 2020

Tağraf H, Arslan NT (2003) Kriz Oluşum Süreci Ve Kriz Yönetiminde Proaktif Yaklaşım. Cumhuriyet Üniversitesi İktisadi Ve İdari Bilimler Dergisi 4(1):149–160

TDK (2019) Türkçe Sözlük, Türk Dil Kurumu Yayınları, Ankara

Tekin ÖF (2015) Kriz Yönetimi Ve Kamu Yönetimi İçin Önemi. Selçuk Üniversitesi Meslek Yüksekokulu Sosyal Bilimler Dergisi 18(2):119–135

TSE (2014) TS En ISO 22301 Toplumsal Güvenlik, İş Sürekliliği Yönetim Sistemleri – Şartlar, Türk Standartları Enstitüsü, Ankara

Yeniçeri Ö (1993) İşletmelerde Yönetim, Organizasyon Ve Davranış, Tutibay Basım A.Ş, Ankara

**Turgay Çağlayan** Internal Auditor at Ministry of National Defense, Ankara, Turkey. Ph.D. student in Audit and Risk Management at Social Sciences University of Ankara. Holds MSc in International Relations and BS in Civil Engineering. He has the title of Certified Internal Auditor (CIA).

**Halis Kiral** is an associated professor at the Social Sciences University of Ankara in Turkey. He is also Head of Audit and Risk Management Department and Director of Center for Audit and Risk Management (ASBÜDRM) at the ASBU. He was a visiting scholar in Duke Center for International Development (DCID) for the 2017–2018 academic year. He has also worked in the Ministry of Finance of Turkey as a state budget expert, public finance expert, head of the department of Central Harmonization for Internal Audit, and head of the Budget Policy Department. He wrote a number of articles, books and book chapters on topics such as public finance, public financial management and control, specifically internal audit and risk management, public budgeting, and applied economics.

# Part II
# Pandemic in Turkish Economy

# Chapter 5
# Financial Measures Taken in Turkey and Selected Countries in Combatting COVID-19 Outbreak

**Tülin Canbay and Hilal Balcı Cura**

**Abstract** In the process passing from past to present, the world history has witnessed many natural and unnatural disasters. Negative events particularly climate change and including outbreaks have caused the world to be affected economically and socially, and caused these said negativities to become global today. The COVID-19 outbreak, which emerged in Wuhan, China's Hubei state, was declared as a "pandemic" in the fourth quarter of 2019, on March 11, 2020, by the World Health Organization (WHO). It is estimated that the economic destruction of the COVID-19 pandemic, as well as its dimension affecting human beings, will be significant by the end of 2020. In addition to the loss of numerous lives around the world, another impact of the virus has been experienced by the global economy. The fact that this flu, which originated in Central Asia, has spread to the USA and Europe has had an impact on the currencies of countries, capital markets, precious metals, barrel oil prices, and even virtual currencies, causing volatile fluctuations in the global markets. In the process that the world is in, COVID-19 has brought the entire world to a significant historical turning point. The entire world has focused on two main issues at this historical turning point. The first of them is to fight the pandemic, to minimize casualties, and to eradicate the pandemic. The second step is to take an action to avoid the crises and damage that will occur in post-epidemic economies. All countries have begun to implement socialization policies in order to protect public health and fight the pandemic when the COVID-19 disease spread around the world. Closures of educational institutions, primarily in trade and tourism, work restrictions, and restrictions on human mobility have had a rapid negative impact on all sectors. Today's economy is a structure where employees, financial institutions, companies, suppliers, consumers, and countries are interconnected. The COVID-19 pandemic has caused the economy to ground to a halt. It is stated that the economy has suffered an unprecedented negative shock as a result of this pandemic. The closure of borders,

T. Canbay (✉)
Department of Finance Theory, Manisa Celal Bayar University, Manisa, Turkey

H. B. Cura
Department of Protection of Ownership and Security Social Security Programme, Manisa Celal Bayar University, Manisa, Turkey
e-mail: hilal.cura@cbu.edu.tr

 
B. Açıkgöz and İ. A. Acar (eds.), *Pandemnomics: The Pandemic's Lasting Economic Effects*, Accounting, Finance, Sustainability, Governance & Fraud: Theory and Application, https://doi.org/10.1007/978-981-16-8024-3_5

restrictions on transportation, the lockdown of people in their homes, the imposition of curfews, the reduction of import and export activities, decrease in both supply and demand, as well as the unprecedented developments in the global economy, distinguished this crisis from others. It could not be avoided that all countries around the world, including Turkey, would be affected by this situation. The economic effect of the COVID-19 pandemic harmed the sectors of the economy that directly benefit from natural resources, particularly agriculture (primary sector), the sector where industrial activities take place (secondary sector), and the industries where all services are provided (tertiary sector) (such as education, finance, and tourism sectors). Countries around the world implement economic measures to mitigate the effects of the economic crisis. Financial measures, which are primarily among the economic measures taken by countries in the fight against the COVID-19 pandemic, are discussed in the study in this context.

**Keywords** Anahtar Kelimeler: COVID-19 · Economic crisis · Financial measures · Outbreak · Tax · Selected countries

## 5.1 Introduction

World has faced many natural and unnatural disasters from past to present. Today, many adversities, including epidemics and particularly climate change, cause the world to be affected economically and socially, and these negativities cause them to become global. The epidemic, which was announced to have emerged in Wuhan City, Hubei Province in China, at the end of 2019, started to affect the whole world as of the beginning of 2020 and soon this was announced to the world as a "pandemic" by the World Health Organization (WHO) in March 2020. From the first emergence of the epidemic until today, it has adversely affected and continues to affect the whole world economically, without exception, and especially the health conditions. As a result of the COVID-19 pandemic, the global economy has stalled. The economies around the world have begun to face a collapse. COVID-19 has brought the whole world to an important historical turn. In this historical turn, the whole world has focused on two main points. The first one is to combat the epidemic, to minimize the loss of life, and to get rid of the epidemic, and the second is to take measures today to prevent the crises and damages that will occur in the post-epidemic economies. This study examines economic and financial measures taken to mitigate the financial impact of the pandemic in Turkey and selected countries after the International Monetary Fund (IMF) and other international organizations declared that the world would go into recession following the pandemic. In the first part of the study, the emergence of the COVID-19 outbreak and the process of reaching a global dimension are discussed. The second part addresses the economic impact caused by the pandemic and the last section reveals the fiscal measures taken against the pandemic in selected countries, particularly Turkey.

## 5.2 COVID-19 Turning into a Pandemic

Today, an economic, political or social event wherever it occurs around the world has the power to affect the whole world at certain levels in a short time. Although the COVID-19 epidemic was initially seen as a virus-induced health problem, over time, it had a great power to affect not only human health, but also economic, social, and political life in different aspects, and it has led to deep and powerful changes that have not been experienced in the world until now.

### *5.2.1 Outbreak of COVID-19*

With Coronaviruses (CoV), which the world is not a stranger to historically, humans have actually faced two members of this large virus family in the twenty-first century before COVID-19. For example, in 2003, it appeared under the name of "Severe Acute Respiratory Syndrome (SARS-CoV)," and in 2012, it appeared on the world stage under the name "Middle East Respiratory Syndrome (MERS-CoV)." However, COVID-19, the type of this family of viruses we encounter today, is quite different from the coronaviruses we have met before, because the transmission rate of this virus was faster than the previous family members and, unlike the other two types, it managed to spread throughout the world in a very short time. COVID-19, the third of the coronavirus species transmitted from animals to humans(zoonotic), first appeared in Wuhan. It is claimed to originate from bats sold in the Huanan Seafood Retail Market (Bruinen De Bruin et al. 2020). Therefore, the first known case of the COVID-19 outbreak is seen in Wuhan City in Hubei Province of China. The first COVID-19 patient was diagnosed on December 10, 2019, and the first death was recorded on January 9, 2020 (The World Bank 2020). China announced the COVID-19 outbreak to the world on December 31, 2019.

### *5.2.2 Global Dimension of COVID-19*

After the first COVID-19 case in China, it was observed that it will spread all over the world in a short time due to the high rate of transmission. WHO declared the COVID-19 cases, which reached a global dimension, as a pandemic on March 11, 2020 (De Vito and Gomez 2020: 1). Figure 5.1 shows the worldwide spread of COVID-19, prepared by WHO.

As of May 21, 2020, according to WHO data, a total of 4,833,186 cases and 323,256 deaths occurred worldwide. According to WHO data, the distribution comparison of COVID-19 cases in terms of continents is given in Fig. 5.2.

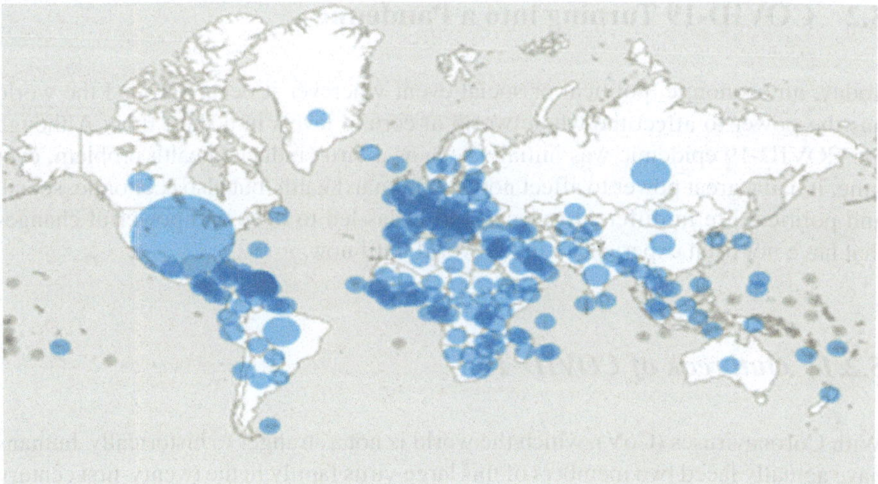

**Fig. 5.1** WHO coronavirus disease (COVID-19) dashboard. *Source* World Health Organization (2020)

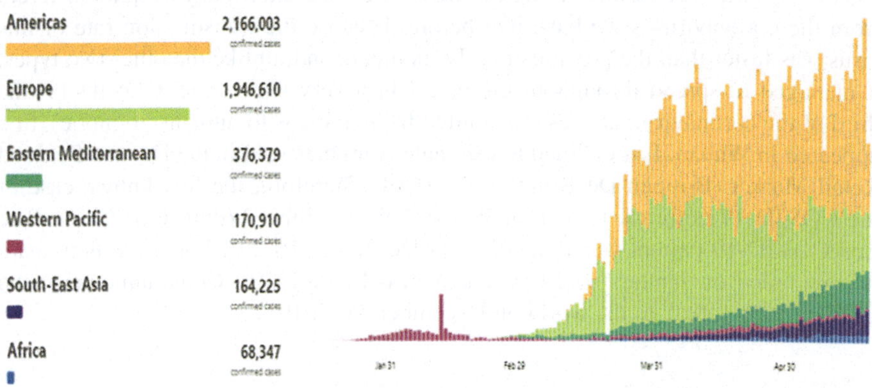


**Fig. 5.2** Situation by WHO region. *Source* World Health Organization (2020)

Examining Fig. 5.2, as of May 21, 2020, Europe had the highest number of cases after the American continent. The countries where the highest number of COVID-19 cases are reported are the USA, Russia, Brazil, the UK, Spain, Italy, Germany, Turkey, France, Iran, India, and Peru. COVID-19 was described as the most seriously threatening epidemic to public health since the Spanish Flu in 1918 (Loayza and Pennings 2020). As of September 2020, the total number of cases worldwide was 28,606,726, 19,288,985 patients recovered and 917,417 people died.

## 5.3 Economic Impact of COVID-19 Outbreak

Although health policies are important in combating the COVID-19 pandemic, it is estimated that there will be a high level of economic stagnation on the basis of both countries and worldwide, according to international economic organizations. With a view to better understanding the financial measures taken by the countries, it would be useful to set out the economic impact of the pandemic on a global level and particularly on Turkey.

### *5.3.1 Global Economic Impact of the Pandemic*

In addition to the death of many people around the world, another effect of the virus was felt in the global economy. The presence of this Central Asia-based flu in the Americas and Europe has been effective on the currencies of the countries, capital markets, precious metals, barrel oil prices, and even virtual currencies, through volatility, with the increasing concerns in the global markets. Perhaps the most resounded of these fluctuations was the declines in Dow Jones and S&P indices, which are traded in financial markets in America. The American Stock Exchange, which closed at negative for seven days in a row, experienced the biggest drop after the 2008 crisis. Likewise, the ounce price of gold, which was seen as a safe haven in times of crisis, increased to one thousand seven hundred dollars and such reactions prompted governments to take action and have to take some measures. When the COVID-19 disease spread all over the world, all countries started to implement *socialization* policies to protect public health and combat the epidemic (Mamoon 2020). The closure of educational institutions, restriction of work, and measures to limit human mobility quickly affected all sectors, especially trade and tourism (Maliszewska et al. 2020).

Today's economy is in a structure where employees, financial institutions, companies, suppliers, consumers, and countries are connected to each other (Gourinchas 2020). The COVID-19 outbreak has led to a sudden halt of the economy. Due to this epidemic, it is stated that there is a negative shock in the economy that has not been encountered before (Özatay and Sak 2020). The economic shock effect of the COVID-19 epidemic negatively affected the sectors that directly benefit from natural resources (primary sector) in the economy, especially agriculture, the sector which includes industrial activities (secondary sector) and the industry where all services are provided (education, finance, and tourism sectors, etc.) (Nicola et al. 2020).

Due to the COVID-19 outbreak, the total demand and supply shrunk first in China and then all over the world. According to the report prepared by the IMF, it is calculated that the world economy will shrink by 3% in 2020. It is suggested that the world economy will grow by 5.8% in 2021, predicting that the impact of the epidemic will decrease (IMF 2020a, b). When Table 5.1. taken from the report prepared by the IMF is examined, it is clearly predicted that recession will be seen in many regions

**Table 5.1** Overview of the world economic outlook projections (percent change, unless noted otherwise)

| (real GDP, annual percent change) | 2019 | PROJECTIONS 2020 | 2021 |
|---|---|---|---|
| World Output | 2.9 | -3.0 | 5.8 |
| Advanced Economies | 1.7 | -6.1 | 4.5 |
| United States | 2.3 | -5.9 | 4.7 |
| Euro Area | 1.2 | -7.5 | 4.7 |
| Germany | 0.6 | -7.0 | 5.2 |
| France | 1.3 | -7.2 | 4.5 |
| Italy | 0.3 | -9.1 | 4.8 |
| Spain | 2.0 | -8.0 | 4.3 |
| Japan | 0.7 | -5.2 | 3.0 |
| United Kingdom | 1.4 | -6.5 | 4.0 |
| Canada | 1.6 | -6.2 | 4.2 |
| Other Advanced Economies | 1.7 | -4.6 | 4.5 |
| Emerging Markets and Developing Economies | 3.7 | -1.0 | 6.6 |
| Emerging and Developing Asia | 5.5 | 1.0 | 8.5 |
| China | 6.1 | 1.2 | 9.2 |
| India | 4.2 | 1.9 | 7.4 |
| ASEAN-5 | 4.8 | -0.6 | 7.8 |
| Emerging and Developing Europe | 2.1 | -5.2 | 4.2 |
| Russia | 1.3 | -5.5 | 3.5 |
| Latin America and the Caribbean | 0.1 | -5.2 | 3.4 |
| Brazil | 1.1 | -5.3 | 2.9 |
| Mexico | -0.1 | -6.6 | 3.0 |
| Middle East and Central Asia | 1.2 | -2.8 | 4.0 |
| Saudi Arabia | 0.3 | -2.3 | 2.9 |
| Sub-Saharan Africa | 3.1 | -1.6 | 4.1 |
| Nigeria | 2.2 | -3.4 | 2.4 |
| South Africa | 0.2 | -5.8 | 4.0 |
| Low-Income Developing Countries | 5.1 | 0.4 | 5.6 |

*Source* (IMF 2020a, b: 7)

of the world considering the projections. It is estimated that the real GDP growth figures of developed economies will shrink by 6.1% on average in 2020. In particular, the expectation of an average of 7.5% contraction in the European region, including Germany, France, Italy, and Spain, can be considered as an indicator of the impact of the shock to the world economy.

It is predicted that negative growth expectation for emerging markets and developing countries will be seen on the basis of regions. In particular, it is above 5% of the expected shrinkage in Brazil, South Africa, Mexico, and Russia.

### *5.3.2 Economic Impact of the Pandemic on Turkey*

Various unprecedented developments have been observed in world economy such as closure of borders, restriction of transportation, isolation of people in their homes, curfews, minimized import and export activities, and contractions in both supply and demand. This crisis is different from other economic crises; all countries around the world and thus Turkey have also inevitably been affected.

When considered in terms of Turkey, in fact, it can be said that the effects of the crisis that had been experienced in the world economy before COVID-19 to be more perceptible in 2018 and subsequently in 2019 when it became more concrete as reflected in numbers. As a matter of fact, although the growth rate was 0.9% in the last month of 2019, the 6% growth rate achieved in the last quarter of the year led to optimistic estimates for 2020, and the growth rate for 2020 was determined as 5%.

Turkey was not much affected by the developments in the December 2019 when COVID-19 was first pronounced and during the first two months of 2020 (perhaps due to being out of China's supply chain), and this optimism continued. However, after the first case was seen in March, there was a slowdown in production in all sectors, especially in the service sector, including industry and construction, manufacturing, education, and production even stopped in some sectors. Significant shrinkage began to be experienced not only in production but also in demand.

The contraction production and demand brought along decline in GDP of Turkey, as was the case for the whole world. Indeed, according to May 2020 data, IMF's forecast for real GDP growth in Turkey is −5%. This will also cause significant decline in tax revenues. The decrease in tax revenues increases the budget deficits and the public sector borrowing requirement. On the other hand, while the unemployment rate was 13.7% in 2019, the IMF's forecast for 2020 increased to 17.2%. Significant increases in the inflation rate continue.

As a result, the economic impacts of the COVID-19 outbreak are expected to be negatively long-lasting and profound. Therefore, financial measures to be implemented by states within the scope of economic policies are important in combating the economic stagnation that the epidemic will cause.

## 5.4 Financial Measures Taken Against the Economic Impact of COVID-19 Pandemic in Selected Countries and Turkey

Countries combatting the COVID-19 outbreak have created effective policies in reducing the spread of the virus by taking measures such as social distancing, closing workplaces, restricting work, and quarantine practices. However, the cost of all these measures is the emergence and deepening of the economic contraction. The countries

**Table 5.2** COVID-19 outbreak status in selected countries

| Countries | Number of case | Number of deaths |
|---|---|---|
| USA | 8.093.600 | 220.900 |
| Brasil | 5.114.823 | 151.063 |
| Russia | 1.340.409 | 23.205 |
| France | 756.472 | 32.942 |
| England | 684.920 | 43.018 |
| Italy | 365.467 | 36.246 |
| Turkey | 338.779 | 8.957 |

*Source* World Health Organization (2020) (October 12, 2020)

have taken and continue to take fiscal measures within the scope of their economic policies in order to eliminate the economic contraction.

Within the scope of the financial measures implemented, the USA, the UK, Italy, Russia, and Brazil, which attracted attention with the increase in the number of cases and mortality rates, were determined as selected country examples. Table 5.2 includes the figures of these selected countries regarding the COVID-19 outbreak.

According to Table 5.2 prepared in accordance with of the data of WHO, USA, Brazil, Russia, France, UK, Italy, and Turkey are seen in terms of the number of cases in selected countries. Besides, USA, Brazil, Russia, France, UK, Italy, and Turkey are ranked in terms of the deaths because of COVID-19 epidemic.

In general, it is seen that countries shaped their economy policies within the scope of monetary policies, fiscal policies, and structural measures during the epidemic period, and practices such as expansionary spending policies, tax concession, and direct income transfer were predominant within the scope of fiscal policy.

### *5.4.1 The USA*

The USA, where more than 8 million cases have been reported and more than 220 thousand Americans died in 50 states, faced the rapid spread of COVID-19. At this point, the USA is the country where the most people died due to the coronavirus epidemic as of October 12, 2020 (Worldometer 2020). In fact, on May 28, 2020, it was announced that the USA left the World Health Organization on the grounds that they did not manage the process well and caused such deaths when they informed the world late.

In addition to the health effects of the COVID-19 epidemic, the USA is considered as reaching the highest level of unemployment since the Great Depression (O'connor et al. 2020: 1). The package of measures taken against the epidemic in the USA is calculated as 2.5 trillion dollars (approximately 11% of GDP). Financial measures taken under the package are listed as follows (OECD 2020):

- Congress provided $116.3 billion to cover individual's current and future bills. 2 trillion dollars of aid has been enacted through the CARES (the Coronavirus Aid, Relief, and Economic Security) Act. An additional support package was announced through the Paycheck Protection and Health Care Enhancement Act,
- Under the CARES Act, $221 billion of tax deductions and tax deferrals—with no late payment fee—was enacted, regardless of the size of the business,
- Employment tax payments of 2020 were postponed to 2021 and 2022,
- Small Business Management announced measures to address the urgent capital and cash needs of businesses affected by the virus. A low interest support of approximately 50 billion euros was announced within this scope,
- Under the CARES Act, the Foreign Exchange Stabilization Fund announced a $500 billion package to support businesses, cities and states.

In addition, the US Revenue Service (IRS) pushed tax payments to June 15. Small and medium-sized enterprises took measures such as applying tax reductions, removing the tax liability of those who cannot work due to quarantine, and delaying the withholding liability of taxpayers in order to quickly compensate the cost of putting workers on leave related to coronavirus (Internal Revenue Service 2020).

### 5.4.2 *Brazil*

On March 20, 2020, Brazilian Parliament declared the epidemic as a natural disaster. The cost of the measures taken against COVID-19 corresponds to approximately 8% of GDP. Financial measures included in these measures are listed as follows:

- Providing income support for three months at $120 per month to households in need of assistance,
- Commencement of short-time working allowance to be covered by the Unemployment Insurance Fund,
- Determining the import and industry taxes as zero on medical equipment import.
- Suspension of tax on bank loans for three months,
- Postponement of air navigation tariffs for six months,
- Postponement of the tax obligations of small and medium-sized enterprises (SMEs) for three months,
- Opening a new line of credit to enterprises by the Brazilian Central Bank, up to 0.6% of GDP.
- Increasing the lending limits of public banks,
- Prohibition of layoffs for two months and covering two-month wages of employees through the Emergency Credit Line.

### 5.4.3 The UK

The UK, which is not a member of the EU, announced a support package for 18.1% of its GDP (approximately 401.5 billion pounds). The financial measures included in this package are listed as follows (IMF 2020a, b):

- Postponing VAT payments (approximately 30 billion pounds sterling) to 2021,
- Compiling an additional £6.2 billion to support the National Health Services and other public services,
- Allocating £30 billion to support businesses and £8 billion for welfare support,
- Guarantee to all employers 80% (up to £2500 per month) of employee salaries until October 2020,
- Postponing tax liabilities of self-employed for three months,
- Postponing tax obligations of income taxpayers until July 31, 2020,
- Transferring an additional 750 million pounds of resources to Research and Development Expenses,
- The application of expanding the loan amounts for SMEs has started. In particular, the loan interest of companies with a business volume of less than £250,000 is covered by the government for twelve months.

### 5.4.4 Italy

The European Union (EU) pledged a 1.7 trillion euro rescue package to reduce the impact of the COVID-19 outbreak on the eurozone. The European Central Bank announced that it would purchase assets worth 750 billion euros (Nicola et al. 2020: 1). An emergency action package of 25 billion euros named "Cura Italia" has been put into effect in Italy. The support package corresponds to 1.4% of GDP. The financial measures taken are listed below (IMF 2020a, b):

- Granting 3.2 billion euros to support the National Health Services and Civil Protection,
- Providing a support of 10.3 billion euros to prevent job loss, support those laid off and self-employed workers,
- Providing 6.4 billion euros of support within the scope of regulations on deferring tax and other liabilities of businesses,
- Providing 5.1 billion euros of support to meet the loan demands of SMEs,
- Postponing of electricity, water, natural gas, and wastewater costs for two months in local governments most affected by the COVID-19 outbreak.

### 5.4.5 Russia

The cost of the package announced by Russia to combat the epidemic was approximately 6.6 billion dollars (2% of GDP). The financial measures taken are listed as follows (OECD 2020):

- Increasing the amount of compensation paid to healthcare workers who performed the first response in the fight against COVID-19 outbreak,
- Making a payment, equal to the minimum wage, until the end of 2020 to those who are quarantined, sick, and recovered,
- Paying a monthly salary equal to the minimum wage for three months to those who are unemployed,
- Financial support for children up to a certain age for three months,
- Supporting SMEs and businesses with key roles,
- Postponing the tax liabilities of businesses most affected by the epidemic,
- Postponing execution and bankruptcy procedures of businesses for six months,
- Postponing the social security premium payment obligations of SMEs for six months,
- Supporting financial institutions by the Federal government for the unpaid loans of SMEs.

### 5.4.6 Turkey

Turkey announced a package named "Economic Stabilization Shield" on March 18, 2020, for combatting COVID-19 in the field of economy (Turan and ve Hamza Çelikyay 2020: 18). The total cost of the package, which includes economic measures, is calculated as 350 billion TL (5% of GDP). Financial measures included in are listed as follows (IMF 2020a, b):

- Reduction or postponement of tax obligations (withholding tax and VAT withholding and SSI premiums for six months, postponing accommodation tax, reducing VAT on domestic flights from 18 to 1%) in many sectors affected by the epidemic, especially tourism,
- Postponing the declarations and tax payments of the taxpayers over the age of 65 and who have chronic diseases, banned from going out on the streets, until the ban is lifted,
- Providing stock financing support to the exporter,
- Postponing bank loan principal and interest payments for three months and providing financial support when necessary,
- Providing additional resources of 3 billion TL to municipalities,
- Provision of capital support by Turkey Assets Fund (TVF) to the three main state-owned banks, amounting to 0.4% of GDP,
- Creating new rights to buy the shares of companies in trouble by TVF,
- Relaxing the short-work allowance criteria,

- Suspension of layoffs for three months,
- Expanding the credit channels of public banks to support individuals,
- Increasing the lowest pension to 1500 TL,
- Providing cash support to families in need through the Ministry of Family, Labour and Social Services,
- Increasing the allowance of healthcare workers who receive allowance according to their performance to the ceiling and employing 32,000 additional health personnel.

## 5.5 Conclusion

As a result of the time that has passed since the emergence of the COVID-19 outbreak, the global economy has stalled. The collapse process of economies in the world has begun. The economic shock effect of the COVID-19 pandemic negatively affected the sectors that directly benefit from natural resources (primary sector) in the economy, especially agriculture, the sector including industrial activities (secondary sector) and the industry where all services are provided (education, finance and tourism sectors, etc.). All developed and developing countries have started to implement measures packages in proportion to their economic capabilities and financial power in order to reduce this recession in the world and start to rise again. Although the financial measures taken by the countries addressed in the study, namely the USA, Brazil, the UK, Italy, Russia, and Turkey, are close to each other, the cost is observed to vary in proportion to the financial capability of each country.

With the thought that the epidemic will cause a worldwide recession, many European countries, as well as the USA, have implemented emergency packages of billions of dollars. These packages include measures such as providing cash aid to those in need, creating liquidity for businesses, providing financial support to major sectors affected by the virus such as tourism and creating rescue packages considering the airline companies canceling their flights.

As a result, the health measures taken and the health system and capacities of countries will play a decisive role in combating the global pandemic. However, the epidemic has also become the cause of the economic crisis affecting the whole world. Therefore, if the results of the fiscal measures announced and put into practice do not create a positive effect as expected, not the country that cannot be successful alone, but the whole world, which is economically integrated with each other, will not quickly exit from the recession. The ability of states to strengthen their own immune systems against this microscopic enemy depends on sound fiscal measures they will take today.

## References

Bruinen De Bruin Y, Lequarre A, Mccourt J, Clevestig P, Pigazzani F, Zare Jeddi M, Colombo C, Goulart De Medeiros M (2020) Initial impacts of global risk mitigation measures taken during the combatting of the COVID-19 pandemic. Safety Sci. ISSN 0925-7535 (online). https://doi.org/10.1016/j.ssci.2020.104773

De Vito A, Gomez JP (2020) Estimating the covid-19 cash crunch: global evidence and policy. J Account Public Policy (2):1–4

Gourinchas PO (2020) Flattening the pandemic and recession curves, mitigating the covid economic crisis: act fast and do whatever it takes (Edt. Richard Baldwin and Beatrice Weder di Mauro). CEPR Press, London, 2020. https://voxeu.org/content/mitigating-covid-economic-crisis-act-fast-and-do-whatever-it-takes. Access on 20 May 2020

IMF (2020a) World economic outlook April 2020: the great lockdown. IMF Publishing, Washington, www.imf.org/en/Publications/WEO/Issues/2020/04/14/World-Economic-Outlook-April-2020-The-Great-Lockdown-49306. Access on 21 May 2020

IMF (2020b) Policy responses to covid-19, www.imf.org/en/Topics/imf-and-covid19/Policy-Responses-to-COVID-19#EU. Access on: 26 May 2020

Internal Revenue Service (2020) Coronavirus tax relief. www.irs.gov/coronavirus. Access on: 24 Mayıs 2020

Loayza NV, Pennings S (2020) Macroeconomic policy in the time of covid-19: a primer for developing countries. The World Bank research & policy briefs, No. 28, Washington. http://documents.worldbank.org/curated/en/951811585836124198/pdf/Macroeconomic-Policy-in-the-Time-of-COVID-19-A-Primer-for-Developing-Countries.pdf. Access on 18 May 2020

Maliszewska M, Mattoo A, Mensbrugghe DV (2020) The potential impact of covid-19 on GDP and trade: a preliminary assessment. The World Bank policy research working paper, No. 9211, Washington, 2020. http://documents.worldbank.org/curated/en/295991586526445673/pdf/The-Potential-Impact-of-COVID-19-on-GDP-and-Trade-A-Preliminary-Assessment.pdf. Access on 21 May 2020

Mamoon D (2020) Health and economic outcomes of covid-19. J Econ Soc Thought 7(1):41–54

Nicola M, Alsafi Z, Sohrabi C, Kerwan A, Al-Jabir A, Iosifidis C, Agha M, Agha R (2020) The socio-economic implications of the coronavirus pandemic (COVID-19): a review. Int J Surgery 78:185–193

O'connor CM, Anoushiravani AA, Dicaprio MR, Healy WL, Iorio R (2020) Economic recovery after the covid-19 pandemic: resuming elective orthopedic surgery and total joint arthroplasty. J Arthroplasty 35(7):32–36

OECD (2020) Key country policy responses. www.oecd.org/coronavirus/en/#country-tracker .Access on 26 May 2020

Özatay F, ve Sak G (2020) Covid-19 Salgını Bir Değil, Bir Kaç Çeyrek Sürerse Ne Olur? TEPAV Politika Notu, No:202015, Ankara, ss. 1–10

The World Bank (2020) Semiannual report of the Latin America and Caribbean region: the economy in the time of covid-19. The World Bank Publishing, Washington, Oct 9, 2020, pp 5–71, https://openknowledge.worldbank.org/handle/10986/33555. Access on 18 May 2020

Turan A, ve Hamza Çelikyay H (2020) Türkiye'de Covid-19 ile Mücadele: Politikalar ve Aktörler. Uluslararası Yönetim Akademileri Dergisi. 3(1):1–25

World Health Organization (2020) WHO coronavirus disease (Covid-19) dashboard. https://covid19.who.int/

Worldometer (2020) ABD coronavirus cases. https://www.worldometers.info/coronavirus/country/abd/. Access on 29 Mayıs 2020

**Tülin Canbay** was born in 1969 in Aydın. After attending Aydın High School, she continued her undergraduate studies at Dokuz Eylül University, Department of Finance. She received her master's degree in Financial Law from Dokuz Eylül University. In 1999, she was awarded her Ph.D. degree from Dokuz Eylul University Department of Public Finance. Her Ph.D. thesis covered the topics of budget reform.

In 2002–2005, she worked as a visiting professor at the Kyrgyz-Turkish Manas University. Professor Dr. Tülin CANBAY has books, articles and papers on tax, budget, women's studies, migration. She is currently working at the Department of Public Finance at Manisa Celal Bayar University/Turkey.

**Hilal Balcı Cura** is a lecturer of Social Security Program at Manisa Celal Bayar University, Kırkağaç Vocational School. She received her bachelor's degree from Faculty of Law, Selçuk University, Konya, Turkey in 2005. Hilal Cura is graduate student of Fiscal Law at Manisa Celal Bayar University, Institue of Social Sciences. Her research focuses on social security, public finance, law and fiscal law. Hilal Cura has authored and contributed to book chapters and articles on these research areas.

# Chapter 6
# Public Transfer Expenditures in Combatting the Economic Impact of COVID-19 Pandemic: Turkey Case and Policy Suggestions

**Yaprak Karadağ Duymazlar**

**Abstract** The supply shocks that emerged with the deterioration of the supply chain and the narrowing of liquidity facilities in the COVID-19 pandemic brought demand shocks by narrowing production and employment. This has taken the epidemic beyond a health crisis. In order to solve the crisis caused by supply and demand shocks, the need to implement expansionary monetary and fiscal policies together has arisen. The most important tool that can be used in fiscal policy is public transfer expenditures. Transfer expenditure is a type of expenditure against which there is no corresponding transfer of goods, services or production factors. Although these expenditures do not directly increase the goods, services or production factors, they can contribute to the accumulation or improvement of outputs/factors in the economy. Social transfer expenditures play a critical role in protecting purchasing power, meeting minimum living standards, expanding the scope of social security; economic transfer expenditures ensure the continuity of production and employment. Unemployment payments, direct income support, social assistance and grants have provided widely in developed countries. Developing countries, on the other hand, have the risk of inadequate demand-side policies due to the financial risks, the narrow fiscal space and the low expenditure multiplier. Turkey, which has determined a demand-oriented economic growth strategy, has faced problems such as high exchange rates, budget deficits, and increase in debt stock for the last few years. The uncertainty and insecurity created by COVID-19 have made this growth strategy of Turkey hard. Shortly after the first COVID-19 case was announced in the country, administrative measures were taken and public life was limited. These measures had negative economic consequences. In the first months of the pandemic, a contraction process was observed in all sectors of the economy. The Economic Stability Shield Package was put into effect for the rapid recovery of the economy. Within the scope of the package, applications such as tax reductions, tax deferrals, deferral of loan and interest payments, loan support packages, increasing pensions, minimum wage support and short-time working allowance can be listed. In the process, sectors such as construction, manufacturing and industry entered into a rapid

Y. K. Duymazlar (✉)
Department of Financial Management, İzmir Kâtip Çelebi University, İzmir, Turkey
e-mail: yaprak.karadag@ikcu.edu.tr



B. Açıkgöz and İ. A. Acar (eds.), *Pandemnomics: The Pandemic's Lasting Economic Effects*, Accounting, Finance, Sustainability, Governance & Fraud: Theory and Application, https://doi.org/10.1007/978-981-16-8024-3_6

recovery process. However, the expected improvement in sectors such as tourism, transportation, accommodation, food, culture, arts, entertainment and sports could not be realized due to the severity of the pandemic. While the new waves of the pandemic continued, public transfer expenditures continued to be presented. Tax, loan and interest payments have been postponed and the duration of the short-time working allowance has been extended. The supports provided in Turkey, it is seen that monetary policy is heavily utilized. Credit support packages such as individual basic needs, tradesmen, housing, vehicle and vacation were provided and the demand side was tried to be kept alive. In the field of social transfers—direct income supports, cash aids and grants—lagged significantly behind credit supports. Considering the projections for Turkey, additional social transfer expenditures should be made ready to be presented in order to protect the purchasing power of households. The sustainability of economic transfer expenditures is critical in maintaining the level of economic growth, employment and output in the long run.

**Keywords** Public transfer expenditures · Social transfers · Economic transfers · Fiscal policy · Turkey · COVID-19

## 6.1 Introduction

Compulsory measures taken to reduce the risk of contagion of COVID-19 pandemics and the problems of the economy over the past few years will result in contraction in the economy in 2020 both on a global scale and in Turkish economy, according to the estimates of international authorities. Governments frequently resort to expansionary monetary and fiscal policies with the aim of overcoming the current conjuncture period. Public transfer expenditures are one of these policy tools.

In this chapter, we will examine the impact of the pandemic on economic growth, sectors and employment in Turkey. Then, the scope and spending dimension of public transfer expenditures offered to the sectors and segments affected by the crisis will be discussed and their role in overcoming the effects of the crisis will be evaluated. In the light of the findings of the case analysis, suggestions that policymakers can stimulate the economy in the short and long term through transfer expenditures will be discussed.

## 6.2 Transfer Expenditures and Their Economic Impact

Transfer expenditure is a type of expenditure against which there is no corresponding transfer of goods, services or production factors. Although these expenditures do not directly increase the goods, services or production factors, they can contribute to the accumulation or improvement of outputs/factors in the economy (Tables 6.1 and 6.2).

**Table 6.1** Classification of transfer expenditures according to Brochier and Tabatoni

| | |
|---|---|
| Direct and in-direct transfer expenditures | While direct transfers increase cash revenues directly, indirect transfers are expenditures that decrease the prices of goods and services that do not increase revenues directly. A large part of public debt interest, social aid and security expenditures are among direct transfer expenditures. Cheap raw materials, tax reductions, tax benefits and financial assistance are indirect transfer expenditures |
| Revenue transfers and capital transfers | It is a distinction made to indicate income transfers that increase the income/profits of consumers and producers directly and indirectly, and capital transfers such as war indemnities, premiums for housing construction, supply of free land |
| Efficient and inefficient transfers | Transfers directed towards production and increasing total revenue are efficient, whereas consumption-oriented transfers are inefficient. In general, economic transfers such as subsidies and research and development expenditures are efficient; social transfers such as widow's and orphan's pensions, retirement pensions and scholarships are considered inefficient |

*Source* Akbulut (2013)

**Table 6.2** Turkey 2020 growth rate forecasts

| | Before COVID-19 | After COVID-19 | Difference |
|---|---|---|---|
| IMF | 3.0 | −5.0 | −8.0 |
| World Bank | 3.5 | 0.5 | −3.0 |
| EIU | 3.8 | −3.5 | −7.3 |
| Average | 3.4 | −2.7 | −6.1 |

*Source* Deloitte (2020a)

Transfer expenditures are also classified as economic, social, financial and debt interest payments according to their purposes. Apart from financial transfers and debt interest payments, which are transfers from the central government to local governments, economic and social transfers stand out in the analyses. Economic transfers are practices such as support and subsidies to businesses/sectors, tax reductions, tax deferrals, which have economic and financial purposes. Social transfers are expenditures that protect individuals and households from certain risks and meet needs in case the risk occurs. Food aid and vouchers, green cards (health card for uninsured people in Turkey), pensions, widow's and orphan's pensions, scholarships, disability pensions, housing benefits and unemployment payments are within the scope of social transfers (Akbulut 2013).

The value of the expenditure multiplier is lower than the consumption and investment expenditures, as the transfer expenditures occur not at the time they are made, but during the consumption of the income. However, the composition of transfer expenditures is also important in terms of its effects on the economy. If the social transfers made in order to ensure a minimum income standard are made to the low-income group, the multiplier effect will be more because this segment has a higher spending tendency. Similar to investment expenditures, economic transfers will support private sector investments and increase supply in the long run (Pınar 2014). Economic transfers contribute to the increase the production of certain goods and services and encouraging their consumption, protection of agricultural areas, improvement of exports and development of underdeveloped regions (Mutluer et al. 2007). With the support and encouragement of public transfer expenditures, bottlenecks on the supply side can be eliminated and the output level can be increased by providing financial assistance to production areas. Thus, inflationary trends can be prevented and long-term supply opportunities can be increased (Tokatlıoğlu and Selen 2017).

The share of current transfers item, which includes economic and social transfers, in the central government budget of Turkey is high, 39% in 2017 and 2018. In 2018, the total budget expenditure was approximately 830 billion TL, of which 323 billion TL was current transfers. The most important item of current transfer expenditures was "*health, retirement and social assistance expenditures*", approximately amounting to 150 billion TL (18% of GDP). 75 billion TL (9% of GDP) was allocated to agricultural and other incentives (Çetinkaya and Aslantaş 2019).

## 6.3 Economic Impact of COVID-19 Pandemic and Transfer Expenditures

The COVID-19 outbreak affects the economy through: (i) the shock caused by the contraction of China in the first quarter of 2020, (ii) the supply shock caused by the disruption of the supply chain, (iii) the demand shock caused by the negative impact on investment plans due to low consumer demand and uncertainties and (iv) the effect of the liquidity restrictions on companies (European Commission 2020).

The emergence and spread of the first case in China required the restriction of trade and circulation with China worldwide. However, the fact that China is the first link of the supply chain in some sectors has caused these restrictions to adversely affect the supply (Gault 2020). Production and employment are decreasing due to the negative supply shock arising from the epidemic. Negative supply shocks cause a greater contraction of demand than the shock itself in production and employment (Guerrieri 2020). As a result, a crisis occurs in supply and demand.

COVID-19 is not only a health problem, but also a cause of an economic crisis that will go beyond the 2008 crisis. Quarantine, restrictions, and prohibitions applied to prevent the spread of the pandemic cause a decrease in economic activities. These effects create more difficult problems for countries with weak financial, macroeconomic, labour and health policies (Loayza and Pennings 2020).

Since the beginning of the crisis, monetary policy practices such as financial expansion, liquidity increases, increasing loan supply, loosening loan payment terms and swap agreements made in developing countries have been followed (IMF 2020a). However, the crisis is not one-sided enough to be solved only by monetary policy. In this struggle, a need emerged for governments to execute their monetary and fiscal policies in coordination.

Expansionary monetary and fiscal policies were advised by international authorities to overcome the negative effects of the crisis. The IMF (2020b) has presented its proposals to increase the total demand by offering additional financial incentives to businesses and individuals affected by the crisis in order to prevent long-term economic damage in the fiscal policy measures to be taken against the COVID-19 virus. OECD (2020) also states the necessity of providing income support to economic actors. It was also stated that income subsidies may increase demand again, but might not compensate for the disruptions caused by mandatory workplace closures and travel restrictions.

Considering the practices during the pandemic, fiscal policy is presented through methods such as transfer expenditures to households and businesses, expansion of health and social security payments, and tax regulations. Some examples are; cash payments and consumption coupons to low-income individuals, wage and rent supports to businesses in South Korea; supports such as expanding short-time working allowance and childcare support in Germany; increasing National Health Service (NHC) funds, tax reductions and deferrals, grants to companies in UK (Elgin et al. 2020).

Income supports, subsidies, tax reductions and deferrals and financial supports are transfer expenditures. Transfer expenditures can be presented as conditional or unconditional transfers in eliminating the stagnation experienced in the COVID-19 process. Conditional transfers are offered to those who previously worked but are unemployed due to quarantine. The logic of both transfer expenditures is to increase decreasing income and liquidity possibilities, thus compensating for reduced consumption expenditures and overcoming the quarantine shock (Bayer et al. 2020).

However, the struggle against the negative effects of COVID-19 becomes difficult due to the high level of informality, deficient labour market and limited financial opportunities in developing countries. While the use of monetary and transfer expenditure mechanisms is recommended in developing countries, considering that the monetary transmission mechanism is weak and the value of the fiscal multiplier is low in these countries, demand-oriented policies also carry the risk of being inadequate to overcome the crisis. Providing income support to people in need and having no social security and protecting their health should be the main objective instead of a multiplier mechanism; bankruptcies and collective layoffs should be prevented by providing support to households and businesses in the short term through economic policies; continuity of public services and social supports should be ensured in the medium term, along with monetary and financial incentives (Loayza and Pennings 2020).

## 6.4 Macroeconomic and Sectoral Effects of COVID-19 in Turkey

The growth rate of Turkey's economy has slowed in recent years, after the exchange rates shock experienced in August of 2018. The growth rate, which was 0.9% in 2019, is estimated at 5.0% for 2020 in the medium-term programme. Domestic demand is considered as the main determinant of the growth target. It is stated that private expenditures, deferred demand, credit and confidence channel are the most important contributors to growth (Strateji ve Bütçe Başkanlığı 2019).

Some restrictions were recorded on the supply side as a result of the administrative measures taken by the companies and implemented by the government following the first COVID-19 case in Turkey was reported on 10 March 2020. Limiting the capacity and ceasing the production in some facilities and the closure of various businesses in service and retail sectors decreased the productive capacity of employment. The squeeze in supply combined with curfews, travel restrictions, remote and flexible working, unpaid leave, and the psychological effects of the pandemic changed the level of demand, leading to a total recession in supply and demand (Deloitte 2020a).

In a short time, the reactions of households and firms started to reflect in economic indicators. Accordingly, household consumption expenditures decreased in Turkey by 34% in 3 April week compared to 13 March week (TEPAV 2020). With this decrease in consumer demand, the supply side was also affected, and the capacity utilization rate in the manufacturing industry was recorded as 61.6%, by 13.7% decrease in April compared to the previous month (TCMB 2020).

Uncertainty and insecurity created by COVID-19 have become an insuperable obstacle in front of Turkey's growth strategy. In a report published in June 2020, IMF estimates that Turkey's economy will experience a negative growth by −5.0% at the end of 2020. Similar to the IMF's forecasts, organizations such as the World Bank and the EIU also expects Turkey will shrink in 2020. Considering the average of all these organizations' forecasts, Turkey's economy will have a negative growth of −2.7%.

Considering the studies examining the sectoral effects of the pandemic; according to the publications of Demir et al. (2020), while sectors such as airline, road transportation, entertainment, tourism-hotel management are damaged, it is expected that there will be an increase in cleaning materials, mask manufacturing, remote shopping and online shopping sectors. The reflections of this change in imports and exports will be similar. The shares of the sectors in GDP, the level they are affected and the time they go back in business are presented in the Table 6.3.

In Table 6.3, according to their shares in GDP in 2018 sectors are 54.26% Services, 22.30% Industry, 7.17% Construction, 5.82% Agriculture, respectively. According to ULISA (2020), main sectors in Turkey except for agriculture will be highly affected by COVID-19. Moreover, the recovery process of these sectors will be slow. Agriculture is expected to be less affected by the pandemic.

In the study conducted by Voyvoda and Yeldan (2020), the top five sectors that will shrink the most compared to 2019 are Accommodation and Food Services by

**Table 6.3** Sectors and COVID-19

| Sector | % Share in GDP (2018) | Level of impact of COVID-19 | Going back in business |
|---|---|---|---|
| Agriculture, forestry and fishery | 5.82 | Low | Fast |
| Industry | 22.30 | High | Slow |
| Construction | 7.17 | High | Slow |
| Services | 54.26 | High | Slow |

*Source* ULISA (2020)

55.6%, Tourism by 51.5%, Construction by 48.7%, Air Transport by 47.7% and Iron and Steel by 40.5%. A loss of 26.7% and 22.8% in employment is expected in GDP; the number of the unemployed is expected to rise from 4.7 million to 11.7 million; household disposable income is expected to decrease by 46% compared to the previous year.

In his study about the effects of pandemic on GDP and employment in Turkey, Taymaz (2020) suggests that household consumption expenditures and exports are the directly affected. The sectors that will suffer the most from the pandemic are accommodation and food services, tour and travel companies, show and performing arts, entertainment sector, cultural services, sports sector, airline companies and betting games. According to the results of the analysis, it is predicted that there will be a decrease of 7.2% in added value and 10.7% in employment.

The reflections of the projections in the studies are seen in the statistical indicators as time passes. In the sub-sectors of industry, the mining and quarrying sector index decreased by 14.5%, the manufacturing industry index decreased by 33.3% and the electricity, gas, steam and air conditioning production and distribution sector index decreased by 14.9% in April 2020 compared to the same month of the previous year (TÜİK 2020). The expectation that the recovery in manufacturing, which is the sub-sector with the highest share in the industrial sector, will continue slowly may have negative consequences for the coming months.

Contractions in the manufacturing sector were also reflected in foreign trade statistics. In April, compared to the same month of 2019, the biggest shrinkage occurred in the manufacturing sector, amounting to 43%, while there was a shrinkage of 30.3% in imports in intermediate (raw materials) goods. The ratio of exports to imports contracted sharply in the light of all these developments. While the foreign trade deficit increased by 67% in April compared to the same month of 2019, it increased by 102.3% in the January–April 2020 period compared to the same period of 2019 (Soylu 2020).

Included in the manufacturing sector, revenues and productive capacity of automotive, textiles and white goods sectors which have a high share in the distribution of export revenues in Turkey have gone downwards in this process.

Automobile sales decreased by 91% compared to the January-April period of the previous year. Again, due to the closed auto factories, a 77% contraction in exports and a 20–30% loss in the year-end export target are expected (OSD 2020; Özarfat 2020).

In April, textiles and ready-made clothing decreased by 60% on an annual basis and retail sales volume decreased by 19.3%. The total production in the white goods sector decreased by 52.3% and domestic sales by 11.4% compared to the previous year. Again, in this period, food sales increased by 12.5%, non-food sales decreased by 36.7% (Adıgüzel 2020).

Civil aviation, accommodation and tourism are the top sectors most deeply affected by the crisis. Restricting national and international circulation, travel restrictions applied to prevent the spread of the virus, flight bans, flight cancellations, closing of border gates ended the flights. Travel restrictions have taken the tourism, accommodation and travel spending to the bottom. According to TURKSTAT statistics, tourism revenues decreased by 11.4%, accommodation expenditures decreased by 15.7%, international transport expenditures decreased by 12.1% between January and April compared to the same period of 2019 (Macit and Macit 2020; Soylu 2020).

80% of the aircraft in the Turkish civil aviation sector landed in March. Although there was no flight, operating and personnel costs caused great losses in the aviation industry. The risk of income and job losses still continue for the civil aviation sector due to the uncertainty in front of the pandemic, stagnation in tourism activities and still limited international circulation (Macit and Macit 2020).

The negative effects of the pandemic on employment reveal themselves in the sectors experiencing the greatest contraction. The areas where unemployment risk is most prominent are: manufacturing, wholesale and retail trade, accommodation and food, real estate activities (Balcı and Çetin 2020) and civil aviation.

It is estimated that 5.6 million employees will be affected in April–June period. It is estimated that approximately 3.1 million of 16.6 million wageworkers, casual workers and self-employed people working in the non-agricultural private sector were directly affected by the measures taken against pandemic, and 2.5 million were directly affected by the pandemic. In the April–June period of 2020, it is estimated that 5 million job losses will be in the service sector and 550 thousand in the manufacturing industry (Yükseler 2020).

## 6.5 Transfer Expenditures Measures Taken Against COVID-19 Pandemic in Turkey

Financial packages implemented during the pandemic can be classified into two categories: budgetary and extra-budgetary measures. Budgetary financial packages are: health spending, tax reductions and deferrals, transfers to households and firms, wage and unemployment subsidies. Extra-budgetary packages are loans and funding, especially financial supports for SMEs and aviation sector, loan guarantees and Central Bank supports (Alberola et al. 2020).

As of 10 March when the first COVID-19 case was seen in Turkey, administrative measures were started to be taken in the areas of health, education, transport, trade and accommodation. Administrative measures were subsequently followed by economic measures. The biggest step regarding economic measures is the *Economic Stability Shield Package* (Ekonomik İstikrar Kalkanı Paketi 2020).

The arrangements in the *Economic Stability Shield Package* announced on 18 March 2020 are briefly as follows:

- April, May and June payments of withholding and VAT withholding tax and SGK premiums in various sectors are postponed for 6 months.
- Application of accommodation tax is postponed.
- April, May and June payments of easement fees and revenue shares related to hotel rentals are postponed for 6 months.
- As for domestic airline transport, VAT which is 18% is decreased to 1% for 3 months.
- Loan and interest payments of companies whose cash flow has deteriorated are postponed and additional financing support is provided when necessary.
- Stock financing support for exporters.
- Loan principal and interest payments of tradesmen and craftsmen is postponed for 3 months without applying any interest.
- The limit of credit guarantee fund is increased and the SMEs are given high priority.
- Housing loan interest rates are cut.
- Loan support packages.
- The lowest pension is increased to 1500 TL and pension promotion payments are brought forward.
- 2 billion TL cash aid support is allocated to those who are already entitled to needs support.
- Providing minimum wage support and short-time working allowance.

The Economic Stability Shield Package includes public expenditures, tax reductions and financial supports. In the context of transfer expenditures, social support programs, raising the lowest pension, bringing forward salary promotion payments paid to retirees during religious holidays, and cash aids for families in need can be examples of social transfers (Table 6.4).

Measures taken for employment in Turkey are: short-time working allowance, unpaid leave practice and layoff bans. The conditions of the short-time working allowance which is applied in times when the business is slowed down and stopped due to a force majeure have been stretched during this period (Kara 2020). Lay-off bans, which started on 16 March, have been extended until 30 June 2021, until going back to normal. Short-time working allowances and unemployment allowances can also be considered as social transfers.

**Table 6.4** Supports provided under social protection shield (as of 18.05.2020)

| | Unift | Household/Person receiving the payment | Amount/TL |
|---|---|---|---|
| Social support program | Household | 5,440,551 | 5,440,551,000 |
| Short-time working allowance | Employee | 3,050,584 | 4,885,413,106 |
| Wage support in cash | Employee | 878,614 | 441,169,757 |
| Unemployment benefit | Person | 591,894 | 730,894,637 |

*Source* Aile, Çalışma ve Sosyal Hizmetler Bakanlığı (2020)

It is also reported that an additional 2 billion lira-resource has been allocated for cash aid to families in need within the scope of the Economic Stability Shield Package. It has been announced that a cash support of 1000 TL will be provided to 2 million households that meet the neediness conditions in the relevant laws in cooperation with the Ministry of Family, Labour and Social Security. The total amount of support provided under the *Social Protection Shield* is approximately 11.5 billion TL.

On the other hand, economic transfers were offered through financing supports, expanding loan opportunities and lowering interest rates, postponing loan payments, tax reductions and deferrals, stock financing supports and loan guarantee fund. In this context, in the aviation sector, which is one of the sectors most affected by the crisis, the VAT rate on domestic flights were lowered, the accommodation tax, the servitude and revenue shares of the hotels were deferred, and the VAT declaration periods and SSI premiums were postponed in various other sectors (Table 6.5).

In addition, in order to support the supply and demand side of the economy, loan support packages with below market interest rates were made available under the leadership of public banks for financing support. These loans for individual basic needs, SMEs, tourism, housing, vehicles and retail sectors were in high demand. Housing sales increased by 209% compared to the same month of the previous year, especially with the housing loan campaign.

These supports provided to stimulate the demand in the market and to ensure the continuity of financing increased the duty losses of public banks. Duty losses are included in the current transfers item in the budget. According to the data of the Presidency of Strategy and Budget, the duty loss of Halk Bank, which is a state bank, increased by 59% and the duty loss of Ziraat Bank, also a state bank, increased by 40% in January-May compared to same period of the previous year.

**Table 6.5** Loan facilities provided during COVID-19

| | Content of loans |
|---|---|
| Individual basic needs support loan | Low-interest-rate loan for those with household income below 5000 TL |
| Tradesmen support loan | Financing for tradesmen and craftsmen |
| Housing loan | Interest rate cut for new and used houses |
| Vehicle loan | Interest rate cut for new vehicles produced domestically and used cars |
| Vacation support loan | Financing support up to 10,000 TL without payment for 6 months for holiday packages purchased at contracted travel agencies |
| Social life support loan | Low-interest financing for products to be purchased from contracted companies in order to meet the financing needs of furniture, electronics, white goods, home textiles, bicycles, dowry, ceramics, door, window systems |
| Stay in business loan support | Low-interest loan support for companies provided that they do not dismiss workers |
| Paying checks support loan and loan support | Loan support for the payment of the checks that the customers have drawn To date and will draw based on their real commercial transactions |

*Source* Created by author benefiting from Bankası (2020) and İZTO (2020)

## 6.6 Policy Suggestions Against Economic Impact of Pandemic

Fiscal policy measures taken against the pandemic have had a rapid response at the global level (Alberola 2020). Additional expenditures and forgone public revenues in Turkey are $ 2 billion, corresponding to 0.2% of national income. Liquidity supports and additional resources are 63 billion dollars, corresponding to 9.1% of national income. In G-20 countries, these rates are 5.78% for expenditures and forgone revenues, while liquidity supports and additional resources are 6.35% (IMF 2020c). In Turkey, main channel used in the fight against COVID-19 pandemics has been loans and monetary channel.

The general opinion in times of crisis is that fiscal policies give effective results compared to monetary policies. In fiscal policy, which can be applied under two main headings as public expenditures and tax incentives, tax reductions have more positive results in developed countries while public expenditures have more positive results in developing countries (Ustaoğlu 2020).

In his fiscal multiplier analysis on Turkey, Ustaoğlu (2020) stated that giving priority to public spending in times of crises would be more effective than some policies such as tax reductions, postponements, deferrals, etc. In their fiscal multiplier analysis on Turkey, Şen and Kaya (2017) also demonstrated that the multiplier effect of public expenditures on GDP is higher than that of taxes. Although transfer expenditures have a less Keynesian effect than public consumption expenditures on the public expenditures side, they emphasized that, any type of public expenditures are more effective in promoting the economy than taxes.

Turkey has followed a similar path with other countries, in this period, in the area of fiscal policy. An important shortcoming of the supports such as tax deferrals, social security premium and loan payments and short-time working allowance is that it could not provide direct income support to employees and SMEs who lost their jobs or were deprived of income flow due to the pandemic (Çakmaklı et al. 2020).

The most comprehensive study on the economic effects of direct transfer expenditures in the current period is made by Voyvoda and Yeldan (2020). The *Labour Income Support Package* is designed in this study which uses the general balance model. In this package, supporting the labour income of households and providing direct income support are examined. Technique of the package is; income transfer of up to 50% of their income to formal wage earners, supporting SMEs and freelancers and increasing the public consumption expenditures by 20%. As a result, it is suggested that a package of 123.5 billion TL provides a 60% gain in GDP relative to the possible impact of the COVID-19 pandemic. At the same time, it is stated that this package will reduce the budget deficit under COVID-19 in the public sector by half and stimulate the sectors producing intermediate and investment goods.

Considering that labour-intensive sectors and small businesses are affected from the COVID-19 measures more than the sectors that create added value, supports such as income supports and minimum working time should be provided without restrictions; income transfers to people with income and job losses should be increased. In this process, the payment ceilings of short-time working allowance and unemployment insurances provided to those who lost their jobs should be increased, and additional income transfers should be offered to retirees and low-income families (Taymaz 2020; Yükseler 2020).

During the pandemic, new business models were adopted, flexible and remote working became widespread, and digitalization gained speed. An analysis demonstrated that the business lines operating through e-commerce were less adversely affected by the pandemic. The non-digitalized business lines have assumed a heavy burden (Deloitte 2020b).

In order for SMEs to adapt to the remote working model and digitalization, a "Digital Enterprise Support Platform" should be created, and the government should reduce adaptation costs and support the process. As for the supports, opportunities such as tax reductions/deferrals and support loans should be provided to businesses that adapt to digitalization (Balcı and Çetin 2020).

Another effect of the pandemic is the debate on shifting the production to countries other than China as a result of the reactions against China. Considering its proximity to G-20 economies and large markets, high labour supply, low labour costs, high quality and safe production, Turkey has the opportunity to turn the crisis into opportunity in the medium term. However, the opportunities may not be used as effective when taken into account the private sector's indebtedness and financing challenges in Turkey. New solutions and international collaborations are needed in this period.

Yet, government spending can also be used to support exports and the private sector (TÜBA 2020).

In order not to increase the debt burden of the enterprises considering their existing loans, it should be considered to delay loan payments again, when necessary. Additional measures and cash supports should be provided for the continuity of employment in SMEs (Taymaz 2020).

VAT and insurance premium payments dates which are postponed especially for the tourism sector may be extended again considering that businesses will face payment difficulties due to the stagnant summer season in 2020 compared to previous years (Yaşar 2020).

Again, the conditions for benefiting from short-work allowance for those working in the tourism sector should be stretched. In short-time working applications made with the effect of COVID-19, it is required to have paid 450 days of premium in the last 3 years (İşkur 2020), as subject to the service contract in the last 60 days of. The seasonal nature of the employees of the tourism sector, which provides an annual input of $40 billion, and the fact that the tourism season has not started at the peak of the pandemic, make it difficult for those working in this sector to benefit from short-time working allowance. The conditions for benefiting from short-work allowance for those working in the tourism sector should be revised (Yaşar 2020).

## 6.7 Conclusion

The public health measures taken in the fight against the pandemic have required temporary closure of some businesses and workplaces or the reduction of existing capacity by disabling vital and essential links of the supply chain. Losses in production damaged the purchasing power of economic units by triggering employment losses. The uncertainty that emerged in this process was reflected in consumption behaviour and resulted in the contraction of demand, which is seen as the driving force of growth. As a result, the supply shock combined with the demand shock, giving rise to insuperable problems.

Turkey got caught by such period with economic problems aggravated over the past few years. Struggling with the exchange rate shock since 2018 high hopes of reducing the current account deficit encountered by the pandemic obstacle in Turkey. Production declined in manufacturing sectors such as automotive, textile and white goods, which have a considerable share in export revenues. Again, tourism revenues, which would greatly contribute to the reduction of the current account deficit, fell sharply upon the restriction of international circulation.

The fiscal space of the government is narrowing in Turkey which had a primary deficit in 2019, for the first time for many years, due to; the increase in debt stock, upward trend in dollarization, high credit risk premiums, decrease in public revenues, increased public spending due to the pandemic.

The narrow fiscal space in developing countries, including Turkey, increasing financing costs of spending and the difficulties in accessing external financing possibilities restrict fiscal stimulus packages and transfer expenditures (Alberola et al. 2020).

Supports implemented to overcome the crisis were offered mainly through credit channels in Turkey. The domestic demand supported growth strategy included in the medium-term programme was tried to be maintained during the pandemic. Direct income support was relatively limited.

The most critical dilemma of the measures taken through credit channels is the uncertainty of the duration of pandemic. The inability to generate income and pay the loan debts in the maturity period increases the default risk of economic agents. For the private sector, which is currently under high debt, the results of loan financing support may differ according to the pace of the economic recovery and slow recovery may result in the non-convertibility of operating debt.

The same risk also applies to the households. Despite the layoff bans and short-time working allowances during the pandemic, supporting 60% of the gross wage by the state reduces the purchasing power of the people. The minimum living standards of the individuals whose disposable incomes are reduced are endangered. Therefore, depending on the course and severity of the crisis, direct income support and additional cash aid-weighted additional transfer expenditure packages should be made available by the government. Projections on unemployment also support this argument.

In addition, the presentation of supply-side transfer expenditures is critical in maintaining the level of economic growth, employment and output in the long run. Considering the fact that the countries are refraining from manufacturing based in China and they search for new centres, Turkey can convert the crisis into an opportunity by reflecting the high exchange rate in lower labour costs, in terms of filling the vacant production place. With its strong stance, particularly, in health care, textile, installation industry and durable goods, Turkey can achieve an economic success, in this period, by meeting the need for protective products and equipment for health personnel, masks and ventilators around the world. This policy should be strengthened with new business lines in the long term; they should be supported with tax exemptions, exceptions, reductions, etc. for international collaborations and direct investments.

New support packages should be developed for the financial sustainability of sectors with high export shares in the manufacturing sector. The decrease in the export revenues of the domestically produced automobile industry can be compensated by stimulating domestic demand with excise duty reduction and replacing the revenue increases in this area.

Construction made the fastest recovery among the sectors. As a result of the attractive design of the loan packages, mortgaged housing sales had historical heights. Tourism and civil aviation, where care is taken to provide support, did not made the expected improvement due to the lack of international demand.

Enterprises in the entertainment sector are still closed as part of health measures against pandemic. Demand continues to decline in the food services, entertainment, culture, arts and sports sectors. The ongoing uncertainty and health risks are delaying the recovery process of the sectors. Following supports can be provided; postponing loan debt payments of the sector employees and business owners, increasing short-time working allowance supports, postponing the submission dates of tax declarations.

## References


Adıgüzel M (2020) Covid-19 pandemisinin Türkiye ekonomisine etkilerinin makroekonomik analizi. İstanbul Ticaret Üniversitesi Sosyal Bilimler Dergisi Covid-19 Sosyal Bilimler Özel Sayısı 19(37):191–221

Aile ÇSHB (2020) Sosyal koruma kalkanı paketi. www.ailevecalisma.gov.tr. Accessed on 27 Nov 2020

Akbulut H (2013) Transfer harcamaları ve büyüme ilişkisi: Gelişmekte olan ülkeler için dinamik panel veri analizi (Unpublished doctoral thesis), Hacettepe Üniversitesi, Türkiye

Alberola E, Arslan Y, Cheng G, Moessner R (2020) The fiscal response to the Covid-19 crisis in advanced and emerging market economies (No 23). Bank for International Settlements

Balcı Y, Çetin G (2020) Covid-19 pandemi sürecinin Türkiye'de istihdama etkileri ve kamu açısından alınması gereken tedbirler. İstanbul Ticaret Üniversitesi Sosyal Bilimler Dergisi Covid-19 Sosyal Bilimler Özel Sayısı 19(37):40–58

Bayer C, Born B, Luetticke R, Müller GJ (2020) The Coronavirus stimulus package: How large is the transfer multiplier? (No. DP14600). CEPR Discussion Paper

Çakmaklı C, Demiralp S, Kalemli Özcan Ş, Yeşiltaş S, Yıldırım MA (2020) Covid-19 and emerging markets: the case of Turkey, (Working Paper No: 2011). Koç University-Tüsiad Economic Research Forum Working Paper Series

Çetinkaya Ö, Aslantaş MF (2019) Merkezi yönetim cari transfer harcamalarının mali büyüklüğünün değerlendirilmesi. Uluslararası Yönetim Akademisi Dergisi 2(1):41–50

Deloitte (2020a) Covid-19 salgınının elektrik talebine olan etkisi ile Türkiye 2020 büyüme beklentilerinin incelenmesi. Retrieved from https://www2.deloitte.com/content/dam/Deloitte/tr/Documents/energy-resources/covid-19-un-turkiye-elektrik-talebi-ve-gsyh-uzerine-etkisi.pdf

Deloitte. (2020b). Küresel Covid-19 salgınının Türkiye'de farklı kategorilere etkileri- II. Retrieved from https://www2.deloitte.com/tr/tr/pages/consulting/articles/kuresel-covid-19-salgininin-turkiyede-farkli-kategorilere-etkileri.html

Ekonomik istikrar kalkanı paketi (2020) https://www.aa.com.tr/tr/info/infografik/17798. Accessed on 30 Apr 2020

Elgin C, Basbug G, Yalaman A (2020) Economic policy responses to a pandemic: developing the COVID-19 economic stimulus index. Covid Econ 1(3):40–53

European Commission (2020) Coordinated economic response to the COVID-19 outbreak. Retrieved from https://ec.europa.eu/info/sites/info/files/communication-coordinated-economic-response-covid19-march-2020_en.pdf

Gault N (2020) Coronavirüs ve küresel ekonomi. Retrieved from https://www.ey.com/Publication/vwLUAssets/Koronavirüs-ve-kuresel-ekonomi/$File/Koronavirüs-ve-kuresel-ekonomi.pdf

Guerrieri V, Lorenzoni G, Straub L, Werninf I (2020) Macroeconomic implications of Covid-19: can negative supply shocks cause demand shortages? (No. w26918). National Bureau of Economic Research

IMF (2020a) A crisis like no other, an uncertain recovery. Retrieved from https://www.imf.org/-/media/Files/Publications/WEO/2020/Update/June/English/WEOENG202006.ashx

IMF (2020b) Fiscal monitor-April 2020. Retrieved from https://www.imf.org/-/media/Files/Publications/fiscal-monitor/2020/April/English/text.ashx

IMF (2020c) Policy steps to address the Corona crisis. Retrieved from http://www.imf.org/-/media/Files/Publications/PP/2020/English/PPEA2020015.ashx

İşkur (2020) Genel bilgiler. Retrieved June 30, 2020, from https://www.iskur.gov.tr/isveren/kisa-calisma-odenegi/genel-bilgiler/

İZTO (2020) Covid-19 tedbir ve destekleri. http://www.izto.org.tr/tr/covid-19-tedbir-ve-destekleri. Accessed on 30 June 2020

Kara E (2020) Covid-19 pandemisi: İşgücü üzerindeki etkileri ve istihdam tedbirleri. Avrasya Sosyal Ve Ekonomi Araştırmaları Dergisi 7(5):269–282

Loayza NV, Pennings S (2020) Macroeconomic policy in the time of COVID-19 : a primer for developing countries. Retrieved from http://elibrary.worldbank.org/doi/abs/https://doi.org/10.1596/33540

Macit A, Macit D (2020) Sivil havacılık sektöründe Covid-19 pandemisinin yönetimi. Avrasya Sosyal Ve Ekonomi Araştırmaları Dergisi 7(4):100–116

Mutluer K, Öner E, Ahmet K (2007) Teoride ve uygulamada kamu maliyesi. İstanbul: İstanbul Bilgi Üniversitesi Yayınları

OECD (2020) Coronavirus: the world economy at risk. Retrieved from https://www.oecd.org/berlin/publikationen/Interim-Economic-Assessment-2-March-2020.pdf

OSD (2020) Otomotiv sektörü aylık değerlendirme raporu 4/2020. Retrieved from http://www.osd.org.tr/sites/1/upload/files/04-2020_OSD_Aylik_Degerlendirme_Raporu-5487.pdf

Özarfat E (2020) Otomotivin kaderini iç pazar belirleyecek. Dünya. Retrieved from https://www.dunya.com

Pınar A (2014) Kamu maliyesi ve maliye politikası. Ankara: Turhan Kitabevi

Soylu ÖB (2020) Türkiye ekonomisinde Covid-19'un sektörel etkileri. Avrasya Sosyal Ve Ekonomi Araştırmaları Dergisi 7(5):169–185

Strateji ve Bütçe Başkanlığı (2019) Orta vadeli program 2020–2022. Retrieved from http://www.sbb.gov.tr/wp-content/uploads/2019/10/YeniEkonomiProgrami_OVP_2020-2022.pdf

Şen H, Kaya A (2017) How large are fiscal multipliers in Turkey? Turk Stud 21(5):772–799

Taymaz E (2020) Covid-19 tedbirlerinin Türkiye ekonomisine etkisi ve çözüm önerileri. https://sarkac.org/2020/04/covid19-tedbirlerinin-turkiye-ekonomisine-etkisi-cozum-onerileri/. Accessed on 23 Dec 2020

TCMB (2020) İmalat sanayi kapasite kullanım oranı. https://www.tcmb.gov.tr/wps/wcm/connect/tr/tcmb+tr/main+menu/istatistikler/reel+sektor+istatistikleri/imalat+sanayi+kapasite+kullanim+orani. Accessed on 30 Apr 2020

TEPAV (2020) COVID-19'un tüketici harcamalarına etkisi. Retrieved from https://www.tepav.org.tr/upload/files/1586499546-0.COVID_19un_Tuketici_Harcamalarina_Etkisi_Bulteni_10_Nisan.pdf

Tokatlıoğlu M, Selen U (2017) Maliye politikası. Bursa, Türkiye: Ekin Yayınevi

TÜBA (2020) Covid-19 pandemi değerlendirme raporu. Retrieved from http://www.tuba.gov.tr/files/images/2020/kovidraporu/Covid-19Raporu-Final+.pdf

TÜİK (2020) Sanayi üretim endeksi, nisan 2020. https://data.tuik.gov.tr/Bulten/Index?p=Sanayi-Uretim-Endeksi-Nisan-2020-33799. Accessed on 30 June 2020

ULISA (2020) Kovid-19 (Koronavirüs) salgınının ekonomik etkileri (ULISA 12, Sayı 1). Ankara, Türkiye: Ankara Yıldırım Beyazıt Üniversitesi Uluslararası İlişkiler ve Stratejik Araştırmalar Enstitüsü

Ustaoğlu M (2020) Covid-19 küresel salgını ve maliye politikalarının etkinliği. In Demirbaş D, Bozkurt V, Yorğun S (ed) Covid-19 pandemisinin ekonomik, toplumsal ve siyasal etkileri. İstanbul, Türkiye: İstanbul Üniversitesi Yayınevi, pp 35–49

Voyvoda E, Yeldan E (2020) Covid-19 salgının Türkiye ekonomisi üzerine etkileri ve politika alternatiflerinin makroekonomik genel denge analizi. Retrieved from https://yeldane.files.wordpress.com/2020/05/covid_voyvodayeldan_v2_31mayis.pdf

Yaşar B (2020) Covid-19 kapsamında turizm sektörü için uygulanan destekler. Dünya. Retrieved from http://www.dunya.com

Yükseler Z (2020) Koronavirüs (Covid-19) salgınının istihdam ve büyümeye etkisi. https://doi.org/10.13140/RG.2.2.23619.96802

Bankası Z (2020). Krediler. https://www.ziraatbank.com.tr/tr/bireysel/krediler. Accessed on 30 June 2020

**Yaprak Karadağ Duymazlar** Research Assistant in Department of Public Finance, İzmir Katip Çelebi University, Turkey. Studies Ph.D. in Public Finance and Financial Management; holds M. Sc. in Public Finance and Financial Management, BS in Public Finance and Economics. She has articles and book chapters about public expenditures, economic crises and local governments.

# Chapter 7
# Effect of COVID-19 Pandemic on Tax Perception: An Empirical Study

**Burhanettin Onur Kireçtepe and Bernur Açıkgöz**

**Abstract** Tax is a financial burden that individuals have to bear as a result of an administrative act carried out by the tax administration. Although 24.1% of taxpayers consider tax as a sacred duty Çoban et al. (Sezgin Vergi Mükelleflerinin Davranışları Üzerine Ampirik Bir İnceleme: Denizli Örneği 777–792, 2004), the European Human Rights Committee (ECHR) states that "…Any law involving some form of tax liability involves deprivation from the relevant assets…". The European Court of Human Rights (ECHR) declared that it accepts the case law of the ECHR by saying "taxation as an intervention to the guaranteed rights" in Article 1 of Protocol 1 Yaltı (Vergi Yükümlüsünün Hakları, 2006). Regardless of how we define the tax, for an ideal tax system, tax compliance of the taxpayer should be ensured at the highest possible level. One of the most important factors affecting tax compliance is tax perception. In this study, we will try to answer these questions and analyse how various demographic differences affect tax perception during the COVID-19 pandemic. In the study, the data of the online survey prepared just for this study will be used and the differences will be determined by this way. It will be important to reveal the changes made by various demographic variables in the perception of tax during the COVID-19 process, in order to shed light on the future steps that the tax administration and the legislator can take regarding taxes.

**Keywords** Tax perception · Tax compliance · Tax law

B. O. Kireçtepe
Faculty of Law Department of Financial Law, Tokat Gaziosmanpaşa University, Tokat, Turkey
e-mail: burhanettinonur.kirectepe@gop.edu.tr

B. Açıkgöz (✉)
Department of Public Finance and Financial Management, İzmir Kâtip Çelebi University, İzmir, Turkey
e-mail: bernur.acikgoz@ikc.edu.tr

 
B. Açıkgöz and İ. A. Acar (eds.), *Pandemnomics: The Pandemic's Lasting Economic Effects*, Accounting, Finance, Sustainability, Governance & Fraud: Theory and Application, https://doi.org/10.1007/978-981-16-8024-3_7

## 7.1 Introduction

Tax is a financial burden that individuals have to bear as a result of an administrative act carried out by the tax administration, which has the public power regarding taxation. Although 24.1% of taxpayers consider taxation a sacred duty (Çoban et al. 2004), the European Commission of Human Rights says, "... any law involving some form of financial liability includes depriving the person of his/her possessions as much as the amount that needs to be paid from the respective assets" (Yaltı 2006). By this, it states that the taxation process is the result of deprivation of property as much as the part that causes a decrease in the assets and may constitute an intervention to the property right. The European Court of Human Rights (ECtHR), on the other hand, stated that it acknowledged the case law of European Commission of Human Rights, saying, "that taxation as an intervention to the rights to give assurance in Article 1 of the Protocol" (Yaltı 2006).

Taxes can be called an administrative act, a sacred duty or an interference with the right to property, and there are many other definitions of taxes. Many of these definitions ignore the fact that taxes are a social event. No matter for what legal or religious reason we rationalize taxes; tax is an economic burden on those exposed to it. In many cases, taxpayers try to reduce the tax they will bear, and some different taxpayers fulfil their tax duties in a timely and complete manner, even if they will face severe economic consequences.

The views that prioritize the socio-psychological aspect of taxes (Sağlam 2013) come to the fore when trying to explain the reason for these two opposite reactions. Research on tax psychology is mainly conducted to understand why taxpayers react differently to tax. In these studies, sometimes a group of taxpayers are dealt with, and sometimes it is tried to understand why the tax efforts of countries differ. Most studies show us the difference between taxpayers or countries is directly related to tax compliance or tax perception of taxpayers.

Tax perception is an important factor affecting tax compliance and, accordingly, tax revenue. In cases where the tax perception is negative, tax compliance decreases and this causes reactions such as tax avoidance or, in more advanced cases, tax evasion. In a crisis, such as the pandemic, when public expenditures are expected to increase, taxpayer compliance will be much more important in collecting taxes that will finance these expenditures. It is known that there are many variables that affect tax perception. In this study, it will be tried to determine how the tax perception is affected by a global crisis, namely pandemic.

## 7.2 Conceptual Overview of Tax Compliance and Tax Perception

Tax compliance or voluntary tax compliance is an important issue frequently encountered in studies conducted especially in the field of tax psychology. Basically, it can be defined as the taxpayers paying their taxes in full and on time without being forced to by the tax administration (Saygın 2013). At this point, we should be considered that even if one of the motivations that ensures compliance is worrying about a forced sanction, the taxpayers have fulfilled their tax liability completely and on time without any direct sanction by the tax administration.

When it comes to tax compliance, studies mention four types of taxpayers. They are called honest or voluntary taxpayers, sincere taxpayers, social taxpayers and tax evaders. An honest taxpayer is defined as a taxpayer who pays tax without being affected by any external stimulus with a very high tax compliance (Tosuner and Demir 2009). Sincere taxpayers are a type of taxpayer who has high personal tax compliance and pay tax regardless of the compliance of other taxpayers or the status of public services but tend to be affected by the attitude and behaviour of the tax administration. A social taxpayer is the type of taxpayer who is affected by the frequency of audits and amnesties, who has the anxiety and embarrassment behind their tax compliance, their tax compliance increases especially in cases where they think that other taxpayers also pay taxes and the taxation is fair, while otherwise it decreases or completely disappears. A tax evader, on the other hand, is the taxpayer with the lowest tax ethics and tax compliance, and this taxpayer, whose basic motivation is not to pay taxes, will try to evade tax regardless of the conditions (Tosuner and Demir 2009). Countries that aim to increase their tax efforts and tax revenues should increase the ratio of honest taxpayers among all taxpayers as much as possible. In addition to that to implement practices that will increase "Tax Compliance" of social and sincere taxpayers is important as well. In most cases, certain behaviours that will increase the harmony of social and sincere taxpayers will also result in the capture and punishment of tax evaders.

There are many factors that affect tax compliance, such as tax ethics, frequency of tax audits, high possible penalties, frequency of amnesty practices, belonging to the country to which tax will be paid, easy understanding of tax regulations and their frequent changes (Taşkın 2012). It is predicted that tax compliance will increase in times such as war and coup. In fact, it has been indirectly demonstrated that the displacement theory in public expenditures is valid in times of coups, as it is predicted to be in other crisis times, and that the public revenues should increase accordingly and therefore tax compliance increases (Kutbay and Gerede 2019). New reasons other than those listed may also arise for each concrete situation.

Some of the variables that affect tax compliance will also directly affect tax perception; the attitude of the tax administration, the demographic structure of taxpayers, the frequency of tax amnesties is just a few of the variables that affect tax perception positively or negatively. Again, the perception that taxes are fair is one of the factors that positively affect both tax perception and tax compliance (Çetin 2007). The concentration of public expenditures on the issues that the taxpayers attach importance to and the low level of claims such as corruption is among the variables that are expected to positively affect tax perception.

Another factor that affects tax compliance and tax perception together is the tax burden. Tax burden is defined in two different ways; the rate at which taxes cause a decrease in the economic power of the taxpayer is called objective tax burden (Çoban et al. 2004), and the extent to which the taxpayer feels the objective tax burden depends on the psychological and demographic structure of the taxpayer and is named as subjective tax burden (Nadaroğlu 1998). In most cases, the taxpayer' perception of the tax is initially bearing the economic burden; as thc magnitude of the impact of this amount on the economic well-being of the taxpayer increases, the subjective burden of the tax will increase more than its objective burden. In fact, according to Laffer (2004), after a certain rate, the subjective tax burden for taxpayers reaches an unbearable dimension and the tax payment behaviour reaches a size that will reduce the tax revenue of the country.

The frequency of tax audits also positively affects tax compliance (Taşkın 2012). As the risk of getting caught as a result of the audit increases and the penalty to be incurred becomes definite, tax evasion becomes economically harmful for the taxpayer and tax compliance increases accordingly. Behind this behaviour lies the idea that the individual tries to maximize his/her economic interest and will do the best for himself/herself as a result of cost–benefit comparison (Doyle et al. 2009).

Increasing tax inspections also contributes to tax compliance by affecting tax perception positively. Since the taxpayer will not face the risk of withdrawing from the competition by paying tax, he will not develop a non-paying-tax behaviour. As a result of these audits, practices such as the disclosing of those found to have evaded taxes may also affect tax compliance (Tosuner and Demir 2009). For a similar reason, the announcement of tax record holders also encourages tax compliance.

Most of the situations mentioned above that affect tax compliance affect one type of taxpayer more than the others. The general tax compliance of the country will increase faster if a good tax administration takes measures that will affect as much of a taxpayer group as possible by observing this situation and recognizing its own taxpayers.

## 7.3 Literature Overview

In addition to many studies on tax compliance and tax perception at home and abroad, there are also many studies focused on understanding the factors that affect them. Some of these studies tend to explain this difference with questionnaires like our study. While some try to compare two different countries, others try to explain the effects of regional differences or economic development levels of countries on tax compliance; there are also studies trying to explain the effect of religious or ethnic differences on tax compliance and tax perception. Most of the studies conducted in our country consist of studies aimed at determining the tax perception of a particular city. However, more extensive studies have been conducted in Turkey, as well.

Studies of a general nature, relatively recently published, which are listed below, have focused on examining whether tax evasion is perceived as ethical. McGee et al. (2014), McGee (2012, 2014), Martin (1944), Torgler (2003), Block (1989, 1993), Leiker (1998), Morales (1998) study are examples of them. Some other studies focus more on the social aspect of taxation. They tried to explain how the question of whether the tax levied on the rich should be used in the financing of the poor citizens, and the question of whether the rich are taxed sufficiently (McGee 2016).

Studies have also been conducted on tax perception in many countries and regions. Ballas and Tsoukas on Greece, (1998), Smatrakalev on Bulgaria, (1998), Vaguine on Russia, (1998), and Murtuza and Ghazanfar, (1998), examining the tax perception and Muslim perspective, can be given as examples of micro-scale studies. Some of these studies are about Turkey. These are: Benk et al. (2009), McGee et al. (2016, 2012, 2011); Gergerlioglu and McGee (2017).

## 7.4 Methodology

In our study, an online survey was preferred to prevent health risks during the pandemic. This surveys aim is to understand whether the tax perception of taxpayers is affected by the pandemic process and if so, in what way. Open-ended questions were not preferred due to the possible problems they may cause in the online survey. The demographics of the participants were determined through the questions in the first part, and the second part questions examined whether the taxpayers adopted the measures taken regarding the COVID-19 pandemic. The third part questions were to understand to what extent the taxpayers were informed about the tax measures taken by the government as a result of the COVID-19 pandemic and whether they support these tax measures. The fourth and final part questions aimed to determine what the taxpayers thought about the macro-level effects of the COVID-19 pandemic.

A total of 291 people responded to the questionnaire. Answers to the questions were first evaluated independently of demographic variables, and then it was determined whether the answers differed significantly according to demographic variables. After determining the difference, it was also analysed.

### *7.4.1 Challenges Encountered Throughout the Study*

In order for the study to have a healthy result, the sampling should have the demographic structure to reflect the population of Turkey. It is also acceptable for this demographic structure to reflect taxpayers in tax-related studies. However, face-to-face surveys to ensure this demographic structure would have created a health risk, during the pandemic period for both the people, who will conduct the survey and the respondents. For this reason, online survey method had to be preferred. Hence, a sample with intense internet access was formed spontaneously. It can be said that this sample unable to fully adapt to the demographic structure of Turkey has created a problematic area in terms of the results of the study. However, considering that there are also studies using face-to-face survey method with a high level of education (Ayrangöl et al. 2019), it can be said that this problem has developed independently from conducting the survey online.

Although the sample we reach out in our study is above the Turkey average in terms of age, it is also impossible to mention that our sample is completely irrelevant in terms of tax liability. Although this result is not intended, it is thought that the demographic structure of the sample obtained is in line with the demographic structure of taxpayers.

### 7.4.2 *Findings of the Study and Evaluation of the Results*

In this part of the study, relevant analyses were made and interpreted through the data obtained from online questionnaires applied by the participants. Data on the demographic characteristics of the participants are given in Table 7.1. While calculating percentages in all tables, the ten thousandth digit, which is the fourth digit after the comma has been rounded to the third digit after the comma, i.e., the thousandth, in accordance with mathematical rules due to numerical reasons.

Women participants constitute 20.6% of the total participants, while men constitute 79.3%; this rate does not reflect Turkey's demographic structure. Although the gender statistics of taxpayers are not kept, it would not be too misleading to mention that the participants in the study have a gender structure close to the gender of taxpayers, given the labour force participation rates (TÜİK 2020).

Another noteworthy demographic data is that 32.6% of the respondents are engaged in a job that has to file an income tax return. Considering the rate based on declaration (GİB 2019) which is lower than 9% in all income taxes, it is observed that the rate of taxpayers who pays tax based on declaration is high in our sample. Due to the high rate of taxpayers directly dealing with tax, it would be possible to say that the study has a sample with a high sensitivity in tax issues.

### 7.4.3 *Evaluation of General Findings and Results*

The tables we will evaluate under this section are in a structure to show general findings, independent of demographic variables. In this context, the general part of the study will be evaluated in this section (Table 7.2).

The rate of support for the measures taken by the government is around 21%. This rate decreases to 13% at the point of supporting economic measures. The low rate of support for economic measures can be interpreted as the government's failure to meet the expectations of the markets. This can also be explained by the higher sensitivity of people towards economic measures. It should not be forgotten that even in the sixteenth century, Machiavelli stated that "people forget losing their fathers more quickly than losing the property they inherited from their fathers" (Machiavelli 1993), expressing that this sensitivity is an issue that administrators should pay attention to.

**Table 7.1** Data on demographic characteristics of participants

| Variables | Number | Percentile |
|---|---|---|
| **Gender** | | |
| Women | 60 | 20,619 |
| Men | 231 | 79,381 |
| Total | 291 | 100 |
| **Marital status** | | |
| Married | 207 | 71,134 |
| Single | 84 | 28,866 |
| Total | 291 | 100 |
| **Age group** | | |
| 18–25 | 24 | 8247 |
| 26–35 | 45 | 15,464 |
| 36–50 | 48 | 16,495 |
| 51–65 | 173 | 59,450 |
| Over 65 | 1 | 0344 |
| Total | 291 | 100 |
| **Educational background** | | |
| Primary school (5 years) | 3 | 1031 |
| Middle-school/primary school (8 years) | 3 | 1031 |
| High school (11 or 12 years) | 16 | 5498 |
| University | 157 | 53,952 |
| Postgraduate (Masters or higher) | 112 | 38,488 |
| Total | 291 | 100 |
| **Occupational background** | | |
| Worker | 52 | 17,869 |
| Civil servant | 94 | 32,302 |
| Tradespeople | 7 | 2406 |
| Self-employed | 71 | 24,399 |
| Owner of SME | 21 | 7216 |
| Large scale enterprise owner | 3 | 1031 |
| Student/working | 8 | 2749 |
| Student/not working | 18 | 6186 |
| Unemployed | 17 | 5842 |
| Total | 291 | 100 |
| **Occupational changes because of the COVID-19 pandemic** | | |
| Used to have a job, not anymore | 27 | 9278 |
| Used to be an unemployed, not anymore | 7 | 2406 |
| Nothing Changed | 257 | 88,316 |
| Total | 291 | 100 |

**Table 7.2** Support rates of the government's struggle against COVID-19

| Variables | Number | Percentage |
|---|---|---|
| Do you support the precautions taken by the government regarding the COVID-19 pandemic? | | |
| I totally support | 11 | 3780 |
| I support | 53 | 18,213 |
| I am indecisive/have no idea | 35 | 12,028 |
| I do not support | 105 | 36,082 |
| I definitely do not support | 87 | 29,897 |
| Total | 291 | 100 |
| Do you support the economic precautions taken by the government regarding the COVID-19 pandemic? | | |
| I totally support | 9 | 3093 |
| I support | 33 | 11,340 |
| I am indecisive/don't know | 18 | 6186 |
| I do not support | 116 | 39,862 |
| I definitely do not support | 115 | 39,519 |
| Total | 291 | 100 |
| Do you find these precautions sufficient? | | |
| I find totally sufficient | 2 | 0,687 |
| I find sufficient | 10 | 3,436 |
| I am indecisive/don't know | 11 | 3,780 |
| I do not find sufficient | 111 | 38,144 |
| I definitely do not find sufficient | 157 | 53,952 |
| Total | 291 | 100 |

Now, challenging measures to prevent the epidemic have started to be expressed more all over the world. In this context, the rate of finding sufficient measures for COVID-19 is slightly above 4%, and the rate of those who do not find these measures absolutely sufficient is around 54%. This situation can be read as that citizens will support a more effective fight against COVID-19 and more stringent measures (Table 7.3).

Taxpayers are highly aware of both the Special Consumption Tax (SCT) increase and the customs duty increase. The rate of those who are aware of the SCT increase is over 93%, and this rate is only 78% for the customs duty. This can be explained by the fact that tax awareness is higher in a tax which is encountered on a daily basis in life and even imposed on soda, even if it is an indirect tax, compared to the customs duty which is relatively less encountered with (Taylar 2010).

Although support for tax increases is low, there is a significant difference in support between the two taxes. At this point, a relatively higher support, i.e., 15%, to the increase in customs duty which can be explained by the low level of awareness, as well as by the fact that the customs duty is less visible than the SCT in daily life.

**Table 7.3** Detailed support status for the financial measures taken by the government during the struggle against COVID-19

| Variables | Number | Percentage |
|---|---|---|
| Do you have any knowledge about the recent increase of custom duties made by the government? | | |
| Yes | 228 | 78,351 |
| No | 63 | 21,649 |
| Total | 291 | 100 |
| Do you support the increase of custom duties? | | |
| I totally support | 8 | 2749 |
| I support | 36 | 12,372 |
| I am indecisive / don't know | 19 | 6529 |
| I do not support | 91 | 31,271 |
| I definitely do not support | 137 | 47,079 |
| Total | 291 | 100 |
| Would you give a different answer if there was no COVID-19 pandemic? | | |
| Yes | 30 | 10,309 |
| No | 261 | 89,691 |
| Total | 291 | 100 |
| Do you have any knowledge about the recent increase at the special consumption tax (SCT) of some goods made by the government? | | |
| Yes | 272 | 93,471 |
| No | 19 | 6529 |
| Total | 291 | 100 |
| Do you support the increase of SCTs? | | |
| I totally support | 4 | 1375 |
| I support | 11 | 3780 |
| I am indecisive/don't know | 7 | 2405 |
| I do not support | 74 | 25,430 |
| I definitely do not support | 195 | 67,010 |
| Total | 291 | 100 |
| Would you give a different answer if there was no COVID-19 pandemic? | | |
| Yes | 18 | 6186 |
| No | 273 | 93,814 |
| Total | 291 | 100 |
| Would you support if the government decided to increase other taxes to tackle down the COVID-19 pandemic? | | |
| I will totally support | 2 | 0.687 |
| I will support | 8 | 2749 |

(continued)

**Table 7.3** (continued)

| Variables | Number | Percentage |
|---|---|---|
| I am indecisive/don't know | 11 | 3780 |
| I will not support | 82 | 28,179 |
| I definitely will not support | 188 | 64,605 |
| Total | 291 | 100 |
| Which taxes would you prefer to increase? | | |
| Income tax/corporate income tax | 220 | 75,601 |
| Expenditure taxes (VAT-SCT etc.) | 71 | 24,399 |
| Total | 291 | 100 |

Again, the rate of those who say "I definitely do not support" in the question about supporting these two taxes varies significantly. The rate of those who do not support definitely which is 47% in customs duty increases to 67% in SCT. Similarly, this can be interpreted as negative thoughts about a tax that is more involved in life are higher than those for a tax that is relatively less in life.

The ratio of those who support the government to increase other taxes due to the struggle against the pandemic remains at a seriously low point of 3.5%. Again, the rate of those who state that they will not support the tax increase is over 64%. We think that this can be explained by the high level of the total subjective burden of taxes, as well as by the fact that taxes are collected at high rates that are close to the tax limit.

Within the scope of the questionnaire, the answer to the question of "which taxes would you prefer to increase" with two options, either one or the other, was the direct taxes expressed as income and corporate income tax at a rate of 75%. The rate of those who preferred indirect taxes expressed by SCT and Value Added Tax (VAT) remained at 25%. Thus, instead of taxes imposed on spending, which are likely to generally increase the cost of living, considered unfair in terms of tax justice and difficult to avoid, they prefer direct taxes that are more appropriate to tax justice and have no direct effect on the general cost of living (Table 7.4).

Thirty of those who answered the question, "Do you support the increase in customs duty?" answered yes to the question "Would your answer have changed without the COVID-19 pandemic?". Understanding whether those who answered yes support customs duty has also gained importance in this context. A total of 10 out of the mentioned 30 people either support or definitely support the tax increase, corresponding to 33%. A total of 10 people among those who say that "my answer would have changed if there was no pandemic" do not support or definitely do no support the tax increase. Conditional support to tax increases in an extraordinary situation such as a pandemic is common, for the reasons explained above, as included in the scientific literature. However, we have not encountered with, in the literature, such a situation as not conditionally supporting tax increases in an extraordinary period such as a pandemic. We believe that a detailed analysis of this situation can be the subject of further studies (Table 7.5).

**Table 7.4** The people who support status of the increase of custom duties will change if there is no COVID-19 pandemic

| To what extent do those who answered yes to the question of whether your answer would have changed if there was no COVID-19 pandemic support the increase of customs duties? | | |
|---|---|---|
| I totally support | I totally support | I totally support |
| I support | I support | I support |
| I am indecisive/don't know | I am indecisive/don't know | I am indecisive/don't know |
| I do not support | I do not support | I do not support |
| I definitely do not support | I definitely do not support | I definitely do not support |
| Total | Total | Total |

**Table 7.5** The people whom support status of the increase of SCT will change if there is no COVID-19 pandemic

| To what extent do those who answered yes to the question of whether your answer would have changed if there was no COVID-19 pandemic support the increase pf SCTs? | | |
|---|---|---|
| I totally support | I totally support | I totally support |
| I support | I support | I support |
| I am indecisive/don't know | I am indecisive/don't know | I am indecisive/don't know |
| I do not support | I do not support | I do not support |
| I definitely do not support | I definitely do not support | I definitely do not support |
| Total | Total | Total |

18 of those who answered yes to the question, "Do you support the SCT increase?" answered yes the question whether your answer would have changed if there was no COVID-19 Pandemic. Similarly, in the distribution of these answers, those who do not support and those who do not definitely support them are in the majority. We could not explain this, and a distinct result occurred in the literature, as is for the results in customs duty (Table 7.6).

The aim of the 4th group of questions is to understand how the economic and democratic effects of the pandemic are evaluated by the taxpayer. To this end, it was tried to understand, in two groups of questions, how the democracy indicators and economic indicators were perceived by the participants in the survey, and, by asking the same questions for 2008, it was aimed to understand whether the perceptions of these indicators were affected in the medium term or the pandemic was the main factor.

While 94% of the respondents stated that the budget deficit increased during the pandemic period, 90% stated that their purchasing power decreased compared to the pre-pandemic period. When we evaluate these two statements together, taxpayers

**Table 7.6** Trust in democratic institutions and economic situation

| Variables | Number | Percentage |
|---|---|---|
| Do you think the budget deficit rise during the COVID-19 pandemic? | | |
| Yes | 276 | 94,845 |
| No | 15 | 5155 |
| Total | 291 | 100 |
| How has your purchasing power changed compared to 2008? | | |
| It became higher | 10 | 3436 |
| It did not change | 17 | 5842 |
| It became lower | 264 | 90,722 |
| Total | 291 | 100 |
| How has your purchasing power changed compared to before the COVID-19 pandemic? | | |
| It became higher | 2 | 0.687 |
| It did not change | 36 | 12,371 |
| It became lower | 253 | 86,942 |
| Total | 291 | 100 |
| How do you think the democracy index of Turkey has changed compared to before 2008? | | |
| It improved | 6 | 2062 |
| It did not change | 15 | 5155 |
| It declined | 270 | 92,783 |
| Total | 291 | 100 |
| How do you think the democracy index of Turkey has changed compared to the pre-COVID-19 pandemic? | | |
| It improved | 4 | 1375 |
| It did not change | 69 | 23,711 |
| It declined | 218 | 74,914 |
| Total | 291 | 100 |
| Do you think that the decisions regarding the measures taken to tackle the COVID-19 pandemic are taken with your democratic participation? | | |
| Yes | 5 | 1718 |
| Partially | 26 | 8935 |
| No | 260 | 89,347 |
| Total | 291 | 100 |

who think that public expenditures are made in order to combat the pandemic and that this increases the budget deficit think that these public expenditures do not increase their purchasing power and even do not ensure that their purchasing power remains constant. This can also be read as the citizens think that some measures should be taken to increase their purchasing power affected by the pandemic.

The rate of those who think that the decisions about the pandemic are made with democratic participation is 89%, but those who think that the democracy index of the country has decreased with the pandemic remains only 75%. As a result of reading these two propositions together, it can be concluded that the decrease in democratic participation in processes such as pandemic is reasonable for 14% of the respondents. However, when interpreting the 92% of the answers to the question "How the democracy index has changed compared to pre-2008?" saying "it has deteriorated", it can be concluded that the democratic participation has remained low for a while, at least for 14% of the participants in the survey.

## 7.5 Evaluation of Findings and Results Differentiated According to Demographic Variables

The tables that we will evaluate under this section are in a structure to show the general findings regardless of demographic variables (Table 7.7).

As for supporting the measures, we observe that the workers expressed 7% more support than the general. Again, it has been determined that workers who say "I am indecisive/Don't Know" are 5% more than the general, and accordingly, the rate of those who do not support the measures is 53%, the lowest among all professions. This decrease, which remained at 15% in the total non-support rate, has been the only group among all professions, realizing below 10%, with a decrease of 20% among those who say they definitely do not support them. In terms of supporting the economic moves, the ratio of workers who indicated a higher support of around 5%, while the ratio of the non-supporting group to total workers is also 5% lower than the general. Just as in the previous question, the rate of those who said they definitely do not support was below 30% and it was the lowest among all occupational groups.

Since the examination of the sociological reasons of the determined differences was considered outside the scope of our study, we have only determined the differences (Table 7.8).

Whether the unemployed differ from the general in the support of the measures taken by the government to combat the pandemic displayed in Table 7.2 is included in Table 7.8. At the point of supporting the measures taken by the government, the support rate of the unemployed decreases to 11% and is 10% lower than the general. The decrease in this ratio increased the rate of the indecisive and the rate of those who absolutely do not support it by 5%, respectively.

**Table 7.7** Analysis of the answers given to the questions in Table 7.2. According to occupations: worker

| Occupation | Worker | | |
|---|---|---|---|
| Variables | Number | General percentage | Special percentage |
| Do You support the precautions taken by the government regarding the COVID-19 pandemic? | | | |
| I totally support | 3 | 3780 | 5769 |
| I support | 12 | 18,213 | 23,077 |
| I am indecisive/don't know | 9 | 12,028 | 17,308 |
| I do not support | 23 | 36,082 | 44,231 |
| I definitely do not support | 5 | 29,897 | 9615 |
| Total | 52 | 100 | |
| Do you support the economic precautions taken by the government regarding the COVID-19 pandemic? | | | |
| I totally support | 3 | 3093 | 5769 |
| I support | 7 | 11,340 | 13,462 |
| I am indecisive/don't know | 3 | 6186 | 5769 |
| I do not support | 24 | 39,862 | 46,154 |
| I definitely do not support | 15 | 39,519 | 28,846 |
| Total | 52 | 100 | |
| Do you find these precautions sufficient? | | | |
| I find totally sufficient | 1 | 0,687 | 1,923 |
| I find sufficient | 2 | 3,436 | 3,846 |
| I am indecisive/don't know | 4 | 3,780 | 7,692 |
| I do not find sufficient | 18 | 38,144 | 34,615 |
| I definitely do not find sufficient | 27 | 53,952 | 51,923 |
| Total | 52 | 100 | |

The point where the unemployed differ from the general in supporting the economic moves made by the government is the increase in the rate of supporters, although the rate of those who definitely do not support has decreased. There was no noticeable change in the total support rate as these changes eliminated each other's

**Table 7.8** Analysis of the answers given to the questions in Table 7.2. According to occupations: unemployed

| Occupation | Unemployed | | |
|---|---|---|---|
| Variables | Number | General percentage | Special percentage |
| Do you support the precautions taken by the government regarding the COVID-19 pandemic? | | | |
| I totally support | 0 | 3780 | 0 |
| I support | 2 | 18,213 | 11,765 |
| I am indecisive/don't know | 3 | 12,028 | 17,647 |
| I do not support | 6 | 36,082 | 35,294 |
| I definitely do not support | 6 | 29,897 | 35,294 |
| Total | 17 | 100 | |
| Do you support the economic precautions taken by the government regarding the COVID-19 pandemic? | | | |
| I totally support | 0 | 3093 | 0 |
| I support | 3 | 11,340 | 17,647 |
| I am indecisive/don't know | 1 | 6186 | 5882 |
| I do not support | 6 | 39,862 | 35,294 |
| I definitely do not support | 7 | 39,519 | 41,176 |
| Total | 17 | 100 | |
| Do you find these precautions sufficient? | | | |
| I find totally sufficient | 0 | 0.687 | 0 |
| I find sufficient | 1 | 3436 | 5882 |
| I am indecisive/don't know | 0 | 3780 | 0 |
| I do not find sufficient | 5 | 38,144 | 29,412 |
| I definitely do not find sufficient | 11 | 53,952 | 64,706 |
| Total | 17 | 100 | |

influence. Apart from this, there is no point where the unemployed differ significantly from the general in terms of economic moves and considering measures being adequate (Table 7.9).

Due to the low rates of each individual rate, tradesmen, SME owners and large business owners are analysed in a single table under the name of business owners.

**Table 7.9** Analysis of the answers given to the questions in Table 7.2. According to occupations: business owner

| Occupation | Business owner | | |
|---|---|---|---|
| Variables | Number | General percentage | Special percentage |
| Do you support the precautions taken by the government regarding the COVID-19 pandemic? | | | |
| I totally support | 1 | 3780 | 3226 |
| I support | 8 | 18,213 | 25,806 |
| I am indecisive/don't know | 4 | 12,028 | 12,903 |
| I do not support | 13 | 36,082 | 41,935 |
| I definitely do not support | 5 | 29,897 | 16,129 |
| Total | 31 | 100 | |
| Do you support the economic precautions taken by the government regarding the COVID-19 pandemic? | | | |
| I totally support | 2 | 3093 | 6452 |
| I support | 5 | 11,340 | 16,129 |
| I am indecisive/don't know | 0 | 6186 | 0 |
| I do not support | 14 | 39,86 | 45,161 |
| I definitely do not support | 10 | 39,519 | 32,258 |
| Total | 31 | 100 | |
| Do you find these precautions sufficient? | | | |
| I find totally sufficient | 0 | 0.687 | 0 |
| I find sufficient | 2 | 3436 | 6452 |
| I am indecisive/don't know | 0 | 3780 | 0 |
| I do not find sufficient | 12 | 38,144 | 38,710 |
| I definitely do not find sufficient | 17 | 53,952 | 54,839 |
| Total | 31 | 100 | |

The rate of business owners who supported the measures taken by the government regarding the pandemic was around 29% in total. While this rate is around 8% more than the support of the general, it was the highest rate among all occupational groups. The total support of business owners in supporting economic moves to combat the pandemic emerged as 22% and was 8% more than the general. This support rate is the highest among all occupational groups in terms of supporting economic measures. There is no significant difference between the owners of the business and the general in terms of the proportion of those who do not support and considering measures being adequate (Table 7.10).

**Table 7.10** Analysis of the answers given to the questions in Table 7.2. According to occupations: tradesperson or self-employed

| Occupation | Tradesperson or self-employed | | |
|---|---|---|---|
| Variables | Number | General percentage | Special percentage |
| Do you support the precautions taken by the government regarding the COVID-19 pandemic? | | | |
| I totally support | 2 | 3780 | 2817 |
| I support | 11 | 18,213 | 15,493 |
| I am indecisive/don't know | 8 | 12,028 | 11,268 |
| I do not support | 21 | 36,082 | 29,577 |
| I definitely do not support | 29 | 29,897 | 40,845 |
| Total | 71 | 100 | |
| Do you support the economic precautions taken by the government regarding the COVID-19 pandemic? | | | |
| I totally support | 2 | 3093 | 2817 |
| I support | 10 | 11,340 | 14,085 |
| I am indecisive/don't know | 3 | 6186 | 4225 |
| I do not support | 22 | 39,862 | 30,986 |
| I definitely do not support | 34 | 39,519 | 47,887 |
| Total | 71 | 100 | |
| Do you find these precautions sufficient? | | | |
| I find totally sufficient | 1 | 0,687 | 1408 |
| I find sufficient | 1 | 3436 | 1408 |
| I am indecisive/don't know | 3 | 3780 | 4225 |
| I do not find sufficient | 25 | 38,144 | 35,211 |
| I definitely do not find sufficient | 40 | 53,952 | 56,338 |
| Total | 71 | 100 | |

Inspired by Income Tax Law, the concept of self-employed is defined as working on behalf and account, and the professionals such as lawyers, doctors and financial advisors are evaluated under this heading.

The total support of the self-employed was 3% less as for supporting the measures taken by the government regarding the pandemic. As a result, the percentage of total non-supporters was high by 3%. Although the difference up to this part is not too big, the main difference is seen in the rate of definitely non-supporters, which is 11% higher and above 40%.

There is no difference between the self-employed and the general population in terms of supporting economic measures, and there is no remarkable difference in terms of considering measures being adequate.

The difference of civil servants from the general population at the point of supporting the measures taken by the government regarding the pandemic is analysed in Table 7.11. The total support of civil servants was 21%. This rate was similar to the general population. However, the rate of those who definitely did not support these measures was 73% in total, 8% higher than the general population. The main difference here lays in the rate of definitely non-supporters. Here, the 8% difference from the general population is the same as the difference in terms of total non-supporters.

The total ratio of those supporting economic regulations remained at 9% and was 5% lower than the general population. The rate of those who definitely do not support these economic measures was 42%, which was 3% higher than the general population. While the rate of those who consider the measures taken against the pandemic adequate was similar to the general population, the total rate of those who consider the measures adequate was 3% lower (Table 7.12).

The students were the most indecisive group with a rate of 23% regarding the measures taken by the government. This rate was 11% higher than the general population. While the total percentage of supporters is 19% lower than the general population, i.e., 3%, the total percentage of non-supporters is 54%, which is 11% lower than the general population. This proportion was slightly higher than workers, and immediately after workers, students were the group being least opposed to the measures.

The rate of those who supported economic moves was over 3%. Although this rate is below 11% of the general population, it is the lowest among all groups. The rate of total non-supporters was also 84%. This rate was the highest among all demographic groups. Students' attitudes did not significantly differ from the general population in terms of considering the measures being adequate.

The responses of the workers to the questions in Table 7.3. Do not contain a great difference compared to the general population. But we will address some relatively minor differences here.

More than 84% were aware of the increase in customs duties, which is 6% points higher than the general population. While the total support for the increase was 6% less, the total non-support rate was 5 percentage points higher. The difference in the answers given to the questions other than this was even less (Tables 7.13 and 7.14).

88% of the unemployed was aware of the increase in the customs duty, i.e., 10 percentage points higher than the general population. While the total non-support

**Table 7.11** Analysis of the answers given to the questions in Table 7.2. According to occupations: civil servant

| Occupation | Civil Servant | | |
|---|---|---|---|
| Variables | Number | General percentage | Special percentage |
| Do you support the precautions taken by the government regarding the COVID-19 pandemic? | | | |
| I totally support | 4 | 3780 | 4255 |
| I support | 16 | 18,213 | 17,021 |
| I am indecisive/don't know | 5 | 12,028 | 5319 |
| I do not support | 34 | 36,082 | 36,170 |
| I definitely do not support | 35 | 29,897 | 37,234 |
| Total | 94 | 100 | |
| Do you support the economic precautions taken by the government regarding the COVID-19 pandemic? | | | |
| I totally support | 2 | 3093 | 2128 |
| I support | 7 | 11,340 | 7446 |
| I am indecisive/don't know | 8 | 6186 | 8511 |
| I do not support | 37 | 39,862 | 39,362 |
| I definitely do not support | 40 | 39,519 | 42,553 |
| Total | 94 | 100 | |
| Do you find these precautions sufficient? | | | |
| I find totally sufficient | 0 | 0,687 | 0 |
| I find sufficient | 3 | 3436 | 3191 |
| I am indecisive/don't know | 2 | 3780 | 2128 |
| I do not find sufficient | 40 | 38,144 | 42,553 |
| I definitely do not find sufficient | 49 | 53,952 | 52,128 |
| Total | 94 | 100 | |

rate with regard to supporting this increase was 94%, the rate of definitely non-supporters was higher than 70%. The opposition to the tax increase, which was 16 and 23 points higher than the general population, respectively, was also the highest among the groups.

**Table 7.12** Analysis of the answers given to the questions in Table 7.2. According to occupations: student

| Occupation | Student | | |
|---|---|---|---|
| Variables | Number | Percentage | |
| Do you support the precautions taken by the government regarding the COVID-19 pandemic? | | | |
| I totally support | 1 | 3780 | 3846 |
| I support | 4 | 18,213 | 15,385 |
| I am indecisive/don't know | 6 | 12,028 | 23,077 |
| I do not support | 8 | 36,082 | 27,586 |
| I definitely do not support | 7 | 29,897 | 26,923 |
| Total | 26 | 100 | |
| Do you support the economic precautions taken by the government regarding the COVID-19 pandemic? | | | |
| I totally support | 0 | 3093 | 0 |
| I support | 1 | 11,340 | 3846 |
| I am indecisive/don't know | 3 | 6,186 | 11,538 |
| I do not support | 13 | 39,862 | 50 |
| I definitely do not support | 9 | 39,519 | 34,615 |
| Total | 26 | 100 | |
| Do you find these precautions sufficient? | | | |
| I find totally sufficient | 0 | 0,687 | 0 |
| I find sufficient | 1 | 3436 | 3846 |
| I am indecisive/don't know | 2 | 3780 | 7692 |
| I do not find sufficient | 10 | 38,144 | 38,462 |
| I definitely do not find sufficient | 13 | 53,952 | 50 |
| Total | 26 | 100 | |

The unemployed people, who are 100% aware of the SCT increase, have been the only group to answer the question "Do you support this increase"? as, "I do not support" and "I definitely do not support". The unemployed, over 88% of whom responded, "I definitely not to support", were the group that certainly did not support the SCT increase at the highest rate.

The rate of support for a new tax increase was also zero, as was the case in the first two tax increases. In addition to the answer that "I do not support", the ratio of which was around 6%, the ratio of the incisive was around 6%, and the rate of the answer, "I definitely not to support", was 88%, being the highest total non-support rate and the highest rate of definitely non-supporters. When asked which taxes would you prefer to be increased, they preferred direct taxes, expressed as income and corporate tax, at the rate of 94%. This may be caused by the fact that they think that they will be affected by indirect taxes, although they will not be dealing with direct taxes as long as they remain unemployed (Table 7.15).

**Table 7.13** Analysis of the answers given to the questions in Table 7.3. According to occupations: worker

| Occupation | Worker | | |
|---|---|---|---|
| Variables | Number | General percentage | Special percentage |
| Do you have knowledge about the recent increase at custom duties made by the government? | | | |
| Yes | 44 | 78,351 | 84,615 |
| No | 8 | 21,649 | 15,385 |
| Total | 52 | 100 | |
| Do you support the increase of custom duties? | | | |
| I totally support | 0 | 2749 | 0 |
| I support | 5 | 12,372 | 9615 |
| I am indecisive/don't know | 1 | 6529 | 5882 |
| I do not support | 19 | 31,271 | 36,538 |
| I definitely do not support | 27 | 47,079 | 51,923 |
| Total | 52 | 100 | |
| Do you give a different answer if there is no COVID-19 pandemic? | | | |
| Yes | 5 | 10,309 | 9,615 |
| No | 47 | 89,691 | 90,385 |
| Total | 52 | 100 | |
| Do you have knowledge about the recent increase at the special consumption tax (SCT) of some goods made by the government? | | | |
| Yes | 49 | 93,471 | 94,231 |
| No | 3 | 6529 | 5769 |
| Total | 52 | 100 | |
| Do you support the increase of SCTs? | | | |
| I totally support | 0 | 1375 | 0 |
| I support | 1 | 3780 | 1923 |
| I am indecisive/don't know | 1 | 2405 | 1923 |
| I do not support | 12 | 25,430 | 23,077 |
| I definitely do not support | 38 | 67,010 | 73,077 |
| Total | 52 | 100 | |
| Do you give a different answer if there is no COVID-19 pandemic? | | | |
| Yes | 2 | 6186 | 3846 |
| No | 50 | 93,814 | 96,154 |
| Total | 52 | 100 | |
| Will you support if the government decide to increase other taxes for tackling down the COVID-19 pandemic? | | | |
| I will totally support | 0 | 0,687 | 0 |
| I will support | 3 | 2749 | 5769 |

(continued)

**Table 7.13** (continued)

| Occupation | Worker | | |
|---|---|---|---|
| Variables | Number | General percentage | Special percentage |
| I am indecisive/don't know | 1 | 3780 | 1923 |
| I will not support | 9 | 28,179 | 17,308 |
| I definitely will not support | 39 | 64,605 | 75 |
| Total | 52 | 100 | |
| Which taxes you would prefer to increase? | | | |
| Income tax/corporate income tax | 42 | 75,601 | 80,769 |
| Expenditure taxes (VAT-SCT etc.) | 10 | 24,399 | 19,231 |
| Total | 52 | 100 | |

**Table 7.14** Analysis of the answers given to the questions in Table 7.3. According to occupations: unemployed

| Occupation | Unemployed | | |
|---|---|---|---|
| Variables | Number | General percentage | Special percentage |
| Do you have knowledge about the recent increase at custom duties made by the government? | | | |
| Yes | 15 | 78,351 | 88,235 |
| No | 2 | 21,649 | 11,765 |
| Total | 17 | 100 | |
| Do you support the increase of custom duties? | | | |
| I totally support | 0 | 2749 | 0 |
| I support | 0 | 12,372 | 0 |
| I am indecisive/don't know | 1 | 6529 | 5882 |
| I do not support | 4 | 31,271 | 23,529 |
| I definitely do not support | 12 | 47,079 | 70,588 |
| Total | 17 | 100 | |
| Do you give a different answer if there is no COVID-19 pandemic? | | | |
| Yes | 1 | 10,309 | 5882 |
| No | 16 | 89,691 | 94,118 |
| Total | 17 | 100 | |
| Do you have knowledge about the recent increase at the special consumption tax (SCT) of some goods made by the government? | | | |
| Yes | 17 | 93,471 | 100 |
| No | 0 | 6529 | 0 |
| Total | 17 | 100 | |

(continued)

**Table 7.14** (continued)

| Occupation | Unemployed | | |
|---|---|---|---|
| Variables | Number | General percentage | Special percentage |
| Do you support the increase of SCTs? | | | |
| I totally support | 0 | 1375 | 0 |
| I support | 0 | 3780 | 0 |
| I am indecisive/don't know | 0 | 2405 | 0 |
| I do not support | 2 | 25,430 | 11,765 |
| I definitely do not support | 15 | 67,010 | 88,235 |
| Total | 17 | 100 | |
| Do you give a different answer if there is no COVID-19 pandemic? | | | |
| Yes | 0 | 6186 | 0 |
| No | 17 | 93,814 | 100 |
| Total | 17 | 100 | |
| Will you support if the government decide to increase other taxes for tackling down the COVID-19 pandemic? | | | |
| I will totally support | 0 | 0,687 | 0 |
| I will support | 0 | 2749 | 0 |
| I am indecisive/don't know | 1 | 3780 | 5882 |
| I will not support | 1 | 28,179 | 5882 |
| I definitely will not support | 15 | 64,605 | 88,235 |
| Total | 17 | 100 | |
| Which taxes you would prefer to increase? | | | |
| Income tax/corporate income tax | 16 | 75,601 | 94,118 |
| Expenditure taxes (VAT-SCT etc.) | 1 | 24,399 | 5882 |
| Total | 17 | 100 | |

All business owners are aware of the increase in customs duties, which is higher than the general population being close to 22%. The ratio of supporters realized above 19% was above 4% than the general population. The total rate of those who do not support was 2.5% higher.

The rate of awareness of the SCT increase was similar to the general population. As for supporting the increase in SCT, the rate of this support, which is over 9%, is 4% higher than the general population. Accordingly, the rate of those who do not support is 3% lower. But the remarkable part in this part of the table is the ones who definitely do not support, amounting to 51%. It is also noteworthy that business owners have a ratio of definitely non-supporters being 16% lower than the general population.

**Table 7.15** Analysis of the answers given to the questions in Table 7.3. According to occupations: business owner

| Occupation | Business Owner | | |
|---|---|---|---|
| Variables | Number | General percentage | Special percentage |
| Do you have knowledge about the recent increase at custom duties made by the government? | | | |
| Yes | 31 | 78,351 | 100 |
| No | 0 | 21,649 | 0 |
| Total | 31 | 100 | |
| Do you support the increase of custom duties? | | | |
| I totally support | 0 | 2749 | 0 |
| I support | 6 | 12,372 | 19,355 |
| I am indecisive/don't know | 0 | 6529 | 0 |
| I do not support | 10 | 31,271 | 32,258 |
| I definitely do not support | 15 | 47,079 | 48,387 |
| Total | 31 | 100 | |
| Do you give a different answer if there is no COVID-19 pandemic? | | | |
| Yes | 5 | 10,309 | 16,129 |
| No | 26 | 89,691 | 83,871 |
| Total | 31 | 100 | |
| Do you have knowledge about the recent increase at the special consumption tax (SCT) of some goods made by the government? | | | |
| Yes | 29 | 93,471 | 93,548 |
| No | 2 | 6529 | 6452 |
| Total | 31 | 100 | |
| Do you support the increase of SCTs? | | | |
| I totally support | 0 | 1375 | 0 |
| I support | 3 | 3780 | 9677 |
| I am indecisive/don't know | 0 | 2405 | 0 |
| I do not support | 12 | 25,430 | 38,710 |
| I definitely do not support | 16 | 67,010 | 51,613 |
| Total | 31 | 100 | |
| Do you give a different answer if there is no COVID-19 pandemic? | | | |
| Yes | 3 | 6186 | 9677 |
| No | 28 | 93,814 | 90,323 |
| Total | 31 | 100 | |
| Will you support if the government decide to increase other taxes for tackling down the COVID-19 pandemic? | | | |
| I will totally support | 0 | 0,687 | 0 |
| I will support | 2 | 2749 | 6452 |

(continued)

**Table 7.15** (continued)

| Occupation | Business Owner | | |
|---|---|---|---|
| I am indecisive/don't know | 0 | 3780 | 0 |
| I will not support | 14 | 28,179 | 45,161 |
| I definitely will not support | 15 | 64,605 | 48,387 |
| Total | 31 | 100 | |
| Which taxes you would prefer to increase? | | | |
| Income tax/corporate income tax | 16 | 75,601 | 51,613 |
| Expenditure taxes (VAT-SCT etc.) | 15 | 24,399 | 48,387 |
| Total | 71 | 100 | |

In the answers given to the government's question "Would you support another tax increase?", business owners differ from the general population as regards not supporting them. This ratio, which was 48%, was 14% lower than the general population.

More than 51% of the business owners answered the question of "Which taxes would you prefer to be increased?" supported direct taxes, being the group supporting direct taxes the least among the whole population and the group preferring indirect taxes the most among the whole population at a rate of at 48%. This can be explained by the fact that the taxes on spending that the business owners can charge to the final consumer are preferred based on more economic rationality than a tax increase that they will be directly assume along with the other population.

The self-employed are aware of the increase in customs duty 8% less than the general population. Those who supported this increase were 18% in total, being 4% higher than the general population, while the ratio of total non-supporters was 69%, being 9% lower than the general population.

The ratio of the self-employed being aware of the increase in SCT was 97%, pointing out a 4% higher awareness level than the general population. Understanding why awareness level of the self-employed, who are less aware of the increase in customs duty compared to the general population, is higher than the general population regarding the increase in SCT requires additional research.

With regard to supporting the SCT increase, the attitude of the self-employed did not differ significantly from the general population when asked whether they would support other tax increases by the government and which tax would they prefer to be increased.

The ratio of civil servants who were aware of the increase in the customs duty was 71%, the lowest among all groups. This is also seven points lower than the general population awareness rate. The total support given to the increase of the customs duty is also three points higher than the rate of the general population, being 18%. Consequently, the total rate of supporters was five points lower than the general population, amounting to 73%.

As for being aware of the SCT increase, civil servants answered yes at a lower rate than the general population. Here, the difference is two points, amounting to 91%. Again, the rate of those who did not support the increase in SCT was 88% for civil servants, remaining four points lower than the general population. Apart from these differences, no significant difference was found between the civil servants and the general population in the responses to Tables 7.16 and 7.17.

**Table 7.16** Analysis of the answers given to the questions in Table 7.3. According to occupations: tradesperson or self-employed

| Occupation | Tradesperson or self-employed | | |
|---|---|---|---|
| Variables | Number | General percentage | Special Percentage |
| Do you have knowledge about the recent increase at custom duties made by the government? | | | |
| Yes | 50 | 78,351 | 70,423 |
| No | 21 | 21,649 | 29,577 |
| Total | 71 | 100 | |
| Do you support the increase of custom duties? | | | |
| I totally support | 5 | 2749 | 7042 |
| I support | 8 | 12,372 | 11,268 |
| I am indecisive/don't know | 9 | 6529 | 12,676 |
| I do not support | 19 | 31,271 | 26,761 |
| I definitely do not support | 30 | 47,079 | 42,254 |
| Total | 71 | 100 | |
| Do you give a different answer if there is no COVID-19 pandemic? | | | |
| Yes | 8 | 10,309 | 11,268 |
| No | 64 | 89,691 | 90,141 |
| Total | 71 | 100 | |
| Do you have knowledge about the recent increase at the special consumption tax (SCT) of some goods made by the government? | | | |
| Yes | 69 | 93,471 | 97,183 |
| No | 2 | 6529 | 2817 |
| Total | 71 | 100 | |
| Do you support the increase of SCTs? | | | |
| I totally support | 1 | 1375 | 1408 |
| I support | 3 | 3780 | 4225 |
| I am indecisive/don't know | 2 | 2405 | 2817 |
| I do not support | 13 | 25,430 | 18,310 |
| I definitely do not support | 52 | 67,010 | 73,239 |
| Total | 71 | 100 | |

(continued)

**Table 7.16** (continued)

| Occupation | Tradesperson or self-employed | | |
|---|---|---|---|
| Variables | Number | General percentage | Special Percentage |
| Do you give a different answer if there is no COVID-19 pandemic? | | | |
| Yes | 3 | 6186 | 4225 |
| No | 68 | 93,814 | 95,775 |
| Total | 71 | 100 | |
| Will you support if the government decide to increase other taxes for tackling down the COVID-19 pandemic? | | | |
| I will totally support | 1 | 0,687 | 1408 |
| I will support | 0 | 2749 | 0 |
| I am indecisive/don't know | 2 | 3780 | 2817 |
| I will not support | 23 | 28,179 | 32,943 |
| I definitely will not support | 45 | 64,605 | 63,380 |
| Total | 71 | 100 | |
| Which taxes you would prefer to increase? | | | |
| Income tax/corporate income tax | 55 | 75,601 | 77,465 |
| Expenditure taxes (VAT-SCT etc.) | 16 | 24,399 | 22,535 |
| Total | 71 | 100 | |

There was no significant difference in the rate of awareness of the increase in customs duties between students and the general population. In terms of supporters of this increase, the ratios of the general population and students were very close to each other. However, while the total rate of non-supporters was 88% for students, this rate remained at 78% for the general population.

In terms of being aware of the increase in SCT, this rate was 84% for students and 93% for the general population, the difference being nine points. There is no serious difference between students and the general population in terms of supporting the SCT increase.

In the context of supporting the government to increase other taxes, the total support and total non-support rates were close to each other in students and the general population. The rate of those who said they definitely would not support was 46%, which made a remarkable difference, being 18 points below the general population (Table 7.18).

**Table 7.17** Analysis of the answers given to the questions in Table 7.3. According to occupations: civil servant

| Occupation | Civil Servant | | |
|---|---|---|---|
| Variables | Number | General percentage | Special percentage |
| Do you have knowledge about the recent increase at custom duties made by the government? | | | |
| Yes | 67 | 78,351 | 71,277 |
| No | 27 | 21,649 | 28,723 |
| Total | 94 | 100 | |
| Do you support the increase of custom duties? | | | |
| I totally support | 3 | 2749 | 3191 |
| I support | 14 | 12,372 | 14,894 |
| I am indecisive/don't know | 8 | 6529 | 8511 |
| I do not support | 30 | 31,271 | 31,915 |
| I definitely do not support | 39 | 47,079 | 41,489 |
| Total | 94 | 100 | |
| Do you give a different answer if there is no COVID-19 pandemic? | | | |
| Yes | 12 | 10,309 | 12,766 |
| No | 82 | 89,691 | 87,234 |
| Total | 94 | 100 | |
| Do you have knowledge about the recent increase at the special consumption tax (SCT) of some goods made by the government? | | | |
| Yes | 86 | 93,471 | 91,489 |
| No | 8 | 6529 | 8511 |
| Total | 94 | 100 | |
| Do you support the increase of SCTs? | | | |
| I totally support | 2 | 1375 | 2218 |
| I support | 4 | 3780 | 4255 |
| I am indecisive/don't know | 4 | 2405 | 4255 |
| I do not support | 25 | 25,430 | 26,596 |
| I definitely do not support | 59 | 67,010 | 62,766 |
| Total | 94 | 100 | |
| Do you give a different answer if there is no COVID-19 pandemic? | | | |
| Yes | 8 | 6186 | 8511 |
| No | 86 | 93,814 | 91,489 |
| Total | 71 | 100 | |
| Will you support if the government decide to increase other taxes for tackling down the COVID-19 pandemic? | | | |
| I will totally support | 1 | 0,687 | 1064 |
| I will support | 3 | 2749 | 3191 |

(continued)

**Table 7.17** (continued)

| Occupation | Civil Servant | | |
|---|---|---|---|
| I am indecisive/don't know | 5 | 3780 | 5319 |
| I will not support | 23 | 28,179 | 24,468 |
| I definitely will not support | 62 | 64,605 | 65,957 |
| Total | 94 | 100 | |
| Which taxes you would prefer to increase? | | | |
| Income tax/corporate income tax | 69 | 75,601 | 73,404 |
| Expenditure taxes (VAT-SCT etc.) | 25 | 24,399 | 26,596 |
| Total | 94 | 100 | |

**Table 7.18** Analysis of the answers given to the questions in Table 7.3. According to occupations: student

| Occupation | Student | | |
|---|---|---|---|
| Variables | Number | General percentage | Special percentage |
| Do you have knowledge about the recent increase at custom duties made by the government? | | | |
| Yes | 21 | 78,351 | 80,769 |
| No | 5 | 21,649 | 19,231 |
| Total | 26 | 100 | |
| Do you support the increase of custom duties? | | | |
| I totally support | 0 | 2749 | 0 |
| I support | 3 | 12,372 | 11,538 |
| I am indecisive/don't know | 0 | 6529 | 0 |
| I do not support | 9 | 31,271 | 34,615 |
| I definitely do not support | 14 | 47,079 | 53,846 |
| Total | 26 | 100 | |
| Do you give a different answer if there is no COVID-19 pandemic? | | | |
| Yes | 0 | 10,309 | 0 |
| No | 26 | 89,691 | 100 |
| Total | 26 | 100 | |
| Do you have knowledge about the recent increase at the special consumption tax (SCT) of some goods made by the government? | | | |
| Yes | 22 | 93,471 | 84,615 |
| No | 4 | 6529 | 15,385 |
| Total | 26 | 100 | |

(continued)

**Table 7.18** (continued)

| Occupation | Student | | |
|---|---|---|---|
| Variables | Number | General percentage | Special percentage |
| Do you support the increase of SCTs? | | | |
| I totally support | 1 | 1375 | 3846 |
| I support | 0 | 3780 | 0 |
| I am indecisive/don't know | 0 | 2405 | 0 |
| I do not support | 10 | 25,430 | 38,462 |
| I definitely do not support | 15 | 67,010 | 57,692 |
| Total | 26 | 100 | |
| Do you give a different answer if there is no COVID-19 pandemic? | | | |
| Yes | 2 | 6186 | 7692 |
| No | 24 | 93,814 | 92,308 |
| Total | 26 | 100 | |
| Will you support if the government decide to increase other taxes for tackling down the COVID-19 pandemic? | | | |
| I will totally support | 0 | 0,687 | 0 |
| I will support | 0 | 2749 | 0 |
| I am indecisive/don't know | 2 | 3780 | 7692 |
| I will not support | 12 | 28,179 | 46,154 |
| I definitely will not support | 12 | 64,605 | 46,154 |
| Total | 26 | 100 | |
| Which taxes you would prefer to increase? | | | |
| Income tax/corporate income tax | 22 | 75,601 | 84,615 |
| Expenditure taxes (VAT-SCT etc.) | 4 | 24,399 | 15,385 |
| Total | 26 | 100 | |

## 7.6 Conclusion

Our study focuses on determining how, in particular, the economic measures taken to combat the pandemic are perceived by the citizens and how an important crisis such as a pandemic affects tax perception of taxpayers. At this point, the first situation that draws our attention is that only 4% of the citizens find the measures taken regarding the pandemic adequate. We can interpret this as the willingness of citizens to comply with stricter measures. Considering that the ratio of citizens supporting economic measures is 13%, it is possible to utter the idea that the government should take more economic measures against the impact of the pandemic.

Another important point we have determined is that a significant proportion of taxpayers are aware of the recent customs duty and SCT increases. However, the awareness rate is not the same for both taxes, while 93% of the taxpayers are aware of the increase in SCT, this rate is 78% for the customs duty. We think that this difference can be explained by the higher sensitivity of the citizens to the changes in taxes which are more regularly encountered in life.

Again, there is a similar difference in the support rates given to the increase of these two taxes. Although the support for the increase in both taxes was low, the support given to the increase in customs duty was 15% higher. We think that one reason for this can be explained by the difference in being aware of the increase in taxes mentioned above, as well as the fact that the SCT is more visible in daily life than customs duty.

The ratio of those who support the government to increase other taxes to combat the pandemic remains at a seriously low point, i.e., 3.5%. This can be explained by the unwillingness of the taxpayers for a new tax, depending on their high subjective tax burden, or it can be evaluated as a taxation close to the peak of the Laffer curve in total taxation.

In the questionnaire, the answer to the question of "Which taxes would you prefer to be increased?", a two-option question, in the form of either one or the other, was the direct taxes, expressed as Income and Corporate Income Tax, amounting to the rate of 75%. The rate of those who preferred indirect taxes expressed by SCT and Value Added Tax (VAT) remained at 25%. Thus, instead of taxes on spending, which are likely to create a general cost of living, considered unfair in terms of tax justice and difficult to avoid, they have preferred direct taxes that are more appropriate in terms of tax justice and have no direct effect on the general cost of living. It is also possible to interpret this situation as taxpayers will prefer the increase in the share of direct taxes in total tax revenue, as happened in developed countries.

While 94% of the respondents stated that the budget deficit increased during the pandemic period, 90% stated that their purchasing power decreased compared to the pre-pandemic period. When we evaluate these two statements together, taxpayers who think that public expenditures are made in order to combat the pandemic and that this increases the budget deficit also think that these public expenditures do not increase their purchasing power and even do not ensure that their purchasing power remains constant. This can also be read as the citizens' wishes for some measures taken in a way to increase their purchasing power affected by the pandemic.

Which profession groups differ from the general is examined in the relevant sections. The point we especially want to emphasize in the conclusion is the existence of a general non-support for tax increases. This can also be evaluated as the need for tax deductions, being taking into account by the legislator and as a requirement of the opposition that is especially concentrated in taxes on spending. This will also serve to the need to increase the share of direct taxes in all taxes, similar to developed countries (Ay and Talaşlı 2008).

As for increasing the tax compliance, it may be beneficial to ensure that citizens, especially those with lower compliance, are represented at a higher rate and their requests are voiced through non-governmental organizations from the point of the legislative commission regarding taxes to the end of the legislative process and in the processes related to collection. Similarly, we think that reducing the high rate of taxes on spending within the collected taxes may increase tax compliance, provided that it is supported by policies such as increasing tax inspections. In order for the tax reporting lines, already established in many developed countries, to become operational and to ensure that the citizens realize that tax evaders steal from their own pockets and to make them report the evaders to the tax administration and also to ensure that the citizens understand that it is very different from spying and it is an important way to broaden the tax to the base and reduce the tax burden on individuals, explaining it to the media and through social media will also have a positive effect on tax compliance. The last and most important issue is the opinion of the taxpayers about the efficient use of taxes. Considering that the budget deficit has reached very serious levels, the taxpayers' expressing their demands during the budget preparation process through non-governmental organizations and the transparency will have positive effects on tax perception.

## References

Athar M, Ghazanfar SM (1998) Taxation as a form of worship: exploring the nature of zakat. J Acc, Ethics Public Policy 1(2):134–161

Ay HM, Talaşlı E (2008) Ülkelerin Ekonomik Gelişmişlik Seviyeleri ve Vergi Yapıları Arasındaki İlişki. Maliye Dergisi 154(1)

Ayrangöl Z, Tekdere M, Çadırcı BD (2019) Mükelleflerin Vergi Algılaması ve Vergi Psikolojisi Üzerine Bir Analiz: Erzurum İli Örneği. 2. Uluslararası Bilimsel Araştırmalar Kongresi, Erzurum

Ballas AA, Tsoukas H (1998) Consequences of distrust: the vicious circle of tax evasion in Greece. J Acc, Ethics Public Policy 1(4):572–596

Benk S, McGee RW, Ross AM (2009) An empirical study of ethical opinion in Turkey. J Acc, Ethics Public Policy 10(1):83–99. http://ssrn.com/abstract=1682606

Block W (1989) The justification of taxation in the public finance literature: a critique. J Public Fin Public Choice 3:141–158

Block W (1993) Public finance texts cannot justify government taxation: a critique. Can Public Adm/Adm Publique du Can 36(2):225–262

Çetin G (2007) Vergi Aflarının Vergi Mükelleflerinin Tutum ve Davranışları Üzerindeki Etkisi. Yönetim ve Ekonomi 14(2)

Çoban S, Çoban H, Sezgin S (2004) Vergi Mükelleflerinin Davranışları Üzerine Ampirik Bir İnceleme: Denizli Örneği. Türkiye'de Vergi Kayıp ve Kaçakları Önlenmesi Yolları. Türkiye 19. Türkiye Maliye Sempozyumu. Yaklaşım Yayınları, Ankara, pp 777–792

Crowe MT (1944) The moral obligation of paying just taxes, The Catholic University of America Studies in Sacred Theology No. 84

Doyle E, Kieran G, Mary C (2009) Procedural justice principles and tax compliance in ireland: a preliminary exploration in the context of reminder letters. J Finan Manage Public Serv 8(1)

Gergerlioglu U, McGee RW (2017) University students' attitudes toward tax evasion: a case study of the faculty of economics at Istanbul university. Researcher: Soc Sci Stud 5(5):383–407. http://rssstudies.com/Makaleler/1948943099_UfukGERGERL%C4%B0O%C4%9ELU-383-407.pdf

GİB (2019) Merkezi Yönetim Gelirleri. https://gib.gov.tr/sites/default/files/fileadmin/user_upload/VI/GBG/Tablo_18.xls.htm. Access date 10 Nov 2020

Kutbay H, Gerede C (2019) Sıçrama Tezinin Türkiye'de Geçerliliği: Darbeler Bakımından Bir Analiz. MANAS Sosyal Araştırmalar Dergisi 8(1)

Laffer AB (2004) The Laffer curve: past, present and future. The Heritage Foundation, No. 1765

Leiker BH (1998) Rousseau and the legitimacy of tax evasion. J Acc, Ethics Public Policy 1(1)

Machiavelli N (1993) Prens, çv. N. Güvenç, İstanbul: Anahtar Yayınevi

McGee RW (2014) Some thoughts on the ethics of parking profits offshore. J Acc, Ethics Public Policy 15(1):165–174
McGee RW, Gelman W, Tarangelo TJ (2014) How serious is tax evasion? An empirical legal answer. Indonesian J Int Comp Law 1(1):218–259
McGee RW, Benk S (2011) The ethics of tax evasion: a study of Turkish opinion. J Balkan Near Eastern Stud 13(2):249–262. https://datapro.fiu.edu/campusedge/files/articles/mcgeer1545.pdf
McGee RW, Benk S (2016) Attitudes toward tax evasion in Turkey: an empirical study. In: Mustafa Erdogdu M, Christiansen B (eds) Handbook of research on public finance in Europe and the MENA region. Hershey, PA: IGI Global, pp 299–318. http://www.researchgate.net303737564
McGee RW, Benk S, Yıldırım H, Kayıkçı M (2011) The ethics of tax evasion: a study of Turkish tax practitioner opinion. Eur J Soc Sci 18(3):468–480. https://datapro.fiu.edu/campusedge/files/articles/mcgeer1535.pdf
McGee RW, Benk S, Ross A, Kılıçaslan H (2012) Cheating on taxes if you have a chance: a comparative study of tax evasion opinion in Turkey and Germany. In: McGee RW (eds) The ethics of tax evasion: perspectives in theory and practice. Springer, New York, pp 357–369. http://link.springer.com/chapter/10.1007%2F978-1-4614-1287-8_22#page-1
McGee RW, Devos K, Benk S (2016) Attitudes towards tax evasion in Turkey and Australia: a comparative study. Soc Sci 5(10):1–13. http://ssrn.com/abstract=2741308
McGee RW (2012) Four views on the ethics of tax evasion. In: McGee RW (ed) The ethics of tax evasion: perspectives in theory and practice. Springer, New York, pp 3–33
McGee RW (2016) Should governments tax the rich and subsidize the poor? An empirical study of opinion in 60 countries. Working Paper. (Nov 24). http://ssrn.com/abstract=2875547
McGee RW (2017) Do the rich pay their fair share of taxes? An empirical study of United States data. Working Paper, (March 11). http://ssrn.com/abstract=2931527
Morales A (1998) Income tax compliance and alternative views of ethics and human nature. J Acc, Ethics Public Policy 1(3):380–399
Nadaroğlu H (1998) Kamu Maliyesi Teorisi. Beta Yayınları, İstanbul
Sağlam M (2013) Vergi Algısı ve Vergi Bilinci Üzerine Bir Araştırma: İktisadi ve İdari Bilimler Fakültesi Öğrencilerinde Vergi Algısı ve Bilinci. SosyoEkonomi Dergisi 19(1)
Smatrakalev G (1998) Walking on the edge: Bulgaria and the transition to a market economy. In: McGee RW (ed) The ethics of tax evasion. The Dumont Institute for Public Policy Research, Dumont, NJ, pp 316–329
Taşkın Y (2012) Vergi Psikolojisi ve Vergiye Karşı Mükellef Tepkileri. Maliye Araştırma Merkezi Konferansları 0/54 (Oct 2012), pp 67–90. https://dergipark.org.tr/tr/pub/iumamk/issue/793/8661 Access date 10 Nov 2020
Taylar Y (2010) Vergi Teorisi Açısından Özel Tüketim Vergileri ve Türk Özel Tüketim Vergisi Uygulaması. Dokuz Eylül Üniversitesi Hukuk Fakültesi Dergisi 12(S):435–467
Torgler B (2003) Tax morale: theory and empirical analysis of tax compliance. Dissertation der Universität Basel zur Erlangung der Würde eines Doktors der Staatswissenschaften
Tosuner M, Demir IC (2009) Vergi Ahlakının Sosyal ve Kültürel Belirleyenleri. Süleyman Demirel Üniversitesi İktisadi ve İdari Bilimler Fakültesi Dergisi 14(1)
TÜİK (2020) İstatistiklerle Kadın. https://data.tuik.gov.tr/Bulten/Index?p=Istatistiklerle-Kadin-2019-33732. (6 Mart 2020). Access date 10 Nov 2020
Vaguine VV (1998) The "Shadow economy" and tax evasion in Russia. In: McGee RW (ed) The ethics of tax evasion. The Dumont Institute for Public Policy Research, Dumont, NJ, pp 306–314
Yaltı B (2006) Vergi Yükümlüsünün Hakları. Beta, İstanbul

**Burhanettin Onur Kireçtepe** was born in 1988 in Erzurum. After high school, he continued his undergraduate education at Eastern Mediterranean University, Faculty of Law. He graduated as an Honour Student in 2009. After that, he also graduated as a High Honour Student from Anadolu University, Department of Public Finance in 2017. He gets his LL.M degree at the University of

Aberdeen in 2019 with the dissertation "How could Turkey's EIA Procedure Improve with the Help of Aarhus and Espoo Conventions?"

Burhanettin Onur Kireçtepe has articles and papers on different areas of tax law. He is currently a Ph.D. candidate at Public Law at Ankara Hacı Bayram Veli University, and He is working as a research assistant at Tokat Gaziosmanpaşa University Law School.

**Bernur Açıkgöz** was born in 1979 in Ankara. After attending Ankara Finance High School, she continued her undergraduate studies at Dokuz Eylül University, Department of Finance. She received her master's degree in Financial Law from Dokuz Eylül University. In 2006, she was awarded her Ph.D. degree from Dokuz Eylul University Department of Public Finance. Her Ph.D. thesis covered the topics of poverty and development. In 2006, she won the Harvard University Project scholarship and worked as a visiting professor at Harvard University. In 2009, she received a scholarship from the Swiss Government for a post-doctorate degree in economics at the University of Neuchatel/Switzerland, and taught courses at Bern Universities. She then began to work in the fields of experimental economics and game theory, and for three consecutive years as a guest lecturer in the economics laboratory of the Montpellier University in Montpellier, France. Afterwards, she went to Missouri University, Indiana University and Arizona University with a scholarship from Missouri University. She then worked as a visiting professor at the University of East Anglia and took some courses from Exeter Universities in the UK with a Tubitak scholarship. Professor Dr. Bernur Açıkgöz has books, articles and papers on foreign direct investments, economic growth, panel econometrics, experimental economics and game theory. She is currently working at the Department of Public Finance and Financial Management at Izmir Katip Çelebi University/Turkey. In addition, Açıkgöz teaches at the Department of International Trade and Finance at Izmir University of Economics/Turkey and the Department of Economics at University of Life Sciences in Poznań (Uniwersytet Przyrodniczy w Poznaniu)/Poland.

# Chapter 8
# COVID-19 Outbreak and Budget Management: An Assessment for Turkey Within the Framework of Selected Country Examples

**Elif Ayşe Şahin İpek and İbrahim Attila Acar**

**Abstract** The COVID-19 pandemic has affected the economy through supply, demand and confidence channels, causing recession. One of the financial tools used in the fight against the economic recession caused by the COVID-19 is the budget. In this study, the content of the budgetary measures, their transparency, legal infrastructure and their impact on the budget performance were evaluated. In this evaluation, the examples of France, Germany, England, Denmark, USA and Turkey were examined. The degree of quarantine measures (full quarantine, partial quarantine, mass immunity, etc.) was effective in the selection of countries. However, the limitation of the study is that the study covers the year 2020 and therefore cannot make cross-country comparisons in terms of the effect of the budgetary measures taken on the budget performance. As a result of the study, it is stated that the pandemic will continue to be effective on the parameters of the budget deficit, debt and interest burden for Turkey. It has been concluded that the differentiation between countries will emerge in terms of the transparency and legal infrastructure of the budgetary measures taken.

**Keywords** COVID-19 · Budget performance · Turkey · Public financial management · Public budget management · Budgetary measures

## 8.1 Introduction

At the end of 2019, COVID-19 outbreak that occurred in Wuhan, China's Hubei Province, affected the whole world and locked life (McKibbin and Fernando 2020). COVID-19 is the ninth epidemic in the last century. Given the health threat posed by COVID-19, it is one of the most serious epidemics since the Spanish flu epidemic in

E. A. Ş. İpek · İ. A. Acar (✉)
Department of Public Finance and Financial Management, İzmir Katip Çelebi University, İzmir, Turkey

E. A. Ş. İpek
e-mail: elifa.sahin.ipek@ikc.edu.tr

 
B. Açıkgöz and İ. A. Acar (eds.), *Pandemnomics: The Pandemic's Lasting Economic Effects*, Accounting, Finance, Sustainability, Governance & Fraud: Theory and Application, https://doi.org/10.1007/978-981-16-8024-3_8

1918 (Loayza 2020). Of course, national economies are also affected in this process. In this respect, it is an international emergency, given that it has gone beyond the effects of the 2008 economic crisis (Loayza 2020). Due to the epidemic, each country is making significant changes in its financial management by allocating some of its activities and budgets to this area in order to prevent and reduce the spread of the virus and to provide assistance to economically affected social groups (Jaelani and Hanim 2020). Approximately 30 million people have been infected as of September 2020 in 213 countries of the world, and the number of fatal cases has reached one million. Of course, it will have important social, political and economic effects, apart from the health aspect of this situation. COVID-19 outbreak, in general,

- Is a pandemic that affects all countries, regardless of whether they are rich or poor.
- Emerged in a period when economies slowed down, oil prices fell and interest rates reached the bottom.
- Triggers anxiety and fear on production supply, logistics and end consumers. Consequently, it creates the biggest break on employment.

The study encompasses the devastating effects of the epidemic as well as the measures taken and an evaluation of the measures taken in Turkey in terms of their budgetary burden. The current debt burden and the impact of the new package of measures on debt burdens will also be evaluated within this scope.

The main thing here is that the epidemic interrupts social life due to the isolation and quarantine measures, thus slowing down the economic life and leading to unfulfillment of liabilities. In this process, for example, while the UK was unresponsive to the epidemic and awaited "herd immunity", life in Denmark was completely stopped; France, Germany and Turkey gradually stopped economic life and restrictive measures were taken. As a result, it does not mean that the liabilities are suspended as the economic life stops. States should postpone its own receivables, give up some of it and make corporate or individual private liabilities sustainable through various financial facilities, and the unemployment problem to be experienced in this process should also be supported by various financing models. The study is important as it examines application of the mentioned various measures and models in different countries and addresses reflection of the measures taken in Turkey on the economy.

## 8.2 Outlook of the Pandemic and Necessity of a Public Intervention

World Health Organization Representative in China was notified of the outbreak on 31 December 2019. WHO named the disease COVID-19 on 11 February 2020, and as of 26 February 2020, the disease was detected on all continents, except for Antarctica. The organization declared a pandemic as of 11 March (McKibbin and Fernando 2020b). As of 20 September 2020, out of 30 million cases in the world 960 thousand people died. The epidemic continues and a second wave is expected.

Due to its epidemic nature, COVID-19 can cause collapse of any health system, as well as increase the mortality rates. Therefore, countries are unprepared and insufficient in terms of the number of hospitals, beds, intensive care units and equipment, and the number of qualified health professionals. This means that the number of patients that can be properly treated at any given time is limited. This scenario indicates that when a country's capacity is exceeded, it carries a higher risk of death. Hence, all countries are trying to reduce the rate of contamination and extend the contamination over time with different measures. This way, the health system will continue to exist and will try to reduce the mortality rates by means of treatment opportunities (Gourinchas 2020).

Although the social measures taken to slow the spread of the epidemic are similar across countries, the degree of these measures varies in terms of stopping economic activities. According to the classification made by Çakmaklı et al. (2020), it is possible to evaluate countries in four different categories, in which the degree of social measures, increasing number of patients and deaths, economic problems and public pressure are also effective:

i. Full quarantine (Denmark, New Zealand).
ii. Mass immunity (UK).
iii. Partial quarantine (France, Germany, Italy, Spain, Iran and Russia).
iv. Advanced partial quarantine (Turkey).

There are practices that differ between states in the USA. However, it is still the country with the most widespread epidemic and the highest number of deaths. Here, the fact that the epidemic is observed more in socio-economically inadequate regions triggers other discussions.

Table 8.1 below includes explanations regarding the social distancing measures taken by the selected countries according to the said classification.

These health measures taken by the public have yielded strong results in the short term. In this respect, these measures appear as correct policies that should be taken in the short term. However, in the short term, the flattening of the epidemic curve inevitably steeps the macroeconomic recession curve. Because of the increasing social distancing measures required the closure of schools, universities, and workplaces that were not a priority for social life, and therefore, most of the working-age population stayed at home. Although some of the active working population could work from home, this constituted a small part of the overall workforce. Even though working from home is an option, the short-term disruption of work and family routines has greatly affected productivity (Gourinchas 2020). This has caused economic recession across the world. However, according to Çakmalı et al. (2020), the economic costs of the epidemic were lower in countries that applied short-term but full restrictions.

**Table 8.1** Social distancing measures taken in selected countries to combat COVID-19

| France |
| --- |
| The COVID-19 outbreak started to spread rapidly in France at the end of February. This resulted in inadequate hospitals due to the relatively limited number of beds in intensive care units in some regions. Nevertheless, the rapid expansion of intensive care capacity and the transfer of some patients to less affected areas alleviated the bottleneck in the health system, but the capacity problem of the health system forced the authorities to take action from mid-March. Within the framework of the decisions taken, non-priority workplaces and entertainment facilities were closed and large-scale meetings were banned. In addition, day care centres, schools and universities were closed, and long-distance travels were banned. It was decided to gradually reduce these restrictions as of 11 May (OECD 2020: 200, 202). As of 22 June, most of the restrictions were lifted. Restrictions regarding large meeting organizations still continue and there is a requirement to use masks in public transportation. On 2 June, the government digital communication monitoring started (IMF Policy Tracker)<br>As 21 June, 160,377 confirmed cases, 29,640 deaths and 74,372 recoveries were reported after hospitalization |
| **Germany** |
| The first COVID-19 case in Germany was reported on 27 January 2020. The German government did not consider special measures necessary in the first place. However, as of 13 March, it resorted to restrictive measures. Accordingly, the German government closed schools and kindergartens, postponed academic terms and banned elder care home visits to protect the elderly. On 22 March, the government declared national curfew, allowing individuals to leave their living quarters for certain activities (shopping, sports, etc.). Public meetings with more than two foreign participants were banned between 22 March and 5 June, although they were implemented by loosening since 6 May. However, restaurants, businesses operating in non-priority sectors, and cultural and entertainment facilities were closed. Regulations on border controls that restrict the domestic mobility of citizens, including special regulations on seasonal agricultural workers and some vehicles, were introduced. Although meetings with broad participation were prohibited until 31 August, gradual opening of workplaces and schools was allowed as of April 20<br>As of June 29, Germany announced only 262 new cases and 4 COVID-19 deaths |
| **The UK** |
| The first case in the UK was reported on 28 February 2020<br>Social distancing restrictions started across the country on 23 March. In this context, all social events and meetings were banned and businesses operating in non-priority sectors were closed. The government announced that as of 13 May all bans will be lifted, with a gradual transition. Accordingly, in the first stage, it was decided to open some schools, open market places and car showrooms as of 1 June, and workplaces in other sectors as of 15 June. In the second stage, it was announced that the public spaces and personal care centres would be opened as of 4 July, provided that they comply with the guidelines on social distancing measures |

(continued)

**Table 8.1** (continued)

| |
|---|
| **Denmark** |
| The first case was reported in Denmark on 27 February 2020, and there was a rapid increase in the number of cases in early March. In the face of this increase, Denmark closed all overseas borders as of 13 March, banned all activities requiring more than 10 participation and closed schools, universities, personal care centres, entertainment canters, etc. Public personnel working in non-priority services went on leave, and all private sector enterprises were directed to work from home. On 6 April, officials announced that the restrictions would be gradually relaxed. Accordingly, in the first phase, some schools and health facilities were opened as well as self-employed workers from mid-April. The second phase started on 11 May and restaurants, retailers, other schools and cultural activities opened. As of June 15, it was announced that the borders with Germany, Iceland and Norway would be opened. In the third phase, it was announced that the 10-person limit previously envisioned for the events was increased to 30–50 people. In addition, the authorities began to work to ensure more populations were tested for COVID-19 as part of the reopening strategy |
| **The United States** |
| The first case was reported in the USA at the end of January, and restrictive health measures were initiated at the state level for the first time in California as of the end of March. Although these measures helped slow the upward trend of the epidemic, the rise in death rates was rapid. Under the measures taken at the state level, schools and workplaces that operated in non-priority areas were closed, and public organizations were prohibited. States have decided to lift restrictions, except for schools, restaurants and entertainment venues, from the end of April. However, it is difficult to say that the epidemic could be controlled |
| **Turkey** |
| The first COVID-19 case was reported in Turkey on 10 March 2020, and all schools and universities were closed on 12 March, distance education system was introduced. Curfew was imposed for people over 65 with chronic diseases as of 22 March. Later, the curfew was imposed for children aged 20 and under. Other measures include: strict restrictions on inter-provincial travel, postponement of all international flights, closure of businesses operating in non-priority areas, closure of recreation and entertainment venues, and prohibition of all meetings and organizations. In addition, public employees started to work from home, and businesses in the private sector were also sensitive to this issue. These restrictions were gradually removed from the beginning of June, provided that the criteria for social distancing rules were followed. The necessity to use masks outside the home continues from the beginning of the epidemic<br>Turkey reported, as of 25 June, that 3.1 million COVID-19 testing was conducted, 193.115 cases were detected and 5405 people died due to COVID-19. The Ministry of Health announced that an antibody test would be applied to 153,000 people randomly selected at the national level as of 15 June. Studies are continuing on alternative measure scenarios against the possibility that the epidemic attacks for the second time |

*Source* OECD (2020a, b); IMF Policy Tracker

## 8.3 Economic Trend of the Epidemic: The Necessity of Managing Expectations

In an idealized world, people will isolate themselves until the rate of contamination drops, and after the epidemic ends, the economic engines will re-engage. That is, workers will return to their jobs, factories will continue to work again, and the national and international trade network will start to function again. The point to note here is that even in an idealized world, the post-epidemic economic damage will be significant (Gourinchas 2020).

The fear of the spread of the epidemic and the health measures taken caused a global supply shock, especially in the manufacturing sector. The isolation of those who are infected has led to less consumption trends in tourism and entertainment sector, as other people reduce social contact. As employees and other consumers remained at home, businesses faced simultaneously falling supply capacity and falling income (Odendahl and Springford 2020). If this is not resolved with appropriate policies, it makes companies to face a decision to lay off or close (Odendahl and Springford 2020). Therefore, mismanagement of the process may cause the economic costs to be much larger and longer lasting (Gourinchas 2020) (Table 8.2).

While there may seem to be a trade-off between health and economic recession, it is not really a trade-off. There is not much to discuss in the face of unemployment and lost lives. In addition, even if there is no restriction, it will still cause an economic recession fuelled by cautious/panic behaviours of households facing the epidemic policy uncertainty where the public is inadequate. Fortunately, economic policy can act decisively to prevent these economic epidemics. The main purpose here has also been to flatten the curve and to keep the economic damage and the decrease in production at a certain level, due to the quarantine of the workforce (Gourinchas 2020).

### *8.3.1 Economic Impact of the Epidemic*

According to (Boone et al. 2020), the epidemic affects the general economy through supply, demand and trust channels to the economy. Accordingly, the COVID-19 outbreak brought supply and demand shocks with it.

**In terms of** supply, workers coming down with the epidemic, babysitters who are no longer needed due to the closure of schools and unfortunately, increasing death rates have led to a decrease in labour supply. However, the main impact of the epidemic on economic activities occurred due to social distancing restrictions and quarantines, leading to large decreases in capacity utilization rates. However, the slowdowns in international trade or the measures taken due to the epidemic have negatively affected the supply chain, increasing the production costs of the companies, resulting in a loss of productivity, and thus a decrease in economic activities. In this regard, China being a supplier of intermediate goods in the electronics, automobile, machinery and equipment industries for a significant part of the world played an important role (Gopinath 2020).

**In terms of demand**, loss of income, fear of epidemics and increased uncertainty have caused people to spend less and increase their tendency to save. Firms have become unable to pay their employees' salaries. These effects have been more severe for some sectors such as tourism and accommodation. In addition to these sectoral effects, the decline in the general consumption trend caused firms to expect lower

**Table 8.2** Economic effects caused by social distancing measures in selected countries

| |
|---|
| **France** |
| The French economy faced a deep recession as consumption and investment fell sharply during the restriction period. If the epidemic is limited to the summer period we are in, the real GDP is expected to decrease by 11.4% and grow by 7.7% in 2021. However, if the epidemic creates a second wave, the GDP is expected to fall by 14.4% in 2020 and will enter a recovery process with a rate of 5.2% in 2021. Increase in unemployment can be prevented with policy measures such as strengthened short-term work allowance. However, it is estimated that the unemployment rate will peak at the end of 2020 with a rate of 12.4% according to the first scenario and 13.7% according to the second scenario<br>Despite government support, investment and consumption will only gradually improve, as high uncertainty will remain. By the end of 2020, the fiscal deficit is expected to be 10.4% and 12.0%, respectively, according to the mentioned two scenarios, and the decline is expected to push the debt/GDP ratio to 116% and 126%, according to both scenarios, by the end of 2021 |
| **Germany** |
| Germany is experiencing a deep recession. If the epidemic is limited to the summer period, the GDP will shrink by 6.6% in 2020. However, in case of a second epidemic wave, it is estimated to shrink by 8.8%. Although the contraction in Germany was smaller than in other major European countries, trade confidence and activity indicators declined to low levels in April. Accordingly, industrial production decreased by 25% in April compared to the same month of the previous year. The share of the automotive sector in this decline is significant. On the other hand, real-time indicators show that economic activity has recovered but still remains below normal, as the restriction measures were eased in May |
| **The UK** |
| It is estimated that GDP will fall by 14% in 2020 in the event of a second epidemic wave in the UK. Even if the epidemic is limited to the summer period, it is estimated that the unemployment rate will double above 10% and the increase will continue until 2021. In this scenario, the measures to limit the effects of the crisis will increase the fiscal deficit up to at least 14% of GDP in 2020. The source of the expected shrinkage in the UK economy is explained by the fact that it is an economy based on the service sector and that this sector is most affected by the epidemic. Sectoral estimates reveal that staying at home measures will reduce production output by at least 1/3 |
| **Denmark** |
| In case of a second epidemic wave in Denmark, it is estimated that the shrinkage in GDP will be over 7% in 2020, and if the epidemic is limited to the summer period, the shrinkage will be 6%. The shorter duration of the restrictions compared to other countries has reduced the economic costs of the epidemic. Foreign demand will significantly affect the recovery path |
| **The United States** |
| The measures taken in the USA have resulted in an unprecedented sharp increase in unemployment, with workplace closures and households staying at home, causing a serious contraction in economic activity. More than 20 million employees lost their jobs in a month, much faster than during the 2008 Crisis or even the Great Depression. The unemployment rate rose to almost 15% in April. In the first quarter of 2020, GDP contracted by 5% on an annual basis |

(continued)

**Table 8.2** (continued)

| **Turkey** |
|---|
| Following the positive growth at the beginning of the year, the contraction in GDP is estimated to be 8% in 2020, in the event of a second wave in Turkey, and if the epidemic is limited to the summer period, the contraction is estimated to be 5%. It is estimated that the recovery will be gradual in 2021 |

*Source* Prepared by the authors using the information obtained from OECD (2020a, b, c, d) and IMF Policy Tracker

demand, and thus reduce their expenditure and investment tendencies. This resulted in business closures and layoffs (Gopinath 2020).

**In terms of confidence in the economy**, uncertainty causes a decrease in consumption of goods and services, and thus a decrease in investments. On the other hand, banks' expectation that individual consumers and companies will not be able to repay their loans on time may increase borrowing costs and tighten financial conditions. High borrowing costs and low interest rates will expose financial security gaps that have accumulated over the years, increasing the risk of non-rollover. The decrease in credit may increase the decline resulting from supply and demand shocks. When these shocks spread to other countries through financial markets, these effects could lead to a decline in global activity (Gopinath 2020).

## 8.3.2 *Combatting Economic Impact of the Epidemic*

### 8.3.2.1 Theory: Policies Suggested

As long as governments put into practice early and aggressive economic policies to support the liquidity of firms, balance workers' wages, protect and promote the financial system, there is a clear path to recovery. The following is necessary to this end: (i) supporting liquidity, (ii) clarifying lost wages, (iii) preserving the financial system and (iv) accelerating economic recovery (Odendahl and Springford 2020).

i. *Supporting Liquidity*

The biggest threat to the economy is the liquidity shortage and bankruptcy of important companies. Accordingly, temporary disruptions can have permanent effects: if companies do not successfully recover from the bankruptcy wave during the pandemic, future wages of the workforce and the companies' loss of information will have a permanent impact on the future level of production.

In order to overcome this risk, cooperation between the institutions that regulate the banking markets of the countries, public investment banks, central banks and finance ministers is important. Banking regulators should encourage banks to transfer existing loans to companies operating in industries severely affected by the recession. However, banks alone will not be able to alleviate companies' liquidity problems.

Extension of credit terms will cause banks to take risks. Public banks should provide incentive loans to more affected parts of the economy (Odendahl and Springford 2020).

Finance ministers should also provide liquidity support through fiscal policy. Companies have to pay labour wages under existing laws, even if they have to reduce production. Governments should consider methods such as short-time working allowances. Although practices such as short-time working allowances provide significant liquidity, they cannot cover all employees. Employees working on temporary contracts, self-employed and workers working without security constitute an important group that cannot be included in this scope. In this framework, in addition to the short-time working allowance, another option is to provide monthly income support to each citizen through private banks (Odendahls and Springford 2020).

On the other hand, to prevent the epidemic, many governments have decided to temporarily close educational institutions such as schools and kindergartens. This decision threatens the financing of families who have to take care of their children and therefore take unpaid leave from work. For this reason, it is necessary to make legal regulations by governments that allow employees with children to take paid leave.

In addition to these supports, further financial support can be provided by deferring the collection of certain taxes for a certain period (Odendahls and Springford 2020).

ii. *Protection of Financial System*

Regulatory and supervisory activities should be carried out with the aim of maintaining the stability and soundness of the banking system and maintaining its economic activities. Ultimately, the economic impact of the pandemic will affect borrowers' loan repayment capacity and reduce banks' earnings, which can undermine bank soundness and stability. Banks should be encouraged to use flexibility in existing regulations and to prudently renegotiate loan terms for problem borrowers. Supervisory authorities, on the other hand, should increase the monitoring of financial soundness and increase the frequency of dialogue with auditees, and prioritize discussions on business continuity planning and operational flexibility (Tosunoğlu and Kasal 2020).

iii. *Accelerating Economic Recovery*

After the epidemic, low demand will continue, especially in the service and tourism sector. Therefore, financial support will be needed especially in these sectors after the epidemic is over. Governments will not encourage people to travel, go to restaurants or attend large gatherings. However, governments could announce that once the epidemic is officially over, there will be, for example, a 6–9 month VAT reduction for the most affected sectors. This will also encourage banks to lend to these businesses (Odendahls and Springford 2020).

However, there is a risk that some governments will not be able to borrow the sums they need because they are already heavily indebted. Given the amounts likely to be required, there is a high risk of another possible loan (Wyplosz 2020).

iv. *Instruments and Budget Management*

In order to combat the economic recession caused by the epidemic, most OECD countries make commitments to support economic activities by increasing public expenditures, as well as resort to various regulatory activities and non-financial instruments. Measures taken be grouped considering what or whom they aim at: (i) the business world and employees, (ii) households and individuals and (iii) sectors (OECD 2020c).

One of the financial instruments is the budget, and countries affected by the epidemic have developed new approaches to budget allocation, depending on their public financial management systems. Ultimately, taking into account the impact of new economic and financial restrictions due to the epidemic, it is necessary to make new arrangements on the revenue side of the budget, on the one hand, and to make quick decisions on the expenditure side of the budget (Barroy et al. 2020).

#### 8.3.2.2 France

As of 24 March 2020, the French Parliament approved a law laying down France's 2-month "Emergency Health Declaration". By this law, the government is empowered to enact such measures, including soliciting people and property needed to combat COVID-19. Based on this mandate, the government is taking many new decisions for budgetary measures it plans to take to combat COVID-19, including the elaboration of supplementary budget laws approved by the parliament (OECD 2020c).

The budgetary measures that the government took to combat the COVID-19 outbreak were announced by the Head of Government on 12 March and became legal with the Supplementary Budget Law adopted on 23 March. A second supplementary budget was adopted in the second half of April.

The first Supplementary Budget Law revised the budget deficit as a ratio of GDP as 3.9% which had been estimated as 2.2% in the current budget. The increase in the budget deficit resulted from the revision of the positive 1.3% growth forecast, which is the basis for the current budget, as -1% contraction. Second Supplementary Budget Law envisaged the ratio budget deficit to GDP as 9%, as a result of the revision of the growth forecast as −8%.

The amount of budgetary measures envisaged by the Supplementary Budget Laws was estimated to be 45 billion euros and 110 billion euros, respectively (1.9% and 4.6% of GDP, respectively) (OECD 2020c). Measures in the said amounts are explained in the table below classified under the groups: measures for the health sector, measures for the business world and measures for employees.

These measures contributed to the 315-billion-dollar bank loan guarantee and insurance program. However, the total financial support increased to around 14% of GDP. The authorities announced that the financial support program would be phased out from June in sectors other than those that had difficulties in reopening the economy, such as tourism that benefits from wage support and solidarity fund, tax and social security premium exemptions for workers employed with reduced hours, and support to these sectors would continue until the end of 2020.

In addition, the authorities announced a second support plan for the most affected sectors. In this context, it was decided to purchase green vehicles and to provide green investment support for automobiles and aviation. However, a third arrangement, which increased the financial support package to 135 billion euros, is planned to come into force after June (IMF Policy Tracker).

#### 8.3.2.3 Germany

The support package named "Protective Shield for Germany" prepared, in two steps, by the Ministry of Finance and Economic Affairs was announced in order to reduce the economic effects of the COVID-19 epidemic. Accordingly, on 13 March, the government announced, as a first step, an initial support package that includes more flexible short-time working allowances, liquidity support through the state bank KfW and tax measures for companies. Ten days later, as a second step, the Protective Shield Package was completed with an expanded aid for the health sector, an emergency aid program for micro-enterprises and the self-employed, and an economic stabilization fund for large companies.

In addition to significant government guarantees, the package resulted in an supplementary budget of 156 billion euros (4.5% of GDP) for 2020. The supplementary budget included € 122.5 billion of additional expenditure and an expected loss of tax revenue of € 33.4 billion (OECD 2020c). As of 25 March, the German Parliament convened urgently and approved the Supplementary Budget Law and the Economic Stability Fund Act. The "debt brake clause" was abolished by parliament as the COVID-19 crisis was considered "an extraordinary situation beyond government control and with a significant impact on the financial situation" pursuant to Article 115 of the German Constitution. Parliament adopted a debt reduction plan that will begin in fiscal year 2023 (OECD 2020c).

Measures for the health sector, measures for households and measures for business provided for in Protective Support Package for Germany are given in the table below. Apart from measures that directly affect the government's financial balance, the Federal Budget provides a guarantee framework of approximately EUR 822 billion to expand the programs carried out by the German Development Bank KfW to provide liquidity to businesses. The KfW package relaxed business loan conditions for existing companies and assumed credit risks. The package includes applications such as "Start-up Loan" for companies under 5 years old, "Growth Loan" for larger companies and "Quick Loan Program" for SMEs with more than 10 employees.

Other financial measures include providing tenants with greater security in the event of delay in rent and utility payments (electricity, gas and telephone) due to the effects of the pandemic. In addition, the government suspended the obligation to file for bankruptcy by September 2020 (OECD 2020c).

#### 8.3.2.4 The UK

The first coronavirus case was reported on 31 January.

On 17 March, the prime minister established a new ministerial structure consisting of four implementation committees on health, preparedness, economy and international relations to coordinate the fight against COVID-19 outbreak. Members of the implementation committees—the Chancellor, the Ministry of Health, the Chancellor of the Duchy of Lancaster and the Minister of Foreign Affairs—attend daily C-19 meeting chaired by the prime minister and report (OECD 2020c).

The British Parliament was closed on 26 March, within the framework of the measures introduced against the COVID-19 outbreak, and on 21 April, and re-gathered in the budget legislative process. Parliament passed two laws which also passed Royal Approval before closing. The first of these laws is the Emergency Fund Law for 2020. This fund enabled the government to spend up to 48% of the 2019–20 expenditures (approximately 266 billion GBP) within the framework of combating COVID-19. The second law approved by the Parliament was the Coronavirus Law. This law identified five areas, namely increasing the capacity of the national health system, reducing the burden on healthcare personnel, reducing social contact, conducting burials of those who died due to the epidemic and supporting citizens, in order to strengthen the epidemic response plans. The law is in force for two years and empowers the government to take measures in these five areas to act on the recommendations of healthcare professionals (OECD 2020c).

The first budgetary measure of the government started on 11 March, which was announced at press conferences on Downing Street on 17, 20, 26 March and 8 April. Within the scope of combating the pandemic, the government announced a financial package estimated to amount to GBP 86 billion (4.1% of GDP) by the UK Budget Office (OECD 2020c). The measures put forward in this framework include extra financing for the health sector and public services, support for individuals, businesses and charities affected by COVID-19 and are explained in the table below. In addition to these budgetary measures, the Bank of England launched the "COVID-19 Corporate Finance Support" on 23 March, to provide liquid support to large companies reporting cash problems. In this way, the shares issued by the companies were purchased by the bank through printing money.

#### 8.3.2.5 Denmark

In Denmark, where the first COVID-19 case was reported on 27 February, all parties in parliament (Folketinget) supported the government's measures to use all necessary tools to combat the COVID-19 outbreak and amended the Danish Epidemic Law by expanding some powers of the prime minister (OECD 2020c).

The government announced the first package of measures to reduce the economic consequences of the spread of COVID-19 on 10 March. Accordingly, approximately 60 billion DKK liquidity support and state guarantee were provided to the economy, with the addition of 10% of GDP to the Consolidated Financial Support Program, which corresponds to 2.7% of GDP. In addition, the government made a commitment to provide the necessary support to the health sector, but did not specify an amount (OECD 2020c).

Four economic packages were implemented to provide direct cash support to workers and companies and to increase access to liquidity. In this context, emergency legislation supporting company liquidity by temporarily postponing compensation of event organizers, VAT and other tax liabilities of event organizers who had cancelled their events also took certain measures targeting the existing challenges in the transportation and tourism sectors (OECD 2020c).

Another financial support to combat the epidemic is expected to come from Denmark's powerful automatic stabilizers. The size of the support to be obtained here is expected to be 2.5% of 2019 GDP. However, postponing the investment programs included in the medium-term programs of local governments created an additional financial resource of 2.5 billion DKK.

Recently, the Danish authorities decided to extend the first fiscal measures until 8 July, resulting in an increase of DKK 30.7 billion in financial support and an increase of DKK 70 billion in guarantee and liquidity measures. On 19 May, the decision was made on the green renewal project of public housing (DKK 30.2 billion) in the period 2021–26. In addition, an additional DKK 0.8 billion was allocated to create public employment in health services and social services in June (IMF Policy Tracker).

#### 8.3.2.6 The USA

In the USA, the White House established the Coronavirus Task Force on 29 January to coordinate the fight by the administrations with the epidemic, following the first COVID-19 case reported in Washington State on 20 January.

On 13 March, the American President declared, based on the provisions of the Stafford Act, that the epidemic was a national emergency and that the federal government would use the Minister's Disaster Relief Fund (US $40 billion) to combat the epidemic. This statement prompted the Federal Emergency Management Authority. On 27 March, when there was a shortage of medical supplies at the national level, the president asked the General Motors Company to prioritize the production of ventilators for use in the treatment process, based on the provisions of the Defense Production Act of 1950.

Budgetary measures of the federal government were made possible by supplementary allocation laws approved by the US Congress. In addition to the Pay As You Go Act enacted in 2010, the enactment of three additional allowance packages provided an exemption from the rule that new expenditures can only be made through spending cuts or income increases. However, new measures were developed to monitor the implementation of allowances (OECD 2020c). In this context, the Independent Committee of Outbreak Healing Inspectors and the Committee for Combating the Outbreak were established under the Council of the Inspectors General on Integrity and Efficiency to monitor how the federal government's funds allocated to combat the epidemic were used (OECD 2020).

In the first stage, Coronavirus Preparedness and Response Supplemental Allowance Law (8.3 billion USD) was enacted; in the second stage, Families First the Fight Against Coronavirus Act (3.5 billion dollars) was enacted; and in the third stage, additional $2.2 trillion was provided for direct payments to taxpayers, emergency loans to distressed businesses, supplementary financing for the healthcare system, suspension of payments for federal student loans and revisions to student aid provisions. The government continues to work on the fourth package of financial measures. In response to the COVID-19 outbreak, the financial measures taken by the Federal Government are estimated to be US $2.2 trillion (10% of GDP). The Parliamentary Budget Office estimates that the country will exceed a $1 trillion budget deficit by the end of the year. In this context, the measures taken in the context of COVID-19 bring along a significant increase in the country's debt levels, reflecting the scale and gravity of the situation (OECD 2020c).

#### 8.3.2.7 Turkey

The first COVID-19 case in Turkey was reported on 10 March, but 31 days before the WHO declared the disease pandemic, the Ministry of Health established an Operations Center, and the Scientific Committee, which provided scientific opinion on the steps to be taken in the COVID-19 process, was established on the same date. According to the pandemic scenarios described, the healthcare professionals have not been allowed to take leaves and healthcare personnel and equipment plans have been made for each region. Thanks to the social distancing measures taken, 40% of the population has been effectively isolated. Curfew has been imposed, since 9 April, on weekends and public holidays for all age groups in 31 metropolitan cities, which constitute approximately 87% of the population, and entering or exiting these cities is not allowed on non-holiday days, as well. This way, it has been possible to control the rate of spread of the epidemic and the rate of increase in mortality.

Although the first peak of the epidemic was passed thanks to these efforts, intensive care bed occupancy rate reached only 6% and the ventilator occupancy rate reached only 5%. COVID-19 has not put pressure on the health system of Turkey (in aktob.org.tr/news(covid-19-salginina-karsi-mucadelede-turkiye-onde). This was mainly because of the fact that Turkey spent the last 15 years restructuring the healthcare system. In this context, new hospital capacities have been built, and thanks to the city hospitals built in recent years, 11 new hospitals with a total of 14,000 beds are planned to be put into service in 2020. In addition, major investments have been made in health information technology (aktob.org.tr/news(covid-19-salginina-karsi-mucadelede-turkiye-onde). In an environment of public health crisis, the Turkish state has prevented a potential crisis in health equipment by adopting the strategy for the development of health technology. Under this strategy, Biyovent domestic respirator was manufactured by Biosys company, as a result of 5 years of design and testing process, with the support of the

Ministry of Industry and Technology, TÜBİTAK and Bilkent University Cyberpark (TÜBİTAK, bilimgenc.tubitak.gov.tr/makale/turkiyenin-ilk-yogun-bakim-tipi-solunum-cihazi). Accordingly, the Ministry of Industry and Technology and the Ministry of Health brought three technology companies (Arçelik, Aseldan and Baykar Savunma) and Biosys company (Bakır 2020). This way, 5,000 ventilators were produced as of May with the purchase guarantee of the Ministry of Health.

The Ministry of Health announced recruitment of 32,000 new personnel.

Within the scope of efforts to improve the additional payments of healthcare personnel, it was decided to make additional payments without being subject to the principles determined by the regulation, for 3 months effective from 1 March 2020, to the personnel and managers working in the medical faculties of universities and health practice and research centres within the scope of research, diagnosis and treatment activities for the COVID-19 outbreak, provided that the scope and rate are determined by the university administrative board in terms of the location and personnel (aa.com.tr/tr/turkiye/saglik-personeline-ek-odeme-yapilmasina-iliskin-yonetmelik-resmi-gazetede-1777971).

On 24 March, Parliament adopted a law providing for amendments to certain laws in the economy under the Economic Stability Shield Program. The size of the Economic Stability Shield Package is 100 billion TL. Detailed information about the contents of the package is given in the table below. In addition, the president called on financial institutions to take the necessary measures to reduce the impact of COVID-19 on the economy, such as expanding credit terms and meeting the liquidity demands of businesses and individuals to sustain growth. Based on this call, three public banks initiated, on 30 March, a 6-month non-refundable Personal Consumer Loan to support households with a monthly income of less than 5,000 TL (OECD 2020c).

In addition to these measures, on April 15, the Ministry of Health launched a successful Contact Tracking Program to monitor the contacts of each new coronavirus case and subsequently prevent the spread of the disease. On 18 April, it launched the Pandemi Isolation Monitoring Project, which aimed to monitor whether the cases comply with the isolation measures. This operational capacity has been achieved thanks to the successful cooperation and coordination between different public and private sector organizations, including the Ministry of Health, Information and Communication Technologies Authority and GSM operators (Bakır 2020).

In June, the authorities stated that the measures taken against the epidemic with additional policy measures rose to 498 billion TL (10.8% of GDP), including deferred loan payments. In order to prevent speculative investments, the Banking and Insurance Transaction Tax rate was increased from 0.2% to 1% in foreign currency and gold purchases, and the withholding tax rate on interest income obtained by banks from commercial bonds was increased from 10 to 15%. Besides, again in June, a new law raised the upper limit of the Treasury's special purpose local government bond issuance from 3% of the 2020 budget revenue forecast to 5% (IMF Policy Tracker) (Table 8.3).

**Table 8.3** Financial support packages in selected countries

| Countries | Measures aiming at health sector | Measures aiming at business world | Measures aiming at employees and households |
|---|---|---|---|
| **France** | (i) Additional liquidity was provided to state hospitals by transferring the unused appropriations from the previous year's budget to the 2020 budget and bringing forward the 2020 appropriations<br>(ii) An additional appropriation of 0.5 billion euros was added to the budget to pay overtime wages of healthcare workers, to purchase sanitary equipment and to cover other health expenses<br>(iii) A 50 million euro Emergency Fund has been established to support research and development activities related to COVID-19 | (i) A "Solidarity Fund" was established to provide subsidies to small businesses with an annual turnover of less than 1 million euros and the self-employed. In order to benefit from the fund, it must be proved that the activities were completely interrupted or the annual turnover decreased by at least 70% compared to March 2019. The size of the fund is 7 billion euros, 5.5 billion euros of which is provided by the central government and 1.5 billion euros of which is provided by local governments<br>(ii) All businesses and the self-employed were granted the right to postpone taxes and social contributions without seeking any criteria. Small businesses can also postpone rent and utilities payments. In addition, the Ministry of Finance made a commitment to speed up the payment of the 2020 CIT and VAT refunds<br>(iii) The Second Supplementary Budget Law introduced a new liquidity support to businesses operating in strategic sectors through equity or nationalization. The budget package is around 20 billion euros | The main measure included in the Supplementary Budget is the payment of the salaries of all employees in reduced hourly employment. Although the reduced hourly employment plan was pre-existing under the French legal framework, salary compensation was exceptionally increased to 84% of each employee's net salary, with a ceiling of 4.5 times the minimum wage. The government's estimate of the cost of this measure in the Second Supplementary Budget Law is 24 billion euros, 16 billion euros of which are financed by central government and 8 billion euros of which by the Social Security Fund for Combating Unemployment |

(continued)

**Table 8.3** (continued)

| Countries | Measures aiming at health sector | Measures aiming at business world | Measures aiming at employees and households |
|---|---|---|---|
| **Germany** | The package allocated € 3.5 billion for information campaigns, the purchase of protective equipment and the promotion of vaccine development and treatment measures. The package also envisions an additional resource of 55 billion euros to give flexibility to the health sector depending on the development of the epidemic. The 2.8 billion euro protective shield envisaged for hospitals is foreseen to alleviate the loss of income and rising costs | (i) Emergency aid program for micro-enterprises and the self-employed (50 billion euros): This measure covers providing support up to 9000 euros to the self-employed and businesses with up to five employees. The main element of the support is that it is a non-refundable grant to cover 3-month operating costs<br>(ii) New Economic Stability Fund for large companies with more than 250 employees: This fund is an aid program that provides liquidity support by the Credit Restructuring Institute: (a) 100 billion euro capital increase, for example state partnership in the company capital to strengthen the company capital structure, (b) 400 billion euro guarantee support for company liabilities and (c) 100 billion euro support to refinance KfW bank programs<br>(iii) Tax measures for business: The government temporarily relaxed the rules on tax payment deferrals, including income tax, corporate tax and VAT. In addition, if the borrower is affected by the economic consequences of COVID-19, sanction measures regarding overdue tax payments were suspended until the end of 2020. On the other hand, some tax types such as energy tax and aviation tax were relaxed | (i) Conditions for short-time working allowance were relaxed to make short-time work flexible<br>(ii) The government compensating for some of the lost earnings of parents who are unable to go to work due to the closure of schools or childcare centres to support families, and facilitating access by short-time working parents to the child support fee for low-income families |

(continued)

**Table 8.3** (continued)

| Countries | Measures aiming at health sector | Measures aiming at business world | Measures aiming at employees and households |
|---|---|---|---|
| **The UK** | Although GBP 14.7 billion was committed as of 13 April with the unlimited commitment of the Chancellor, 5 billion GBP was allocated from the budget for the national health system and social services for patients | A budget of GBP 7 billion was allocated to support companies and employees. Later, this budget was increased through interest delays for companies and grants to small companies<br>With the Coronavirus Business Attendance System, measures such as 80% of workers' wages up to GBP 2500 per month are covered by the state, and support for the self-employed workers has been put into effect<br>Tax-related measures such as the postponement of VAT payments and tax benefits for the self-employed were also introduced<br>It aims to provide small companies access to financing by guaranteeing 80% of the loans used by SMEs within the scope of the Coronavirus Work Interruption Loan Program announced in the Budget. The scope of the program has been expanded with the Coronavirus Large Companies Loan Program | A GBP 750 million support package has been announced that provides cash support to aid organizations to help them continue their work during the COVID-19 outbreak<br>Measures were also taken to protect tenants and landlords. Accordingly, it was announced that out of those using mortgage, the loan payments of those who were in difficulty with payment loans would be postponed for 3 months, and then, this support was extended to landlords whose tenants had financial difficulties due to the epidemic |

(continued)

**Table 8.3** (continued)

| Countries | Measures aiming at health sector | Measures aiming at business world | Measures aiming at employees and households |
|---|---|---|---|
| **Denmark** | No amount available | In order to prevent large-scale job terminations, it was decided to cover up to 75% of the company's employee salaries and up to 90% of the wages of hourly employee<br>A total of DKK 10 billion was provided to the self-employed and a total of DKK 40 billion was provided to companies that lost income<br>Among the measures, there is support of 165 billion DKK, including 30-day VAT deferral and 4-month labour contributions and labour taxes cancellation<br>Under the envisaged support, access to the Export Credit Program and government guaranteed borrowing limits were expanded to assist small and medium-sized export companies. It was ensured that large companies had the opportunity of an additional credit of DKK 60.7 billion and through the Danish Export Credit Agency, medium and small-scale exporter companies were provided with an additional loan of 1.3 billion DKK within the scope of liquidity guarantees | A total of DKK 1.5 billion was designed to increase students' access to student loans<br>In case of bankruptcy of tour operators, a liquidity guarantee of 10 billion DKK was provided to SAS airline, which allowed Danish tourists to return home, and a state guarantee of 1.5 billion DKK was provided to the Denmark Travel Guarantee Fund |

(continued)

**Table 8.3** (continued)

| Countries | Measures aiming at health sector | Measures aiming at business world | Measures aiming at employees and households |
|---|---|---|---|
| **The USA** | With the coronavirus preparedness and response supplemental appropriations act, an emergency financing of USD 8.3 billion emergency financing was provided to federal agencies to develop vaccines and to provide medical supply and support to public health institutions and to support the health system<br>180 billion dollars were allocated for the funding of hospitals, public health institutions, community health centres and for the expansion of health insurance coverage<br>$150 billion was earmarked for local governments' efforts to combat the pandemic | A total of $959 billion, including $377 billion for small businesses and $582 billion for large businesses, was allocated to provide grants, tax cuts, loans and loan guarantees to distressed companies<br>$300 billion was reserved for tax cuts for individuals ($20 billion) and businesses ($280 billion) | With the Family First in Combating Coronavirus Act, an additional $3.5 billion was provided for free COVID-19 testing, paid sick leave, improved unemployment insurance, expanded food safety measures and increased the Federal Medical Assistance Fund. $592 billion was reserved to support household incomes. In addition, $260 billion was allocated for the expansion and extension of unemployment benefits and $42 billion for measures such as food stamps and housing support.<br>$32 billion were earmarked for the establishment of the Education Stabilization Fund for states, school districts and higher education institutions, as well as support for federal student aid |

(continued)

**Table 8.3** (continued)

| Countries | Measures aiming at health sector | Measures aiming at business world | Measures aiming at employees and households |
|---|---|---|---|
| **Turkey** | Grant support of 6 million TL to companies manufacturing local medical supplies (disinfectants, protective clothing, glasses and masks)<br>Completing city hospitals<br>Investments in information technology such as the establishment of an epidemic tracking system<br>Supporting ventilator manufacturing | VAT and social security payments were postponed for various sectors including retail, iron-steel, automotive, logistics-transportation, cinema-theatre, accommodation, food-beverage, textile-apparel and event-organization<br>Postponement of loan/debt repayments for companies affected by the crisis for at least 3 months<br>Extension of financial support for exporters, suspension of tourism accommodation tax until November, and reduction of VAT rate from 18 to 1% for domestic air transportation<br>The Treasury-backed "Credit Guarantee Fund" limit for the guarantee loans given to SMEs was increased to 50 billion TL<br>Providing a credit card with a limit of 25.000 TL to all tradesmen and traders<br>Turkey Wealth Fund was authorised to purchase shares of the distress firms | 2 billion TL additional cash assistance was provided to approximately 2 million families in need and 7 billion TL minimum wage support to minimum wage employees, according to the criteria determined by the Ministry of Family, Labor and Social Policies<br>On 7 April, a social transfer of 1000 TL was provided for 2.3 million households that did not meet the previously announced criteria and employees who lost their jobs<br>The lowest pension was raised to 1500 TL and a health program was developed for citizens over the age of 80 who live alone at home<br>The holiday bonus payments envisaged for retirees were taken forward from June to April<br>Application conditions for short-time working allowance were simplified |

*Source* Prepared by the authors using the information obtained from OECD (2020a, b, c, d) and IMF Policy Tracker

## 8.4 Evaluation

### 8.4.1 *In Terms of Legal Infrastructure of Budget Management*

In public financial management, flexibility and accountability in utilisation of budget appropriations are more important than ever under the exceptional conditions caused by the epidemic. Under these exceptional circumstances, governments and legislatures should ensure adequate budgetary funding by reprogramming existing appropriations and/or allocating additional funds. On the other hand, effective expenditure monitoring mechanisms should be established to ensure efficient use of resources and accountability. Finally, it is suggested that countries turn to external resources in line with certain objectives, while rapidly turning to budgetary processes in order to get a rapid response from internal resources (Barroy et al. 2020).

(i) In many countries affected by the epidemic, public financial management systems provide some flexibility for the executive to use budgeted appropriations. This flexibility is provided, for the budget and between administrations, through provisions that allow for allocation transfers between expenditure items or programs. In some countries, however, the existing legal framework allows some funds to be mobilized by the executive in emergencies. For example, the declaration of a national emergency by the president allowed the US administration to apply the Stafford Act, which regulates disaster relief efforts, allowing it to direct $50 billion of emergency funding to the states (Barroy et al. 2020).

(ii) In some countries, the top members of the executive, such as the head of state or the finance minister, exercise their regulatory authority to approve spending decisions for emergency response through existing budgets and simplified approval mechanisms. Indeed, in some European countries, heads of state or finance ministers have regulated the use of some allowances in combating the epidemic through decrees and other legal regulations (Barroy et al. 2020).

(iii) In some countries, state budget flexibility allows for increased financial transfers to local governments and procurement agencies. For example, state units in China were authorized for health expenditures, which increased the central budget transfers to the state of Hubei. Under normal circumstances, powers at this level should be evaluated within the state budget process or in a separate budgetary process. For example, in France, a separate legislative process is required for the National Health Insurance Fund, and France has approved a temporary budget increase of 2 billion euros in the fund to finance masks and tests (Barroy et al. 2020).

(iv) Existing flexibility in the use of budget resources can facilitate the spending process and the rapid response to the epidemic. However, the size of the resource needed often requires supplementary budgets. In some countries, the supplementary budget process has been accelerated, and the supplementary budget has been quickly approved by the legislature. However, from the perspective of budget formulation and structure in this process, the supporting documents should be as robust as possible (Barroy et al. 2020).

(v) In some other countries, spending plans are put into effect through the executive body using exceptional procedures without a new budget. For example, the process in China is managed by the Ministry of Finance Communiqués. With the communiqué published on 31 January 2020, it was clearly stated that the funds allocated to local governments should be used only for the control and prevention of the epidemic (Barroy et al. 2020).

(vi) It is important to use budgetary resources in a timely and effective manner in combating the epidemic. For this reason, some countries also facilitate the procedural steps related to the release of allowances. France, for example, has adopted a rapid expenditure authorization procedure to speed up the release of funds. According to the revised law, all allowances are automatically released. Other countries regulate such rapid spending authorization methods through supplementary budget laws.

However, despite the facilitation regarding the release of such appropriations, risk-based and/or ex-post controls are emphasized, especially for large-scale public procurement (Barroy et al. 2020). In addition to these controls, countries should strengthen their reporting and accountability mechanisms for resource use, while accelerating the release of funds and smoothing spending procedures. In this respect, a budget and reporting system based on program classification may be useful. However, here, it is also important to determine the program officer correctly. Ultimately, an expenditure program for combating the epidemic requires multi-actor cooperation, and more than one ministry and administration spend under this program. The general trend in determining responsibility is to assign the fiscal responsibility for the anti-epidemic program to the ministry of finance (budget) or to the prime minister. China, Germany and France have chosen this method. The new budget program in France is under the budget ministry, and the expenditures are carried out by various ministries and administrations and are accounted under the budget code declared by the budget ministry (Barroy et al. 2020).

### *8.4.2 In Terms of the Content of Budgetary Measures*

How the support provided by governments to combat the economic consequences of the COVID-19 pandemic is designed is important for the success of the post-crisis recovery process. OECD (2020d) recommends support packages that are time-limited, targeted, cash-based and consistent with long-term goals, in terms of sustainability. Accordingly, the seeds planted by the support programs carried out by the governments should not be of nature to create permanent market distortions in the future. Therefore, priority should be given to supporting the small enterprises operating in the service sector, and public investments should be focused on health and social security areas that initiate final consumption and benefit the whole society:

(i) One way to ensure that the necessary economic stimulus does not disturb the long-term market equilibrium is to provide the supports in a time-limited manner. This will help reduce the risk of support becoming established and going beyond its purpose.

(ii) Another point to note is that the supports should target the sector(s) and/or companies most affected by the epidemic, and it should exclude companies that would fail, even if there was no pandemic. This will reduce the risk of the stimulus leading to corporate structures that can limit competition, reduce domestic productivity growth, prevent economic recovery and increase economic inequalities. For example, the German Development Bank KfW provided guarantees of up to 90% for financially sound companies before 31 December 2019.

(iii) Who benefits from the supports is also important. In terms of demand, governments should turn to direct cash benefits from which end consumers can directly benefit, without interfering with the content of the demand. In terms of supply, attention should be paid to the market size and position of the companies in the supply chain when deciding on the companies to provide support. In terms of the market size of the company, it is recommended to support small and medium-sized companies, as they are not an impressive force in the market balance, despite the positive effect they create in terms of employment and social stability.

(iv) However, governments should consider support measures that have a double effect, without sacrificing long-term policy objectives for short-term economic incentives. Accordingly, even if countries try to control the economic and social consequences of the COVID-19 epidemic, for example, the change in shape continues to be a cause for concern. In this context, governments should align support measures more broadly with climate and environmental targets. More generally, support for companies should be designed to contribute to the maintenance of existing production capacity and innovation efforts to recapture R&D and personnel training expenditures that many companies have cut back during the pandemic. This approach can help minimize the damage that short-term shocks can bring to long-term growth and development potential. For example, many European countries announce their green purchasing policies in this process.

### *8.4.3 In Terms of Transparency of Budgetary Measures*

Perhaps the most important aspect of providing government support to a crisis is that governments are transparent about the measures they have adopted as well as their impact. Transparency is valuable for many reasons, including managing business prospects and focusing on guiding the actions of economic actors. Knowing that taxpayers' money is directed not only to large multinational companies but also to small and medium-sized companies, transparency about who benefits from support programs will contribute to public support.

More importantly, being transparent and knowing what countries are doing to stimulate the economy allow experience exchange. Detailed information on policies implemented and funds mobilized can help assess actual cost of government support and it can also provide lessons and insights about its efficiency (OECD 2020d).

## 8.5 In Terms of Budget Performance and Its Macroeconomic Results

The pandemic process stopping life, which is an important obstacle to the economy, is tried to be controlled all over the world through the measures taken. This way, it is intended to stimulate economic life and particularly unemployment. The most important tool for this is demand-side policies. Maintaining the purchasing power, production and demand is considered lifesaver for the economy.

The economic stimulus packages announced all over the world provide for compensation of the compulsory liabilities of the enterprises during the pandemic, no job loss in employment and supporting the segments with reduced purchasing power. Stable and regular income promises of some countries are stuck to various management levels.

Indicators in the economy will provide information about the actual situation from past to present. The determining effect of economic expectations, moral values and other intangible factors on the economy should not be neglected as well as the actual situation. This is also observed in many studies on the effect of the trust atmosphere on the economy. Therefore, the opinions that explain the economy as a result of expectations and positive developments are remarkable. The behaviours of the owners of the factors of production, formed by the information and impressions they receive from the markets, also shape the economy. The behaviour of decision-making units in the economy will also be a guide about developments. In this part of the study, evaluations will be made on Confidence Indices, Capacity Utilization Rates and Budget Balances.

### *8.5.1 Evaluation on Confidence Indexes*

We can have an opinion about the effect of the support structures in Turkey, by referring to the developments in Real Sector Confidence Index, Consumer Confidence Index and Economic Confidence Index. It is important, for the evaluations to be made by sectors, in terms of showing which sectors it affects. The great impact of

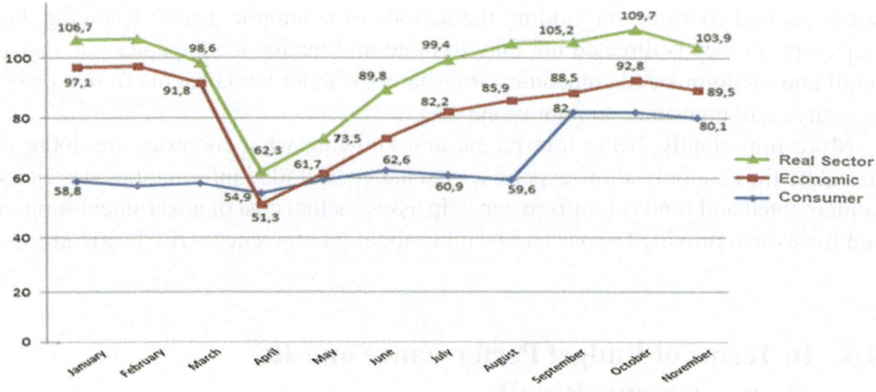


**Fig. 8.1** Trends of confidence index. *Source* It was compiled from TUİK data and prepared by US

the epidemic showed itself by stopping life in the second quarter of the year. Therefore, the pessimistic outlook drawn by all three confidence indices examined can be seen in the figure below (Fig. 8.1).

The first index to be evaluated under this title is the Consumer Confidence Index, which has been followed since the beginning of the pandemic, since all citizens are essentially consumers. Seasonally adjusted net consumer trends survey conducted in cooperation with Turkish Statistical Institute and the Central Bank of Republic of Turkey, monthly measures, by means of consumer trends survey, financial situation of consumers and current situation assessments of the overall economy. Future expectations, spending and saving trends are also included in this index. Confidence index reacted in the same way in times of great breakdowns during the pandemic. Its weight in the Economic Confidence Index is 20%.

All confidence indices calculated from the survey results take values between 0 and 200. 100 represents the mean. The fact that the consumer confidence index is above 100 reflects optimism in consumer confidence. A value under 100 indicates a pessimistic situation in consumer trust. The recovery in domestic demand is directly reflected in consumer confidence. The low level of consumer confidence compared to all other indicators for a long time caused the intervention by those concerned with the indicators and distribution. It is observed that the results of the new data set developed since September are also reflected in the index.

The second index to be considered is the Real Sector Confidence Index (RSCI). It is a survey that gives an idea about the general impression of real sector representatives on the economic outlook. In the real sector confidence index, which has a share of 40% in Economic Confidence, the answers given to different questions under the Business Tendency Survey are evaluated together. Considering the developments in Fig. 8.1, it is clear that industrial production continues to increase with the liberalization following the measures in the second half of the year. Especially since July, the reference value has been exceeded. It is observed that the demand has increased with

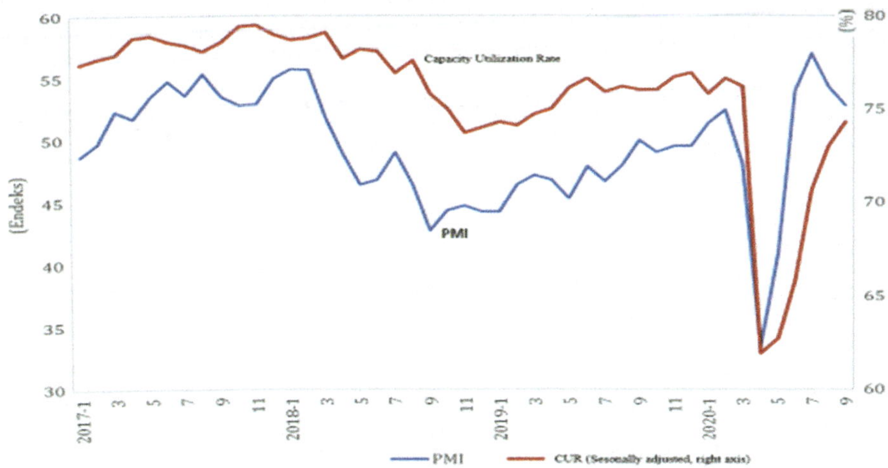


**Fig. 8.2** PMI and capacity utilization rate. *Source* Republic of Turkey Presidency Strategy and Budget Directorate (2020)

the effect of the economic support packages provided. As a result, the RSCI score exceeded 100 even in the pandemic period (Fig. 8.2).

Developments in Capacity Utilization Ratios also support RSCI developments. These developments in capacity utilization are important in showing how prepared the economy is to respond positively. The slowdown seen in all sectors during the pandemic process resulted in a rapid recovery response for some sectors. These observations for 24 sub-sectors show that 21 sub-sectors have recovered positively.

The developments, which include the developments in Capacity Utilization Ratios, together with the Purchasing Managers Index (PMI) results announced by the Istanbul Chamber of Industry, show that the process is parallel to each other.

The favourable outlook of the data on RSCI, PMI and Capacity Utilization Rates for the third quarter of the year is a result of optimistic expectations in industrial production. This will affect other developments in the manufacturing industry.

The recovery in domestic demand is observed towards the end of the second quarter, when the pandemic bans were relatively lifted, reflected in the figures. Growth figures from the second half have also accompanied this revival.

Undoubtedly, low levels of interest rates have been the trigger for economic activity. Thus, a consumption-side demand increase is observed in loan utilization rates. Especially, the cuts in loan interest rates in June, a development that affects many sectors together, increased sales from automotive to housing, from white goods to furniture and even to the tourism sector (Fig. 8.3).

However, considering to Turkey's employment structure, the largest share of employment belongs the services sector (55%). As regards the share of other sectors in employment, it is seen that the share of industry is 20%, agriculture 19% and construction 6%. Consequently, the services sector is naturally the sector that is highly affected by the pandemic process, since it includes tourism, entertainment,

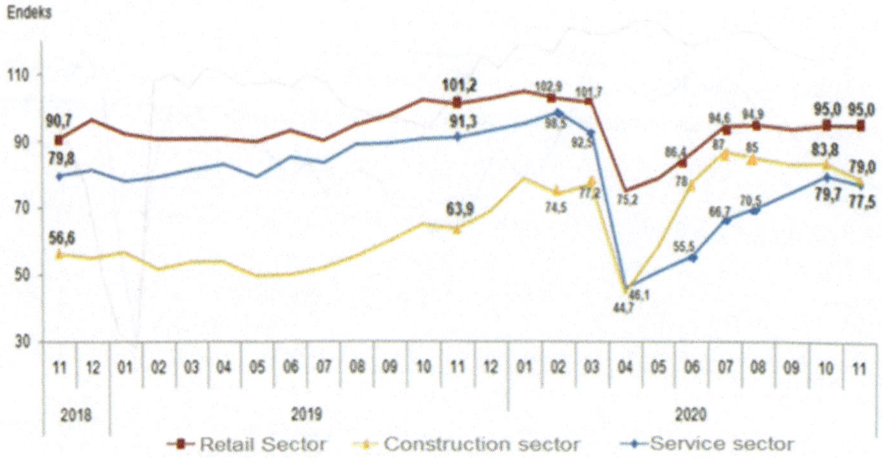


**Fig. 8.3** Sectoral confidence index. *Source* Prepared by the authors with the data obtained frım Turkish Statistical Institute

food and beverage. 2020 is a lost year for the industry. It is not possible to meet the expectations.

### *8.5.2 Evaluations on Credit Usage Rates and Tourism Data*

The recovery in domestic demand started to be reflected in controlled environments as of the second half of the year. Growth will be supported in this process. The reduction in loan rates, especially in June, has been a sign of revival, especially in automobile and white goods sales. The deferred consumption demand has also improved with low loan rates. In this period, it was observed that the Central Bank of Republic of Turkey interest rate cuts created an abundance of liquidity and limited the negative impact on funding costs. Consumption trend limited due to the pandemic has entered an increasing trend with low interest loans, whose usage have been facilitated. However, the negativity and uncertainties prevailing in the international markets undoubtedly suppress the domestic market.

As regards the loans/deposits balance, which shows how much of the deposits in banks are used as loans and which is one of the indicators of the long-term liquidity position of the sector, the deposits have been below the loans since the exchange rate spikes in 2018. It is observed that loans, which were above deposits in previous years, increased significantly, and it is led by the public banks during the pandemic (Fig. 8.4).

Tourism revenues, which have been deemed as *smokeless industry* for years and considered as an important revenue factor in the current account deficit, are far from expectations in 2020. Considering 2020 Tourism data, the number of tourists

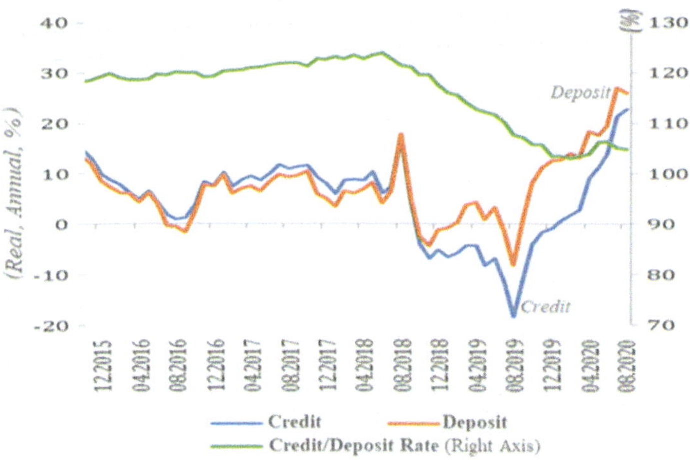


**Fig. 8.4** Credit and deposit rates balance. *Source* Republic of Turkey Presidency Strategy and Budget Directorate (2020)

and tourism revenues declined by 70% as of September compared to 2019, due to closures and since the tourists could not come. Year-end tourist expectation also increases the negativity in employment data. As a result, 3.5 million people actively working in tourism are either employed in other sectors or willing to agree to partial work allowance.

Achieving one-third of the Turkey's $50 billion tourism potential should even be seen as a great success for the current pandemic period. However, the weight of service sector in employment is considerably high in Turkey, as noted above. The sector most affected by the pandemic is the travel and tourism sector due to restrictions.

The tourism sector contributes to the current account balance, which should be evaluated separately. Especially in foreign trade, deficits arising from the balance of goods can reach 100 billion from time to time. However, tourism is an important resource in compensating these amounts. In this period, due to insufficient resources from tourism, it can be expected to have a negative result on the 2020 current account deficit balance of 20 billion dollars for now (Fig. 8.5).

### *8.5.3 Evaluations on Public Balances*

When Turkey faced the pandemic in 2020, along with the rest of the world, it had already been making effort, in 2018, to overcome the effect of the exchange rate experienced in 2019. Fight against inflation, which was the Turkey's main focus, was suddenly put to the backburner, and combatting the pandemic and its consequences came to the fore. However, the fragile nature of the ongoing financial stability and

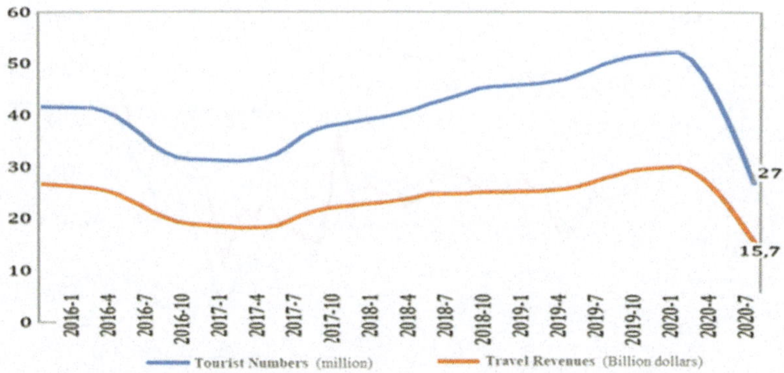


**Fig. 8.5** Tourist numbers and tourism revenue. *Source* Republic of Turkey Presidency Strategy and Budget Directorate (2020)

vulnerability, ongoing due to Turkey's geopolitical risks, has led to an exchange rate-interest impasse. As a result, an interest rate increase has become inevitable. In the short term, this will mean inflation. This means that all financial policy scenarios will have to be handled from scratch. It will not be easy to focus on growth on the one hand and become vulnerable to interest pressure on the other to curb the exchange rate and use all these tools during such a pandemic process.

It is not easy to combat the socio-economic effects of the pandemic that has been going on since March 2020, to manage this without cutting expenses while having income losses. The wide-ranging tax and cash supports announced by the state mean the state gives up some revenues, and cash supports can be interpreted as the continuation of expenditures. In addition, cheap loans offered with a low interest policy can be considered a kind of support. All these combatting policies have an aspect to increase budget expenditures and decrease the revenues. The compensation for declining budget revenues is also made through borrowing, which increases the state's debt burden (Fig. 8.6).

The pandemic process has caused a significant erosion in the state's revenue sources. Tax amnesty announced as required by the period will not be sufficient to compensate for the revenue. The budget deficit will continue, which is already seen in the 2020 realization estimates and projections for 2021.

The Maastricht Criteria, which the government has long regarded as a criterion, has been exceeded for 2020. The share of budget deficits in GDP is 4.9%. The general government deficit is 6.1%. Although 3% has been maintained for 2019, it does not seem easy to overcome the effects of this pandemic process in a short time.

The interest burden is increasing. The share of interest in budget expenditures is 11.3%. The interest approached again the main budget items such as education and health expenditures. Approximately 1/5 of the taxes is spent for interest, which means both insufficient tax collection and high interest expense. Decreases in the collection/accrual rates of taxes, especially during the pandemic, may also mean revenue and service weakness for the state. It is inevitable for the state which cannot

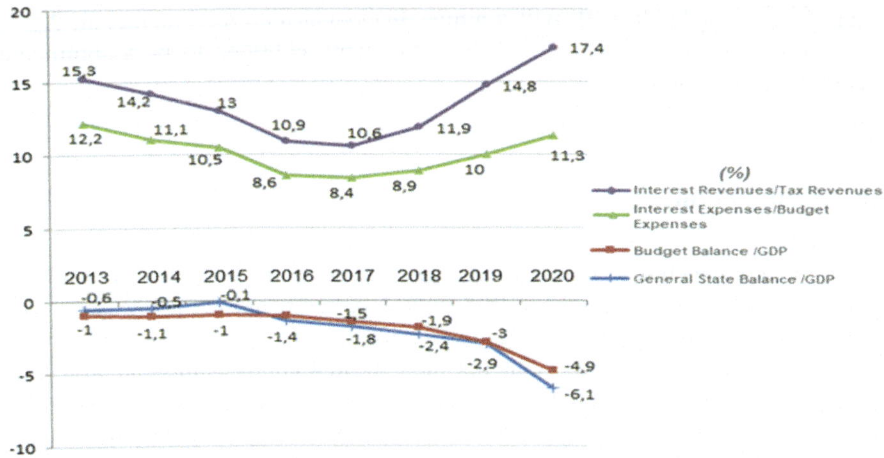


**Fig. 8.6** Budget balance and interest expenses. *Source* Republic of Turkey Presidency Strategy and Budget Directorate (2020)

collect taxes to borrow in this period. Therefore, borrowing will also increase interest expenditures.

### *8.5.4 Managing the Risks*

All the economies hurled by the pandemic in 2020 had the risk of losing their assets first. They could not fulfil their due obligations as well as their normal current liabilities. Speaking of loans, instalments and taxes, they also could not pay their dated cash debts. First of all, the businesses that defer their obligations due to the state both for themselves and through support packages have been effective in declining collection/accrual rates. This led the state, as the biggest decision-making unit and managing the crisis, to be more cautious and make controlled decisions considering its current revenue losses.

While businesses are trying to survive, "concentration in the service sector", which is a general trend in the employment of all developed economies, has been effective in the service sector coming to the fore as the most affected sector of the pandemic process. This rate is 52%, even for Turkey. Although it varies from country to country in Europe, the share of the services sector, which reaches 60%, in total employment, has decreased to 40% in this process. Job losses at the level of 15% are well above the current unemployment figures.

Although the positive atmosphere of the vaccine is promising, the destructive effects of the epidemic do not seem to easily recover in a short time. Even 2021 contains signs that this struggle will continue. Inadequate demand and income distribution disorders, especially ongoing unemployment, continue to be a significant threat (Pehlivanlı 2020).

## 8.6 Conclusion

The pandemic, which has created great economic pressures on states and millions of people across Europe and the world, will be remembered for many years with severe economic damage and the deaths it caused. While the first measures were taken against the epidemic, especially in China, the news of measures and protection packages were announced from the Eurozone and the European Central Bank (ECB), the Fed and from all over the world. New packages were announced before the other one was finalized. The packages announced in the first half of March 2020 have not been interrupted and it seems that they will continue. As the epidemic continues, it is necessary to develop compensation programs. On the one hand, continuing the economic activities and, on the other hand, the epidemic concern necessitates an international fight as well as a domestic one.

In this case, economically:

- The state will enter the market as a distributor and stabilizer, preventing the destructive damage.
- Tax revenues will not be collected, rather be postponed.
- The deterioration of budget balances will not be considered.
- Businesses and their employees will be protected.

New ones have been added to the protection and support measures of countries and supranational organizations. Although some countries are indecisive about the amount and scope of the new support, the support will continue.

Economic measures were also taken in Turkey while struggling for the prevention of the pandemic. State aids and credit opportunities were kept open. However, the devastating effect of the pandemic will still be seen after it is over. For now, lost jobs and closed businesses continue to be a problem. Although the state has given up taxes, as the pandemic continues, the due day is coming for deferred taxes. What matters is cash positions. The number of cities in Turkey capable of tax collection below 10% approaches to 20.

Stopping the epidemic and ensuring resuming the normal life is the primary goal. As the epidemic continues, the effectiveness of the support packages will decrease. Suspending the production is a temporary solution. Simply "stopping the life" without sticking to the measures against the pandemic will have many unintended consequences. Financial fluctuations from manufacturing to distribution and even to the retail sector must be brought under control.

Sectors such as automotive, white goods, clothing, airline, travel, iron and steel, which constitute the main branches of the industry, have certainly suffered greatly from this process. Naturally, the banking sector, which is fed by the real sector, seems to have been adversely affected by this process.

Cautious optimism will be the source of the upward movement for the markets. The second half of the year was more productive considering the BIST index. Recovery in financial sector is as much essential as it is in the retail, food and pharmaceutical sectors.

## References

Bakır C (June 2020) The Turkish state's responses to existential COVID-19 crisis. Policy Soc 1–18

Barroy H, et al. (2020) How to budget for COVID-19 response? A rapid scan of budgetary mechanisms in highly affected countries. March p4h.word/node/8821. Access Date 5 July 2020

Boone L, Haugh D, Pain N, Salins V (2020) Tackling the fallout from COVID-19. In: Baldwin R, di Mauro BW (eds) Economics in time of COVID-19. CEPR Press, UK, London, pp 37–44

Çakmaklı C, et al (2020) COVID-19 and emergency markets: the case of Turkey. Koç University—TÜSİAD economic research forum, Working Paper No: 2011, April

Gopinath G (2020) Limiting the economic fallout of the coronavirus with large targeted policies. In: Baldwin R, di Mauro BW (ed) Mitigating the COVID economic crisis: act fast and do whatever it takes. CEPR Press, UK, London, 41–47

Gourinchas PO (2020) Flattening the pandemic and recession curves. In: Baldwin R, di Mauro BW (ed) Mitigating the COVID economic crisis: act fast and do whatever it takes. CEPR Press, UK, London, 31–39

https://grcmngmnt.com/2020/12/24/2021-riskleri-ve-otesi

IMF, policy tracker. https://www.imf.org/en/Topics/imf-and-covid19/Policy-Responses-to-COVID-19

Jaelani A, Hanim TF (2020) Sustainability of public finances during the COVID-19 outbreak in Indonesia. Al-Amwal: Jurnal Ekonomi Dan Perbankan Syari'Ah 12 (1):109–123

Loayza NV (2020) Macroeconomic policy in the time of COVID-19: a primer for developing countries. WB research and policy briefs no: 28, March

Odendahl C, Springford J (2020) Bold policies needed to counter the coronavirus recession. In: Baldwin R, di Mauro BW (ed) Mitigating the COVID economic crisis: act fast and do whatever it takes. CEPR Press, UK, London, 145–150

OECD (2020a), OECD economic outlook, preliminary version, June

OECD (2020b) Tackling coronavirus (covıd 19): contributing to a global effort, https://www.oecd.org/coronavirus/country-policy-tracker/

OECD (2020c) Initial budget and public management responses to the coronavirus (COVID-19) pandemic in OECD countries, GOV/PGC (2020)/14, April

OECD (2020d) Government support and the COVID-19 pandemic

Pehlivanlı D (2020) Türkiye risk raporu

Republic of Turkey Presidency Strategy and Budget Directorate (2020) 2020 Annual Economic Report and Budget Statement for 2021

Tosunoğlu Ş, Kasal S (2020) Yeni koronavirüs (Covid-19) Salgını ve Sağlıklı Küresel Ekonomi İçin Politika Uygulamaları: IMF'nin Rolü. Anadolu Üniversitesi İktisat Fakültesi Dergisi 2(1):35–49

Warvick M, Fernando R (2020a) The economic impact of COVID-19. In: Baldwin R, di Mauro BW (ed) Economics in time of COVID-19. CEPR Press, UK, London, 45–51

Warvick M, Fernando R (2020b) The global macroeconomic impacts of COVID-19: seven scenarios. CAMA working paper, working paper no. 19/2020

Wyplosz C (2020) So far, so good: and now don't be afraid of moral hazard. In: Baldwin R, di Mauro BW (ed) Mitigating the COVID economic crisis: act fast and do whatever it takes. CEPR Press, UK, London, 25–29

**Elif Ayşe Şahin İpek** is an Associated Professor Doctor of Public Finance at İzmir Katip Celebi University, Faculty of Economics and Administrative Sciences. As of 2013, she started to work as head of Public Financial Management Chair at the Department of Public Finance. Her research focuses on public budgeting, public financial management and audit, strategic planning and performance management.

**İbrahim Attila Acar** has books, articles and papers on public strategic management, public financial management and control law (Law No: 5018), health and education economy, refugees crisis, auditing, financial management and budgeting. He was a member of the Specialization Commission in the Development Plans of 9–10 and 11 and involved in quality, effectiveness, university rankings, European University Association higher education assessment and rating studies in higher education. He worked as a panelist and independent evaluator of TÜBİTAK and Development Agencies. He participated in programs in written and visual media. He prepared and presented the Economic Agenda program at TRT for many years. The analyzes are located in its own website, acarhoca.com. He worked at Süleyman Demirel University for 10 years. And he is currently working at the Department of Economics, Faculty of Economics and Administrative Sciences at Izmir Katip Celebi University. He was the Vice Rector and the founding dean at the same university.

# Part III
# Pandemic and New Financial Trends

# Chapter 9
# Effects of COVID-19 Pandemic on Robot Employment and Digitalization in Employment

**Abdulcelil Gazioğlu, Zeynep Demirci Çakıroğlu, and Alper Doğan**

**Abstract** The COVID-19 pandemic has significantly affected all countries of the world in many areas since the first day it was seen. The virus, which was first seen in China, spread to other countries over time and was declared a pandemic on March 11, 2020. In order to tackle the virus, people were prevented from being in groups; events, sports competitions and conferences were cancelled; and distance education was started by using technology. The aim was to prevent people from coming together and to reduce the spread of the virus. As a result of the measures taken within the scope of struggling the COVID-19 pandemic, practices such as social distancing, lockdown and quarantine caused significant changes in social life, and also their reflections on the economy were negative. The slowdown in production, the increase in unemployment and the recession can be given as examples of these negative results. In this context, sectors that want to continue their economic activities have resorted to policies such as creating an unmanned work environment by making use of digital technologies or enabling people to work from home with the remote working method instead of working in the office. This situation has led to an increase in digitalization and automation in employment, which had a positive momentum before the pandemic. In the last twenty years, technology has reached a very advanced level in economy and employment, as in all areas of life. Digitalization in employment and employment of robots increase significantly every year, thanks to technological advances such as artificial intelligence, cloud technology and the Internet of Things. On the basis of these technologies, whose importance has increased considerably today, there is the knowledge and technology accumulation created by the industrial revolutions. All industrial revolutions, from the first industrial revolution to the present, have produced economic and social consequences.

A. Gazioğlu (✉)
Department of Budget and Financial Planning, İzmir Katip Çelebi University, İzmir, Turkey
e-mail: abdulcelil.gazioglu@ikcu.edu.tr

Z. D. Çakıroğlu · A. Doğan
Department of Fiscal Theory, İzmir Katip Çelebi University, İzmir, Turkey
e-mail: zeynep.demirci@ikcu.edu.tr

A. Doğan
e-mail: alper.dogan@ikcu.edu.tr

 
B. Açıkgöz and İ. A. Acar (eds.), *Pandemnomics: The Pandemic's Lasting Economic Effects*, Accounting, Finance, Sustainability, Governance & Fraud: Theory and Application, https://doi.org/10.1007/978-981-16-8024-3_9

Especially, the mechanization in agriculture has caused many people to be unemployed. Today, the advancement of automation and robotic technologies has increased the use of these technologies in employment. As a natural consequence of this, as many international research institutions have reported, it is predicted that in the near future, occupations made by people today will be completely automated and unemployment will increase. Since applications such as social distance, full closure and quarantine, which entered our lives due to the COVID-19 pandemic, have brought production to a halt, many sectors have sought ways to carry out their activities with as few people as possible by shifting their investments to digital technologies. In this context, while unmanned aerial and ground vehicles are used more widely for contactless delivery, it is planned to meet the needs of people without creating crowded environments with measures such as remote working and online trade.

In accordance with these policies carried out to prevent the COVID-19 pandemic, remote working has been adopted in many sectors and has brought the necessity of robots to the agenda. In this context, the question of "should robots be taxed", which started to be discussed before the COVID-19 pandemic, becomes more important. In addition, whether or not to pay social security premiums for robots has been one of the issues that started to be discussed. At the same time, due to the possibility of unemployment of a large part of the population with the increase in robot employment, the issue of providing a certain amount of monthly income to people to meet their basic needs with the universal basic income application is emphasized. A financing is needed for this income transfer to the unemployed population. In this context, it is claimed that robots should be taxed. One of the reasons for the taxation of robots is that robots do the same work with people who work in the factory and are subject to tax on their income. Another reason is stated as ensuring the equality of competition between the company that employs the robot and the company that does not. However, besides these views, there are also those who argue that robots should not be taxed. As automation increases, production volume will increase, so it will positively affect economic growth. In addition, since more production means purchasing more raw materials, finished products and semi-finished products, people who employ robots will indirectly pay more taxes. It can be seen that taxation of robots is a new discussion topic. If digitalization and automation continue at the speed it has reached with the effect of COVID-19, it will be discussed more and its theoretical foundations will be completed in the near future.

**Keywords** Industry 4.0 · Automation · Digitalization · Robot employment · Robot tax · COVID-19

## 9.1 Introduction

The COVID-19 outbreak, which has become the most important agenda item in the world after its emergence, has had significant effects on economy and social life. This outbreak emerging in December 2019 and spreading to millions of people all around the world except for a few countries costed hundreds of thousands of lives by March 2020. Each country has implemented various measures by creating its own policies in order to, first, slow down and stop the spread of the COVID-19 outbreak which is spreading very quickly and against which there is no treatment methods such as vaccines or drugs. As a result of measures such as quarantines, curfews, social distance, hand hygiene and the obligation to use masks, social life has changed and restricted considerably. Naturally, these restrictions also affected working life, resulting in new working arrangements. Digital service and employment of robot workers, which is on the rise with the introduction of the Fourth Industrial Revolution, played a key role in the efficient use of production facilities in this new working order. In this part, we will briefly mention industrial revolution, the development of the Fourth Industrial Revolution and the progress of robot employment and digitalization in employment, especially over the last 20 years. We will discuss how the changes in working methods resulting from the measures taken against COVID-19 outbreak, such as working from home and digital services, have affected the rising graphic of digitalization in employment and robot employment. We will also suggest some solutions for possible economic problems that may arise with the increase of robot employment.

The COVID-19 outbreak, which affects the whole world and introduces new concepts and practices into our daily life, has not only had great effects in health and social life, but also brought many new practices in the economy. The measures taken in Turkey to reduce the rate of spread and stop the outbreak set by "Coronavirus Science Committee", namely quarantine, social distancing, hygiene and mask, have adversely affected the economy in the short term. In many sectors operating efficiently in the economy, primarily in the food and accommodation sectors, services and activities were temporarily suspended and partially reopened after the effect of the virus began to decrease. In this process, important developments have been made in the field of employment. Many working models such as working from home, digital service and online commerce have been used more widely than ever before. The importance of robot employment has been recognized in heavy industry, which has been adversely affected by the COVID-19 outbreak and where production has almost stopped.

This study mentions industrial revolutions and technological innovations brought along and then focuses on the participation of robots in economic and daily life. The study examines the places that robots have been given in employment and their development in this field. The effects of the COVID-19 outbreak on the economy, digitalization in employment and robot employment are discussed. In addition, public intervention scenarios regarding the solution of problems that will possibly arise as a result of robotization in employment and the unemployment that it will cause are evaluated.

## 9.2 Industrial Revolutions and Robots

The concept of robot was first used in a theatre play written by Karel Capek in 1921 (Barutçuoğlu 2001: 1). Robot can be named as machines that have the ability to perceive, learn, plan and act in order to interact with their environment (Gök 2019). At the same time, robots can work directly under the control of an executive, as well as at the command of a standalone computer software or with artificial intelligence.

Although robotization seems to have increased rapidly over the last two decades, it is essentially the last part of a much longer process/evolution. Robotization is the last point of the ongoing stages since the First Industrial Revolution. The foundation of the First Industrial Revolution is based on the invention of the steam engine by Thomas Newcomen in England in 1712. The use of the steam engine invented by Newcomen in the textile industry is called the First Industrial Revolution. The production that was previously carried out on weaving looms was quitted, and machine production was started after the First Industrial Revolution. Upon including the machinery in production, iron and steel and textile production increased, while overproduction has accumulated significant capital in industrializing countries. In the same period, the development of railway networks also caused the effect of the revolution to spread and further increase in production (Alçın 2016: 20).

The mechanization of production after the First Industrial Revolution and the continuous advancement of technology in the following years paved the way for the Second Industrial Revolution. For this reason, the Second Industrial Revolution that occurred between 1840 and 1870 is also known as the technological revolution. With the development of technology, the development of transportation networks, the provision of raw materials in a shorter time and the provision of access to distant markets are due to the effects of the Second Industrial Revolution. At the same time, the development of electrical technology and its use in transportation enabled the development of mechanization that emerged with the First Industrial Revolution. Considering the widespread use of iron and steel as raw materials, it can be said that the heavy industry developed with the Second Industrial Revolution (Eğilmez 2017).

Two world wars and the 1929 Economic Depression in the first half of the twentieth century slowed down the technological developments, but in the 1950s, digital technology started to develop and the foundations of the Third Industrial Revolution were laid. Computer and digital production technologies started to be used in production, and technological small household appliances started to be used in homes. In other words, with the development of computer and information technologies, mechanization leaving the factories and taking its place in daily life also coincides with this period (EBSO 2015: 6).

With the technology that has remarkably changed and developed in the last decade, discourses of the transition to the Fourth Industrial Revolution, also known as Industry 4.0[1], have started to emerge, because the machines managing themselves and their

[1] Industry 4.0 is a concept that begins with shifting from the invention of steam machines to the process where the machines are able to manage themselves and their production processes without the need for manpower in the industry and is expressed in 2011 Hannover Fair (EBSO 2015: 7).

production processes without the need for manpower show that we have gone beyond the Third Industrial Revolution and passed to the Fourth Industrial Revolution. With the Fourth Industrial Revolution, systems that require serious technology such as robots leaving factories and entering daily life, cloud technologies, big data and cyber-physical systems started to be made and used. However, these developing technologies bring some problems with them (EBSO 2015: 7).

The production style that changed with the First Industrial Revolution mechanized the workforce to a great extent and caused a decrease in the need for manpower, leaving workers unemployed for a long time, especially in the agricultural field (Küçükkalay 1997: 62). It can be predicted that a similar process can be repeated with the Fourth Industrial Revolution, because the use of mechanization to a large extent and the intensive use of robots in production and in daily life may leave employees unemployed in the future, as was the case in First Industrial Revolution.

According to the studies of the World Economic Forum, within the next 5 years, too many working people face the possibility of unemployment due to the increase in the inclusion of robots in production. Many companies will reduce the number of people they employ due to the decrease in the need for people in certain occupational groups or such professions will completely disappear. However, there will be professions that are emerging or developing due to the developing technology. These data were obtained as a result of the survey conducted by the World Economic Forum on 371 companies. World Economic Forum researchers evaluated the results by taking into account the possibility of unemployment due to technological transformation, as well as conditions such as climate changes and natural resources constraints (WEF 2016: 50). Occupational groups expected to shrink according to the results of this research: office and administration, manufacturing, construction and mining, painting, design, entertainment, sports and media, law, assembly, and maintenance and repair. New professions predicted to be born or professions predicted to develop are education sector, computer and mathematics, sales and management, architecture and engineering, trade and financial transactions (WEF 2016: 11–12).

Considering the report of the World Economic Forum, a similar unemployment problem that occurred in the First Industrial Revolution seems likely to emerge in terms of our recent past. Especially, the technological transformation experienced with the Fourth Industrial Revolution is the signal of innovation and change to a great extent. Because robots may appear in many different areas in daily life. However, certain issues have begun to be discussed around the world since they will be used intensively in production. As a matter of fact, the starting, development and completion periods of the industrial revolutions have been shorter with each new revolution. While the first two revolutions completed these processes within a period of nearly a century, the Third Industrial Revolution developed and completed in a relatively short time. The Fourth Industrial Revolution, on the other hand, radically changed the production facilities and daily life activities in a very short time compared to other revolutions.

## 9.3 Place of Robots in Employment and Their Development

Robot technology has been used in employment since the day it was developed and has been a part of the production factor. Artificial intelligence, automation and robotic technologies, which have reached a very advanced level with Industry 4.0, have begun to replace human power, and the emerging new economic system has been defined as "robonomics" (Ivanov 2017: 284). New generation robots, defined as collaborative robots and expressed with the term cobots (are the assistant of workers, especially in the automotive sector), significantly increase both speed and efficiency (Kurt and Bozoklu 2019: 28). Boston Consulting Group, conducting revolutionary work in this technological field, sees autonomous robots as the power to change industrial transformation. In addition, it is told that the technology of "Internet of Things"[2] may leave millions of people unemployed, primarily unskilled workers, in the future. The increase in industrial robot purchases confirms this. It is understood from the reports of international financial associations such as the World Economic Forum and the International Monetary Fund that the share of these technologies in employment is increasing. According to the report of the International Federation of Robotics (IFR), the number of expert service robots increased to 271,000 in 2018, with a 68% increase compared to 2017, which was 168,000 back then. Market sales values reached 9.2 billion dollars. The sectors where this increase was experienced the most were the logistics and production sectors, where the use of autonomous vehicles increased by 41% (IFR 2019a: 11). In 2018, the world average of the number of industrial robots used for every 10,000 employees was 99. The fact that the world average, which was 48 in 2010, increased more than 100% in 8 years indicates that robots will spread rapidly in production and other sectors in the future. In this area, Singapore is at the top with 831 robots, while South Korea follows it with 774 robots. Germany, one of the countries with the largest production capacity, ranks first with 334 robots in Europe. In the same report, it was estimated that the number of robots, which was 422,000 in 2018, will reach 584,000 in 2022 (IFR 2019b).

In order to understand the position of robots in employment, it would be appropriate to mention Amazon GO, the unmanned store established by Amazon. This store, where every transaction in the store with no check-out or cashier is carried out by cameras and sensors and shopping is completed through the application, gives some clues about the future. Likewise, the autonomous robots used by AliExpress, one of the largest online shopping sites in the world, in storage and logistics prove that worker robots are being used more effectively. However, it is not possible to say that robot employment always produces satisfactory results. In Henn Na Hotel, which was established in Japan in 2015 and had only 7 human employees, many services such as guest welcoming, luggage carrying and reception services were provided by robots, but this application was abandoned after a short time due to the low performance of robots (Zeng et al. 2020: 6). Although robots are not considered

[2] Internet of Things can be defined as, "*a network structure where devices or machines communicate data, collect information and decide with the collected information without the need for human intervention and manual input of any data*" (Gündüz ve Daş 2017:328).

sufficient, they successfully perform services such as cleaning, catering and carrying luggage in many hotels with the developing technology. In addition, considering that significant progress has been made in studies on unmanned aerial, land and sea vehicles, it is predicted that in the near future, we may come across with many more servant robots in daily life.

It is estimated that this transformation will cover 50% of the current world economy and affect more than 1 billion employees, especially in countries such as the USA, China and India. In some studies, it is thought that the number of employees who will be dismissed by 2030 will be between 400 and 800 million, while it is predicted that 75 to 375 million of these employees will find new job opportunities (Manyika et al. 2017: 11). If 41% of the employees in the USA cannot gain new competencies according to the new working order by 2026, it is expected that they will have narrow job opportunity, such as only three business lines, at best (Gökalp et al. 2019: 207). In fact, besides all these predictions, the report prepared by the World Economic Forum best summarizes how the new order will change the world. In the said report, it is estimated that 65% of the children who attend primary school today will not work in current jobs (WEF 2016: 32).

Industry 4.0 made a rapid development compared to previous industrial revolutions and covers many sectors. While the First Industrial Revolution affected the transportation sector and agriculture sector, the Second Industrial Revolution had its effect on heavy industry. However, the Fourth Industrial Revolution, which was realized by using the knowledge and technology accumulation created by the prior industrial revolutions, made great and important changes in every field from agriculture to heavy industry, from tourism to food sector and from transportation to service sector in a period as short as ten years. With the COVID-19 outbreak, the use of autonomous robot technology and digital service understanding introduced by the Fourth Industrial Revolution has peaked.

The pandemic period in which robot employment or digitization in employment increased rapidly, in fact, has proved that the economy has an infrastructure in this regard. It would be appropriate to discuss to what extent the role of robot employment and digitization in employment has changed in reducing economic impacts in the case of COVID-19 outbreak and similar outbreaks.

## 9.4 Economic Impact of COVID-19 Outbreak

The COVID-19 outbreak, which emerged in China in December 2019 and spread globally in a very short time, has become the world's most important agenda item due to its medical, economic and social effects. In fact, this pandemic has introduced bans, restrictions and new regulations all over the world in many areas from education to health, from economy to social life. The impact on employment of the outbreak whose economic, political and social consequences are discussed to be too large to be compared with previous outbreaks, may be the most striking issue during the peak periods of the pandemic. Within the scope of the measures taken in this process, many workplaces were closed, and many continued their activities with limited production opportunities. The importance of the issue is quite apparent at this point. While some of the institutions or organizations that continue their activities digitally (such as online trade websites, banks, retail sector, technology sector, e-government and many public institutions serving on the Internet) have made a significant growth compared to the pre-pandemic period, there are also companies continue to operate at the same or lower capacity than the pre-pandemic period. The reflection of this situation in the economy has gradually emerged with the end of the first quarter of 2020. As a matter of fact, the USA, which leads the countries most affected by the pandemic, and Italy experienced an economic contraction of 4.8% and 4.7%, respectively, in the first quarter of 2020 (OECD 2020).

Another macroeconomic indicator through which the impact of COVID-19 outbreak is felt significantly in the world economies is unemployment. Employees in sectors that experienced moderate and high levels of decline in production levels due to the pandemic took unpaid leave or lost their jobs. Although employers were supported to stop layoffs in many countries of the world with the economy recovery packages, unpaid leaves and layoffs could not be prevented at the desired level. Unregistered workers, which are common especially in developing countries, are the employees most affected by the pandemic (Kara 2020: 272). Another group most affected has been the "Gig"[3] economy, which includes short-term jobs created by the increase in freelance opportunities and available through digital platforms. In this economy, which covers short-term and project-based jobs such as freelance photography, caregiving and house cleaning, the number of employees in the USA reached 55 million in 2018 (ILO 2018). In the study conducted on the pandemic, it was revealed that more than half of the workers (52%) in the global gig economy lost their jobs and 26% started to work for a shorter time (Kara 2020: 273).

The COVID-19 outbreak, which brought many innovations to our social life, also brought innovations to business life. As a matter of fact, many private and public institutions have made it compulsory to work from home in order to maintain social distance and prevent people from coming together and creating a crowded environment. Before the pandemic, the number of people working from home was quite low in the world economy, in countries other than Denmark, Sweden and Norway. In fact, according to the research conducted in OECD countries in 2015, the rate of those who work from home at least once a year is 20%, while the rate of those who work from home at least once a month is only 5% (OECD 2016: 6). In the USA, this rate is 24.8% for 2017 and 2018 (U.S. Bureau of Labor Statistics 2020). However, with the measures taken during the pandemic, there has been a significant increase in the number of people working from home. The rate of working from home rose to 39% in March and April 2020, when the effects of the crisis were the highest in the USA. Considering that not all professions and jobs are suitable for working from home, the increase in this ratio becomes even more meaningful. Finance, insurance, education, scientific and technical services, and company and

[3] It is the economy of freelance people working on digital platforms that allow short-term and project-based jobs in many sectors, with the development of digitalization.

**Table 9.1** Impact of COVID-19 Outbreak on Sectors

| Sectors | Level of Impact |
|---|---|
| Accommodation and Food | High |
| Production | High |
| Wholesale and retail trade | High |
| Art-Sports-Entertainment and other services | Medium-High |
| Transport and Communication | Medium-High |
| Construction | Medium |
| Finance and insurance services | Medium |
| Agriculture and forestry | Low-Medium |
| Education | Low |
| Human health and social security services | Low |

*Source* ILO Monitor: COVID-19 and the World of the work

business management have been the most suitable working areas for working from home. Transportation, construction, agriculture and forestry are among the jobs that are not suitable for working from home (Kara 2020: 275). Table 9.1 is created using the report prepared by the International Labour Organization on the exposure levels of the production activities of the sectors during the COVID-19 outbreak.

As shown in Table 9.1, sectors that require human labour such as accommodation and food sector wholesale and retail trade have been the sectors most affected by the crisis. Sectors such as arts-entertainment-sports and transportation that bring people together and provide services that people can benefit from in large groups are among the sectors most affected by the crisis. Sectors such as the banking and finance sector and the education sector that can continue their activities through digital channels were among the least affected by this crisis. The fact that they have digital service opportunities such as mobile banking, Internet banking and distance education that people can easily benefit from has contributed that. The digitalization in employment, the increase in robot employment and the fact that the sectors that are compatible with new service activities are much less affected by the crisis caused by the COVID-19 outbreak will lead other sectors to prefer to be more compatible with these new service and production activities.

Digitalization and the increase in robot employment will change the perspective of sectors towards these production elements, perhaps in the period when similar epidemics are predicted every decade in the future (WEF 2019: 6), because today's cloud data storage system, Internet speed and widespread network, Internet of Things, unmanned aerial vehicles, driverless private and public transport vehicles, 3D printers, the technology of humanoid robots and autonomous robots show that digitalization in employment and robot employment can be used much more widely in many more sectors. In the light of these predictions, new and modern policies should be followed in addition to traditional policies for unemployment or new employment order to be created by robots and digitalization.

As seen and happened in the COVID-19 outbreak, digitalization and robot employment continue to be actively used in various sectors. In fact, the pandemic has seriously increased robot employment. This increase in robot employment requires predicting the possible effects on the economy and making arrangements accordingly. In this context, it would be beneficial to address the robot tax issue, which was highly emphasized and discussed in 2017.

## 9.5 Robot Tax

With the technology brought by the Fourth Industrial Revolution, robots and digital service activities that are included in every moment of our daily lives have brought the employment of robots onto the agenda, and the necessity of robots and their advantages compared to human employees in the new working order created as a result of the measures taken against the COVID-19 outbreak started to draw more attention. At this point, the measures that can be taken against the problems that new members of employment will cause in the economy, such as unemployment, have been among the most discussed topics in recent years.

One of the most striking suggestions on robot-related issues that started to be discussed before the COVID-19 outbreak was Bill Gates' proposal that "robots should also be taxed" in an interview he gave to the Quartz news site in 2017.[4] Apart from this, the necessity of paying the social security premium for robots is another matter of discussion (Worstall 2016). At the same time, it is recommended to put in place a "Universal Basic Income" in order to prevent the population from being unemployed due to the development of robots. Universal Basic Income practice means every citizen of a country receives a certain amount of monthly wage that they can use to meet their basic needs (Riley 2017). However, it is important to keep track of the monthly income provided to the people or to ensure that people who are likely to be unemployed maintain their lives with this wage at a minimum level. For this reason, the robot tax application is also discussed for financing the income transfer to the unemployed.

Before evaluating the necessity/justification of robot tax, it is necessary to remember the classical taxation understanding and taxation principles. Tax is the monetary amount received from real and legal persons, based on the right of sovereignty, as non-quid pro quo and on the basis of law, in order to meet the public expenditures of the state or organizations authorized by the state (Çakır et al. 2006: 154). Although the purpose of tax collection is mostly financial, taxes are also collected for non-financial purposes such as combating cyclical fluctuations, reducing injustice in income distribution, combating environmental problems and supporting population policies.

---

[4] https://www.ft.com/content/d04a89c2-f6c8-11e6-9516-2d969e0d3b65 Date of access: 05.08.2020.

There are certain principles that must be followed in order to avoid any mishaps when collecting the taxes. These principles can be broadly divided into two: the classical principles determined by Adam Smith and today's modern taxation principles.

There are four classical taxation principles determined by Adam Smith: equality (fairness), certainty, convenience and efficiency (Ay 2014: 168–169). Apart from these four principles determined by Adam Smith, there are also principles accepted in today's modern taxation understanding. These principles are principles of generality, fairness, efficiency, legality, certainty, stability in tax, economic efficiency and flexibility (Bilici and Bilici 2011: 140–141).

In the 2000s, some changes were experienced due to technological development. The widespread use of electronic commerce has brought about structural changes in taxation. In addition, not being indifferent to technical developments, states have also developed applications such as e-government, e-finance and e-tax (Hepaksaz 2011: 1).

The developments in the Fourth Industrial Revolution and the widespread use of robot technology have brought up the issue of whether robots can be taxed.

As stated, Bill Gates came up with the idea of collecting some kind of tax on robots considering too many robots employed in companies (Delaney 2017). In other words, companies will pay taxes and social security premiums for the robots they employ in their companies, and the state will be able to make human capital investments such as health support, retirement, social security and education for people with these taxes collected from companies. The basic logic of Gates in this regard is that a robot that can do the same job should be taxed in the same way as the human labour working in return for a certain wage in a company or factory and taxed at a certain rate. After Gates' comment, many people around the world started to discuss the issue of taxation of robots. However, although this proposal is accepted by certain groups, there are also those who oppose this view.

The discussion on "Should the robots be taxed?" did not remain on the philosophical or theoretical grounds and was carried to the European Parliament in 2017. In the draft text submitted to the European Parliament, it was stated that robots should be given identification numbers and classified as "electronic persons" in order to be subjected to social security premium payment, and the employers or owners of robots considered as electronic persons should be obliged to pay taxes. However, while saying yes to the robot law, the European Parliament rejected the robot tax by majority vote.[5] Even if it was rejected by the European Parliament, the issue of the taxation of robots continues to be discussed by all parties.

First of all, in the classical economic system, production factors consist of labour, capital, natural resources and enterprise. Technology has also been added to these production factors in recent years. Tax is imposed on the income, wealth and expenditures obtained from these factors. In this sense, in the classical taxation approach,

---

[5] http://www.ticaretgazetesi.com.tr/indexx.php?f=3bd704e38fe839ba454b3702e36cc6b3&l=1&sayfa_id=666&g_id=&id=420713 Date of access: 05.08.2020.

as mentioned above, there are taxes levied on expenditures, taxes levied on income and taxes levied on wealth.

If tax is collected from robots, this tax can be considered as taxation on income, because as for the taxes on income, the taxable event is the income of the person. In this sense, taxation can be made by assuming that the robots earn an income as a result of working in a factory or a company.

Another method of taxation might be quota application. The maximum amount of production that can be reached through human labour should be determined and it should be ensured that this amount is subject to a regular taxation for robots. For the portion exceeding this amount, taxation can be made from the upper tranche, similar to the progressive tariff. This is also important in terms of ensuring the principle of fairness in taxation.

Taxing the robots can be beneficial to ensure equality of competition between the company that employs robots and the company that does not. Apart from robot tax, mechanical security premiums, similar to social security premiums, can be collected from robots in order to cover costs such as breakdowns, replacement of parts and renewal and maintenance of robots. However, it should be ensured that mechanical security premiums are paid to a separate insurance institution to be established, similar to the social security institution, and spent for robots. However, it does not seem possible to establish and manage such an institution.

In terms of collecting robot taxes, as unconscious robots cannot be indirectly taxed, tax can be collected from those who employ the robots or their owners.

When the increase in production volume with robotization in production is deemed positive, not collecting any taxes from robots can be considered more logical, because more production means the use of robots as a tool to make the economic growth more possible. Taxation of robots can be an obstacle to further production. However, producing more is not a sufficient criterion alone for the growth of the economy. There must also be demand meeting that production. If demand is not sufficient, excess supply occurs and the economy may enter a recession period. Moreover, too many people may be unemployed as a result of the increase in robotization. Even within the scope of a "Universal Basic Income Practice", it may not be possible for those people to create enough demand to meet the production of robots. For this reason, it is not very meaningful to think that it is efficient as production will increase and that no tax should be collected from robots.

At the same time, a company employing robots produces more than a company that does not employ robots, but, for the said overproduction, it also pays more tax and price for the raw materials, finished products, semi-finished products, spare parts, seeds, etc. For this reason, it can be said that this overproduction is already taxed indirectly.

From two different angles of view, there are conditions that require taxation of robots, as well as negative consequences as a result of collecting such tax. Taxes on robots would be reasonable and logical if they were actually used for human capital, such as the care of the elderly and retirees, education of people, and to finance public expenditures that may arise from hiring of robots instead of humans, provided that it ensures fair competition. However, in the future, it is also possible that robots that can make robots emerge as a result of the development of technology. In such a situation, the labour trained with robot tax may not have a business line left to practise that training. Or for limited employment, only a small fraction of the large number of trained people may be hired. Although it may seem utopian, these are possible scenarios. For these reasons, it is thought that robots can imperil the jobs of not only blue-collar workers but also white-collar workers.

As Bill Gates suggests, the use of robot tax for human capital contradicts the principle of "tax is a non-quid pro quo payment".[6] Certain revenues cannot be allocated to some specific expenditures, as a tax must be non-quid pro quo payment. If it will be collected for this purpose, it should be taken under another revenue title (fund, etc.). If there will be a use in the form of robot tax, this revenue should be collected to be used in general public expenditures.

The involvement of robots in the economy can adversely affect the supply-demand balance. In such a case, the robot tax can be used as a balancing instrument to restore deteriorated economic balances. States can keep the robot market under control through regulatory and supervisory institutions that it will establish with the function of "arbitrator state". At the same time, public administrations may oblige that company to provide public service by taking a certain amount of goods as tax in kind, depending on the amount of goods produced by companies using robots, or companies that use robots for more than certain working hours can have the robots used in public service in proportion to their working hours, considering their bodies as taxes. This suggestion, which is theoretically appropriate, seems difficult to implement given that taxes are collected in cash.

As a result, it seems that robotization and robotic developments are a very new discussion topic. The theory of robotization and robot taxes is not yet grounded, but it is likely to develop in the near future. For this reason, it is not possible to certainly conclude that robots should or should not be taxed. However, when the issue regarding the taxation of robots is on the agenda, it is clear that comprehensive studies need to be carried out. It is expected that new legal arrangements will be made, a renewed understanding of taxation and taxation principles will be introduced, a suitable financial environment will be prepared, multifaceted regulations regarding the economy will be developed and a new generation of taxes will be allocated.

## 9.6 Conclusion

It took three centuries from the First Industrial Revolution, which started with the invention of steam machines in 1712, to the Fourth Industrial Revolution, in which cloud systems were used, big data, cyber-physical systems and robots emerged. Today, in the economic crisis caused by the COVID-19 outbreak, the production

---

[6] Taxes being a non-quid pro quo payment: For paying the taxes, the taxpayers cannot purchase public goods and services in return for the tax have paid. That is, there is no direct relationship between purchasing public goods and paying taxes (Altay 2016: 150).

and service shortage experienced by the sectors dominated by the human factor in employment have highlighted again the importance of robots and digitalization in employment again.

With the use of robots in production, the risk that many working people will be unemployed in a very short time and the danger of extinction of some professions emerged, and these risk factors were confirmed by the research conducted by the World Economic Forum on the subject. According to the surveys and interviews conducted by the World Economic Forum with 371 companies, it is predicted that in the next five years, a large number of people will be unemployed and the employment in business lines such as office management, production, construction and mining, painting, design and entertainment will decrease or even disappear. Besides, according to the mentioned research, employment will increase in fields such as education sector, computing and mathematics, sales and business management, architecture and engineering, commerce and financial transactions.

The first issue that is considered to overcome the unemployment problem, which is expected to arise with the widespread use of robots, is the application of the "Universal Basic Income Policy" to all people in the countries. Universal Basic Income policy is the monthly payment of a determined amount of money to all citizens of the country. Thus, it is predicted that the unemployment problem to arise can be alleviated to some extent. However, due to the difficulty of keeping track of this monthly income and/or if people cannot live with the specified amount, robot tax has come up as another solution proposal.

Robot tax was transferred to the European Parliament and rejected there. However, it is still up-to-date. It may seem reasonable to impose a robot tax for certain reasons. Robots used in a workplace can be considered as an employee working there and subject to taxation on a salary determined accordingly. Another method of taxation might be quota application. The maximum amount of production to be made by manpower can be determined, and a different rate of taxation can be made for the part exceeding this production amount as in the progressive tax tariff. Apart from that, companies employing the robots may also be asked to pay mechanical safety premiums for issues such as breakdown of robots, replacement of their parts, maintenance and repair.

It is predicted that the mass production volume will increase significantly with the increase in the efficient use of robots. More production means robots become an important tool in achieving national growth targets. However, in order for excess production to positively affect growth, there must be a demand to meet this production. With the spread of robotization in production, people who are unemployed may not be able to demand those goods and disclose their demands for them, so there may be an excess supply. This situation is thought to lead economies to recession. Given this situation, imposing a robot tax would not make much sense. At the same time, the company that currently produces more with robots pays more tax when purchasing necessary for production such as finished products, raw materials and semi-finished products. In addition, taxing robots may negatively affect the performance of the country imposing such a tax in terms of competition in the technological race of global markets. In this case, countries may need to use tax incentives for the robot maintenance and repair, renovation, scrapping, scrap disposal, recycling, creation and renovation of robot graveyards, such as auto graveyards.

It is understood that different positive and negative situations may arise in cases where states impose or do not impose robot tax. At the same time, since robot taxes are a very new topic of discussion, their theoretical foundations have not yet been developed. For this reason, making precise judgements such as robots can or cannot be taxed can lead to wrong results.

It is estimated that imposition of a robot tax will bring about very radical changes. The tax systems of the countries are likely to change completely. The ability to make the robots to be subject to taxes may require the change of tax laws in accordance with the principle of legality of taxes. In addition, it is considered that the necessary control mechanisms should be established for the follow-up of robot tax and economic indicators should be examined very carefully. For the robot security premium system similar to social security premium, it is anticipated that it would be correct to develop a new generation parafiscal security system for robots.

## References


Alçın S (2016) "Üretim için yeni bir izlek: sanayi 4.0. J Life Econ 3(2):19–30

Altay A (2016) Kamu Maliyesi: Teorisi, Gelişimi, Kapsamı. Seçkin Kitabevi, Güncellenmiş 2. Baskı, Ankara

Ay H (2014) *Kamu Maliyesi*, Nobel Yayıncılık, Gözden Geçirilmiş 2. Baskı, Ankara

Barutçuoğlu EI (2001) *Robotların Tarihçesi*, July 2, Retrieved 16 Mar 2020, from http://robot.cmpe.boun.edu.tr/593/history.pdf

Bilici N, ve Bilici A (2011) *Kamu Maliyesi*, Seçkin Yayıncılık, Ankara

Çakır T, Moğol T, Ataç E, Heper F, Dönmez R, Ataç B, ve Varcan N (2006) *Kamu Maliyesi*, Anadolu Üniversitesi Yayınları, Yayın No: 1682, Eskişehir

Delaney KJ (2017) Robot that takes your job should pay taxes, says Bill Gates. Retrieved 18 July 2020, from https://qz.com/911968/bill-gates-the-robot-that-takes-your-job-should-pay-taxes/

EBSO (2015) *"SANAYİ 4.0"*, İzmir

Eğilmez M (2017) "Endüstri 4.0", Kendime Yazılar. Retrieved 18 Mar 2020, from http://www.mahfiegilmez.com/2017/05/endustri-40.html

Gök KÖ (2019) Robot Nedir? Retrieved 18 Mar 2020, from https://blog.universal-robots.com/tr/robot-nedir

Gökalp E, Gökalp MO, Çoban S, Eren PE (2019) Dijital dönüşümün etkisinde verimli istihdam yönetimi: yol haritası önerisi. Verimlilik Dergisi 3:201–222

Gündüz MZ, Daş R (2018) Nesnelerin İnterneti: Gelişimi, Bileşenleri, Uygulama Alanları. Pamukkale Üniversitesi Mühendislik Bilimleri Dergisi 24:327–335

Hepaksaz E (2011) *Türkiye'de E-Maliye Uygulamaları*, Gazi Kitabevi, Ankara

IFR (2019a) Executive summary world robotics 2019 service robots. Retrieved 16 June 2020, from https://ifr.org/downloads/press2018/Executive_Summary_WR_Service_Robots_2019.pdf

IFR (2019b) IFR press conference. Retrieved 30 April 2020, from https://ifr.org/downloads/press2018/IFR%20World%20Robotics%20Presentation%20-%2018%20Sept%202019.pdf

ILO (2018) Helping the gig economy work better for gig workers. Retrieved 10 July 2020, from https://www.ilo.org/washington/WCMS_642303/lang--en/index.htm

Ivanov S (2017) Robonomics-principles, benefits, challenges, solutions. Yearb Varna Univ Manage 10:283–293

Kara E (2020) COVID-19 pandemisi: İşgücü üzerindeki etkileri ve istihdam tedbirleri. Avrasya Sosyal Ve Ekonomi Araştırmaları Dergisi 7(5):269–282
Kurt D, ve Bozoklu Ü (2019) Robot Ekonomisinin Yükselişi. *Sosyal Bilimler Metinleri* 1:25–47
Küçükkalay M (1997) Endüstri Devrimi ve Ekonomik Sonuçlarının Analizi", *SDÜ İİBF Dergisi*, Sayı 2:51–68
Manyika J, Lund S, Chui M, Bughin J, Woetzel J, Batra P, Ko R, Sanghvi S (2017) Jobs lost, jobs gained: Workforce transitions in a time of automation. McKinsey Global Institute 150
OECD (2016) Family-friendly workplace practices. Retrieved 12 July 2020, from http://www.oecd.org/els/family/LMF_2-4-Family-friendly-workplace-practices.pdf, Erişim Tarihi
OECD (2020) OECD Economic Outlook (2020) (2). Retrieved 12 Dec 2020, from https://www.oecd-ilibrary.org/sites/39a88ab1-en/1/3/1/index.html?itemId=/content/publication/39a88ab1-en&_csp_=fd64cf2a9a06f738f45c7aeb5a6f5024&itemIGO=oecd&itemContentType=issue
Riley K (2017) Taxing robots and "Free money" in a future of job automation. Retrieved 5 Aug 2020, from https://futurism.com/taxing-robots-and-free-money-in-a-future-of-job-automation/
U.S. Bureau of Labor Statistics (2020) Workers who could work at home, did work at home, and were paid for work at home, by selected characteristics, averages for the period 2017–2018. Retrieved 12 July 2020, from https://www.bls.gov/news.release/flex2.t01.htm
World Economic Forum (2016) The future of jobs employment, skills and workforce strategy for the fourth industrial revolution. Global challenge insight report, Geneva
World Economic Forum (2019) Outbreak readiness and business impact; Protecting lives and livelihoods across the global economy. White Paper
Worstall T (2016) More EU lunacy: Robots should pay social security taxes for the pensions they won't get. Retrieved 5 Aug 2020, from https://www.forbes.com/sites/timworstall/2016/06/23/more-eu-lunacy-robots-should-pay-social-security-taxes-for-the-pensions-they-wont-get/#3ec13eba1060
Zeng Z, Chen PJ, Lew AA (2020) From high-touch to high-tech: COVID-19 drives robotics adoption. Tourism Geographies 1–11

## *Internet Sources*

Retrieved 5 Aug 2020, from http://www.ticaretgazetesi.com.tr/indexx.php?f=3bd704e38fe839ba454b3702e36cc6b3&l=1&sayfa_id=666&g_id=&id=420713
Retrieved 5 Aug 2020, from https://www.ft.com/content/d04a89c2-f6c8-11e6-9516-2d969e0d3b65

**Abdulcelil Gazioğlu** Research Asistant in Department of Public Finance, İzmir Katip Çelebi University, İzmir, Turkey. Studies Ph.D. in Public Finance and Financial Management; holds M.Sc. in Public Finance and Financial Management, B.S. in Business Administration. He has book chapters, articles and papers on public finace, Industry 4.0, State budget, financial crisis, tax.

**Zeynep Demirci Çakıroğlu** Assistant Professor in Department of Public Finance, İzmir Katip Çelebi University, İzmir, Turkey. Holds Ph.D. in Public Finance and Financial Management, M.Sc. in Public Finance, B.S. in Public Finance. She has book chapters, articles and papers on global public goods, refugee protection, international tax agreements, tax audit and other fiscal theory research areas.

**Alper Doğan** Alper Doğan received his B.A. from the Department of Public Finance, Celal Bayar University, Manisa, Turkey in 2003. He received Ph.D. in Public Finance with his thesis entitled as "Gender Budgets: An Evaluation for Turkey" from Celal Bayar University, Manisa, Turkey in 2012. He presently serves as an associate professor at Izmir Kâtip Çelebi University, Faculty of Economics and Administrative Sciences, Izmir, Turkey. He was also a visiting fellow at the University of Utah, Salt Lake City, USA between 2009 and 2010. Dr. Doğan's research interest includes Fiscal Theory, Gender Studies, Industry 4.0, International Taxation.

# Chapter 10
# Liquidity Steps: Policy Actions Taken by Central Banks During Coronavirus Pandemic

**Ümit Çevik and Belgin Yakışan Mutlu**

**Abstract** This article, it is aimed to examine the primary actions taken by central banks to support the sectors, businesses, and individuals in difficulty during the epidemic process. In line with this purpose, we compiled actions of the US Federal Reserve (FED), the European Central Bank (ECB), the Bank of Japan (BoJ), Bank of China (PBoC), and the Bank of England (BoE) as leading central banks, as well as many countries including Turkey. While the main framework of the moves made in this process is to keep the liquidity abundant by creating a low-interest environment, it can be summarized as providing the banks with the necessary flexibility to open credit channels and support the tradesmen and individuals. Quantitative easing was one of the main policies applied during the epidemic. In addition to this, facilitating the access of countries to dollars and euros through swap agreements was among the policies implemented. Looking at all these steps taken by the central banks from January to mid-June, it was seen that the moves stimulated the flow of credit towards the real economy and the employment market, while on the financial side, it had an effect on reducing the volatility in the markets. While it is agreed that the problem in the liquidity flow has been eliminated and the pressure on the supply of dollars has been alleviated through the swap channel, it is considered that the extent to which the measures and incentives will weaken the financial side will depend on how to further the outbreak will last.

**Keywords** Central banks · Epidemic · US Federal Reserve FED · European Central Bank ECB · Bank of Japan (BoJ) · Bank of China (PBoC) · Bank of England (BoE) · Liquidity · Economy

---

Ü. Çevik (✉) · B. Y. Mutlu (✉)
Ziraat Participation Bank, İstanbul, Turkey



B. Açıkgöz and İ. A. Acar (eds.), *Pandemnomics: The Pandemic's Lasting Economic Effects*, Accounting, Finance, Sustainability, Governance & Fraud: Theory and Application, https://doi.org/10.1007/978-981-16-8024-3_10

## 10.1 Introduction

After the 2008 global financial crisis, which is described as one of the most important economic disasters in the world history, there were debates about what the role of central banks should be, and in this context, many economists agreed that the pre-crisis central banking paradigm was insufficient. After these criticisms, we witnessed a transition period in which price stability and financial stability were addressed together in targeting by central banks and reflected in monetary policies.

While the paradigm shift in central banking after the global economic crisis made its effects felt again after every unpredictable development such as natural disaster and epidemic, we observe that the novel coronavirus (COVID-19) emerging in China recently shaped monetary policies. The spreading of problems in any country to the whole world as a result of globalization in this period also brought with it that the central banks to be alert to all kinds of economic downturns and also to support the markets by opening up "room for manoeuvre" in monetary policy and resorting to unconventional methods.

In this process, which brings the widespread use of concepts such as quantitative easing and negative interest, the concerns that unforeseen developments would lead to a slowdown in economic activities beyond expectations and the risk of deflation were prevalent.

At this point, concerns about the impact of COVID-19, which emerged in China and spread rapidly around the world, on global trade are on the agenda of central banks. Central banks, which took many measures together aggressively during the epidemic, took measures to increase liquidity through various channels in order to support sectors, businesses and individuals in difficulty. In this context, the US Federal Reserve (Fed), the European Central Bank (ECB), the Bank of Japan (BoJ), Bank of China (PBoC) and the Bank of England (BoE) as leading central banks, as well as many countries including Turkey, followed the epidemic closely and took quick steps through extraordinary meetings.

While the main framework of the moves made in this process is to keep the liquidity abundant by creating a low interest environment, it can be summarized as providing the banks with necessary flexibility to open credit channels and support the tradesmen and individuals. The quantitative easing, which was first applied by the Chairman of Fed, Ben Bernanke, during the 2008 global financial crisis, was one of the main policies applied during the epidemic. On the other hand, facilitating the access of countries to dollars and euros through swap agreements was among the policies implemented.

## 10.2 Fed: The Flagship

After the first coronavirus incident in the USA, the extent of the damage in the financial markets and real economy brought with it the same high amount of measures and incentives taken. Three separate measures announced by the government to combat the crisis accounted for more than 10% of the country's national income. Although these measures, which were taken under the largest stimulus package in US history amounting to 2 trillion dollars, helped to limit the depth of the economic shock in the country, they increased financial risks, and the downside risks to growth remained high.

In this process, while it was observed that the income flow of the consumers who stayed home and limited their spending was disrupted and the job losses increased, while the liquidity flow of the enterprises decreased significantly. In the face of this situation, the Fed, which is described as the flagship in the world financial markets, has implemented many measures.

Fed Chairman Jerome Powell, who first pointed to the seriousness of the epidemic in his speech after the monetary policy board meeting on 29 January 2020, stated that the uncertainties stemming from COVID-19 on global growth continued and said, "The virus is a very serious issue. it is unclear how far the epidemic could spread and what effects could be. We are observing the situation closely" (Anadolu Ajansı 2020a–g).

At the end of February, Powell stated that they were closely monitoring the developments regarding COVID-19 and the effects of the epidemic on the economic outlook, and gave the message that they would take appropriate steps to support the economy. The same day, Fed St. Louis Branch Chairman James Bullard also stated that if the epidemic spreads further, the Fed was likely to cut interest rates (Anadolu Ajansı 2020a–g).

Not even a week after the statements by Powell and Bullard, the Fed surprisingly cut rates on 3 March. Upon this decision taken before the Federal Open Market Committee (FOMC) meeting on 17–18 March, the bank cut the policy rate by 50 basis points to the range of 1–1.25% (Federal Reserve 2020a–l). The decision went down in history as the Fed's interest rate action before its scheduled meetings for the first time since the 2008 global crisis.

This decision, which was taken during the period when the economic effects of the virus were discussed and uncertainties were intense, actually caused panic in the markets in the first place. The impact of the decision was first seen on the US 10-year bond rates. The US 10-year bond yields, which are globally important and closely monitored as a risk measure, fell below 1% for the first time in history.

The first move regarding the liquidity squeeze after the rate cut came from the New York Branch of the Fed on March 12. In this context, it was announced that a total of 1.5 trillion dollars of liquidity will be offered to the markets where unusual fluctuations were observed due to the COVID-19 epidemic through 1-month and 3-month repo transactions (Federal Reserve Bank of New York 2020).

On 15 March, the Fed cut the rates for the second time before the FOMC meeting on 17–18 March to mitigate the economic impact of the COVID-19 outbreak and took the policy rate down to the range of 0–0.25%. Fed Chairman Jerome Powell pointed out that the interest rates would be kept at this level for a long time after the decision, and said that they would keep the interest rate at 0–0.25% until after they were sure that the economy survived the latest events and they could achieve their maximum employment and price stability targets (Federal Reserve 2020a–l).

On the same date, the ECB decided to expand the swap line with the Fed and BoJ, as well as the central banks of Canada, England and Switzerland, to secure dollar liquidity supply on a global scale. Within the scope of the joint decision taken in order to act in a coordinated manner to increase the dollar-denominated liquidity supply of the markets, in addition to its current operations for one week, it started to give weekly dollars on overnight index swaps (OIS) with a maturity of 84 days at 25 basis points (Federal Reserve 2020a–l).

The Fed, which continues its actions without interruption, announced on March 17 that it would restart the opportunity for US companies, which are in a difficult situation under the economic impact of the COVID-19 outbreak, to borrow through the commercial securities market. In this context, the bank re-commissioned the Commercial Paper Funding Facility (CPFF), which was established to increase liquidity in short-term funding markets during the 2008–2009 global financial crisis (Federal Reserve 2020a–l).

On the other hand, with a decision taken on March 18, the bank initiated the *Primary Dealer Credit Facility (PDCF)* to support the loan needs of households and businesses (Federal Reserve 2020a–l), which was implemented during the 2008 global financial crisis to open a new liquidity window for market makers. Mentioned facility, which was restarted due to COVID-19, supported the good functioning of the markets and provided loans to businesses and households. The Fed stated that the PDCF, which started on March 20, would be in place for 6 months and could be extended, if necessary.

Three days after the decision to expand the swap line with major central banks, the Fed made another move in this regard. In this context, the Fed established new swap lines with 9 central banks, including Australia, Brazil, Denmark, Korea, Mexico, Norway, New Zealand, Singapore and Sweden, on 19 March. With the swap lines in question, it was announced that nearly USD 60 billion of liquidity would be provided for each of the central banks of Australia, Brazil, Korea, Mexico, Singapore and Sweden, and USD 30 billion for each of the central banks of Denmark, Norway and New Zealand (Federal Reserve 2020a–l).

The Fed took its actions to an "unlimited" dimension as the economy faced serious problems despite all the mentioned steps and the manufacturing industry indexes in many states fell to historically low levels in this process. In order to mitigate the damage caused by the epidemic and provide support to the economies, the Fed, which took new measures, including unlimited asset purchases, on 23 March, announced that it would purchase securities based on treasury bonds and mortgages in order to ensure smooth functioning of markets and effective transmission of monetary policy.

On the other hand, the bank has included commercial mortgage-backed security purchases in its residential mortgage-backed security purchases.

Although the Fed's unlimited asset purchase move was welcomed in the markets, it revealed the necessity of taking aggressive measures in the public and private sectors to limit job losses and ensure rapid recovery. Within the same statement, the bank also stated that credit flows to employees, consumers and businesses would be supported by creating new programs and approximately 300 billion dollars of new financing would be provided. In this context, it was also announced that the Ministry of Treasury Exchange Stabilization Fund would provide 30 billion dollars equity. In addition, the Fed's New York Branch simultaneously announced that it would purchase USD 75 billion in treasury bonds and USD 50 billion mortgage-backed securities every day that week (Federal Reserve 2020a–l).

On the last day of March, the Fed launched a temporary repo facility for foreign central banks and international financial institutions to help the smooth functioning of financial markets. In this context, foreign central banks and international financial institutions had the opportunity to temporarily exchange their US Treasury securities for dollars (Federal Reserve 2020a–l).

In early April, when the spread of the outbreak accelerated and peaked in many countries, the Fed temporarily eased the additional leverage ratios that major banks had to hold for a year. This decision was reported to aim to facilitate lending by banks while supporting their liquidity.

Deciding to take additional actions to provide up to USD 2.3 trillion in loans to support the economy on April 9 due to the pandemic, the Fed announced the details of support to households, businesses of all sizes, and local governments. In this context, the Fed announced that up to USD 600 billion loans would be purchased to ensure credit flow to small and medium-sized enterprises, while the US Treasury Department would provide USD 75 billion in equity. On the other hand, it was announced that the scope of 3 loan programs to increase credit flow to households and businesses would be expanded and support up to USD 850 billion would be provided. It was reported that states and local governments would receive loans of up to USD 500 billion and they would work with banks to provide 4-year loans to the companies with a revenue of less than USD 2.5 billion or up to 10,000 employees (Federal Reserve). The scope of this liquidity facility for municipalities, which was put into practice in the last days of April, was expanded by lowering the lower population threshold.

Although it was open to debate whether the Fed, which greatly reduced its arsenal in terms of near-zero interest, unlimited bond purchases, and credit channels, would apply negative interest rates in May, President Powell put an end to this debate with a statement and said that this was not a tool they consider.

At its monetary policy meeting held on 18 May, the Fed continued to keep the policy interest rate in the range of 0–0.25, as previously signaled. In the text of the decision, it was promised that the Fed would use all the tools it had to support the US economy in such a difficult period. In June, the prominence of verbal guidance was noteworthy, and the frequency of President Powell's evaluation increased. Powell reminded in each of his evaluations that they reduced the policy interest rate to almost zero, and conveyed the message that they would keep their interest rates at this level until they were sure that the economy had overcome these events and achieves the targets of maximum employment and price stability.

At the meeting held on June 10, the bank kept the interest rates in the range of 0–0.25, while the Fed's long-term growth expectation for the US economy was reduced to 1.8% (Federal Reserve 2020a–l).

On the other hand, it was estimated that the US economy could contract by 6.5% in 2020, grow by 5% in 2021 and 3.5% in 2022. "We don't even think about raising rates. What we are thinking about is supporting the economy. We think it will take some time," said the Fed Chairman, who held a post-decision press conference, on interest rates. By making this statement, he once again gave the message that they would maintain the "long-term close to zero interest rate" stance. The Fed's semi-annual monetary policy report, prepared twice a year and published on 12 June, warned that there was an extraordinary uncertainty over the economic outlook and the damage of the economic recession could be quite permanent (Federal Reserve 2020a–l).

The bank started to receive applications from banks on 15 June, within the scope of the loan program for small and medium-sized enterprises, which it announced on 9 April and implemented to mitigate the economic effects of the outbreak. With the support announced as the "**Main Street Lending Program,**" it is envisaged to provide loans of up to 600 billion dollars for small and medium-sized enterprises. In addition, the Fed announced that it would start buying corporate bonds on 16 June, while Powell reaffirmed its commitment to using all tools (Federal Reserve 2020a–l).

Looking at all these steps taken by the Fed from January to mid-June, it was seen that the moves stimulated the flow of credit toward the real economy and the employment market, while on the financial side, it had an effect on reducing the volatility in the markets. While it is agreed that the problem in the liquidity flow has been eliminated and the pressure on the supply of dollars has been alleviated through the swap channel, it is considered that the extent to which the measures and incentives will weaken the financial side will depend on how further the outbreak will last.

## 10.3 ECB: The Roof of Europe

While the ECB did not make any changes in interest rates in line with market expectations on 23 January 2020, it announced that the strategic review started. The content of the strategic review consisted of "price stability," "monetary policy toolkit," "economic and monetary analyses" and "quantitative formulation of communication practices" (European Central Bank 2020a–i).

The first serious warning of the bank within the scope of COVID-19 was made by ECB President Christine Lagarde on 5 February. Stating that the coronavirus outbreak contributed to global economic uncertainty, Lagarde did not give a clue about the monetary policy to be adopted against this new risk. Lagarde repeated the same warning a day after this announcement (Hürriyet, 2020). On 3 March,

ECB President Lagarde stated that they were ready to take "appropriate and targeted measures" to combat the negative impact of the COVID-19 outbreak on the economy (Financial Times 2020a, b).

When the calendars showed 4 March, the Finance Ministers of the Euro Group member countries stated that they were ready to use all policy tools that included financial measures to support economic growth in the face of the risks posed by the coronavirus.

In March, when the effects of the outbreak were seen seriously and around the middle of March when the economies closed one by one, the ECB took its first serious step. The bank announced, on 12 March, that it planned to purchase additional temporary assets of 120 billion euros by the end of the year, although the interest rates remained unchanged (European Central Bank 2020a–i).

In the statement made regarding the decision, it was stated that temporary new long-term refinancing operations (LTRO) would be provided to support the ECB's Euro Zone financial system, which would provide bank loan support for SMEs affected by the spread of the coronavirus. In her post-decision statement, ECB President Lagarde stated that the spread of the COVID-19 outbreak had a negative impact on the growth of the Eurozone, that the risks were downside for the region, and that an assertive and coordinated fiscal policy response would be needed, and if interest rate cut was needed, they would do it (Anadolu Ajansı 2020a–g).

On 16 March, the ECB decided to expand the swap line with the Fed and BoJ, apart from the central banks of Canada, UK and Switzerland, to secure dollar liquidity on a global scale (European Central Bank 2020a–i).

On 18 March, the ECB issued a new statement, announcing that the economic consequences of the spread of the coronavirus outbreak were closely monitored and they were ready to adjust all measures taken against the epidemic, when deemed appropriate. On the other hand, on 20 March, the bank decided to re-activate the swap line with the Danish Central Bank to expand its access rights from 12 billion euros to 24 billion euros. Thus, the bank supported the provision of euro liquidity with its successive swap moves (European Central Bank 2020a–i).

On 20 March, the European Central Bank announced that Eurozone banks struggling with the economic impact of COVID-19 would be given more flexibility in audits. With this measure, it was aimed to make it easier for banks to provide funds to individuals and companies in difficult times. Meanwhile, the leaders of 9 European Union (EU) countries, including France, Italy, Spain, Greece, Belgium, Ireland, Portugal, Slovenia and Luxembourg, called for the establishment of a joint borrowing instrument to finance the policies implemented against the pandemic. However, on 27 March, it was reported that leaders could not agree on a common policy against the economic effects of COVID-19. On the same day, the ECB advised, due to the novel coronavirus (COVID-19) outbreak, banks in the Eurozone not to pay dividends, not to buy back shares until October and to use their profits to support the economy against the impact of the pandemic. (Anadolu Ajansı 2020a–g).

In April, the ECB postponed the strategic review it announced in January, which aimed to redefine the tools to achieve the bank's main goal, for 6 months due to the pandemic. The completion of the strategic review was postponed from the end of

2020 to mid-2021 (European Central Bank 2020a–i). The bank announced on April 15 that it freed up more than 20 billion euros in banks in the Eurozone (European Central Bank 2020a–i).

On April 30, the ECB announced that it facilitated the conditions of Targeted Longer-Term Refinancing Transactions (TLTRO), while keeping interest rates unchanged in line with market expectations. In this context, interest rates in TLTRO were reduced by 50 basis points from the average interest of Eurosystem's refinancing transactions from June 2020 to July 2021 (European Central Bank 2020a–i).

Following the decisions, ECB President Lagarde said that the pandemic caused an unprecedented decline in the Eurozone economy, and that it was difficult to predict the time of recovery. In May, the professional forecasters survey of the ECB for the second quarter had a result similar to Lagarde's statements and it was concluded that the recovery in the economy would be slow and gradual (Anadolu Ajansı 2020a–g).

In the written statement made on 5 May, it was emphasized that the bank was determined to do everything to bring inflation back to the targeted level, while the update report published on 14 May stated that an unprecedented contraction in the Eurozone economy was expected in the second quarter due to the pandemic (European Central Bank 2020a–i). The ECB, which could not achieve the desired recovery in the economy after the 2008 global financial crisis due to the Brexit deadlock, political developments and geopolitical risks, reached even more stalemate with the pandemic. With the reflection of this situation on the expectations and clear expression of it, the ECB's monetary policy minutes published in mid-May signaled that the Pandemic Emergency Asset Purchase Program could be expanded.

Lagarde shared the forecast on 27 May that the Eurozone economy would shrink between 8 and 12% in 2020 (Reuters 2020). By 4 June, the expected step was taken and the ECB increased Pandemic Emergency Asset Procurement Program by €600 billion and took it up to €1 trillion 350 billion (European Central Bank 2020a–i).

Before the end of first week of June, ECB President Lagarde took the stage once again and, verbally, emphasized that the ECB's crisis-related measures were temporary, purposeful and proportionate. Finally, the bank launched the Eurosystem repo facility for central banks (EUREP) on 25 June to meet the euro liquidity needs of central banks outside the Eurozone (Bloomberg HT 2020).

The ECB announced that it had launched a new repo program to provide euro liquidity to central banks outside the Eurozone. With the program that will last until the end of June 2021, the ECB aimed to meet the liquidity needs of central banks outside the Euro Zone.

## 10.4 PBoC: Country Where the Virus First Emerged

While discussing the extent to which the coronavirus will affect the global supply chain as China has a say in world trade and how it will direct world growth, the support of the central banks and the incentives of the Chinese authorities have reflected positively in the markets.

The Central Bank of the People's Republic of China (PBoC) stepped in to dispel the panic atmosphere in the market. The bank, which injected 1.2 trillion yuan of liquidity into the market first, also cut the 7- and 14-day reverse repo interest rates. The bank then provided another 400 billion yuan of liquidity to the market. Finally, PBoC cut 1-year interest by 10 basis points and 5-year interest rate by 5 basis points to 4.05% and 4.75% respectively (Anadolu Ajansı 2020a–g).

PBoC, which frequently applied to its "wait-and-see" policy in this process compared to other countries, reduced the required reserve ratio by 50–100 basis points for some banks that were considered qualified on 13 March. Stating that the discount would provide a total of 550 billion yuan of long-term funding, PBoC gave the message that they would maintain liquidity at the appropriate adequacy. On the other hand, the bank stated, after this announcement, that they would implement a prudential monetary policy and increase flexibility (Bloomberg HT 2020).

Following this decision, the bank left the policy rate unchanged at 4.05% at the meeting held on 20 March and gave the message that the required reserve ratio move was sufficient (investing.com 2020).

On the other hand, on 25 March, the press reported that the central bank officials were considering lowering the benchmark deposit interest rate (Financial Times 2020a, b). Having made the second rate cut decision on April 20, the bank cut its benchmark 1-year basic loan prime rate (LPR) by 20 basis points from 4.05 to 3.85% (China Banking News 2020). On June 2, the bank stated that they faced downside risks for the economy, but that there was room for monetary policy, while leaving the policy rate at 3.85% at its meeting on 22 June. (Forex Live 2020).

## 10.5 BoJ: Center of Unusual Methods

In Japan, which is among the countries most affected by the coronavirus outbreak, the country's central bank gave the message that they were following closely and would take steps if necessary, although the country's central bank did not take a clear step against the devastating effects of the epidemic at its meeting on 21 January. Stating that the impact of the novel coronavirus on China and the world economy was a cause of concern, BoJ President Haruhiko Kuroda also said, "The Chinese economy has a large share in the global economy. Therefore, the effects of the virus can be great. We can go to monetary easing without hesitation, if necessary, but it is too early for this" (Bank of Japan 2020a–j).

In a later statement, Kuroda also stated that if the coronavirus pandemic threatened Japan's economy and price trends significantly, the central bank would not hesitate to evaluate additional mitigation steps.

The BoJ announced a series of measures to increase monetary easing by meeting extraordinarily on 16 March, just before the 18–19 March monetary policy meeting. In this context, BoJ announced that it would carry out various operations including Japanese government bond purchases and dollar-based fundraising transactions. The bank also took measures, including the launch of a new operation to facilitate corporate finance. Within the scope of the measures to facilitate the financing of the companies, the bank started a new operation to provide loans as collateral against corporate debts until the end of September, with a maturity of up to 1 year with zero interest rate. Increasing the upper limit in corporate bonds and bills purchases to 2 trillion yen in total, the bank also increased the amount of purchases of exchange traded funds (ETF) from 6 trillion yen annually to 12 trillion yen, and Japan real estate investment funds (J-REIT) purchases from 90 billion yen annually to 180 billion yen (Bank of Japan 2020a–j).

At its meeting which ended on 27 April, the bank further loosened its monetary policy and announced that it would purchase unlimited amount of government bonds. Removing the upper limit for purchases of government bonds, which was previously 80 trillion yen per year, the bank announced that it would buy corporate bonds and bills totalling approximately 20 trillion yen. BoJ also stressed that private fundraising processes could be strengthened to facilitate financing against COVID-19. According to the text of the decision, the maximum maturity of corporate bonds to be purchased by BoJ would be increased to 5 years. On the other hand, 12-trillion-yen annual exchange traded funds (ETF) and 180-billion-yen annual Japan real estate investment funds (J-REIT) would be purchased (Bank of Japan 2020a–j).

By May, while the bank did not change interest rates and monetary policy, it introduced an interest-free and unsecured loan fund of about 30 trillion yen to support the financing of small and medium-sized enterprises. It was stated in the text of the decision published in this context, "We have announced about 20 trillion yen of corporate bonds and bills purchases, and secondly, fund guarantee programs against private sector debts of about 25 trillion yen, within the scope of the financing package that we have commissioned against the negative effects of the coronavirus, with a total size of 75 trillion yen. Today, as a third measure, we have taken a new financing measure, which will provide approximately 30 trillion yen of interest-free and unsecured loan funds to support the financing of SMEs. On the other hand, we decided to continue with the previously announced package until March 2021 by extending the duration of the measures by 6 months" (Bank of Japan 2020a–j).

On 16 June, BoJ made a commitment that it would not hesitate to take additional expansion measures in the face of the effects of the novel coronavirus (COVID-19) pandemic, while not making changes in interest rates and monetary policy. The bank announced that it would continue to buy 2-trillion-yen corporate bonds and 3-trillion-yen corporate bills, and would make additional purchases of 7.5 trillion yen each by the end of March 2021 (Bank of Japan 2020a–j).

## 10.6 BoE, Coming Down with the Pandemic While in Brexit Pincer

England, which has the second largest economy in Europe, has come down with the coronavirus outbreak during the economic recession that started with the process of leaving the European Union. The quarantine measures taken within the scope of the fight against the pandemic made the country's economy, which was already struggling with the recession, confront with a more difficult crisis to manage. In a statement regarding this process, the international credit rating agency Moody's warned that a no-deal Brexit would seriously affect Britain's recovery from its deepest recession in the last century (www.bloomberght.com).

During the period when difficult times awaited the country's economy due to Brexit and the pandemic, the Bank of England implemented a series of measures simultaneously with the central banks of the developing countries. The Bank of England (BoE) gathered extraordinarily on 11 March and cut the policy interest rate from 0.75 to 0.25% by a 50-basis point reduction to combat the pandemic. The said rate cut was BoE's first rate cut since August 2016. In its statement, the bank also decided to implement a new term funding scheme for SMEs and to continue the asset purchase program at the level of £435 billion (Anadolu Ajansı 2020a–g).

BoE, which convened extraordinarily for the second time in March, reduced the policy interest rate by 15 basis points to 10% 10 days after the first meeting. At the same meeting, the asset purchase program, which was at the level of 435 billion pounds, was increased by 200 billion pounds to 635 billion pounds. BoE, which kept the policy interest rate constant at 0.10% at the April, May and June meetings, increased its asset purchase program by another £ 100 billion at the meeting in June (www.dunya.com).

The UK economy, which had a tough second quarter as was the case in the world economies, contracted by 6% in March and 20% in April. While the Bank of England warned that the country's economy could face the deepest crisis of the last 300 years in its predictions at the beginning of the outbreak, officials stated that the measures taken started to show signs of growth for the ongoing period (Anadolu Ajansı 2020a–g).

The virus, which spread throughout the world in March, significantly increased the downside risks on the global economic outlook. Due to the increasing volatility in international markets, developed and developing countries started to adopt unconventional expansionary monetary and fiscal policies.

## 10.7 CBRT, at the Center of Actions

As for the Turkey's economy, a significant improvement was recorded in macroeconomic indicators, and the Central Bank of the Republic of Turkey (CBRT) cut the policy interest rate by 125 basis points in January and February by taking into account factors affecting the inflation outlook. By March, in order to reduce the effects of the pandemic on economic activity, the CBRT took a series of measures in the monetary policy channel to ensure efficient working of credit channel and that the uninterrupted and smooth running of cash flow of companies.

In this scope, the CBRT advanced, for the first time, the Monetary Policy Committee meeting, which was initially scheduled to convene on 19 March, by two days and convened extraordinarily on 17 March, and the policy interest rate was cut by 100 basis points to 9.75%. In addition to this decision, the measure packages taken to limit the economic and financial impacts of the coronavirus were shared with the public on 17 March, 31 March and 17 April (www.tcmb.gov.tr).

The measures focusing on four main objectives were listed as: providing flexibility in banks' TL and foreign currency liquidity management and increasing predictability, ensuring credit flow to the real sector and supporting exporting companies, supporting the cash flow of exporting companies with rediscount credit arrangements and supporting the Government Domestic Borrowing Securities market (www.tcmb.gov.tr) (Fig. 10.1).

Evaluating limiting the negative impact of the pandemic history of the pandemic on Turkey's economy, keeping the credit channel open, and smooth continuing of firms' cash flows and downward risks in the inflation outlook, CBRT kept reducing the rates until May. Thus, the CBRT reduced the policy rate by 300 base points since the beginning of 2020 and by 150 basis points since March, when the effects of the coronavirus began to be felt (www.tcmb.gov.tr).

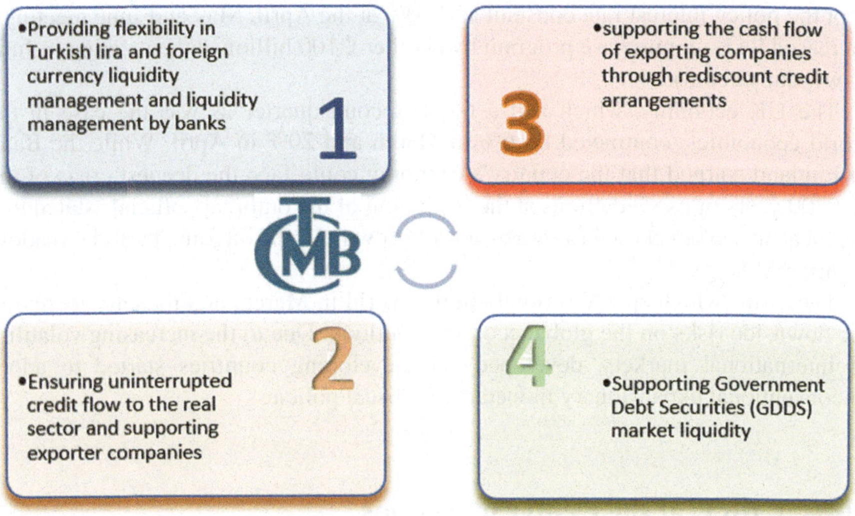


**Fig. 10.1** Package of measures taken to limit the economic and financial effects of the coronavirus. *Source* (Central Bank of Republic of Turkey 2020)

Due to the pandemic, economic activity decreased significantly around the world, while the supply and demand side decreased significantly. For this reason, this period enabled implementing unique preventive policies.

Implementing a lot of actions and measures in the process, CBRT amended swap agreements signed earlier with Qatar and China to meet Turkey's short-term foreign currency need arising from sharp decline in exports and tourism, country's important foreign currency income channels, and thus, took the amounts to a higher level. With the amendment made with the Central Bank of Qatar on 17 August 2018, the amount of the swap agreement was increased from USD 5 billion equivalent of Turkish lira and Qatari rial to USD 15 billion equivalent of Turkish lira and Qatari rial.

The first usage of the Chinese Yuan (CNY) funding under the swap agreement signed between the Central Bank of the Republic of Turkey (CBRT) and the People's Bank of China in 2019 had been realized on 18 June 2020. In this way, similarly, within the framework of the swap agreement renewed in 2019 between the CBRT and the PBoC, the first usage of yuan funding was made on 18 June 2020. In this way, Turkish companies in various sectors paid their import bills from China using yuan through relevant banks. In the statement made by the CBRT regarding the swap agreement, it was stated that the use of swap agreement resources was important in terms of the use of local currency in international trade payments and access of Turkish companies to international liquidity, and should also be considered as a step to strengthen financial cooperation between both countries (www.tcmb.gov.tr).

Although the global pandemic caused long-lasting damage to the economies, intense efforts were made to limit these effects by means of the extraordinary measures repeatedly announced by the central banks. The CBRT took part at the "Center" of actions with nearly 50 measures as of 16 March in coordination of economy management, together with the Banking Regulation and Supervision Agency.

## 10.8 Conclusion

While the virus, which was initially thought to have limited effects at the regional level, caused a serious health threat all over the world, its economic impact was unfortunately devastating for both developed and developing countries. It was aimed to reduce the impact of the pandemic on economies with the voluminous liquidity measures of the central banks against the virus whose economic effects were stated to be seen more clearly by the second quarter of 2020.

In this process, the countries' competent authorities took measures against the pandemic with a wide set of economic tools. Among the aims of these measures were reducing the volatility which is almost unprecedented in the markets, contributing to financial stability in economies, supporting economic activity by keeping credit channels open and keeping the loss of workforce at a low level.

The first and clearest response of developed and developing countries to the pandemic was the sharp cut in policy interest rates with extraordinary meetings and the simultaneous commissioning of other policy tools. During the pandemic, both fiscal and monetary policies were eased as much as possible. While policy rates, which were at low levels in developed countries before the pandemic, approached to zero with the spread rate of the pandemic, developing countries used the area opened during this cutting process without hesitation. The pandemic brought with it a period in which extraordinary policies were quickly implemented. Countries have struggled intensely to keep their economies alive with interest rate cuts, bond purchases, additional liquidity supports, dollar swap agreements, loan restructuring and postponement and additional loan support programs.

The global pandemic has been a sad development for all people. Although the large-volume liquidity measures announced by governments and central banks limited the panic that occurred at the first time in the markets, 2020 went down in history as economically the most difficult period of the last 100 years.

## References

Anadolu Agency (2020a) https://www.aa.com.tr/tr/ekonomi/fed-faiz-oranini-sabit-tuttu/1718437. Accessed 30 Mar 2020

Anadolu Agency (2020b) https://www.aa.com.tr/tr/ekonomi/fed-yetkilisinden-kovid-19-nedeniyle-faiz-indirimi-sinyali/1749044. Accessed 30 Mar 2020

Anadolu Agency (2020c) https://www.aa.com.tr/tr/ekonomi/ecb-koronaviruse-karsi-avro-bolgesi-bankalarina-esneklik-gosterecek/1773428. Accessed 12 May 2020

Anadolu Agency (2020d) https://www.aa.com.tr/tr/ekonomi/ecb-baskani-lagarde-ekonomideki-toparlanmanin-zamanini-tahmin-etmek-zor/1824556. Accessed 15 May 2020

Anadolu Agency (2020e) https://www.aa.com.tr/tr/analiz/merkez-bankalari-politikalarina-koronavirus-ayari/1742927. Accessed 01 May 2020

Anadolu Agency (2020f) https://www.aa.com.tr/tr/dunya/ingiltere-merkez-bankasi-politika-faizini-50-baz-puan-indirdi/1761763. Accessed 11 Mar 2020

Anadolu Agency (2020g) https://www.aa.com.tr/tr/ekonomi/ingilterede-612-bin-kisi-isini-kaybetti-/1878617. Accessed, 16 June 2020

Bank of Japan (2020a) https://www.boj.or.jp/en/mopo/mpmdeci/state_2020/k200121a.htm/. Accessed 21 Jan 2020

Bank of Japan (2020b) https://www.boj.or.jp/en/announcements/release_2020/rel200316c.pdf. Accessed 18 Mar 2020

Bank of Japan (2020c) https://www.boj.or.jp/en/announcements/release_2020/rel200316d.pdf. Accessed 18 Mar 2020

Bank of Japan (2020d) https://www.boj.or.jp/en/announcements/release_2020/rel200316f.pdf. Accessed 18 Mar 2020

Bank of Japan (2020e) https://www.boj.or.jp/en/announcements/release_2020/rel200316i.pdf. Accessed 18 Mar 2020

Bank of Japan (2020f) https://www.boj.or.jp/en/announcements/release_2020/k200427a.pdf. Accessed 01 May 2020

Bank of Japan (2020g) https://www.boj.or.jp/en/announcements/release_2020/rel200427j.pdf. Accessed 04 June 2020

Bank of Japan (2020h) https://www.boj.or.jp/en/announcements/release_2020/rel200427i.pdf. Accessed 04 June 2020

Bank of Japan (2020i) https://www.boj.or.jp/en/announcements/release_2020/rel200501d.pdf. Accessed 04 June 2020

Bank of Japan (2020j) https://www.boj.or.jp/en/announcements/release_2020/k200616a.pdf. Accessed 25 June 2020

Bloomberg HT (2020) https://www.bloomberght.com/amb-euro-bolgesi-disindaki-merkez-bankalarina-euro-cinsinden-likidite-saglayacak-2258736. Accessed 25 June 2020

Central Bank of Republic of Turkey (2020) http://www.tcmb.gov.tr

China Banking News (2020) http://www.chinabankingnews.com/2020/04/20/chinas-one-year-loan-prime-rate-drops-to-3-85/. Accessed 04 May 2020

European Central Bank (2020a) https://www.ecb.europa.eu/press/pr/date/2020/html/ecb.mp200123~ae33d37f6e.en.html. Accessed 04 Apr 2020

European Central Bank (2020b) https://www.ecb.europa.eu/press/pr/date/2020/html/ecb.mp200312~8d3aec3ff2.en.html. Accessed 04 Mar 2020

European Central Bank (2020c) https://www.ecb.europa.eu/press/pr/date/2020/html/ecb.pr200318_1~3949d6f266.en.html, Accessed 29 Apr 2020

European Central Bank (2020d) https://www.ecb.europa.eu/press/pr/date/2020/html/ecb.mp200430~1eaa128265.en.html. Accessed 13 May 2020

European Central Bank (2020e) https://www.ecb.europa.eu/press/pr/date/2020/html/ecb.pr200402~942a1358ee.en.html. Accessed 30 Apr 2020

European Central Bank (2020f) https://www.ecb.europa.eu/press/pr/date/2020/html/ecb.pr200415~96f622e255.en.html. Accessed 30 Apr 2020

European Central Bank (2020g) https://www.ecb.europa.eu/press/pr/date/2020/html/ecb.pr200430_1~477f400e39.en.html. Accessed 30 Apr 2020

European Central Bank (2020h) https://www.ecb.europa.eu/press/pr/date/2020/html/ecb.pr200430~fa46f38486.en.html. Accessed 30 Apr 2020

European Central Bank (2020i) https://www.ecb.europa.eu/press/pr/date/2020/html/ecb.mp200604~a307d3429c.en.html. Accessed 04 June 2020

Federal Reserve Bank of New York (2020) https://www.newyorkfed.org/press. Accessed 01 Apr 2020

Forex Live (2020) https://www.forexlive.com/centralbank/!/china-pboc-interest-rate-decision-due-monday-22-june-2020-preview-on-hold-expected-20200621. Accessed 22 June 2020

Federal Reserve (2020a) https://www.federalreserve.gov/monetarypolicy/files/monetary20200303a1.pdf. Accessed 01 Apr 2020

Federal Reserve (2020b) https://www.federalreserve.gov/monetarypolicy/files/monetary20200315a1.pdf. Accessed 01 Apr 2020

Federal Reserve (2020c) https://www.federalreserve.gov/newsevents/pressreleases/monetary20200315c.htm. Accessed 01 Apr 2020

Federal Reserve (2020d) https://www.federalreserve.gov/newsevents/pressreleases/monetary20200317a.htm. Accessed 02 Apr 2020

Federal Reserve (2020e) https://www.federalreserve.gov/newsevents/pressreleases/monetary20200318a.htm. Accessed 02 Apr 2020

Federal Reserve (2020f) https://www.federalreserve.gov/newsevents/pressreleases/monetary20200319b.htm. Accessed 02 Apr 2020

Federal Reserve (2020g) https://www.federalreserve.gov/newsevents/pressreleases/monetary20200323a.htm. Accessed 02 Apr 2020

Federal Reserve (2020h) https://www.federalreserve.gov/newsevents/pressreleases/monetary20200331a.htm. Accessed 02 Apr 2020

Federal Reserve (2020i) https://www.federalreserve.gov/newsevents/pressreleases/monetary20200409a.htm. Accessed 02 Apr 2020

Federal Reserve (2020j) https://www.federalreserve.gov/newsevents/pressreleases/monetary20200610a.htm. Accessed 03 Apr 2020

Federal Reserve (2020k) https://www.federalreserve.gov/newsevents/pressreleases/monetary20200610b.htm. (Accessed: 03 Apr 2020

Federal Reserve (2020l) https://www.federalreserve.gov/newsevents/pressreleases/monetary20200615b.htm. Accessed 03 Apr 2020

Financial Times (2020a) https://www.ft.com/content/98fb0c6a-5cd4-11ea-b0ab-339c2307bcd4. Accessed 12 May 2020
Financial Times (2020b) https://www.ft.com/content/6d1725be-5e9d-11ea-b0ab-339c2307bcd4. Accessed 03 May 2020
Hürriyet (2020) http://bigpara.hurriyet.com.tr/haberler/ekonomi-haberleri/lagardedan-koronavirus-uyarisi-ekonomik-belirsizlige_ID1460024/. Accessed 05 Apr 2020
Reuters (2020) https://www.reuters.com/article/us-ecb-policy-lagarde/euro-zone-economy-to-shrink-between-8-and-12-in-2020-lagarde-idUSKBN2330WU. Accessed 27 May 2020
www.bloomberght.com https://www.bloomberght.com/moody-s-ingiltere-yi-anlasmasiz-ayrilik-konusunda-uyardi-2257568. Accessed 01 April 2020
www.dunya.com https://www.dunya.com/finans/haberler/boe-faizi-yuzde-01e-cekti-haberi-465377. Accessed 19 Mar 2020
www.investing.com.tr (2020) https://tr.investing.com/economic-calendar/pboc-interest-rate-decision-1083. Accessed 01 May 2020

**Ümit Çevik** works as Financial Analyst in Ziraat Participation Bank, İstanbul, Turkey in the SME and corporate segment department. He consults as a financial analyst in the fields of financial analysis/credit evaluation of companies. His specialized areas are financial reporting standards, project analysis, financial analysis, loan allocation. He joined a lot of training in the field of cash flow analysis and he has graduation from MBA programme in Bahçeşehir University.

**Belgin Yakışan Mutlu** is working as a Business and Financial Correspondent, Anatolian Agency. Through her work, Ms. Yakisan Mutlu engages with the economic and financial ministries of the government as well as a multitude of state-owned financial institutions and private financial institutions. She was deemed worthy of awards in the categories of financial research by MUSİAD. She worked as a Private Consumer Representative at Garanti Bank between 2010–2012, as a trainee in the Communications and Foreign Relations Department at Central Bank of the Republic of Turkey in 2010, as an analyst at Association of Economic Enterprise and Business Ethics between 2008–2010. She has had a bachelor's degree from the Faculty of Economics and Administrative Sciences, Marmara University in 2010. She has presented her study titled "Using Weak Instrumental Variables Method for Investigation of the Effect of Education on Income" at the International Symposium on Econometrics Statistics and Operations Research of Pamukkale University in Denizli, Turkey.

# Chapter 11
# The Effect of COVID-19 on Electronic Currencies as They Become Common Payment Methods

**Doğancan Akata**

**Abstract** Social events or disasters have caused changes in the materials that individuals use in daily life. On the other hand, technological developments have also affected these changes. Nowadays, this situation is often referred to as digital transformation. Digital transformation is a fundamental process that uses digital tools, through technological and cultural changes. This process has affected the world of finance as well as in all areas of life. The most important effects are the transfer of payment systems and markets to the Internet. The use of electronic money by individuals in daily life is increasing. Electronic money refers to a certain amount of cash or deposits exchanged from the financial institution through the fast payment service initiated by banks and third parties using certain electronic channels (credit cards, etc.). This study evaluates the effect of the COVID-19 pandemic, on the use of electronic money. The course of digital transformation in financial instruments has changed after COVID-19. It is particularly important to assess, in a realistic way, the risks of contamination through cash, as avoiding cash can have distributional consequences. After the outbreak of the pandemic, the increase in online shopping rates and the electronic payment preferences of individuals also increased. However, some companies that place an online order apply to the cash on delivery method because they cannot accept online payments or because most of their customers cannot pay electronically. States are also developing projects to adapt to this new payment system. Problem is that infrastructure investments that require high amounts of public expenditure are investments that the state and international organizations (for developing countries) can afford and require time.

**Keywords** COVID-19 · Digital transformation · Electronic money · Financial systems · Pandemic · Payment methods

D. Akata (✉)
Department of Public Finance and Financial Management/Post-Graduate Study, İzmir Katip Çelebi University, İzmir, Turkey



B. Açıkgöz and İ. A. Acar (eds.), *Pandemnomics: The Pandemic's Lasting Economic Effects*, Accounting, Finance, Sustainability, Governance & Fraud: Theory and Application, https://doi.org/10.1007/978-981-16-8024-3_11

## 11.1 Introduction

The invention of paper and technological developments in printing machines are indisputably the most important factors in the use of paper money. However, there is another factor that is often overlooked and that many scientists have defended: The Black Plague. The clothes left over from millions of people who lost their lives in this epidemic have become a very low-cost raw material source for papermakers, and a high amount of paper was used in various areas with the produced papers. Thus, this epidemic has become one of the factors that do not come to the fore in the spread of paper money, yet important.

About 670 years after the Black Plague, on 17 November 2019, the first case of a new epidemic that would sweep the world in the Far East emerged. The name of this new epidemic was COVID-19. In a period of ongoing digital transformation, the impact of the COVID-19 outbreak, which affected the world in a very short time, on social and economic areas was enormous. The strict implementation of hygiene and social distancing rules, especially in the social field, has brought a new order to social life.

The measures implemented in social life to prevent the spread of the epidemic also have effects in the financial field. Even the preference of payment in cash (paper and coins) in daily life has changed. In order to minimize the spread of the virus, debit-credit cards, mobile payments and electronic currencies (digital, virtual currencies, etc.) used in a more limited environment have come to the fore, instead of money. Contrary to the Black Plague epidemic, COVID-19 will be listed among the main components such as development of financial technology and mass media, as regards the spread of electronic currencies today.

This section will, firstly, explain the concept of money within the framework of the views of various economists. Then, the milestones of the concept of money will be explained as a summary from the past to the present. Finally, the usual impact of digital transformation in the financial field on money and the extraordinary impact of the COVID-19 pandemic on this process will be discussed.

## 11.2 Money from the Perspectives of Various Philosophers

It would not be an academic approach to make a definite statement about the concept of money and present a generally valid definition. Because money has adapted to the system like a living organism shaped in accordance with the needs of the society, according to the geography and period in which it is in use. Throughout the history, depending on the advancement of financial technology, its structural forms have varied, and it has acquired various functions depending on the growth/development/change of the trade volume. In this context, various definitions and views on money in the literature are provided below. A. Smith, A. Marshall, K. Marx, J. M. Keynes, Paul A. Samuelson, William D. Nordhaus, M, Friedman,

Anna J. Schwartz, M. Ray, D. Anderson and G. Simmel who have been influential on the literature with different approaches on "*money*" in the History of Economics are addressed.

In the book titled "*A Study on the Nature and Causes of the Wealth of Nations*" written by Adam Smith in 1776, the development of money under the control of various civilizations throughout history is addressed under the section titled "*The Origin and Use of Money*". The mentioned section explains the role of money in social life in its own period by stating, "*… money has become a universal means of trade in all civilized nations, mediating the purchase and sale of all kinds of goods or being exchanged between themselves*" (Smith 2019).

In Alfred Marshall's book "*Principles of Economics*", first published in 1890, he described money as a "means" with a view parallel to A. Smith regarding money by stating "*Money is a means towards ends, and if the ends are noble, the desire for the means is not ignoble. The lad who works hard and saves all he can, in order to be able to pay his way afterwards at a University, is eager for money; but his eagerness is not ignoble. In short, money is general purchasing power, and is sought as a means to all kinds of ends, high as well as low, spiritual as well as material. Thus though it is true that 'money' or 'general purchasing power' or "command over material wealth," is the centre around which economic science clusters; this is so, not because money or material wealth is regarded as the main purpose of human effort…*", in the chapter entitled "*The Essence of Economy*".

In his book "Capital (Vol-1)" published in 1867, Karl Marx defined the condition of the commodity as being a measure of value and means of circulation as money and approached this with a critical point of view: "*Commodity that functions as a measure of value and functions as a means of circulation by itself or by a representative is" money ". Gold (or silver) therefore means money. On the one hand, gold functions as money, on the other hand, it comes into being as a commodity. (…) In other words, they play the role of pure and simple use values as the only appropriate existence form of exchange values against all other commodities*" (Marx 1976).

In his book of 1914 titled "A Treatise on Money (Volume-1), John M. Keynes claimed, regarding the concept of money: "… debt and price contracts are paid, the form and character of General Purchasing Power derive from its relation to being the Money-of-Account, because prices and debts must first be expressed under certain conditions…" (Keynes 2017). Keynes explained that in addition to being a concrete expression of purchasing power as a means of payment, money also functions as a money of account.

Regarding money in the "*The Modern Mixed Economy*" section of the book "*Economics*" first published in 1948 by Paul A. Samuelson and William D. Nordhaus: "*Money is an oil that facilitates change. When everyone trusts and accepts; trade is facilitated when money is accepted as payment for goods and debts. Imagine how complicated the economic life will be if you have to trade goods every time you want to buy pizza or go to a concert. What services can you offer at Sal's Pizza? What can you trade with your university to cover your tuition? Money acts as a matchmaker between buyers and sellers, and effortlessly influence mutual personal interests and petty marriages billions of times each day*" (Samuelson and Nordhaus

2009). They explained, through examples, that money is a tool that facilitates the exchange of services and goods in our daily life.

Regarding money, the book "*Monetary Statistics of the United States: Estimates, Sources, Methods*" published by Milton Friedman and Anna Jacobson Schwartz in 1970 explained that money can be defined according to various forms: "*… it doesn't matter how money is defined. Different definitions can be placed by changing the equations that determine the equilibrium values of the variables at the same time*" (Friedman and Anna 1970).

In the "*Definition and Measurement of Money*" section of Margaret Ray and David Anderson's book "*Krugman's Economics for Ap* * 2nd Edition", which was first published in 2010, which is an adaptation of "*Economics*" by Paul Krugman and Robin Wells, a definition of money is used that is not different from the previous literature examples: "*Money is defined by the job it does: money is an asset that can be easily used to purchase goods and services…if an asset is defined as liquid if it can be easily converted into cash. Money consists of cash that is liquid by definition and other assets with liquidity feature*" (Ray and Anderson 2011).

As a different point of view, in the book "*The Philosophy of Money*", first published in 1900 by the German sociologist and social philosopher Georg Simmel: "*Money is measured by the goods with which it is exchanged and also by the money itself. Because money is not paid only in money, as shown by the money market and lending with interest, but a country's currency becomes a measure of value for another country's currency, as foreign exchange transactions show*" (Simmel 2018: 83). Simmel, in his study where he addressed the concept of money philosophically, did not consider money only as an expression of a concrete quantity, but explained that its main value took its final form by assuming abstract qualities and with the effect of independent variables.

## 11.3 Journey of Money from Its Brief History to Internet

While it is so difficult to unite even on a general definition of money, arranging a detailed title on the history of money will drag the study into a scope beyond its purpose. Examining the studies in the literature about the history of money, it is observed that, on the one hand, generalizations involving the life and nature of human beings were put forward, and on the other hand, the positioning of money in various cultures and societies was discussed. On the other hand, it was deepened by economic historians through statistics and general theories based on pure economics. Accordingly, the concept of money is not only seen as the transformation of any substance according to social acceptances throughout history, but also the ways in which this value is registered and the way in which the controlling sovereign power evolves according to its political purposes have been adopted in a broad perspective. In this respect, it will focus on certain milestones that will not harm the purpose of the study, but will facilitate the understanding of the transition to electronic-based currencies (Fig. 11.1).

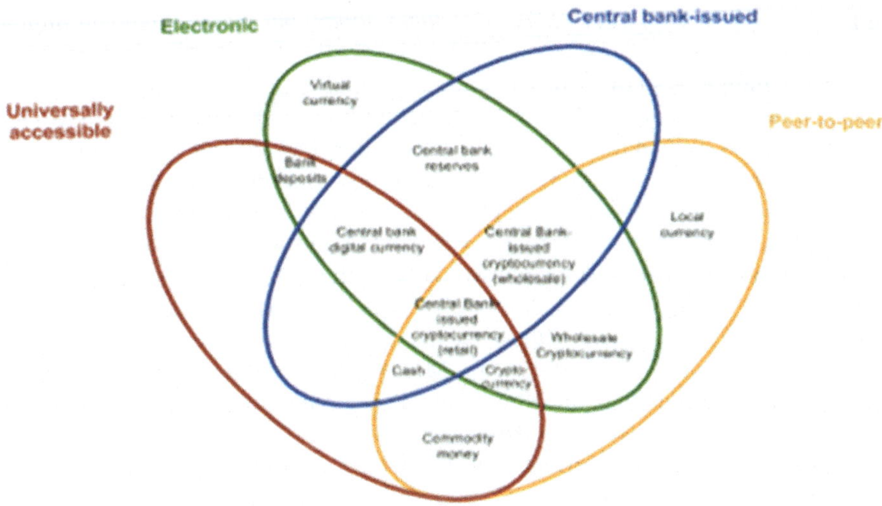


**Fig. 11.1** Money flower: a taxonomy of money. *Source* Bech and Garratt (2017)

## *11.3.1 The Order Before Money*

The value represented by money can be described as abstract and concrete. In concrete terms, it is important which materials that the money is made of. There are many types from various mines to electronic form nowadays, with the development and spread of technology (see Bech and Garratt 2017). The enormous increase in the rate of use over time also adds new functions of money (promoting economic activities, redistribution of income, etc.). In an abstract evaluation, the principle of acceptability and trust in money are manifested itself in society (s) and, today, even in the global framework. The fact that these and many similar variations increase by changing over time leads to the conclusion that money should not be limited to a single definition as it is always dynamic and adapt to the environment and period in which it is accepted.

Ludwing von Mises' book "*The Theory of Money and Credit*", first published in 1912, explained the situations where money is not needed by the individual and/or society by stating: "*Money is not a need where there is no free exchange of goods and services. At the same time, if the production and consumption of only local resources take place in the same household in a society, money becomes an unnecessary phenomenon as much as what it expresses to an individual living in isolation from society. Moreover, even in an economic order based on division of labour, money would still be unnecessary if the means of production were socialized, control of production and distribution of finished products were in the hands of a central body and individuals were not allowed to exchange their allocated consumer goods for consumer goods allocated to others. The phenomenon of money foresees an economic order in which production is based on the division of labour and private property is formed not only in first order goods (consumer goods) but also in goods of higher orders (goods of production)*" (Mises 1954).

The **Exchange System**, which is one of the most primitive financial systems, provided the functioning of economic life before trade and the use of money. Our distant ancestors wanted to exchange the excess they had and get other things they needed. However, this system has encountered a bottleneck over time. It was not always easy to find what you want and someone who is looking for what you have, in the right amounts, in return for what you want. As a solution, some objects were considered markers that most people would be willing to trade for something else in the future. At first, salt or ox skins were examples of such a practice; over time some metals were used, because these metals were scarce, useful, durable, portable and divisible. In general, in everyday life "Money" succeeded because it fulfilled the superior exchange function, valued not only as a commodity in itself but also as a ready-made medium of exchange (Hart 2005).

Although it is not at the forefront of the financial system, exchange trade somehow continued to exist in the background. However, it would not be rational to think of this system as independent from technology today, at least in countries where technology is advancing. When we think that the states are now in collective exchange of technological progress and even ideas in some communities (Digital Nations), it is not an assumption that they adapt to the new order and survive as was the case in history. One-way interactions with the digital transformation of individuals (Peer to Peer, P2P), companies (Business to Business, B2B) and governments (Government to Government, G2G) will be the trigger for this adaptation (Table 11.1).

**Table 11.1** Digital development of the government phenomenon

| | Gov 1.0 | Gov 2.0 | Gov 3.0 |
|---|---|---|---|
| Main goal | Better services | Openness and collaboration | Societal problem solving, citizen well being, optimization of resources |
| Main method | Connected governance | Open and collaborative governance | Smart governance |
| Usual application level | National | National and local | Local to international |
| Key tool | Portal | Social media | Ubiquitous smart services/devices/apps |
| Key obstacle/risk | Public sector mentality | Public sector mentality | Public sector mentality |
| Key ICT (information and communication technology) area | Infrastructures and organisation | People and data | Machine intelligence and IoT (Internet of Things) |
| Most needed discipline, beyond ICT | Management | Sociology | Everything |

*Source* Charalabidis (2015)

As a pre-money system, the **Gift Economy** is considered as a sub-branch of the economy. However, this concept is put forward to refute the planned economy, which believes that human behaviour is a result of rational calculations. The gift economy refers to the providers of goods or services that do not have a clear expectation of what to return or what they expect to return. There are many sharing behaviours based on non-standard habits. At the same time, giving and receiving gifts has turned into an unspecified obligation, creating a confidential relationship between buyer and seller.

### *11.3.2 Commodity (Good) Money and Shifting to Paper Money*

With the spread of **Commodity Money** and the development of trade and productivity over time, people immediately needed a tool for change that they could widely use. The exchange tool to meet these requirements should not be relatively difficult to obtain, not easy to damage and rot, easy to process and suitable for payment in a variety of sizes. After people tried various items, almost all civilizations in the world chose two metals as "*money*": gold and silver. It is difficult to obtain gold and silver; they are suitable mines due to their relatively soft and easy-to-cut properties, although they are not easy to destroy.

In the economy, if the objects used as money are related to other uses as well as their properties as goods, the commodity monetary system is considered to be in place in that economy. This system developed spontaneously and there is no state intervention at any stage of development. At this point, another issue is that paper money may be mistaken for commodity money. The commodity value of a piece of paper used as money is much lower than its value as money. In other words, the value of paper money has taken on a different quality by completely separating it from its essence. In this case, the monetary value included in the commodity money definition is valid for goods with equal relative values as goods (Parasız 2013).

The first examples of **Paper Money** have a history dating back to the seventh century, the Tang Dynasty in China. That its actually active use developed in the Song Dynasty in the eleventh century is the prevalent view in the sources. It is accepted that it later spread to China and the Mongol Empire through the Yuan Dynasty. The recognition of this system by Europe dates back to the thirteenth century, when explorers like Marco Polo mentioned it in their travel notes.

Although the origin of paper money is considered to be China, it was mentioned by the Lombards in the West. Lombards, of Italian origin, spread all over Europe and became bankers who kept the money of those dealing with trade. The functions these bankers have undertaken over time roughly summarize the development of paper money. These bankers, who facilitate trade significantly, have credited or debited these accounts according to the trade between merchants through the checking accounts they open for their customers.

In this process, turnover transactions emerged for the first time. Subsequently, deposit transaction, lending to custody money against interest, certificates with the statement of immediate payment in case of debt instead of coins, and finally, as some of the certificates issued and released to the market were returned, debt certificates were started to be issued on the deposits they consigned, and the foundation of modern banking was laid (Paya 2013).

The origin of banknotes in their current form is based on the certificates of gold and silver coins accumulated in gold and silversmiths (goldsmith-bankers), in the example of England, where the origin of the banknotes is not so independent from commodity currencies. London's first bankers are these goldsmiths. Goldsmiths eagerly embraced the banking role. The first goldsmith's certificate for precious metal deposits was issued in 1633 by the goldsmith Lawrence Hoare. However, most of the wealthy merchants kept their commodity money in the mint located in the Tower of London. When King Charles I seized £ 200,000 worth of commodity money in 1640, trust in the state was lost and wealthy merchants turned to goldsmiths. This event is considered as a historical event in terms of acting like a bank.

As a result, the position of paper money became one of the instruments of intervention in government-run markets. The amount of paper money used by individuals in the market as a medium of exchange and the amount of "cash" along with the coins has become a very small part of the total money offered over time. The amounts that are created as bank money which are only included in the bank records started to quit being the equivalent of a precious metal, which is the logic of paper money's emergence, and created its own identity with the trust mechanism; it began to turn into bank money, first in bank books and then on computer screens.

### *11.3.3 Electronic-Digital-Virtual Confusion and Plastic Period*

Increasing dependence on machines, especially computers, has led to significant social effects. A generation ago, computers were cumbersome but were built-in tools for data computing and word processing; that is, it was not found in every workplace or home. Today, computers can be accessed everywhere, from mainframes computers to smart phones, from desktop computers to laptops and even from visible to invisible technology, and today's computers are intelligent machines powered by artificial intelligence. Thanks to the high-speed connection and Internet, anyone with a computer or a smart phone can access information, services and entertainment in many parts of the world. In summary, just as people changed computers, computers changed people (Lin 2013).

Expectations from the digital system come to the fore in areas such as data storage, processing speed and accessibility. There is an uninterrupted digital revolution in the global economy. According to a recent study, this amount, called the global data sphere, will increase from 16.1 trillion gigabytes in 2016 to 163 trillion gigabytes

**Table 11.2** Money matrix

| | | Form | |
|---|---|---|---|
| | | Physical | Digital |
| Legal status | Irregular | Some local currencies | Virtual currencies |
| | Regular | Banknotes and coins | Digital currencies |
| | | | Deposit account in commercial banks |

*Source* European Central Bank (2012)

(163 Zettabytes) by 2025. This tenfold increase will encompass data held everywhere from cloud systems to handheld devices (Zhang 2018). This means that the pool, which includes from personal data to the private sector and even government data, is now transferred from the physical environment to the digital environment.

Today, payment cards are a more preferred method than cash payment system, through a bank deposit or credit account. Being individually configurable, they make it possible to pay, transfer and split into instalments the high amounts via a small plastic card. Despite the presence of sub-types that serve many purposes, debit card and especially credit card are the prominent payment cards. These plastic cards, which became more popular towards the end of the twentieth century, started with telephone lines, which were the minimum technological need in this period, and the use of the blessings of the Internet in the data sharing of mass media in the twenty-first century and its spread to wider circles expanded the usage areas of payment cards (Table 11.2).

When looking at the equivalents used in the literature regarding the concept of digital money, it is possible to see that electronic (electronic money, electronic currency, e-money) expressions are also preferred in some studies. However, in a wider perspective, as a result of a detailed research, it was observed that there were small differences between the phenomena represented by each concept. Electronic money refers to a certain amount of cash or deposits received and given from a financial institution through the fast payment service initiated by banks and third parties through the use of certain electronic channels (credit cards, etc.). It turns out that digital currencies, unlike electronic money, are not based on bank money and are created completely independently in the digital environment. The most important criterion they expressed in general terms, be it the concept of digital or electronic money, is that money has undergone a new change.

## 11.4 New Catalyst in Financial Transformation: COVID-19

### *11.4.1 Digital Transformation*

Before the COVID-19 pandemic, technological developments in mass media entered a rapid pace of change, especially towards the end of the twentieth century, as was the case in all areas of life. In this new digital age, in the fields of economy and finance, there have been areas getting their share from the transformation and have adapted themselves to innovations quickly. These developments triggered the transformation process of factors such as trade, economic-financial planning and even taxation within the framework of economic activities. These requirements have been able to function properly with the registration of the economy in a certain order (Harford 2019).

The common denominator of all new developments is a phenomenon of "*digital transformation*" that started from the beginning of the twentieth century and has recently made itself felt more intense. Many authors and researchers have focused on a key concept in transformation since the mid-twentieth century. We see important events occur today in society and economy similar to those occurred, throughout history, upon the changes that started with the agricultural revolution and, much later, with the industrial revolution. In this context, Space, Information and Electronic ages are mentioned. While Zbigniev Brzezinski was talking about the "*Technotronic Age*", sociologist Daniel Bell described the "*Post-Industrial Society*". Soviet futurists spoke of the "*Scientific Technological Revolution*". Alvin Toffler calls it "*Super Industrial Society*" (Toffler 1981). An economic manifestation of this new order put forward from different segments has inevitably started to occur.

### *11.4.2 Modern Payment Systems*

In the booklet issued in 2014, the Central Bank of Turkey expressed payment system as, "*... covers the tools which facilitate the exchange of goods and services between economic units, regulations and standards, institutional and organizational framework, the operating processes and communication network*" (TCMB 2014). This expression has taken a broad perspective to encompass individuals in economic life, the state as a legislator, on the other hand, financial institutions (Banks and Stock Exchanges) and mass communication technology. The "*exchange*" of goods and services in the daily life of individuals has been carried out for a long time with the use of money consisting of banknotes and coins. However, from the second half of the twentieth century onwards, use of credit-debit cards that require the authorization of the financial institution as a third party has increased rapidly.

As of the twenty-first century, there are also electronic methods that function as an exchange between economic units such as banknotes and coins, but not put into circulation by any government and not organized and managed by any financial institution.

**Table 11.3** Ratio of use of cash in 2018 (%)

| Country | Cash (%) | Country | Cash (%) |
|---|---|---|---|
| Australia | 37 | Italy | 86 |
| England | 42 | South Korea | 14 |
| Finland | 54 | Spain | 87 |
| France | 68 | Sweden | 20 |
| Germany | 80 | USA | 32 |

*Source* G4S Cash Solutions and Payments Advisory Group (2018)

In all this framework, a payment instrument recognized by a state, which is a legal payment (legal tender), is cash; that is, it a means of payment recognized by a legal system to be valid for the fulfilment of a financial obligation. As mentioned earlier, paper money and coins are common legal forms of payment in many countries. This feature of cash distinguishes it from personal checks, credit cards, debit cards and similar non-cash payment methods. However, it is observed that in countries with intense digital transformation, the rates of cash usage in daily life have decreased, and non-cash payments are becoming more common. It is observed that non-cash payment tools such as credit cards, debit cards, mobile payments and electronic money, albeit limited, are beginning to replace cash (G4S Cash Solutions and Payments Advisory Group 2018) (Table 11.3).

### *11.4.3 COVID-19 Being Included in the Process*

With the COVID-19 epidemic turning into a global pandemic, it is inevitable that in the future perspective, production, consumption and trade data for 2020 and 2021 will be examined and the shock and recovery processes will be monitored by many researchers (Mann 2020). However, the transformation process in financial instruments, which continues routinely, has begun to follow a different course with an extraordinary factor. The impact of the pandemic required sharp measures and rapid adaptation of individuals, governments and financial institutions to these measures. The interconnection of financial markets can show a domino effect and make it inevitable that the entire economy will be driven into an impasse.

As an example, in the opinion presented by the World Bank, it was emphasized that properly functioning money markets are of critical importance for well-functioning capital markets. During the COVID-19 pandemic, the authorities stated that they should focus on efforts to improve the functioning of the money market in order to create adequate bases for capital markets recovery (The World Bank 2020a).

On the other hand, it was estimated by the World Bank that international remittances would be declined sharply by about 20% in 2020 due to the economic crisis caused by the COVID-19 pandemic and the closure at the borders of the country. Projected as the sharpest drop in recent history, it is emphasized that this will largely stem from a decrease in wages and employment of migrant workers, who are more vulnerable to loss of employment and wages during the economic crisis in a host country. As a result, it is estimated that remittances to low- and middle-income countries will decrease by 19.7% to 445 billion dollars (The World Bank 2020b).

In the last report published by G4S Cash Solutions and Payments Advisory Group in 2018, just before the COVID-19 outbreak, the increase in the use of mobile phones and electronic wallets also encourages the use of electronic payments over cash. Combination of these technologies and devices allows it to quickly complete transactions in a consumer-to-consumer (C2C) or face-to-face, electronically and instantly in retail environment. These forms of electronic payment are increasingly taking over the valuable features of payment tools that previously only received cash, such as direct placement, availability and convenience/ease of use (G4S Cash Solutions and Payments Advisory Group 2018).

Some companies that switch to online orders resort to cash on delivery as they cannot accept online payments or most of their customers cannot pay electronically. The most recent World Bank Findex study revealed that 31% of adults worldwide still do not have access to a financial account. Cash on delivery may be the second best option, especially given the need for social distancing. Contactless online payment can eliminate the need to exchange cash in person. In the COVID-19 process, governments can support the use of contactless payments by raising awareness of public health benefits and working with financial institutions to ensure everyone has access to these payment methods (Ungerer and Portugal 2020).

Table 11.4 displays the use of credit card (physical environment) in domestic shopping in Turkey for the first six months of 2019 and 2020. The epidemic began in the fourth quarter of 2019. After this period, in the period until the second quarter of 2020, a decline of 10–15% has started in both the number of transactions and the transaction amount of the credit card

Table 11.5 displays the payment card transactions made in the Internet in Turkey for the first six months of 2019 and 2020. Unlike the use of credit cards in the physical environment, payment card transactions in the Internet environment have started to

**Table 11.4** Using credit cards in domestic shopping (Turkey)

| *2019* | | |
|---|---|---|
| Period | Transaction volume | Transaction amount (Million TL) |
| Q1 | 975,991,684 | 18,296,036 |
| Q2 | 1,046,732,719 | 20,167,001 |
| Q3 | 1,078,479,573 | 21,481,951 |
| Q4 | 1,107,724,879 | 22,078,497 |
| *2020* | | |
| Q1 | 1,074,369,726 | 21,484,870 |
| Q2 | 868,998,414 | 19,667,648 |
| Q3 | 1,194,696,353 | 28,971,244 |

*Source* Merkezi (2020a)

**Table 11.5** Pay online with debit or credit cards (Turkey)

| Period | Transaction volume | | Transaction amount (Million TL) | |
|---|---|---|---|---|
| | Domestic and international use of domestic cards | Domestic use of domestic and foreign cards | Domestic and international use of domestic cards | Domestic use of domestic and foreign cards |
| *2019* | | | | |
| Q1 | 155,590,067 | 136,322,574 | 3,810,963 | 40,66,018 |
| Q2 | 162,187,236 | 143,506,689 | 4,181,144 | 4,544,439 |
| Q3 | 166,217,766 | 150,687,618 | 4,762,610 | 5,147,780 |
| Q4 | 195,088,989 | 176,555,913 | 5,073,699 | 5,252,812 |
| *2020* | | | | |
| Q1 | 194,431,546 | 173,999,121 | 5,002,779 | 5,131,158 |
| Q2 | 217,815,440 | 187,873,124 | 5,665,238 | 5,529,670 |
| Q3 | 248,847,008 | 222,186,362 | 7,135,732 | 7,227,720 |

*Source* Merkezi (2020b)

increase with the COVID-19 outbreak in the fourth quarter of 2019. Shopping habits' tendency to the Internet shopping has increased in Turkey.

Of course, non-cash use with the epidemic process brings some negativities that affect this transformation process. In his speech at the Consensus Blockchain Conference, Kenneth Blanco, President of the Financial Crimes Enforcement Network (FinCEN), which operates under the US Treasury, listed the cybercrime types rising during the COVID-19 outbreak (Blanco 2020) as follows:

- Using COVID-19 information as a bait;
- Targeting vulnerabilities in applications that support remote work such as virtual private networks and remote desktop software to steal information and compromise transactions;
- To exploit COVID-19 for the sale of fraud, extortion, ransomware and fraudulent medical products;
- Digital images use "filing credentials" attacks to facilitate "deepfake" manipulation and account takeover.

### 11.4.4 Technological Competence

It is particularly important to assess, in a realistic way, the risks of contamination through cash, as avoiding cash can have distributional consequences. If cash is not accepted as a means of payment across the community, it can lead to an inequality "*payments divide*" among those who have access to digital payments. This can have a particularly serious impact on non-bank and senior consumers. It is expected that digital payments will be used more by the economic authorities in the near future. However, in the emerging market and most emerging economies, access to such alternative payment instruments seems far from universal (Auer et al. 2020). There are profit-oriented investment strategies in countries where telecommunications industry is not under the state administration. The industry's reluctance to make a significant investment in markets that represent a small percentage of the revenue stream is quite obvious. Therefore, it is likely that technical problems will continue to hinder rural access for a while; the cost of equipment and monthly expenses pose a problem with low socio-economic groups in both rural and urban areas (Cullen 2001).

However, with the pandemic, the first trend has been towards the social protection and social assistance programmes that can be expanded rapidly and whose scope can be expanded. Many developing countries have already tried and tested programmes from the past to the present. Cash transfers and public spending programmes can be strengthened for this purpose. Such programmes can be supported through mobile or digital payment channels where such platforms have sufficient coverage, can establish their identity and have beneficiaries' accounts (The Word Bank 2020c). This way, the rate of access to digital and the usage rates of electronic payment methods may be increased.

As an example of this, millions of US taxpayers had to wait a long time for promised incentive payments of up to $1200 per person as the COVID-19 outbreak turned into an economic crisis. Payments are still expected to be made to those married to immigrants who have not received tax returns in recent years and who do not have a bank account or a registered bank account with the Internal Revenue Service (IRS). On this very situation, the advocates of the Digital Dollar and Central Bank Digital Currencies believe that a digital currency system can solve the logistical problem of how to quickly distribute large sums to many individuals with access to diversified banking services (Thiruvengadam 2020).

This move towards digital money has gained rapid momentum with the COVID-19 outbreak. Although the risk of transmission is low, societal concerns that the virus can be transferred in cash are expected to result in individuals making less preference for cash currencies. This trend towards digital payments is growing worldwide; many countries, including Australia, Sweden, South Korea, Russia and the UK, are seeing a transition towards a cashless society. However, China is at the forefront of the transformation in digital payments. People living in major cities of China usually pay for goods and services through smartphone applications such as AliPay or WeChat, which are linked to their bank accounts (Freidin 2020).

## 11.5 Conclusion

Wars, diseases and inventions have always been the determining factors that started and ended an era in human history. However, from today's perspective, it is an indisputable fact that the frequency of these events increases even more. Because of the development of mass media, increasing population density, easy and fast transportation have turned the world into a small village with a population of 6 billion.

Now, inventions are more towards comfort, wars are more deadly, and diseases spread faster. The inevitable impact area of the variables of all these equations is economics.

Increasing trade volume in parallel with the population requires financial-technology cooperation that can meet the needs of the society without interruption. The phenomenon of digitalization mentioned under the title of "Transformation" comes to the fore at this point, because the unit that will handle the capacity and density in data exchange is no longer the speed of electricity, but the speed of light. However, each unit in the society must be able to provide the minimum components (computer, smart phone, Internet, etc.) to meet this infrastructure. Even if the money phenomenon takes on a digital form, it will cease to function if individuals cannot access this money. While the provision of technological infrastructure and the evolution of social habits in this direction were the subjects of ongoing debate, the COVID-19 pandemic, which broke out suddenly and affected the world, changed the course of the process. The measures taken to prevent the spread of the pandemic also require changing payment habits.

The sudden acceleration of digital transformation has resulted in cash usage not being preferred due to the transmission risk. Despite the increasing demand, digital infrastructure must be provided and digital currencies must be both accepted and functional throughout the society. Another problem is that infrastructure investments that require high amounts of public expenditure are investments that the state and international organizations (for developing countries) can afford and require time.

The fact that the telecommunications industry, which is mentioned under the title of technological competence, is not under state administration, that is, it lacks the quality of public expenditure, creates the danger of deprivation of digital infrastructure in low socio-economic regions in rural and urban areas. While the state is performing digital transformation phases within its own structure, each individual receiving service on the opposite side must be integrated into this transformation with a minimum technological infrastructure. For example, digitizing the taxation process plays an important role in increasing efficiency and making audits more comprehensive and efficient. However, the lack of technical infrastructure and the individuals deprived of that technology to provide this service will make coordination between the administration and the taxpayer difficult. At the same time, it will not be possible to fully realize digital transformation in taxation and audit processes. However, the physical elements (related forms, audit personnel, etc.) in the taxation and audit processes will need to be continued so that taxpayers who do not benefit from digital services are not excluded.

The COVID-19 outbreak has caused companies and factories in many sectors to shrink and many people to lose their jobs. In order for these people to survive, the state has made transfer expenditures to the households. Ideas about making these aids to the individuals in a digital system rather than in cash through the bank come to the fore. This is considered as a development that will change the cash habit in daily life. With the COVID-19 outbreak, if retail shopping evolves in this direction and the private sector's digital payment applications are accepted by the society, it will be inevitable for electronic currencies to become widespread.

## References


Auer R, Cornelli G, Frost J (2020)Covid-19, cash, and the future of payments. BIS Bulletin, No: 3. Retrieved from Bank for International Settlements website: https://www.bis.org/publ/bisbull03.pdf. (Accessed on 5th Dec 2020)

Bech ML, Garratt R (2017) Central Bank cryptocurrencies. Retrieved from Bank for International Settlements website: https://www.bis.org/publ/qtrpdf/r_qt1709f.htm. (Accessed on 3rd Oct 2020)

Blanco K (2020) FinCEN director identifies virtual currency compliance risks and COVID-19 related issues at consensus 2020 conference. Retrieved from https://www.crowell.com/NewsEvents/AlertsNewsletters/all/FinCEN-Director-Identifies-Virtual-Currency-Compliance-Risks-and-COVID-19-Related-Issues-at-Consensus-2020-Conference. (Accessed on 15th Nov 2020)

Charalabidis Y (2015) What is Government 3.0. Retrieved from http://hraweb.aegean.gr/islab/index.php?option=com_content&view=article&id=262:what-is-government-30&catid=35:2010-03-26-11-56-09&Itemid=69. (Accessed on 8th Nov 2020)

Cullen R (2001) Addressing the digital divide. Retrieved from https://files.eric.ed.gov/fulltext/ED459714.pdf. (Accessed 8th on Dec 2020)

European Central Bank (2012) Virtual currency schemes. Retrieved from European Central Bank website: https://www.ecb.europa.eu/pub/pdf/other/virtualcurrencyschemes201210en.pdf. (Accessed on 18th Dec 2020)

Faure AP (2013) Money creation: genesis 2: goldsmith-bankers and bank notes. Retrieved from https://www.researchgate.net/publication/256056664_Money_Creation_Genesis_2_Goldsmith-Bankers_and_Bank_Notes/references. (Accessed on 13rd Dec 2020)

Freidin E (2020) The e-RMB: China's digital currency in The COVID-19 Era. Retrieved from https://foreignbrief.com/asia-pacific/china/the-e-rmb-chinas-digital-currency-in-the-covid-19-era/. (Accessed on 22th Dec 2020)

Friedman M, Anna JS (1970) Monetary statistics of the United States: estimates, sources, methods. (Business Cycles Ser.: No. 20). Columbia University Press, New York

G4S Cash Solutions and Payments Advisory Group (2018) World cash report 2018. Netherlands

Harford T (2019) Modern Ekonomiyi Şekillendiren Elli İcat. Pegasus Yayınları, İstanbul

Hart K (2005) Money: one anthropologist's view. In: Carrier JG (ed) A handbook of economic anthropology. Edward Elgar Publishing, UK, pp 160–176

Keynes JM (2017) A treatise on money, vol. 1. Retrieved from https://archive.org/details/in.ernet.dli.2015.45480/page/n25/mode/2up. (Accessed on 20th Nov 2020)

Lin TCW (2013) The new investor. 60 Ucla Law Rev 678, 680–734

Mann CL (2020) Real and financial lenses to assess the economic consequences of COVID-19. In: Baldwin R, Mauro BW (eds) Economics in the Time of COVID-19. CEPR Press, London

Marshall A (2013) Principles of economics (Eighth Edition: 1920). Retrieved from http://www.library.fa.ru/files/Marshall-Principles.pdf. (Accessed on 22nd Nov 2020)

Marx K (1976) Capital—a critique of political economy—Volume One (B. Fowkes, Trans.). Penguin Books in association with New Left Review. (Original work published 1867), England

Merkezi BK (2020a) Kredi Kartlarının Yurtiçi Alışverişte Kullanımı. Retrieved from Bankalararası Kart Merkezi website: https://bkm.com.tr/yerli-ve-yabanci-kredi-kartlarinin-yurt-ici-kullanimi/. (Accessed on 15th Nov 2020)

Merkezi BK (2020b) İnternetten Yapılan Kartlı Ödeme İşlemleri. Retrieved from Bankalararası Kart Merkezi website: https://bkm.com.tr/internetten-yapilan-kartli-odeme-islemleri/. (Accessed on 8th Dec 2020)

Mises L (1954) The theory of money and credit, (J.E. Batson. Trans). Yale University Press. (Original work published 1912), Connecticut

Mühleisen M (2018) The long and short of the digital revolution. Financ Dev 55(2):4–8

Parasız İ (2013) Para Teorisi ve Politikası. Ezgi Kitabevi, Bursa

Paya MM (2013) Para Teorisi ve Para Politikası. Türkmen Kitabevi, İstanbul

Polo M (1818) The travels of marco polo, a venetian, in the thirteenth century: being a description, by that early traveller, of remarkable places and things, in the eastern parts of the world (W. Marsden, Trans.). Cox and Baylis. (Original work published n.d.), London

Ray M, Anderson DA (2011) Krugman's economics for Ap* 2nd Edition. Worth Publishers, New York

Samuelson PA, Nordhaus WD (2009) Economics, 19th Edition. McGraw Hill Education, New York

Simmel G (2018) Paranın Felsefesi (Y. Alogan, Ö. D. Aydın, Trans.). İthaki Yayınları. (Original work published 1900), İstanbul

Smith A (2019) An inquiry into the nature and causes of the wealth of nations. Retrieved from http://www.gutenberg.org/files/3300/3300-h/3300-h.htm. (Accessed on 23rd Dec 2020)

The World Bank (2020a) COVID-19 outbreak: capital markets implications and response. Retrieved from The World Bank website: http://pubdocs.worldbank.org/en/776691586478873523/COVID-19-Outbreak-Capital-Markets.pdf. (Accessed on 28th Dec 2020)

The World Bank (2020b) World bank predicts sharpest decline of remittances in recent history. Retrieved from The World Bank website: https://www.worldbank.org/en/news/press-release/2020/04/22/world-bank-predicts-sharpest-decline-of-remittances-in-recent-history. (Accessed on 16th Dec 2020)

The Word Bank (2020c) The economy in the time of COVID-19. Retrieved from The World Bank website: https://openknowledge.worldbank.org/bitstream/handle/10986/33555/9781464815706.pdf?sequence=5&isAllowed=y. (Accessed on 22nd Dec 2020)

Thiruvengadam M (2020) How the COVID-19 crisis revived the digital dollar debate. Retrieved from https://www.coindesk.com/coronavirus-what-is-digital-dollar-cbdc-explainer. (Accessed on 18th Dec 2020)

Toffler A (1981) Üçüncü Dalga. (A. Seden, Trans). Altın Kitaplar Yayınevi. (Original work published 1980), İstanbul

Türkiye Cumhuriyet Merkez Bankası (2014) Ödeme Sistemleri—Türkiye'de Ödeme Sistemleri. Retrieved from https://www.tcmb.gov.tr/wps/wcm/connect/73289f67-d210-4f49-8902-6e14ecae055d/OdemeSistemleri.pdf?MOD=AJPERES&CACHEID=ROOTWORKSPACE-73289f67-d210-4f49-8902-6e14ecae055d-m5lk6L-. (Accessed on 5th Nov 2020)

Ungerer C, Portugal A (2020) Leveraging e-commerce in the fight against COVID-19. Retrieved from https://www.brookings.edu/blog/future-development/2020/04/27/leveraging-e-commerce-in-the-fight-against-covid-19/. (Accessed on 17th Dec 2020)

Zhang T (2018) Digitization of money and finance: challenges and opportunities. Retrieved from https://www.imf.org/en/News/Articles/2018/05/08/sp050818-digitization-of-money-and finance-challenges-and-opportunities. (Accessed on 4th Nov 2020)

**Doğancan Akata** is Ph.D., graduated from İzmir Katip Celebi University, Faculty of Economics and Administrative Sciences. His research focuses on Public Finance, Economic Crises, Digital Currency, Cryptocurrency and High-Frequency Trading. Dogancan Akata has contributed to book chapters on Payment Methods and Electronic Currencies research areas. His doctoral thesis on Cryptocurrency and High-Frequency Trading is still ongoing.

# Chapter 12
# Health and Refugee Protection as a Global Public Good: Evaluation of COVID-19 in Terms of Refugees

**Zeynep Demirci Çakıroğlu**

**Abstract** Global public goods: it is defined as goods and services whose benefits or harms exceed national borders and affect countries located in more than one geographical region and even the whole world, that not competition and exclusion in their consumption, and extending to future generations as well as the present generation. One of these goods is health. Pandemic, which is a global problem, emerges when the infectious diseases emerging in the countries go beyond the borders of the country and spread to other countries. The countries of the world have faced many epidemic diseases from past to present. Diseases such as Ebola, plague, polio, H1N1 and Zika are some of these epidemics. The last epidemic we have witnessed is COVID-19. The COVID-19 pandemic has seriously affected all countries of the world with the effect of globalization. Along with the health sector, there are difficulties in many different sectors, because countries have implemented various policies to control the pandemic, and the main purpose has been to reduce the risk of contamination by restricting people's movement. Although the measures taken are successful in controlling the pandemic, there are negative economic consequences. In this context, it is observed that the macroeconomic indicators of many countries have changed negatively. Another dimension of the COVID-19 process, which causes serious problems all over the world, is the refugees' conditions. In a globalizing world, the refugee problem is a global public bad, and providing protection to refugees in order to solve this problem is also a global public good. In this sense, it is necessary to pay attention to the living conditions of refugees in the measures taken regarding COVID-19. Around 20 million people around the world have left their homes due to war, violence or oppression in their country and continue their lives as refugees. Refugees face a series of difficulties following their asylum in various countries. Language barriers, difficulty in accessing information, sociocultural differences, close contact with people and inadequate access to health services are some of these difficulties. With these difficulties, refugees already live in overcrowded environments without access to basic health care. Conditions such as lack of clean water and soap, insufficient health personnel, overcrowding and malnutrition are the

---

Z. D. Çakıroğlu (✉)
Department of Fiscal Theory, İzmir Katip Çelebi University, İzmir, Turkey
e-mail: zeynep.demirci@ikcu.edu.tr

 
B. Açıkgöz and İ. A. Acar (eds.), *Pandemnomics: The Pandemic's Lasting Economic Effects*, Accounting, Finance, Sustainability, Governance & Fraud: Theory and Application, https://doi.org/10.1007/978-981-16-8024-3_12

problems experienced in refugee camps. At the same time, it is not possible to comply with social distance in the camps. In this context, refugees who encounter various difficulties even under normal conditions are more likely to become more vulnerable due to COVID-19, and the risk of contracting COVID-19 disease in refugee camps increases. Apart from refugees, the COVID-19 pandemic also negatively affects asylum seekers, forced migrants, illegal immigrants and the homeless, because these people live in environments with a high risk of contracting an epidemic disease. Their access to cleaning and basic living supplies is limited, or in some cases non-existent. Due to overcrowded prisons, poor health conditions, inadequate health care and lack of social distancing, the virus can spread easily among these people. Within this scope, although aid is provided by various organizations to protect refugees, asylum seekers and forced migrants from the pandemic, it can be said that these aids are not very sufficient. Since it is not possible to prevent diseases without considering the health of everyone in the society, measures should be taken to cover the whole society in the actions to be carried out to prevent COVID-19. Among these measures, refugees and immigrants should not be ignored. In the ongoing pandemic, no one is immune, including these vulnerable groups. Therefore, special measures should be taken to slow down and prevent the spread of the epidemic, including refugees and migrants. Since there can be no public health without refugee and migrant health, they must be included in national public health systems. It should be ensured that the information requested to reach the public about the epidemic reaches these groups by removing the language barriers. If measures are not taken to improve camp conditions, it is likely that COVID-19 will emerge in the camps and spread very quickly. For this reason, if the pandemic is to be prevented, an approach that will include refugees and migrants is needed.

**Keywords** Global public goods · Health · Refugee problem · Refugee protection · Refugees' conditions · COVID-19

## 12.1 Introduction

The COVID-19 outbreak has significantly affected the global world. In fact, we have been going through a process which may have results that go beyond the 1929 Great Depression, which is the most important depression in world history. One of the important areas where these problems can be experienced is the lives of refugees and refugee camps.

The communities in countries have focused on measures to be taken to find a solution to the COVID-19 outbreak. However, if the preparation plans do not take migrants and refugees and their needs into account, these people face the risk of contracting many diseases, especially COVID-19, because refugees and migrants have already been trying to live in overpopulated conditions without reaching basic health conditions (Kluge et al. 2020: 1238).

Many people affected by humanitarian crises live in host countries or camp-like environments. These overcrowded camps pose a serious health risk to the host population and residents. Lack of clean water and soap, lack of medical staff and limited access to health information are serious problems in these environments. Maintaining basic hand hygiene and social distance in refugee camps is either impossible or extremely difficult. In addition, international migrant workers and refugees may also be affected by loss of income, health care insecurity and decisions related to deferring their legal status or reducing employment, legal and administrative services. If urgent measures are not taken to improve the conditions, it is predicted that COVID-19 can spread very quickly in the camps and reach dangerous levels (Kluge et al. 2020: 1238).

In this context, humanitarian organizations state that people in camps should not be forgotten while taking public health measures (Lacobucci 2020). United Nations High Commissioner for Refugees (UNHCR) states that efforts are being made to set up portable hand washing facilities, within the scope of efforts to increase hand washing in the field, and the World Health Organization (WHO) reports that COVID-19 testing has started in camps (Vince 2020).

With the measures to be taken, it will be possible for refugees to be less affected by the COVID-19 pandemic and to reduce its rate of spread. For this reason, countries should take decisions in a way that includes refugees and migrants, should not resort to repatriation and should not discriminate on the grounds that these people spread disease, and the concept of public health should be evaluated in a way that includes refugees and migrants (Kluge et al. 2020: 1239). Only this way, the harmful effects of COVID-19 on refugees can be reduced.

After giving general information on GPGs, this part of the book will provide the theory of GPGs of health and refugee protection. Afterwards, we will evaluate with what kind of policy the refugee protection is approached in the COVID-19 outbreak and how the refugees are doing during the pandemic. In this context; in addition to the decisions made by the countries regarding the refugees after the COVID-19 outbreak, we will address how some situations that the refugees living in the camps face such as limited access to facilities, namely clean water, soap, cleaning materials, etc., and not being able to maintain social distance affect the risk of pandemic. In this sense, the study will make a significant contribution to the literature in terms of evaluating the situation of refugees, during the pandemic, who already had to live under difficult conditions before the pandemic, showing that the countries' COVID-19 outbreak policies should also include refugees. At the same time, being one of the pioneering studies, it will be a reference for those who will work in this field in the future.

## 12.2 General Framework of the Concept of GPG

GPGs can be defined as goods and services whose benefits or harms exceed national borders and affect countries in more than one geographical region and even the whole world, reaching out not only the present generation but also the next generations, in whose production or financing the countries' own resources are inadequate and therefore require global cooperation (Rao 1999: 68).

GPGs must, by definition, have the characteristics of publicity and globalism. What is meant by the publicity feature is that nobody can be excluded from the consumption of goods and there is no competition in their consumption, just like the case for public goods. Its globality feature means that GPGs affect countries in more than one region, more than one population group and not only this generation, but also future generations in terms of their benefits or harms (Akdemir and Şahin 2006: 4). What can be inferred here is that GPGs must meet at least these two criteria. Other features of GPGs are that they cause free rider problems, are consumed collectively and require public financing.

Although GPGs appear to cause positive externalities in general, there are many cases where they also cause negative externalities. It can be said that these negative externalities, emerging especially in parallel with globalization, increased. As a result, GPGs emitting positive externality are defined as GPG, and GPGs emitting negative externality are defined as global public bads by some authors in the literature. Problems that usually arise due to the unintended consequences of GPGs are called global public bads. In fact, it is used to express the spread of negative externalities across borders that arise due to a good and service (Güler 2012: 636).

For example, when combatting infectious diseases in a country, it is possible to prevent the spread of that disease to other countries. In this sense, it can be a positive externality as the disease does not spread. Otherwise, if no fight is made against the diseases, the epidemics will spread to other countries, and thus negative externalities of public goods will be called GPGs, global public bads (Coyne and Ryan 2008: 4–6).

Due to the global dimension of GPGs, even if countries alone can produce some GPGs, it will not be possible to provide these goods at an adequate level. For this reason, the actor involved in the production and presentation of GPGs is not just a single country; many organizations in different fields also take part in this process as an important actor (Mutlu 2006: 55).

The actors playing the most active role in the provision of GPGs are undoubtedly nation states and international organizations. But apart from these actors, non-profit organizations such as academic institutions, independent foundations, non-governmental organizations and profit-making organizations such as private companies also carry out various activities within the scope of social responsibility projects and make significant contributions to the presentation of GPGs. Research, development and environmental protection activities are supported by foundations. Foundations have played a significant role in the protection of biological diversity and the development of vaccines against diseases. Non-governmental organizations such as Greenpeace and Amnesty International as well as university research centres are non-profit organizations that play a significant role in the presentation and financing of GPGs. Profit-making organizations, on the other hand, can allocate large resources to research and activities on that subject, especially in the sector they operate in (Turan 2010: 125–127).

International organizations such as the International Monetary Fund (IMF) and the World Bank, as well as organizations such as multilateral development banks, can also be considered among these actors. The IMF basically contributes to preventing crises and ensuring financial balance; multilateral development banks contribute to capacity building and institutional development. The World Bank, on the other hand, contributes to the presentation of GPGs in several dimensions such as acting as a bridge by creating inter-country policies for global purposes, establishing partnerships to strengthen the financial mechanisms of countries and helping the development of countries through their experts (Turan 2010: 132–133).

Multilateral international communities formed by international and regional organizations are at the focal point of presenting GPGs. Communities such as the International Labour Organization (ILO), the World Health Organization (WHO), Food and Agriculture Organization (FAO) and the United Nations High Commissioner for Refugees (UNHCR) that operate under the United Nations (UN) and the United Nations effectively serve at global level. Apart from these, the International Maritime Organization (IMO), the North Atlantic Alliance (NATO) and the International Organization for Communication via Satellites (INTELSAT) are among other communities considered within this group (Turan 2010: 134–137).

Since there are so many actors in the presentation of GPGs and all actors have different expectations, there are problems in decision-making and inadequate presentation problem arises for GPGs (Sagasti and Bezanson 2001: 10). In order to solve this problem, to find more comprehensive and effective solutions and to implement them, countries need to act together, establish common policies and act in accordance with them (Löschel and Rübbelke 2014: 195). For this reason, a supranational institution is needed for the effective delivery of GPGs.

### *12.2.1 Health and Refugee Protection as GPGs*

Since its first use, the concept of GPG has been subjected to various classifications and divided into many sub-branches. Any public good can be considered as a GPG if it has certain characteristics. Health and refugee protection from these GPGs will be examined within the context of the study. The reason for including these two GPGs in the study is the fact that the COVID-19 outbreak is closely related to the health, a GPG, and the situation of the refugees during this pandemic requires examining refugee protection, another GPG, within the scope of the study.

#### 12.2.1.1 Health as a GPG

Health has the characteristics of both public and private goods. Also, it is accepted as a GPG due to the potential of infectious diseases to cross national borders with globalization. The risk of spreading of infectious diseases to all countries, preventing the emergence of infectious diseases, controlling and eliminating the infectious diseases, inability to exclude anyone from health public goods and not being competitive in their consumption point out that they are GPGs (Yılmaz and Yaraşır 2011: 9).

Health GPG constitutes two important externalities, both positive and negative. The negative externality constitutes the first externality in the form of spreading of infectious diseases to other countries and people due to its global feature, and the second type of externality is the positive externality that occurs by treating infectious diseases or by protecting people from diseases by reducing the risk of disease for other countries or people (Mutlu 2006: 198–199). In this context, measures should be taken to provide health globally and to prevent the spread of infectious diseases.

Infectious diseases have emerged as a problem faced by people in many stages of history. Diseases such as AIDS, tuberculosis and malaria have caused millions of people to become infected and die (World Bank Development Committee 2001: 3). The important point about infectious diseases is that, in addition to causing deaths, they may also result in disintegration of families, the emergence of some negative situations reflected in social and economic life and their transmission to generations (Yılmaz and Yaraşır 2011: 11).

Issues such as trade, travel, immigration, asylum, communication and food security also have direct or indirect effects on health. With the increasing trade, easy access to unhealthy goods causes health problems. In addition, as a result of travels, millions of people every day can cause the spread of many diseases between countries by means of transportation vehicles. In this context, asylum movements also have the potential to reveal adverse health effects. Especially with globalization, the excessive and misuse of global common goods, the decrease in clean water resources, the increase in infectious diseases due to polluted air and the role of ozone depletion in the increase of cancer diseases are issues that need to be addressed in terms of health (Yılmaz and Yaraşır 2011: 11–12).

The expenditures required to prevent, control and eliminate infectious diseases can become an unbearable burden especially for developing countries, and failure to take the necessary measures due to the lack of sufficient resources in these countries may cause infectious diseases to spread to developed countries and thus, all countries of the world may face this threat. This will result in higher costs (Yılmaz and Yaraşır 2011: 12). If even one country is insufficient in combating epidemic diseases, it may cause the whole world to be exposed to the disease (Oral 2014: 84).

The COVID-19 outbreak, which started recently and was accepted and declared as a pandemic by the WHO, is also an issue that should be evaluated in this context. When evaluated in terms of health, which is accepted as a GPG, the COVID-19 pandemic started in China and affected all the countries of the world in a very short time after the necessary measures were not taken and spread rapidly. In other words, with its negative externality, it has the characteristics of global public bads.

However, with the practices and measures that are tried to be carried out in line with the decisions taken by countries within the scope of combating COVID-19, necessary efforts are taken to treat the disease and slow down its spread. With these steps taken, people will be protected and negative externality can turn into positive externality by reducing the risk.

#### 12.2.1.2 Refugee Protection as a GPG

In the history, it is seen that wars or internal conflicts have occurred for many reasons and obligations. Many people had to leave their country due to these conflicts or wars. Apart from the reasons of war or internal conflict, people can migrate due to various compelling factors in their country. Feelings of pressure due to blood feud, language, religion, race, sect differences as well as climate changes, etc., are among reasons that direct people to seek asylum (Roberts 1998: 378). In this sense, refugee is a person who has lost his trust in his own state by feeling under pressure in his country due to his race, religion, language, social position, political opinion or national identity, who leaves his country with the thought that his state would not be impartial towards him, seeks asylum in another country and is "accepted" by that country (Landgren 1998: 417).

Those who have to leave their country for compelling reasons settle in various countries. The needs that arise after the settlement are met by the country of asylum, except for the aid received from some countries and international organizations (Teyyare and Sayaner 2017: 449). However, the refugee problem, which emerges for compulsory reasons, affects not only that country but also other countries (Risse 2008: 26). Although the burden mostly remains in the country of residence, the refugee problem affects the whole world as we live in a global world. First of all, the cheap labour force that will emerge in the country where the refugees have settled affects the employment in that country, and then, this spills over to other countries. Although refugees first go to neighbouring countries with the concern of safety of life, they use these countries as step (crossroad) countries,[1] and at the first opportunity they go to developed countries for better living standards. The important point here is that while their country of departure is certain, the country where the refugees will seek asylum and settle in is not certain. This is why, in case of a possible refugee problem, all countries of the world become a potential asylum country. This makes the refugee problem a globalized one and requires providing refugee protection at a global level.

Due to its mentioned features, refugee protection is a GPG. It has the characteristics of non-rivalry in consumption and non-excludability from consumption, which are the two basic characteristics of public goods. Non-rivalry in consumption means that one person's consumption of any good does not reduce another person's consumption of the same (Samuelson 1954: 387). Non-excludability means once a

[1] The concept of step (crossroad) country is used to refer to the countries where refugees first sought asylum and see as a stage for their transition to developed countries.

public good is produced, nobody can be excluded from the consumption of that good and the consumption of that good cannot be prevented (Musgrave 1959: 9–11).

It can be said that refugee protection has these two features, albeit partially. Accordingly, the refugee problem or the solution of these problems, in other words, providing protection to refugees; has the feature of non-excludability, such that contribution by a country to refugee protection does not reduce the contribution required to be made by other countries or because many states benefit from the benefits arising from the solution of the problems independently of their contribution (peace, order, stability, etc.), and it also has the characteristic of "non-rivalry in consumption" such that the benefit of a country does not reduce any benefit by another country. At the same time, the "free rider problem", which is frequently encountered in public goods, also manifests itself in refugee protection (Bursalıoğlu 2016: 28–29). Those who do not participate in the costs make use of the benefits such as international order, stability, peace and security created by the refugee protection, and on the other hand, they may suffer from the chaos, instability and conflicts that will occur if the problems are not solved and the refugees are not protected (Suhrke 1998: 398). For these reasons, refugee protection has these two basic features of public goods.

At the same time, refugee protection affects not only the countries in the region but also the countries outside the region both financially and in terms of hosting. Refugee protection has global effects that go beyond the responsibility of the host country. Resolving the refugee problem or providing refugee protection not only benefits the host country, but also benefits other countries nearby and countries further away (outside the region), in terms of stability, trust, human rights, peace, etc. (Mottaghi 2018: 1).

The fact that refugees are not a lost generation depends on how host country policy-makers and international and human development agencies respond to this issue. If problems of refugees such as access to health, education, employment and livelihoods are not resolved, this can lead to long-term crises such as infectious diseases, loss of human capital in education and long-term world stability, peace and restructuring processes, immigration to other countries with constant dissatisfaction in employment (Mottaghi 2018: 2). For this reason, the damages will be on a global scale.

Assistance and funding to host countries to bear the costs to avoid hosting refugees also show that refugee protection is a GPG. Because when the aid is sent, the investments required by the donor country may not be made or the implementation plans of certain projects, programmes or processes related to the country may be postponed. Since the country cannot use the financing it provides to develop its own economy, it is obvious that this will affect future generations by causing the loss of welfare of future generations. This applies to all funding countries, neighbouring or not. On the contrary, there are global effects if the costs brought by refugees to the host country are not borne and no aid is received by the host country. Because the host country cannot meet this problem alone, this will fuel the refugee problem and cause refugees to seek asylum in more countries. It should be noted here that refugees can gradually create a global impact since they go not only to neighbouring countries but also to countries further away (Teyyare and Sayaner 2017: 439). In addition, if the costs are not borne, the country crushed under this burden may face economic stability problems, and, as a result of the stability being a GPG, the country's deteriorating economy may disrupt the economies of other countries, lead to a domino effect and globally affect the whole world. The fact that countries develop specific policies regarding refugee problems also shows that refugee protection has GPGs characteristics. For example, a country in Europe in the mass refugee influx that arose due to a war in the Middle East should not develop a policy on not accepting refugees into its country. Since such policies are preferred by countries in today's refugee flows, it would not be wrong to say that refugee protection shows the characteristics of GPGs.

Finally, even if a refugee who leaves his country and seeks asylum firstly in neighbouring countries, he can go to countries farther from neighbouring countries in the following years. Although the refugees are predominantly in neighbouring countries, a considerable number of them live in countries outside the region. The fact that more than one region is affected or the spreading of the externality to more than one region, which is a requirement for GPGs, becomes apparent in refugee protection. In this sense, refugee protection has global effects.

For the reasons explained, it is seen that the refugee problem affects not only the country of asylum, but also other countries. The main characteristics of the GPG, which are the non-excludability and non-rivalry in consumption and the fact that they cause cross-border positive and negative externalities, are also the case for refugee problem. For this reason, in a globalizing world, the refugee problem is actually a global public bad, and providing protection to refugees to solve this problem is a GPG. Considering that there is war in different geographies of the world and tens of thousands of people seek asylum every year, it is obvious that refugee protection is an issue that concerns the whole world. In this sense, within the scope of the COVID-19 outbreak, the living conditions of the refugees should also be considered and the measures should be evaluated in a wide framework.

### *12.2.2 Nature of COVID-19 Outbreak*

The COVID-19 outbreak is estimated the most significant global health disaster of this century and the biggest challenge humanity has faced since World War II. The origin of the outbreak is linked to cases defined in Wuhan, the capital of Hubei Province in central China, and the disease has been named COVID-19 by the WHO (Chakraborty and Maity 2020: 1). Over time, this disease spread to other Chinese provinces and other countries internationally (Chen et al. 2020: 1).

As for the COVID-19 outbreak, global spread has been extremely rapid, and COVID-19 has now globally become a major health threat (Sirkeci and Yüceşahin 2020: 380). The World Trade Organization (WTO) and the Organization for Economic Cooperation and Development (OECD) identified the COVID-19 outbreak as the biggest threat to the global economy since the 2008–2009 financial emergency

(Chakraborty and Maity 2020: 4). It is also thought that poor countries will be affected worse by the COVID-19 outbreak (Sirkeci and Yüceşahin 2020: 385).

The current COVID-19 outbreak has affected more than 20 million people in more than 200 countries worldwide and caused the deaths of approximately 800 thousand people. To date, no clinically approved drug or vaccine that is effective against COVID-19 has been reported. It quickly spread all over the world and created economic, health, social and environmental challenges for the whole human population (Chakraborty and Maity 2020: 1).

When it comes to human history, there are serious disease outbreaks caused by some viruses. Except for COVID-19, there have been at least five other epidemics in this century. These are: H1N1 in 2009, polio in 2014, Ebola in 2014, Zika in 2016 and recurrent Ebola in 2019 (Chakraborty and Maity 2020: 2). Later, the COVID-19 pandemic was declared by WHO as a Public Health Emergency of International Concern (PHEIC) on 30 January 2020 and was described as an pandemic on 11 March 2020 (Dikmen et al. 2020: 329). Thus, it was the sixth epidemic in this century.

These worldwide outbreaks have caused billions of dollars in costs as well as many deaths. COVID-19 causes more people to suffer from infectious diseases compared to other diseases worldwide and their associated burdens. In addition, COVID-19 has the potential to significantly slow down the economy not only in China, the USA or India, but in the world as a whole, as well as its distressing effects on human life. Therefore, governments, the public and health personnel should show solidarity in general and fight shoulder to shoulder to prevent and control the epidemic (Chakraborty and Maity 2020: 2). Consequently, unlike past humanitarian disasters, this epidemic is global (Vince 2020).

As the GPGs literature was examined in the previous section, COVID-19 is a global public bad, and the interventions to be made, the decisions to be taken and the policies to be implemented in this context should be on a global scale.

It is necessary to accelerate the containment of the disease in order to control the COVID-19 crisis, to protect the economy, to alleviate the subsequent social, economic and financial impacts and to ensure the continuity of some activities. Refugees and the unprotected population are another issue that should not be ignored while working in this context (Alqutob et al. 2020).

### *12.2.3 Refugees' Conditions During COVID-19 Outbreak*

COVID-19 has proven that all people on the move are vulnerable to disease (Igoye 2020: 1). The disease is transmitted by droplets. In addition, it is transmitted as a result of contact with the droplets that sick people scatter through sneezing and coughing. The best way to prevent disease is to avoid exposure to the virus. Since the virus is transmitted from person to person, close contact should be avoided, attention should be paid to keep social distance, hands should be washed with plenty of water and soap, and frequently touched surfaces should be constantly cleaned and disinfected (Dikmen et al. 2020: 329).

However, when the COVID-19 pandemic enters vulnerable places such as refugee camps, practices such as hand washing, social distancing and isolation become difficult.

In 2019, about 123,700 refugees and migrants reached Greece, Italy and Spain over three Mediterranean routes from Turkey and North Africa. While the COVID-19 deaths and cases in Italy and Spain increased, the arrival of migrants and refugees to Mediterranean countries continued and increased to over 15,000 in the first two months of 2020. In addition, UNHCR has reported a much higher number of migrants entering the Western Balkan countries in recent months, contrary to the decreasing numbers since 2015 (Julia et al. 2020).

Considering that refugee and migrant mobility is still continuing, the situation of these people in the face of the COVID-19 outbreak is worth examining. This group, which is currently facing difficulties in many issues, has the potential to become even more vulnerable with COVID-19, because refugee camps and camps-like environment are socially built and generally accepted as temporary places. But some of them have existed for decades and accommodated several generations. The COVID-19 outbreak poses a huge danger to these places (Raju and Karlsson 2020). However, it can be said that no official measure has been announced for these camps for now (Clarke 2020: 16).

There are currently several challenges that refugees face. The first of these is access to language and knowledge. The second challenge relates to sociocultural differences between refugees and host countries and health practices that do not conform to their cultural or religious beliefs. The third challenge is overcrowding and close contact with people. The fourth challenge is that in host communities, health systems and local refugee volunteer organizations are overloaded, particularly in mental health care, due to the large number of refugees, because very few doctors in camp clinics have to deal with thousands of refugees (Junior, et al. 2020).

For such reasons, refugees are at high risk of contracting COVID-19 disease and developing psychiatric disorders that are worsened by the epidemic. Overcrowding, sewage problems, poor hygiene standards, malnutrition, lack of access to shelter, public services, healthcare and security-related problems are risk factors for COVID-19 and can accelerate the spread of the disease (Kluge et al. 2020: 1238).

Around 68.5 million people around the world have had to flee their homes due to violence, war or repression. About 21.3 million of them are refugees. In addition, 40.8 million people were internally displaced. For internally and externally displaced people (refugees, forced migrants, asylum seekers, etc.), the mobility process and the post-settlement process involve a number of challenges. Especially in the host countries where refugees are seeking asylum, they face various problems including bureaucratic procedures, mixing with different cultures, poverty and even racism as well as problems such as overcrowding, sewage problems, poor hygiene standards, malnutrition, lack of access to health care, shelters and public services, and security. Especially, the lack of access to health services and clean water and living in crowded shelters make refugees more vulnerable to infection (Junior et al. 2020). For example, in slums in Dhaka and Mumbai, a household can have a population of 15 people. In addition, these houses do not have doors or windows, and many sleep in the same bed. Thousands of settlers share the same several public baths (Raju and Karlsson 2020). In addition, a UK-based aid organization that provides healthcare services to those living in Europe's largest refugee camp warned that overcrowding could create a humanitarian disaster after the COVID-19 outbreak. It was also reported that strategies to reduce personal care and social distance were designed for 3,000 people in the Moria camp on the island of Lesvos in Greece, but more than 20,000 refugees had to live in these camps (Lacobucci 2020: 368). In this case, it is emphasized that in some parts of the camp, there is only one faucet for a large number of people and there is no soap; people live among the garbage without sewage systems (Hargreaves et al. 2020a).

It is also stated that migrants living in India are also subjected to reverse migration and set out to return to their homes, and this reverse migration is described as the second largest mass migration in its history after the division of India in 1947 (Mukhra et al. 2020). Another example is seen in Lebanon. Lebanon, a country that hosts an estimated 1.5 million Syrian refugees, has faced a very serious economic crisis—though it is mitigated recently—civil unrest, as well as struggling with the COVID-19 outbreak (Kassem 2020). Similarly, Cox's Bazar, Bangladesh's second poorest region, is home to more than 855,000 Rohingya refugees from neighbouring Myanmar. Refugees living in this region live in places that can be described as slopes, sleep in a room made of plastic woven walls and covered with plastic sheets, and sewage problems are increasing in these places (Vince 2020). It can be said that immigrants living in Venezuela also live in the same conditions (Daniels 2020: 1023).

Since 17 March 2020, New York has been fighting against the COVID-19 crisis. This metropolis is also home to Latin immigrant communities. These immigrant communities have faced problems such as access to health care, difficulties arising from immigration status, financial and workforce instability for a long time. The COVID-19 pandemic has aggravated these current problems of vulnerable immigrant communities. At the same time, it is very difficult for these groups to access COVID-19 treatment, testing and assistance programmes, as the public information is published in Portuguese and Spanish (Behbahani et al. 2020: 3). For all these reasons, the already fragile situation of refugees is evolving into more difficult conditions due to the COVID-19 outbreak.

While the struggle of refugees under difficult conditions is getting more difficult due to the COVID-19 pandemic, this may also be the case for migrants. With the correct expression used extensively, immigration defines people who change cities, countries or regions with their own will due to economic conditions. However, examining the types of migration, it can be seen that the concept of forced migration is also included in this issue. In fact, forced migrations are population movements that take place in search of a safe place due to population exchanges, fear of punishment, limitation of individual freedoms such as repression and humiliation, border changes, terrorist incidents, wars and natural disasters (Ruiz and Silva 2013: 772). In this sense, it is seen that forced migration takes place in two ways. In the first group of forced migration, people tend to flee to other countries and seek asylum in order to escape from the aforementioned dangers, and those who migrate in this way are called refugees. The second group of forced migration, on the other hand, consists of migrations that take place under the supervision of the official authority and in this direction enable people to move from one place to another (Hajiagha 2007: 75). As can be seen, the concept of migrant may correspond to the concept of refugee in some cases. Therefore, within the scope of this study, it will be useful to examine the situation of forced migrants against COVID-19.

Even in the best of times, global societies face great difficulties in meeting the social care and health needs of migrants, racial, ethnic and other minority groups. Migrant workers are among the vulnerable populations most affected by national quarantines worldwide to mitigate the effects of the epidemic (Lodge and Kuchukhidze 2020: 249). The desperate situation of migrants and refugees is apparent, especially in camps and detention centres, where their seek for asylum await evaluation (Bhopal 2020a: 161). Immigration prisons face some challenges such as overcrowding, poor health conditions, inadequate health care and infectious diseases. It is not possible to keep distance and take other necessary measures to prevent the spread of COVID-19 in immigration prisons. These detention facilities pose a great risk of contamination. It has also been reported that many personnel in different immigration detention centres have tested positive for COVID-19 and the prisoners were exposed to infection. It is also stated that there may be a potentially dangerous epidemic spread at the US-Mexico border. The fact that asylum seekers live in these camps until their asylum applications are accepted and that these camps are overcrowded and unhealthy increases the risk of epidemics (Keller and Wagner 2020: 245).

The difficulties in refugee camps are identified by a wide variety of individuals. However, it is also stated that illegal (undocumented) immigrants face more difficulties. Undocumented persons do not have a legal right to reside in the country they currently live in; they are also in danger of coming down with COVID-19. Although the exact number of these persons is not known as they are not registered, authorities estimate that hundreds of thousands of people are in this situation in the UK. The fact that these people do not have a trust relationship with the authorities, lack of information communication, the inability to maintain social distance and the obstacles in front of getting minimum rights in health services are the case all over the world. At the same time, xenophobia and racism make the conditions even more difficult. Studies show that the epidemic adversely affects all immigrant and ethnic minority groups, but statistical information on illegal immigrants is not available (Bhopal 2020b).

COVID-19 affects homeless people as well as refugees and migrants. This will become a serious problem in North America, where there is a large population of homelessness in almost every metropolitan city in Canada and the USA. Homeless people live in favourable environments for epidemics, similar to refugees. These people have limited or, in some cases, no access to essential living supplies and cleaning products. This can facilitate the spread of the virus among these people (Tsai and Wilson 2020: 186).

However, it is doubtful that nobody has ever had COVID-19 in refugee camps. This may be due to three reasons: refugees' lack of information about symptoms and infection, lack of access to tests and fear of stigmatization (Kassem 2020). Because migrants and refugees may be stigmatized and unfairly discriminated against for spreading disease. These attitudes can prevent refugees and migrants from seeking treatment or cause them to hide their symptoms. This increases public health risk in a wider community, including host populations (Kluge et al. 2020: 1239).

As can be seen from all these mentioned above, efforts to prevent the COVID-19 outbreak should include a collective effort not only to contain the virus, but also on behalf of vulnerable populations (Junior et al. 2020). Refugees and migrants should not be ignored in efforts to combat COVID-19 (Lancet 2020: 1).

It is stated that very limited state financial assistance is given to refugees to assist with food, shelter, local language training, clothing, employment counselling, medical care and education in the USA to overcome these problems faced by refugees and immigrants. UNHCR is accepting funds to combat the COVID-19 outbreak around the world. Their purpose is to provide medical supplies and tests for the treatment of patients affected by COVID-19, conducting information campaigns, sending materials to regions in need and transporting medical work teams between regions (Junior et al. 2020). In addition, in April, the European Union promised 350 million euros to support refugees and asylum seekers, including those in Greece (Subbaraman 2020: 18).

At the same time, a provisional technical guide was prepared by the Inter Agency Standing Committee (IASC) to advise governments and institutions dealing with the large immigrant population. This guide recommends strategies to support outbreak preparedness and response among migrants in high-risk camps and slum environments. The living conditions mentioned are extremely favourable for infectious diseases to turn into epidemics. Immigrants in these environments are sensitive to COVID-19 due to overcrowding, poor hygiene and malnutrition. The guide recommends the countries that the immigrants should not be scapegoated, stigmatized or targeted with discriminatory measures. In addition, the recommendations highlight the positive points, including practical interventions to maximize site planning to maintain distance and promote infection prevention and control standards (Hargreaves et al. 2020b: 645).

The ongoing COVID-19 outbreak continues to progress every day. No individual, society, population group or nation is immune to this disease. Migrants and refugees constitute vulnerable population groups, which requires the urgent inclusion of migrants and refugees in the action plan to contain infection and no compromise on their right to the highest level of mental and physical health. In this context, even though certain efforts have been taken for refugees and migrants, they are not quite sufficient. However, special measures should be taken in vulnerable groups such as refugees and migrants in order to slow down and prevent the spread of the epidemic. In the global COVID-19 outbreak, host countries should not ignore ensuring the safety and health of immigrants. Immigrants remain an important part of many countries' development paths. For this reason, they deserve equal treatment from their host countries, including economic livelihoods and mental issues (Mia and Griffiths 2020: 23).

In addition, refugees and migrants should be included in national public health systems without financial and legal risks. This approach is very important, as public health cannot be achieved without immigrant and refugee health (Kluge et al. 2020: 1239).

Good planning and management of health services for refugees and migrants and meeting the health needs of migrants are of great importance. In order to eliminate language barriers, materials should be provided in languages that migrant groups can understand, and it should be ensured that all information expected to reach the public about the epidemic reaches vulnerable groups. It should be ensured that all the proposed measures are applied to all people living in camps and similar environments. It is important that the legal fears of some immigrant groups should not prevent them from seeking for health care. Stigmatization and discrimination of refugees and immigrants should also be prevented (Dikmen et al. 2020: 329).

The success of measures to control the COVID-19 outbreak will only be possible by including all populations in international and national responses. Moreover, excluding refugees and immigrants would be unfair. The principles of equality, solidarity and human rights should be at the centre of the COVID-19 response (Orcutt et al. 2020: 1482).

Concerns about the outbreak of COVID-19 in the camps will be justified if urgent action is not taken to improve conditions. Therefore, transparent and comprehensive research is required, along with preventive and inclusive control measures, to control and/or prevent the spread of COVID-19 to refugee camps (Kassem 2020).

As a result, if the intention is to overcome the COVID-19 pandemic, an approach, which mainly includes migrants and refugees and where partnerships with various sectors and the whole society are considered within this scope, is necessary. The policy that is required now is to spread all prevention and control activities to vulnerable population groups and to minimize the risk of infection or transmission (Shrivastava and Shrivastava 2020: 163).

## 12.3 Conclusion

The COVID-19 outbreak affects the whole world on a global scale. Countries are taking efforts to minimize the economic, environmental, health and social effects of the pandemic and to protect these areas. However, vulnerable groups such as refugees, asylum seekers and forced migrants should also be included in the efforts and the measures to be taken, because these groups do not live in suitable places where the protection methods required to prevent the disease can be provided. Although their number varies and regardless of the policies of the countries, there are refugees in many countries of the world. In this sense, it is very important that the living conditions of the refugees in their countries and how the diseases can spread with their movements between countries is very important.

Considering that the facilities such as cleaning, food and medical equipment in the camps are limited, it is obvious to what extent the refugees will be affected by the

COVID-19 pandemic. Many people affected by humanitarian crises in host countries live in camps or camp-like environments. These overcrowded camps pose a serious health risk to the host population and residents. Lack of clean water and soap, lack of medical staff and limited access to health information are serious problems in these environments. Maintaining basic hand hygiene and social distance in refugee camps is either impossible or extremely difficult. With the measures to be taken, it will be possible for refugees to be less affected by the COVID-19 outbreak and to reduce its rate of spread.

In this sense, the measures that can be taken during the COVID-19 pandemic for refugee protection can be discussed under the following headings:

- First of all, the movement areas of refugees should be limited.
- Countries should evaluate their decisions to prevent the pandemic in a way that includes refugees and migrants.
- The concept of public health should be addressed to include refugees and migrants.
- Materials that the refugees and migrants can understand should be created by removing language barriers.
- It should be ensured that all the information planned to reach the public about the pandemic reaches these groups as well.
- It should be ensured that all the proposed measures can be applied to the segments living especially in the environments such as camps.
- Finally, these people should not be discriminated on the ground that they spread the disease.

As long as those listed above are achieved, the effect of COVID-19 will be minimized in the refugee protection, which is a GPG and has the potential to affect the whole world.

## References

Akdemir A, Şahin M (2006) Küresel kamusal mallarin üretim ve yönetim dinamikleri bağlaminda siniflandirilmasi. Maliye Dergisi 150:1–24

Alqutob R, Nsour MA, Tarawneh MR, Ajlouni M, Khader Y, Aqel I, Kharabsheh S, Obeidat N (2020) Covid-19 crisis in Jordan: Response, scenarios, strategies, and recommendations. JMIR Publication Preprints

Behbahani S, Smith CA, Carvalho M, Warren CJ, Gregory M, Silva NA (2020) Vulnerable immigrant populations in the New York metropolitan area and COVID-19: lessons learned in the epicenter of the crisis. J Assoc Am Med Coll 3–16

Bhopal RS (2020a) COVID-19: Immense necessity and challenges in meeting the needs of minorities, especially asylum seekers and undocumented migrants. Pub Health 182:161–162

Bhopal RS (2020b) Covid-19: undocumented migrants are probably at greatest risk. BMJ-Br Med J 369. Retrieved from https://doi.org/10.1136/bmj.m1673. 11 June 2020

Bursalıoğlu SA (2016) Migration in the global public good literature: Syrian refugees and Turkey. IOSR J Humanit Soc Sci 21(10):27–36

Chakraborty I, Maity P (2020) COVID-19 outbreak: Migration, effects on society, global environment and prevention. Sci Total Environ 728(138882):1–7

Chen H, Chen Y, Lian Z, Wen L, Sun B, Wang P, Li X, Liu Q, Yu X, Lu Y, Qi Y, Zhao S, Zhang L, Yi X, Liu F, Pan G (2020) Correlation between the migration scale index and the number of new confirmed coronavirus disease 2019 cases in China. Epidemiol Infect 148:1–7

Clarke K (2020) Covid-19 threat adds to refugee suffering in Greece, Turkey, Syria. America 16–17

Coyne CJ, Ryan ME (2008) Foreign Intervention and Global Public Bads. Mercatus Center at George Mason University, Working Paper, pp 08–21, 1–34

Daniels JP (2020) Venezuelan migrants "struggling to survive" amid COVID-190. The Lancet 395(28):1023

Dikmen AU, Budak SN, Budak B, Özkan S, İlhan MN (2020) Covid-19 Salgınında Savunmasız Gruplardan Biri: Göçmenler. GMJ 31:328–330

Güler H (2012) Küresel Kamusal Bir Kötü Olarak Dezenformasyon. Prof. Dr. Aytaç Eker ve Yrd. Doç. Dr. Ayşegül Eker'e Armağan, Dokuz Eylül Üniversitesi Yayınları, İzmir, pp 635–644

Hajiagha M (2007) Türkiye'deki İranlı Göçmenlerin Kimlik, Aidiyet ve Uyum Sorunları (1979 İran Devrimi Sonrası), (Unpublished doctoral thesis), Ankara Üniversitesi, Türkiye

Hargreaves S, Kumar BN, Mckee M, Jones L, Veizis A (2020a) Europe's migrant containment policies threaten the response to covid-19. BMJ-Br Med J 368. Retrieved from https://doi.org/10.1136/bmj.m1213. 5 May 2020

Hargreaves S, Zenner D, Wickramage K, Deal A, Hayward SE (2020b) Targeting COVID-19 interventions towards migrants in humanitarian settings. The Lancet 20:645–646

Igoye A (2020) Migration and immigration: Uganda and the COVID-19. The State of the Republic: A Dialogue Series, Pandemic, Public Integrity, pp 1–4

Julia B, Alberine B, Alexandra K, Nicole R (2020) The global COVID-19 response must include refugees and migrants. Swiss Med Wkly

Junior JG, Sales JP, Moreira MM, Pinhero WR, Lima CKT, Neto MLR (2020) A crisis within the crisis: the mental health situation of refugees in the world during the 2019 coronavirus (2019-nCoV) outbreak. Psychiatry Res 288:11300. Retrieved from https://doi.org/10.1016/j.psychres.2020.113000. 24 June 2020

Kassem II (2020) Refugees besieged: The lurking threat of COVID-19 in Syrian war refugee camps. Travel Med Infect Dis. Retrieved from https://doi.org/10.1016/j.tmaid.2020.101736. 5 June 2020

Keller AS, Wagner BD (2020) COVID-19 and immigration detention in the USA: time to act. The Lancet 5:245–246

Kluge HHP, Jakab Z, Bartovic J, D'Anna V, Severoni S (2020) Refugee and migrant health in the covid-19 response. The Lancet 395:10232, 1237–1239

Lacobucci G (2020) Covid-19: doctors warn of humanitarian catastrophe at Europe's largest refugee camp. BMJ-Br Med J 368

Landgren K (1998) The future of refugee protection: four challenges. J Refug Stud 11(4):416–432

Lodge W, Kuchukhidze S (2020) COVID-19, HIV, and migrant workers: the double burden of the two viruses. AIDS Patient Care STDS 34(6):249–250

Löschel A, Rübbelke D (2014) On the voluntary provision of international public goods. Economica 81:195–204

Mia A, Griffiths MD (2020) The economic and mental health costs of COVID-19 to immigrants. J Psychiatr Res 128:23–24

Mottaghi L (2018) Refugee welfare: a global public good. MENA Knowl Learn Quick Notes Ser 167:1–4

Mukhra R, Krishan K, Kanchan T (2020) Covid-19 sets off mass migration in India. Arch Med Res. Retrieved from https://doi.org/10.1016/j.arcmed.2020.06.003. 7 July 2020

Musgrave RA (1959) The theory of public finance (a study in public economy). McGraw-Hill Press, New York

Mutlu A (2006) Küresel kamusal mallar bağlaminda sağlik hizmetleri ve çevre kirlenmesi: üretim, finansman ve yönetim sorunlari. Maliye Dergisi 150:53–78

Oral BG (2014) Sağlık hizmetlerinin küresel kamusal mal olarak değerlendirilmesi: uluslararasi örgütler. Finans Politik Ekon Yorumlar 51(588):79–96

Orcutt M, Patel P, Burns R, Hiam L, Aldridge R, Devakumar D, Kumar B, Spiegel P, Abubakar I (2020) Global call to action for inclusion of migrants and refugees in the COVID-19 response. The Lancet 395:1482–1483
Raju E, Karlsson S (2020) COVID-19: how do you self-isolate in a refugee camp? Int J Publ Health. Retrieved from https://doi.org/10.1007/s00038-020-01381-8. 26 June 2020
Rao JM (1999) Equity in a global public goods framework. In: Kaul I, Grunberg I, Stern MA (eds) Global public goods: international cooperation in the 21st century. Oxford University Press, Oxford
Risse M (2008) On the morality of immigration. Ethics Int Aff 22(1):25–33
Roberts A (1998) More refugees, less asylum: a regime in transformation. J Refug Stud 11(4):375–395
Ruiz I, Silva CV (2013) The economics of forced migration. J Dev Stud 49(6):772–784
Sagasti F, Bezanson K (2001) Financing and providing global public goods: expectations and prospects. Institute of Development Studies, Development Financing 2000, Study 2001: 2, Sweden
Samuelson PA (1954) The pure theory of public expenditure. Rev Econ Stat 36(4):387–389
Shrivastava SR, Shrivastava PS (2020) Effective containment of the COVID-19 pandemic among migrants and refugee: World Health Organization. TJFMPC 14(2):163–165
Sirkeci İ, Yüceşahin MM (2020) Coronavirus and migration: analysis of human mobility and the spread of Covid-19. Migr Lett 17(2):379–398
Subbaraman N (2020) Refugee camps race to avert coronavirus catastrophe. Nature 581:18
Suhrke A (1998) Burden-sharing during refugee emergencies: the logic of collective versus national action. J Refug Stud 11(4):396–415
Teyyare E, Sayaner K (2017) Suriye İç Savaşı Sonrası Ortaya Çıkan Göç Hareketinin Kamusal Mallar Teorisi Çerçevesinde Değerlendirilmesi. Bartın Üniversitesi İktisadi Ve İdari Bilimler Fakültesi Dergisi 8(15):429–453
The Lancet (2020) COVID-19 will not leave behind refugees and migrants 395, 1090
Tsai J, Wilson M (2020) COVID-19: a potential public health problem for homeless populations. The Lancet 5:186–187
Turan D (2010) Küresel Kamusal Mallar ve Finansmanı. Dora Basım Yayın, 1. Baskı, Bursa
Vince G (2020) The world's largest refugee camp prepares for Covid-19. BMJ-Br Med J 368. Retrieved from https://doi.org/10.1136/bmj.m1205. 28 June 2020
World Bank Development Committee (2001) Poverty reduction and global public goods: a progress report. Retrieved from http://documents1.worldbank.org/curated/en/290411468780341185/pdf/306550v-10DC2001000070E00GPG.pdf. 27 June 2020
Yılmaz BE, Yaraşır S (2011) Bir küresel kamusal mal olarak sağlik ve finansmaninda resmi kalkinma yardimlarinin rolü. İstanbul Üniversitesi İktisat Fakültesi Maliye Araştırma Merkezi Konferansları

**Zeynep Demirci Çakıroğlu** Assistant Professor in Department of Public Finance, İzmir Katip Çelebi University, İzmir, Turkey. Holds Ph.D. in Public Finance and Financial Management, MSc in Public Finance, BS in Public Finance. She has book chapters, articles and papers on global public goods, refugee protection, international tax agreements, tax audit and other fiscal theory research areas.

# Chapter 13
# Analysis of Selected Twitter Headers During the Pandemic Using Big Data Method

**İbrahim Attila Acar and Volkan Altıntaş**

**Abstract** The behaviours and shares of social media users have recently been closely followed by governments, institutions and companies. Governments/companies determine some of their strategies by processing the "big data" created by the shares made by users. Big data analysis has been used extensively lately. During the pandemic period, people shared their ideas and experiences on social media platforms. Twitter is one of the most popular worldwide Online Social Network (OSN). One of these sharing platforms is Twitter Social Media Platform. In this study, between 1 and 31 May 2020, user posts containing keywords related to COVID-19 were collected. The analysis of the shares was made using natural language processing and text mining techniques on the corpus. In this paper, we use topic identification and sentiment analysis to explore a large number of tweets in Turkey. We investigate 19.199.490 tweets in Turkish, and we analyse comparing the effectiveness of topic identification and sentiment analysis in the messages in pandemic days.

**Keywords** Natural language processing · Data analysis · Text mining · Data visualization · Social networks · Twitter · Survey · Social graph · Sentiment analysis · Pandemic · Economics of COVID-19 pandemic

## 13.1 Introduction

All the humanity surrendered to a virus identified as COVID-19 in early 2020. Life slowed down. Although the measures taken increase each day, the contamination continues to spread increasingly. It seems that the "Coronavirus" continues to threaten people. Neither normal working life, nor marketplaces, nor streets, places of worship

İ. A. Acar (✉)
Department of Economic Policy, İzmir Katip Çelebi University, İzmir, Turkey

V. Altıntaş
Akhisar Vocational High School Computer Technologies Programme, Manisa Celal Bayar University, Manisa, Turkey



B. Açıkgöz and İ. A. Acar (eds.), *Pandemnomics: The Pandemic's Lasting Economic Effects*, Accounting, Finance, Sustainability, Governance & Fraud: Theory and Application, https://doi.org/10.1007/978-981-16-8024-3_13

… nor the crowds can resist this. First, the Pope's traditional "Sunday Prayer" in the Vatican held online revealed the gravity of the event. Iran's request for help saying, "1/3 of the people got the virus" even it had not cared at first, calling it just a rumour, turned out to be a complete despair. Finally, in 2020, the Kaaba was closed to visitors. And nobody was able to made pilgrimage in 2020.

On the one hand, businesses shut down, halted working life and employees unable to work… on the other hand, lives going on… Ongoing economic liabilities, the ongoing struggle to survive, economies have been challenged. Workplaces that were closed, educational institutions that could not provide service, curfews and travel bans completely suppressed life. The whole goal has become to prevent the spread of the epidemic.

The process is uncertain. Optimistic news continues to come, although not very positive about the vaccine. States announced packages of measures one after another. Each package became a reference for another country. New ones were added to the packages, but the pandemic is not over.

In addition to many heads of state in the world, many internationally recognized personalities were tested with this virus. There were people who lost their lives. There were also those who did not care. However, the measures taken by the states were violated in the street. The people did not give up on the street. Anti-measures protests never ended. The street started protests, first against the closure and then against the mask. Communities coming together on social media expressed their demands and objections. Social media has become a new medium for those who want to defend their rights and express themselves. Many headers/hashtags were opened for discussion in all social media. It was spoken, objected and even made fun of.

Social media has become a means of public expression amidst pandemic bans. The issue of "social distancing", which the authorities especially emphasize, has been effective in the people's orientation to such socialization channels. As an environment where they feel safe, social media allows sharing at any time of the day. From the first periods of the epidemic, people shared their ideas and information they obtained/read from social media channels. Everything from the experiences of those affected to the protection measures was written down in these environments. Sometimes hundreds of comments were made especially for the posts made via the Twitter application. Thousands of support messages came to a thread created. Instant entertainment, excitement and emotion sharing turned into a means of information during this period.

Due to social distancing, rotating work and work from home became common. All education services from primary education to university were carried out through various distance education platforms. It can be observed from the intensity of use of social media programmes and the increasing content sharing that the majority of the remaining time is spent on social media channels.

The Coronavirus epidemic caused people to be isolated in their homes in our country as is the case around the world. Due to the spread of the epidemic, people had to be more careful with each other. In the later stages of the epidemic, the public could not leave the house due to the restrictions, which negatively affected many sectors economically. However, companies serving in the technology sector turned this crisis period into an opportunity, because the people staying at home have spent most of their time with technological devices, whether they are compulsory or not. The reason for this is that training meetings, business meetings and family meetings cannot be held face to face. Hence, humanity's bond with technology has increased even more in this period.

The increasing use of technology also increased the use of social media platforms. People contribute to the formation of the agenda by sharing on social media platforms. In addition, people constitute an example of the data community called "big data" with their shares. The process of producing meaningful results by processing this "big data", which has been obtained recently, is deemed important by states, institutions and companies.

The behaviour of social media users during the pandemic period is remarkable. As time spent increased, so did the contents. Twitter has become one of the most common social media tools with its 340 million users. The analysis of the message content of some parts of the posts related to the economy reflecting COVID-19 or the pandemic is the subject of this study. By collecting data on the Twitter platform for the last month, during which the bans were ongoing, the posts collected with the help of keywords determined between 1 and 31 May 2020 are the subject of the analysis.

The topics on which the headers determined during the pandemic process concentrated, other titles associated, tagging and people have been analysed using text mining and natural language processing techniques. A data analysis study has been conducted on the titles and associated tagging in the COVID-19 process, by analysing these posts made on Twitter through a text data set (corpus).

## 13.2 New Socialization and Setting the Agenda on Twitter

In the past 15 years of social media, the peak period is after 2010 (Bozkurt 2018). Tagging, making headers, replies, rejections, likes, even emojis… Each of them offers its users the opportunity to express themselves. Shared contents, likes and the notes make the user experience a different feeling in terms of both being popular and cared for. Sharing a photo from another page or even with your own picture, including someone else's post on their page or replies, enables users to produce content. The social media soon turns into a self-published newspaper. With the content and posts it produces, issues that will constitute the agenda can be put forward.

In addition to following celebrities, following the topics and the agenda gains importance in social media environments (Ceyhan 2019). With their comments, acceptance and objection, the social media shows that the masses express themselves and are happy to express themselves; it even turns into an environment where they can be heard and socialize through social media. Especially, the impetus the technology has gained by in mobile phones is an important factor in obtaining these opportunities easily.

It is more appropriate to consider social media as "new socialization tools" rather than "alternative channels". The new socialization is transforming from becoming a follower by reading the agenda to becoming a part of the agenda. Their instant reactions, comments, two lines of articles in the headers and even expressions allow users to reproduce the agenda together. The opportunities offered by digital media with audio and video in reaching target audiences also increase the effectiveness of social media. Selecting the target audience, advertising opportunities, gain factor and instant uploading of content are effective in increasing usability. Even a sharing of a public official or even the president in the middle of the night instantly awakens the social media accounts and thousands of comments and discussions may continue till dawn.

There is only a media difference between looking again and again at the content shared by a person, checking the likes and comments, stating it numerically and interpreting the reactions to an event he/she describes in a community. Moreover, social media environments offer the opportunity to reach thousands of people (Bıçakçı 2019).

The fact that Twitter mainly contains written and visual content in social media and its ease of use has been effective in its being a widely used social media tool. The most popular artist or athlete can also use it, and the most authorized persons of the state can use it; ordinary citizens can also get the opportunity to express themselves in this environment. Especially recently, it has become a social media tool that both politics and public executives frequently use and give messages. Twitter's power and influence are in its widespread use.

According to statistics in October 2020, Turkey was among the countries where people spend the most time on social media in the world, with an average of above 3 h per day. October 2020 figures revealed that the number of users on Twitter is 13.5 million in Turkey. In this regard, it seems possible to reach meaningful data from Twitter posts of Turkish users.

Being on the agenda and setting the agenda have become the dream of every political, art and sports man. The most common means of the saying by famous film producer Andy Warhol, "Everyone will be famous one day for 15 min", who drew attention to this "visible" feeling in all people, are social media environments. It doesn't surprise anyone to see a new quote, a picture or a short video go viral every day, even if for a moment. Therefore, it would be a great loss not to take advantage of Twitter's agenda and agenda-setting features. It is an important means of "reaching the masses" for those who carry out public relations work, communicators and of course advertisers (Fig. 13.1).

Especially after the adoption of Public Financial Management and Control Law No. 5018 in 2003, public institutions have created their own websites and opened social media accounts connected to them, as a requirement of the law. Thus, institutions also carry out the task of informing the public through their websites and social media accounts. Public institutions consider this as a transparency tool. Twitter draws attention with its increasing number of users in this process. Many contents are shared both to give information and to set the agenda. Reducing the voting age and age of candidacy to 18 is important in attracting the attention of the young population.

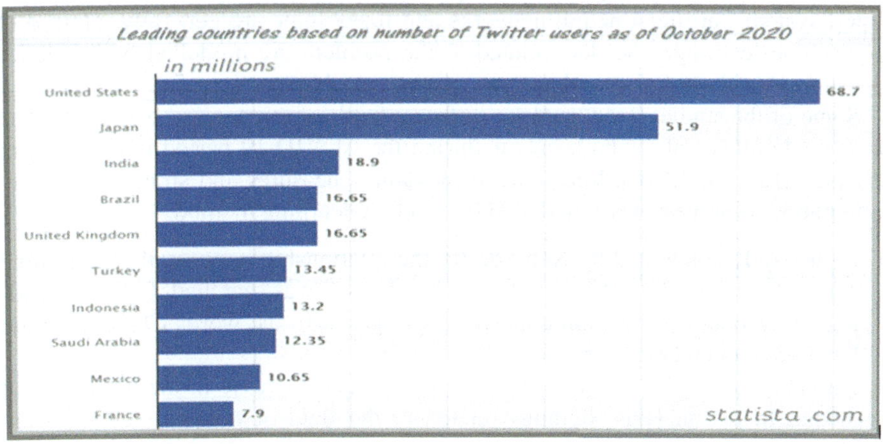


**Fig. 13.1** Number of active twitter users. *Source* Created by the author using the data on website "Statista"

For this purpose, it is normal for official institutions and organizations to show more interest in this field in order to win young people, even if it is for informative purposes.

The subject of this study is examining, by means of selected headers, Twitter messages on curfews, in the last month, introduced due to the Coronavirus cases detected in Turkey. Based on these Twitter posts between 1 May 2020 and 31 May 2020, a "big data analysis" was performed in Twitter users' posts on issues related to the agenda and pandemic. The size of the data analysed consists of approximately 20 million shares and 110 GB of data. The terms used in the posts of Twitter users and the interactions (RT, likes, comments, quotes, retweets) received by the tweets in a period of 31 days were examined.

## 13.3 Studies on the Literature

During the COVID-19 pandemic, people are using social media to obtain different types of information on an unprecedented scale. During the ongoing COVID-19 pandemic, it is necessary to understand the spread strategies of correct information, correct responses and sharing. This study aims to classify and make sense of the concepts, labels and contents related to COVID-19 through keywords selected from among them. It is aimed to analyse Twitter data and natural language processing techniques in accordance with the concept determined here. Similar methods have been used in many studies in the literature. Based on machine learning, it is still interesting to scientists, accepting the human brain as a model and producing solutions for the problems of daily life by taking machine learning as basis. Çelik (2020) draw attention to the fact that machine learning is frequently used for problems such as prediction, classification and clustering. Algorithms such as genetic algorithms, expert systems, artificial neural networks and fuzzy logic are generally referred to as machine learning. The data related to the problem are modelled by computer algorithms for the solution and analysis of many problems.

Some of the studies conducted for different fields of science are as follows: The posts made on social media accounts during the COVID-19 period in China were analysed (Li et al. 2020). Reactions to incidents, measures and strategies used to raise public awareness were modelled by machine learning method.

- In the study conducted by Koh (2020), the relationship between the quarantine applied in the COVID-19 period and "loneliness" was searched. Different findings were obtained by examining the messages with the words COVID-19 and loneliness together.
- Fernando et al. (2019) drew attention to the rapid increase in the use of social media. In his analysis, findings related to the field of political science were obtained, and a proposal was made for the Large-Scale Twitter Observatory.
- Sinnoth et al. (2016) focused on whether human emotions were affected by the weather. They concluded that a big data processing infrastructure, which scales to changing moods of people over time and correlates this with comprehensive, disaggregated weather data, would be necessary.
- Zhang et al. (2020) carried out a big data application in studies for businesses over a period of ten years. It has been observed that big data is still not used enough for businesses.
- Antonakaki (2020) sought to analyse online behaviour patterns, social responses, sensitivity to various entities and the nature of malicious attacks in a live network with hundreds of millions of users. Sensitivity analysis and threats such as spam, bots, fake news and hate speech were examined in the model, which they thought would help create the conceptual model of Twitter.
- Another study was carried out in the field of health by Million et al. (Million et al. 2020). A meta-analysis was conducted on the effects of chloroquine derivatives in patients based on published and unpublished reports that are publicly available on the Internet for one day (27 May 2020) for the COVID-19 outbreak. Ultimately, a meta-analysis of public clinical reports observed that chloroquine derivatives were effective in improving clinical and virological outcomes, and additionally reduced mortality in COVID-19 patients by 3 times.
- Antenuci et al. (2020) used data from Twitter to create job loss, job hunt and job posting indexes. Data were obtained by counting business-related statements such as "I lost my job" in the tweets. Social media indexes are formed of the basic components of these signals.
- In another study examining the relationship between data culture and decision-making performance on 108 companies in China, structural equation modelling was used to test the hypotheses. This study contributed to the literature of big data management and governance mechanisms by establishing the relationship between decision-making performance and big data contractual and relational governance directly and through BDA capabilities (Shamim et al. 2020).

- In the study conducted for Brazil by De Melo and Figueiredo (2020), approximately 4 million tweets and 18 thousand news were examined. First of all, in the study made by creating a series of keywords; users' tweets containing hashtags, media and retweets were defined. These are also classified within themselves. All data were collected between January and May 2020. It was determined that the users make more informative postings and some drugs and active substances entered as keywords do not return much results in postings.
- Cepeda-Bolzman (2020) discussed the issue of refugees on the Twitter agenda in his study. The focus is on knowledge production and consumption. The findings highlight recurring issues related to sociocultural factors, human rights, economy news, critical thinking and religious issues. The originality of the refugee study, social sciences-related sociocultural factors derived from the tweets of minority groups were also observed.
- Using all geolocated photo tweets shared on Twitter in 2012–2013, Indaco (2020) reveals that tweet volume is a valid indicator for country-level GDP forecast. It has also shown that the geographic detail characteristics of social media posts are sufficient for predicting GDP, as specific to US cities.
- Calic-Ghasemaghaei (2020) wanted to prove the relationship between big data usage and financial performance. Whether the firms use big data to improve social performance is the research question of the study. It has been observed that these improvements are realized through organizational innovation in business practices, workplace organization and external relations.
- Durahim-Coşkun (2015) conducted user tendency and emotion analysis to determine the emotional well-being of citizens with Twitter's voluntary information sharing structure. In this context, they worked on a sensitivity analysis model to calculate Turkey's Gross National Happiness (GNH). More than 35 million tweets posted in 2013 and the first quarter of 2014 were collected. The emotion analysis and the reliability of the data set were tested, and the results were found to be similar to the results of the GNH survey results of Turkish Statistical Institute by provinces and the 2013 sensitivity analysis results.
- Yu-Wang (2015) study collected real-time tweets from US football fans at five 2014 FIFA World Cup matches (three matches between the US team and another opponent and two between other teams) using the twitter search API. Sensitivity analysis has been used to examine emotional responses in tweets from US football fans, particularly emotional changes (their or opponent's) after goals. It has been observed that in the matches played by the USA team, negative emotions are fear and anger and generally increase when the opponent team scores and decrease when the USA team scores.

## 13.4 Big Data and Following Twitter Agenda (1–31 May 2020)

Big data analysis has been used extensively in analysis and evaluations in recent years. It is possible to reach results that attract the attention of many areas from politicians, economists, health care to environmentalists on observing and guiding trends and preferences. As a result, it is the human being who is dealt with and whose behaviour is observed. The demands, reactions and expectations of large masses are both being understood and directed. In this sense, it can be said that it is one of the areas that attract the most attention of public relations groups.

The first response of the economy to exogenous negative shocks is withdrawal into itself. Individuals tend to reduce their expenses and postpone their obligations; companies give up investment decisions. It is inevitable that this situation will prevent employment as well as affect total supply and demand. It would not be surprising that a situation where labour is negatively affected will create a slowdown in the economy as a whole. This continues until the uncertainty ends (Steel 2020, p. 318).

In this part of the research, developments in this direction will be observed through the behaviour of Twitter users.

### *13.4.1 Research Results*

The following questions were sought within the scope of the research:

- How did the headers used on Twitter change during the pandemic period?
- Which accounts have Twitter users tagged/mentioned or shared or together with which headers did they use their messages?
- Which titles were the most preferred? and
- What is the level of emphasis on daily life and economic difficulties in their topics?

### *13.4.2 Method*

The "*content analysis method*", one of the quantitative research methods, was used in the study. Content analysis draws attention as a method that reveals the closed areas of texts in media messages instead of the visible and easily determined content (Bilgin 2014). Content analysis ensures that opinions and information are revealed objectively and systematically by digitizing the discourse in the text (Altunışık et al. 2010). Koçak and Arun (2006) define this method as "*a quantitative research method that enables the scientific evaluation of the judgments put forward by the researcher in the light of clearly formulated rules to classify the signs and to reveal which judgments these signs contain*".

### 13.4.3 Preparing Data Set

One of the most used social media platforms today is Twitter social media platform. Social media platforms are used more intensely by the users day by day. People shared their experiences about the disease and their opinions about the restrictions taken during the pandemic in the social media environment. By commenting on the posts of other users, users can act positively/negatively or objectively to the subject as well as remain indifferent.

Within the scope of this study, users' posts were collected from the Twitter social media platform by means of the keywords determined regarding the pandemic. The determined keywords are shown in Table 13.1. The "Twitter API" (Twitter 2020) provided by the Twitter platform was used for data collection. Necessary permissions ("key" and "tokens") were created. "Tweepy" library in Python language (Tweepy 2020) was used for these actions. A data set was obtained with a total of 19,199,490 user posts between 1 and 31 May 2020.

Approximately 150 "key" expressions created for the big data screening were broadened considering the epidemic and its effects. A screening set was created in a way to include issues related to daily news, trade, general economy, violence, worship and staying at home.

The number of posts collected daily between 1 May 2020 and 31 May 2020 is shown in Fig. 13.2.

During the period under review, an average of 535 thousand tweets per day were posted. 1 and 19 May are the dates with the lowest number of Twitter messages. 694 thousand tweets belonging to 23 May exceeded the average by 30%. Although

**Table 13.1** Words scanned in big data

| Keywords in Turkish |
|---|
| 'Covid19', 'corona', 'coronavirus', 'covid19tr', 'coronavirus', 'virus', 'microbe', 'corona', 'coronavirus', 'epidemic', 'death', 'intensive care', 'mask', 'hygiene', 'cleanliness', 'number of deaths', 'mortality rate', 'new case', 'recovery rate', 'healing number', 'medical staff', 'doctor', 'Cemal Taşçıoğlu', 'world health organization', 'WHO', 'firms will go bankrupt', 'unemployment', 'stagnation', 'economy will collapse', 'debt', 'tourism', 'hunger', 'production', 'consumption', 'food', 'support', 'bread', 'help', 'daily workers', 'agriculture', 'production', 'harvest time', 'crop in the field', 'grocer', 'market', 'bakery', 'Market', 'restaurant', 'cafe', 'restaurant', 'service sector', 'Precaution', 'panic', 'fear', 'state financial protection', 'power', 'SME', 'support', 'subsidy', 'credit', 'bankrupt', 'bankrupt', 'production', 'loan debt', 'installment', 'tax', 'social security premium', 'salary', 'wage', 'layoffs', 'unemployed', 'paid leave', 'unpaid leave', 'short work allowance', 'loan', 'bank', 'interest', 'Internet', 'e-education', 'commerce', 'home office', 'flexible working', 'entertainment', 'social media', 'fun', 'no time', 'boredom', 'sports', 'weight gain', 'walking', 'feed the cat', 'feed the dog', 'fasting', 'prayer', 'worship', 'Friday', 'tarawih', 'mosque', 'church', 'Iran', 'mullah', 'pope', 'Sunday ritual', 'Friday prayer', 'family', 'child', 'violence', 'violence against women', 'e-school', 'iftar', 'insult', 'swearing', 'lie', 'slander', 'thieves', 'panic', 'fear', 'concern', 'deaths has increased,' 'turkey actual figures conceals', 'true number of deaths' |

*Source* Created by author

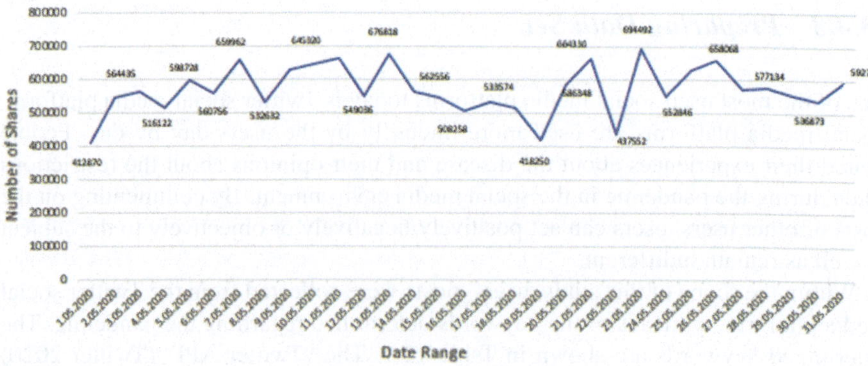


**Fig. 13.2** Number of shares collected daily. *Source* Created by author

Twitter users have an average daily message habit in the relevant date range, it can be said that they use Twitter intensively depending on the situation and the agenda.

## 13.5 Data Pre-processing and Clearance

The unnecessary data and attributes in posts should be pre-processed before analysis. However, before the pre-process, the repetitive data were cleaned in the posts and the posts containing slang/inappropriate, hate speech was detected and cleaned. It was seen that the users made a lot of posts in the mentioned period, relevant or not, in order to stand out in the trending topics. Word groups included in these posts were determined, and these posts were excluded from the data set. In addition, it was observed that there were posts that contain the keywords determined in the data set process and might constitute a crime. Rules were created for these posts, and relevant shares were excluded from the data set within the framework of these rules. To make analysis easier and simpler, unnecessary words and characters were removed from the posts. Accordingly, the following operations were performed on the data set.

- Uppercase letters were converted into lowercase letters in order to prevent differences that may arise as a result of the analysis.
- Different characters (special characters/numbers, etc.) contained in the posts were removed from the data set.
- URL information in the post, if any, was removed.
- Stop words that are commonly used in every language were removed from the data set. NLTK (2020) library was used to exclude these words from the data set.

## 13.6 Data Analysis

With the help of text mining methods, the most frequently tagged accounts/(mention), the most used hashtags and the highest number of repeated words in the data set were determined on the data set. It reveals which subject the posts made by users are related to. With a feature of the Twitter platform, it lists the most shared topics by country every day. Some users publish some posts including these hashtags after having looked at this list, to stand out or advertise. The data with this feature in the data set were deleted according to the rule created during the data cleaning phase.

The pandemic has changed many things, at the centre of our ongoing lives. Therefore, as it is the main agenda itself, the events that it affects can also find a place in Twitter messages. When the subjects that are tagged the most through the data set are examined, it is seen that the "#yks" topic is tagged at the highest rate. The reason for this is that the date of collecting the data set is the Higher Education Institutions Examination (YKS), which is the university entrance exam. Changing the YKS exam date due to the pandemic shows that this tag is used in large amounts in the collected data. The fact that the selected "#ykstarihinedokunma" (do not touch my YKS) header is among the most tagged headers is an important indicator of this (Fig. 13.3).

Coronavirus and similar headers are the most tagged titles, although they are used with different expressions. It is seen at the top of our epidemic data set, albeit with a few different hashtags. It is observed that the topics "#corona", "#corona", "#covid" and "# coronavirus" are predominant in the data set due to the different topics used by the users. Examining the other topics tagged by users, "#avmler", (*malls*) "#evdekal" (*stayhome*), "#maske" (*mask*) and "#bayram" (*holiday*) topics, draws attention. These topics include the concepts started to be commonly used in our lives after the pandemic.

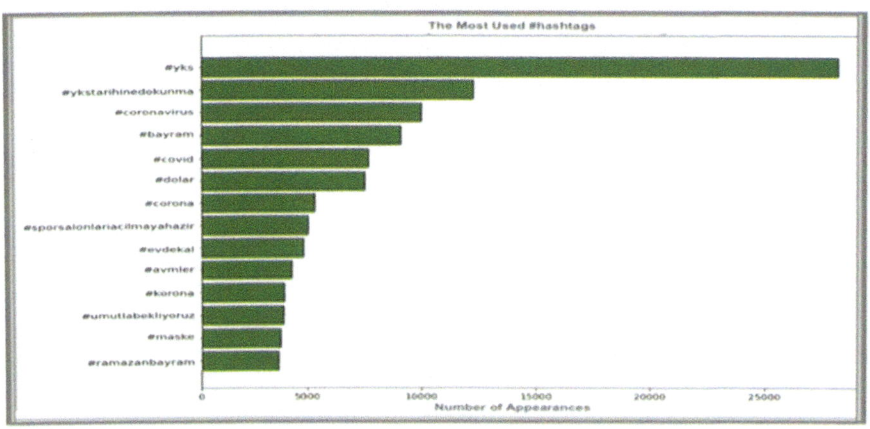


**Fig. 13.3** Most mention and hashtags. *Source* Created by author

Figure 13.4 contains the most frequently tagged account names by users. The most frequently tagged account names by users are the personal account of President Recep Tayyip Erdogan and the personal account of Minister of Health Fahrettin Koca. The highest-level officials of the state are sought as the addressee of the issue

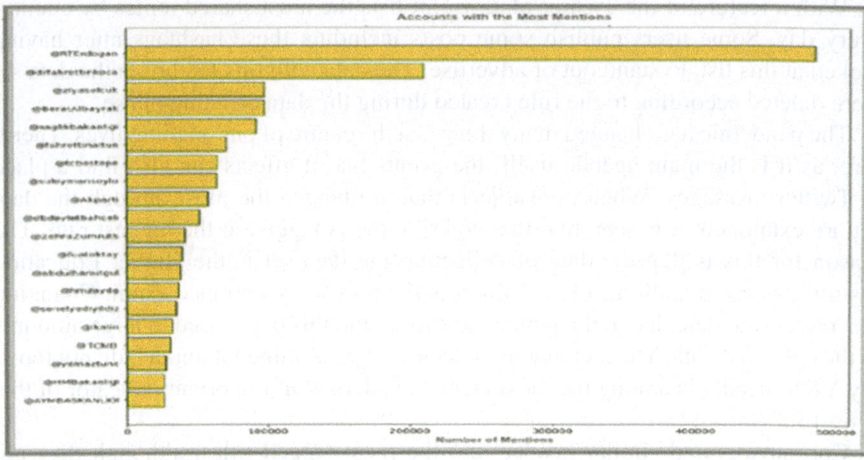


| Account Name | Title/Institution |
|---|---|
| @RTErdogan | President of the Republic of Turkey |
| @drfahrettinkoca | Minister of Health of the Republic of Turkey |
| @ziyaselcuk | Minister of National Education of the Republic of Turkey |
| @beratAlbayrak | Minister of Treasury and Finance of the Republic of Turkey |
| @saglikbakanligi | Ministry of Health |
| @fahrettinaltun | Communications Director, Republic of Türkiye |
| @tcbestepe | Presidency of the Republic of Turkey |
| @suleymansoylu | Minister of Interior of the Republic of Turkey |
| @Akparti | Adalet ve Kalkinma Party |
| @dbdevletbahceli | Chairman of Milliyetci Hareket Party |
| @zehrazumruts | Minister of Family and Social Services of the Republic of Turkey |
| @fuatoktay | Vice President of the Republic of Turkey |
| @abdulhamitgul | Minister of Justice of the Republic of Turkey |
| @hmzaydg | Republic of Turkey Ministry of National Education General Manager of Personnel |
| @senelyediyildiz | Member of Parliament of the Adalet ve Kalkınma Party |
| @ikalin1 | Spokesperson of the Presidency of the Republic of Turkey |
| @TCMB | Central bank of the Turkish Republic |
| @yilmaztunc | Chairman of the TBMM Justice Committee |
| @HMBakanligi | Republic of Turkey Ministry of Treasury and Finance |
| @AYMBASKANLIGI | Presidency of the Constitutional Court |

**Fig. 13.4** Accounts with the most mentions. *Source* Created by author (explanation of account can be find in the table)

in the tags used. It is normal for President Recep Tayyip Erdogan to appear at the top in the titles and tags examined in the study, since he has many followers on the Twitter platform and his posts interact with his followers too much.

Health Minister Fahrettin Koca drew attention with his intensive Twitter use during the pandemic process. In fact, this busy Twitter use became the subject of another research (Atila 2020). With the contribution of the minister's announcement of the daily cases on his social media account and his posts about the pandemic during the day, he ranked second among the most tagged accounts. When the posts of the users who shared the most used "#yks" hashtag in Fig. 13.4 are examined, it was seen that they tagged more than one account name. In addition, the personal Twitter account of the Minister of National Education Ziya Selçuk is among the most tagged due to the fact that the schools continued in the form of remote education and the school term was terminated. As a corporate account, it is seen that "saglikbakanligi" (Ministry of Health) and "tcbestepe" (Republic of Turkey Beştepe) accounts are heavily tagged. Looking at the labels in general, it is seen that the messages are directed to the top management of the state. President and Minister of Health Twitter accounts are the most tagged accounts. The Twitter accounts of ministers, ruling parties, vice president, presidential spokesperson and head of communication, which are always in the spotlight in the process and are on the agenda, are among those that have been intensely tagged.

As shown in Fig. 13.4 data, it is clear that unrelated words and accounts are also tagged in the list. Here, Twitter's own agenda comes into play; more words can be tagged than the words we have specified. However, it seems that this remains only a limited day and event.

The number of words in the data set is shown in Fig. 13.5. The account names and hashtags shown in the previous graphics were removed when determining the number of words in the data set.

Since different words related to Coronavirus were used in the data analysis, all words were added separately to the data set. The numbers are scattered because the words pointing to the virus are different. However, if these expressions are combined in a single account, the most common expression in the messages is again the words that point to the pandemic. The words health, death and mask also reflect the realities of the pandemic period. Even the mask emoji is among the most used emojis in the relevant period.

It has been observed that the messages containing the words support, help and social mostly draw attention to the difficulties of economic life. The economic measures of the pandemic period are also discussed within these messages. During this period, the Eid El-Fitr was among the most used words. Children and holidays are among the top shares.

**Additional explanation of Fig. 13.5 (Turkish/English)**

Destek: support

Yardım: help

Çocuk: kid

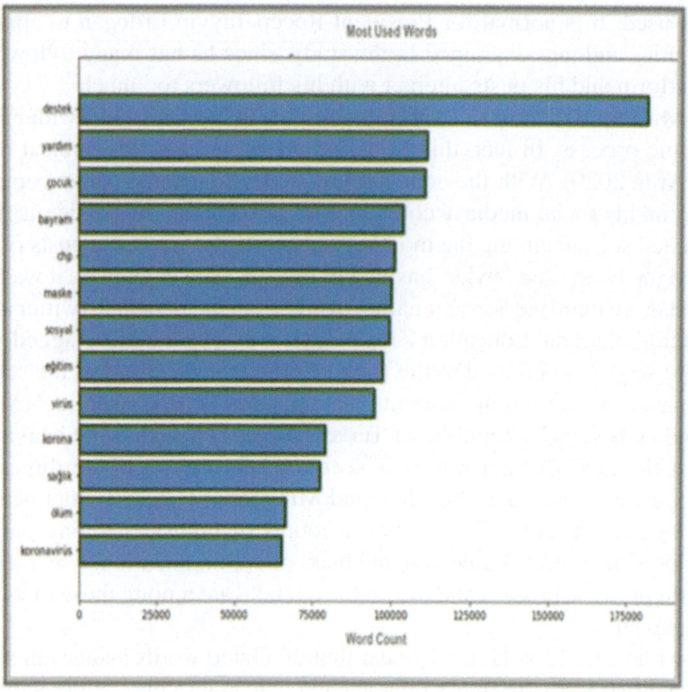


**Fig. 13.5** Maximum number of words in messages. *Source* Created by author

Bayram: festival (religious festival)

CHP: main opposition party

Maske: mask

Sosyal: social

Eğitim: education

Virüs: virus

Sağlık: health

Ölüm: death.

## 13.7 Conclusion

In the analysis of the Twitter agenda covering the period 1–31 May 2020, real-life data were reflected in twitter messages. It was observed that the selected keywords were the expressions that occupied the agenda the most and were frequently included in the messages. As Twitter progressed on its agenda, the compatibility of the keywords scanned within the scope of the research with the agenda has been deemed important.

According to the keywords determined in this study, the data set obtained from the Twitter platform was analysed using natural language processing and text mining techniques. According to the analysis results, it was observed that sharing about the "YKS" exam was intense at the dates when the data set was created. At the same time, it is seen that the posts about "Coronavirus" epidemic come to the fore according to the keywords specified. Based on these results, it was seen that the university entrance exams came to the fore among the pandemic issue in our country on the dates specified on the Twitter social platform.

The messages of the period reflecting the pandemic period and examined under the research cover the last month of the curfews. Although there are complaints of isolation at home and fear of catching Coronavirus, the messages and tags about the virus also include spreading concern and panic.

Economic concerns and the difficulty of liabilities of the ongoing life are reflected in the content of the message. There are economic difficulties, expectations and social supports included in the topics in the tagging and topics. These issues are also tagged for the president's own account, the institution, the relevant ministries and the ministers' own accounts. Even though political parties and their leaders were not determined as keywords, it was observed that they often rank high on the Twitter agenda. The political power, which was moved higher by Twitter users in this process, became the president and relevant ministers.

## References

Antenuci D (2020) Using social media to measure labor market flows. https://www.nber.org/papers/w20010. Accessed on 5 Dec 2020

Antonakaki D (2020) A survey of Twitter research: data model, graph structure, sentiment analysis and attacks. Expert Syst Appl 164:114006. https://doi.org/10.1016/j.eswa.2020.114006

Atila S (2020) Sağlık Bakanı Fahrettin Koca'nın Twitter analizi: Takipçi sayısı 391 binden 5 milyona çıktı, yaklaşık 4 milyon kez retweet edildi. https://medyascope.tv/2020/04/30/saglik-bakani-fahrettin-kocanin-twitter-analizi-takipci-sayisi-391-binden-5-milyona-cikti-yaklasik-4-milyon-kez-retweet-edildi/. Accessed on 15 Nov 2020

Bıçakçı B (2019) Post-truth Çağında Halkla İlişkiler'in "Hakikat Yöneticiliği" Rolü: Gıda ve Beslenme Alanındaki Yalan Haberlere Yönelik Stratejiler. Kurgu 27(4):61–78. https://dergipark.org.tr/tr/pub/kurgu/issue/54877/752382. Accessed on 21 Dec 2020

Bozkurt Ö (2018) Sosyal Medya ve Kültürel Yansımaları. Gazi Üniversitesi Sosyal Bilimler Dergisi 5(14):406–417. https://dergipark.org.tr/tr/pub/gusbd/issue/39212/370186

Calic GMG (2020) Big data for social benefits: innovation as a mediator of the relationship between big data and corporate social performance. J Bus Res. https://doi.org/10.1016/j.jbusres.2020.11.003

Cepeda MP, Bolzmann LGA (2021) Refugee information consumption on Twitter. J Bus Res 123:529–537. https://doi.org/10.1016/j.jbusres.2020.10.029

Ceyhan A (2019) Dijital İletişim Çağında Siyasetin Dijitalleşmesi Üzerine Bir İnceleme: post-truth ve Dijital Siyasetin Sahte Haber Ekseninde Analizi. Kurgu 27(4):1–17. https://dergipark.org.tr/tr/pub/kurgu/issue/54877/752377

Çelik N (2020) Belirsizliklerin Dünya Ekonomisine Yönelik Yansımaları: COVID-19 Salgını Öncesi ve Sonrası Dünya Ekonomisi, Polat M, Aslantaş M (eds) Bir Virüsün Öğrettikleri, (içinde): Nobel Yayıncılık, Ankara, pp 315–330
de Melo T, Figueiredo CMS (2020) A first public dataset from Brazilian twitter and news on COVID-19 in Portuguese. Data Brief 32:106179. https://doi.org/10.1016/j.dib.2020.106179
Durahim A, Coşkun O-M (2015) #iamhappybecause: gross national happiness through Twitter analysis and big data. Technol Forecast Social Change 99:92–105. https://doi.org/10.1016/j.techfore.2015.06.035
Fernando S (2019) Towards a large-scale twitter observatory for political events. Future Gen Comput Syst September 2020 110:976–983. https://doi.org/10.1016/j.future.2019.10.013
Indaco A (2020) From twitter to GDP: estimating economic activity from social media. Reg Sci Urban Econ 85:103591. https://doi.org/10.1016/j.regsciurbeco.2020.103591
Koh JX, Liew TM (2020) How loneliness is talked about in social media during COVID-19 pandemic: text mining of 4,492 Twitter feeds. J Psychiatr Res. https://doi.org/10.1016/j.jpsychires.2020.11.015
Li L (2020) Characterizing the propagation of situational information in social media during COVID-19 epidemic: a case study on Weibo. IEEE Trans Comput Social Syst 7(2):556–562. Article number 9043580
Million M (2020) Clinical efficacy of chloroquine derivatives in COVID-19 infection: comparative meta-analysis between the big data and the real World. New Microbes New Infect 100709. https://doi.org/10.1016/j.nmni.2020.100709
NLTK (2020) NLTK
Shamim S (2020) Big data analytics capability and decision making performance in emerging market firms: the role of contractual and relational governance mechanisms. Technol Forecast Social Change 161:120315. https://doi.org/10.1016/j.techfore.2020.120315
Sinnoth RO (2016) Chapter 15—a case study in big data analytics: exploring twitter sentiment analysis and the weather. Big Data Principles Paradigms 357–388. https://doi.org/10.1016/B978-0-12-805394-2.00015-5
Statista (2020) Twitter user statistics. https://www.statista.com/statistics/242606/number-of-active-twitter-users-in-selected-countries/
Tweepy (2020) https://www.tweepy.org/. Accessed on 29 Nov 2020
Yu Y, Wang X (2015) World cup 2014 in the twitter world: a big data analysis of sentiments in U.S. sports fans' tweets. Comput Human Beh 48:392–400. https://doi.org/10.1016/j.chb.2015.01.075
Zhang Y (2020) A bibliometric review of a decade of research: Big data in business research—setting a research agenda. J Bus Res. https://doi.org/10.1016/j.jbusres.2020.11.004

**İbrahim Attila Acar** CAR has books, articles and papers on public strategic management, public financial management and control law (Law No: 5018), health and education economy, refugees crisis, auditing, financial management and budgeting. He was a member of the Specialization Commission in the Development Plans of 9–10 and 11 and involved in quality, effectiveness, university rankings, European University Association higher education assessment and rating studies in higher education. He worked as a panelist and independent evaluator of TÜBİTAK and Development Agencies. He participated in programs in written and visual media. He prepared and presented the Economic Agenda program at TRT for many years. The analyzes are located in its own website, acarhoca.com. He worked at Süleyman Demirel University for 10 years. And he is currently working at the Department of Economics, Faculty of Economics and Administrative Sciences at Izmir Katip Celebi University. He was the Vice Rector and the founding dean at the same university.

**Volkan Altıntaş** is a Lecturer in the Computer Programming department at Manisa Celal Bayar University. He got his Ph.D., from Suleyman Demirel University in 2020, M.Sc. and B.Sc. from Suleyman Demirel University in 2012, 2005 respectively. His research focuses on Natural

Language Processing, topic modeling, big data analysis, text mining and machine learning. Recently, his research is on web ontology.

# Discussion

While man, who is supposed to have developed considerably throughout history, gained the power to dominate nature, and he also endured the negative consequences of living in a community and settled life. The most important of these are deadly epidemics. Epidemics have many direct and indirect effects, both visible and invisible. The epidemics that changed the ages, affected the course of wars, and shaped the destruction of the economic order and understanding to a great extent throughout history, are the ancient despair of humanity for which they paid many social, psychological, economic and financial costs.

The pandemic we are experiencing is a very serious crisis and much more devastating effects are predicted when compared to the 2008 Global Economic Crisis. In addition, being unable to predict when the epidemic will end and the uncertainty that the subsequent epidemic waves will create a much deeper impact, drag the policies of economic and political actors into uncertainty. COVID-19 has brought the whole world to an important historical turn in its process. In this historical turn, the whole world has focused on two main points. The first one is; to combat the epidemic, to minimize the loss of life and to get rid of the epidemic, the second is to take measures today to prevent the crises and damages that will occur in the post-epidemic economies.

In this context, due to the COVID-19 epidemic that has affected the whole world, states and international organizations have had to put into effect various economic and financial practices in order to combat the epidemic and to prevent the bad course of economies in this process. In particular, it is necessary to establish an environment in which the market and households are supported by public expenditure instruments. Considering the course of decrease in foreign capital investments, the increase in public expenditures instead of private sector expenditures is a harbinger of new bottlenecks. In this context, it is seen that many countries have developed policies in this direction. On the other hand, the increase in spending tendency increases the income need, and the taxation and borrowing tendencies of the public also increase. However, the ongoing uncertainty and health risks delay the recovery processes of the



B. Açıkgöz and İ. A. Acar (eds.), *Pandemnomics: The Pandemic's Lasting Economic Effects*, Accounting, Finance, Sustainability, Governance & Fraud: Theory and Application, https://doi.org/10.1007/978-981-16-8024-3

markets. The necessity of providing support such as postponing loan debt payments of the sector employees and business owners, increasing short-time working allowance supports, and delaying the submission of declarations will further increase the need for public financing.

The last vaccination studies and the transition to phase 3 level for 11 vaccines have given hope to the whole world in combating this microscopic enemy. However, vaccination will also entail serious costs and create serious financial burdens on states. In Turkey, where how many people have survived this disease and developed up immunity are not fully known. However, since at least two doses of vaccine are required per person, even for the vaccination of half of the population, we need at least 80 million doses of vaccine. The main problem is how much funding the government should allocate as these 80 million doses of vaccine will be available to citizens for free. The US government made an agreement to receive 100 million doses of vaccine (mRNA vaccines) developed by Pfizer and Biontech as early as July. Again, EU officials announced that they could purchase vaccines worth of 10 billion dollars from the same two companies and pay 15.50 euros per dose. Again, the UK has already signed contracts for 30 million doses of vaccine, while Canada has signed contracts for 20 million and New Zealand for 1.5 million doses of vaccine. Today, price of the vaccine called Sinovac (inactivated vaccine), which Turkey began to purchase, is $29 in China. Turkey is required to make a huge amount of payment for 80–100 million doses of vaccine, if we consider the unit price of the vaccine as $20. The problem of where to find this resource also shows the seriousness of the issue. Storage and distribution costs will be added other than obtaining the vaccine. In other words, vaccine costs have begun to be included in the expenditure items by which the states weighed down.

In this book, the epidemic problem that we address in various aspects, in particular for COVID-19 is deemed to be a problem that a single country cannot solve alone. The epidemic problem that goes beyond borders affects every aspect of people's lives. In this process, the issue should not be seen as a health issue per se. It is obvious that the subject has many psychological, social, economic and even technological reflections. It is insufficient for states to fight alone against all these variables. The new era after the epidemics, in which the world is affected globally this way, comes with new offers. A new period will begin when the habits of the pre-epidemic will change completely.

Even if the measures proposed by states and international organizations are necessary and sufficient to combat Covid 19 in the short term, the dangers that we do not know yet and that we cannot predict, called "black swan", are at the door. It seems compulsory, for long-term solutions, that the states and international organizations make preparations today and establish strong cooperation networks as well as common funds. Therefore, if the results of the fiscal measures announced and put into practice do not create a positive effect as expected, not the country that fails alone, but the whole world, which is economically integrated with each other, will not come out of the recession quickly. The ability of states to strengthen their own immune systems against this microscopic enemy depends on sound financial measures to be taken today and close cooperation between countries to be established.

2021 has started to be experienced as a year in which negative expectations from 2020 continue, but the conditions for the management of the process are met. The most important indicator of this is that the vaccine has been developed. State support, civil society and solidarity approaches will have an impact on the correct management of 2021 risks. The world is at the edge of the patience limits regarding the pandemic. However, with the diminishing effects of this pandemic, a new recovery move will not be far. However, in solidarity societies, the negative effects of this process are expected to end with a rapid decrease.

İzmir
March 2021
Prof. Dr. İbrahim Attila ACAR
Prof. Dr. Bernur AÇIKGÖZ

# Index





B. Açıkgöz and İ. A. Acar (eds.), *Pandemnomics: The Pandemic's Lasting Economic Effects*, Accounting, Finance, Sustainability, Governance & Fraud: Theory and Application, https://doi.org/10.1007/978-981-16-8024-3

The manufacturer's authorised representative in the EU is Springer
Nature Customer Service Centre GmbH, Europaplatz 3, 69115 Heidelberg,
Germany. If you have any concerns regarding our products, please
contact ProductSafety@springernature.com

Printed and bound by CPI Group (UK) Ltd, Croydon, CR0 4YY
30/09/2026
02225297-0015